Handbook of Deep Learning Models

This volume covers a comprehensive range of fundamental concepts in deep learning and artificial neural networks, making it suitable for beginners looking to learn the basics.

Using Keras, a popular neural network API in Python, this book offers practical examples that reinforce the theoretical concepts discussed. Real-world case studies add relevance by showing how deep learning is applied across various domains. The book covers topics such as layers, activation functions, optimization algorithms, backpropagation, convolutional neural networks (CNNs), data augmentation, and transfer learning – providing a solid foundation for building effective neural network models.

This book is a valuable resource for anyone interested in deep learning and artificial neural networks, offering both theoretical insights and practical implementation experience.

Handbook of Deep Learning Models

Volume One: Fundamentals

Authored by Parag Verma,
Er. Devarasetty Purna Sankar, Anuj Bhardwaj,
Vaibhav Chaudhari, Arnav Pandey and
Ankur Dumka

CRC Press
Taylor & Francis Group
Boca Raton London New York

CRC Press is an imprint of the
Taylor & Francis Group, an **informa** business
A CHAPMAN & HALL BOOK

Designed cover image: Shutterstock

First edition published 2026
by CRC Press
2385 NW Executive Center Drive, Suite 320, Boca Raton FL 33431

and by CRC Press
4 Park Square, Milton Park, Abingdon, Oxon, OX14 4RN

CRC Press is an imprint of Taylor & Francis Group, LLC

ISBN: 978-1-041-10268-7 (hbk)
ISBN: 978-1-041-10270-0 (pbk)
ISBN: 978-1-003-65421-6 (ebk)

DOI: 10.1201/9781003654216

Typeset in Palatino
by Apex CoVantage, LLC

Contents

Biography

Anuj Bhardwaj is a distinguished author, educator, and entrepreneur, currently serving as the director, IQAC, and professor of computer science and engineering at Chandigarh University, and Founder of Data Matrix Experts Pvt. Ltd. With over 17 years of academic and research experience, he holds a PhD in computer science and a master's from BIT Mesra. Dr. Bhardwaj has authored six books with leading publishers, filed multiple patents, contributed nine book chapters, and published over 56 research papers. His expertise spans AI, neural networks, parallel computing, and computer vision. A mentor to many MTech and PhD scholars, he actively contributes to educational initiatives and continues to inspire through his work in advancing education technology.

Vaibhav Chaudhari obtained his integrated dual degree in BE computer science and MSc physics from BITS Pilani K.K. Birla Goa Campus in 2022. Vaibhav is currently working as a member of Technical Staff-3 in Nutanix. He is a member of the AHV Management team and works on distributed systems and VM Management Lifecycle. He has done multiple interdisciplinary projects in the fields of artificial intelligence, astrophysics, high-throughput biological analysis, and satellite data analysis, and his research interests lie in the field of application of artificial intelligence tools to solve real-world problems. He has published 12 research articles and two patents under his name.

Ankur Dumka is an associate professor with additional responsibilities as the dean (academic and research) and head of department, Computer Science and Engineering, the Women Institute of Technology, Dehradun. He has more than 14 years of experience and contributed 140 research papers, 15 book chapters, seven authored books, eight patents granted under his name, and seven patents published. Currently, he holds one R&D project with a grant exceeding ₹10 lakh and has completed one consultancy project of Government Medical College, Haldwani. Also, he was the coordinator of Smart City Dehradun for the drafting of the proposal.

Arnav Pandey is a graduate of St. Joseph's Academy, Dehradun, and has been accepted into the University of California, Los Angeles (UCLA), USA, as a bachelor of technology student majoring in computer science. He has more than three years of experience in the field, with his primary areas of research being deep learning, artificial intelligence, and machine learning. He has authored four research papers, two authored books' proposal accepted, two book chapters, and has one patent filed under his name. He is currently serving as a research trainee on a project exceeding ₹10 lakh in value and is actively working in the domain of generative AI.

Er. Devarasetty Purna Sankar is a seasoned senior software engineer at Data Foundry Pvt. Ltd., specializing in machine learning solutions for the health and finance sectors. With over seven years of experience and a postgraduate diploma in artificial intelligence and machine learning from IIIT Bangalore, he has contributed to impactful projects for Fortune 500 companies. Purna is an award-winning professional recognized for innovation, performance, and excellence in hackathons. Moreover, he is AWS certified, demonstrating strong expertise in cloud-enabled ML solutions. Beyond work, he enjoys hiking, playing badminton, and blending his technical acumen with creativity as an author, aiming to inspire and explore AI's societal impact through his writing.

Parag Verma is an accomplished AI data scientist and technical lead, associated with AIGC, a vertical of Algihaz Holding. With over a decade of experience in artificial intelligence and machine learning, he has specialized in delivering cutting-edge solutions across healthcare, life sciences, and robotics. His professional journey includes impactful roles at Data Foundry Pvt. Ltd., R2E Technologies, and Yuvayana Tech and Craft, along with contributions to various government projects with DST, UCOST, and UBMS. Dr. Verma holds a PhD in artificial intelligence and machine learning, a postgraduate degree in robotics engineering, and a bachelor's in computer science. His work is backed by multiple certifications from renowned institutions such as Stanford, Duke, Google Cloud, and the University of Pennsylvania. A recognized innovator and hackathon winner, he continues to push the boundaries of AI through research and real-world application.

Preface

In recent years, deep learning has revolutionized the field of artificial intelligence, empowering machines to perform tasks that once required human intelligence – from image recognition and speech processing to decision-making and predictive analytics. As this transformative technology continues to evolve, the need for a structured, hands-on approach to learning deep learning models has become more important than ever.

Let's WorkOut With Deep Learning Models is designed to bridge the gap between theoretical foundations and real-world applications. This book offers a comprehensive exploration of deep learning and artificial neural networks, making it an ideal companion for students, researchers, and professionals alike. Whether you are new to deep learning or looking to refine your model implementation skills, this book provides a balanced mix of conceptual understanding and practical application.

Utilizing the intuitive and widely used Keras API in Python, we present practical examples that reinforce theoretical concepts. Real-time use case studies further illustrate how deep learning is being effectively deployed across domains such as healthcare, finance, computer vision, and natural language processing.

The book is structured to take readers on a journey from the fundamentals of neural networks – including layers, activation functions, and backpropagation – to more advanced concepts like convolutional neural networks (CNNs), transfer learning, optimization algorithms, and data augmentation.

Our aim is to empower readers not only to understand how deep learning models work but also to build and fine-tune their own models with confidence. By the end of this book, readers will have gained the foundational knowledge and hands-on experience necessary to apply deep learning techniques to solve complex problems in their own fields of interest.

We hope this book serves as a valuable resource and a stepping stone for your deep learning journey.

Let's dive in and work out with deep learning models!

Part I

Fundamentals of Deep Learning

Chapter 1

Introduction to Deep Learning

1.1 Artificial Intelligence, Machine Learning, and Deep Learning

The chapter provides an introduction to the field of deep learning, starting with an overview of artificial intelligence (AI), machine learning, and deep learning. It explores the relationship between artificial intelligence (AI), machine learning (ML), and deep learning (DL), by providing an overview of these concepts, explaining how they are interconnected and how DL is a subset of ML, which in turn is a subset of AI. It explains the historical context of DL by tracing the evolution of ML and highlighting the key milestones in the field.

The chapter explores what sets DL apart from traditional ML approaches, emphasizing its ability to learn and extract complex patterns and representations directly from raw data. It discusses the modern landscape of ML, including the popularity and widespread adoption of DL in various domains. Moreover, it discusses the advances in related fields that have contributed to the rise of DL, such as computer vision, natural language processing, and speech recognition. The chapter highlights the interconnectedness of these fields and how they have influenced the development of DL techniques. To embark on the journey of DL, the chapter outlines the prerequisites that will help readers grasp the concepts effectively. This includes a basic understanding of linear algebra, calculus, and probability theory. Additionally, the chapter provides guidance on installing the required libraries and frameworks, ensuring readers are ready to dive into hands-on implementation.

Overall, this chapter establishes a solid foundation for understanding DL. It clarifies the relationship between AI, ML, and DL, provides historical context, highlights the unique characteristics of DL, explores the modern landscape, outlines prerequisites, and sets the stage for the subsequent chapters in the book.

1.1.1 Artificial Intelligence

Artificial intelligence (AI) refers to the development of intelligent computer systems that can perform tasks that typically require human intelligence. These tasks encompass a wide range of activities, including speech recognition, decision-making, problem-solving, natural language processing, computer vision, and more. AI aims to create machines that can mimic and replicate human cognitive abilities.

There are two main subtypes of AI:

a) *Narrow AI:* Narrow AI, also known as Weak AI, refers to AI systems that are designed to perform specific tasks with a high level of proficiency. These systems are designed

DOI: 10.1201/9781003654216-2

to excel in a particular domain, such as voice assistants, recommendation systems, or autonomous vehicles. Narrow AI systems are limited in scope and focused on solving specific problems.

b) *General AI:* General AI, also known as Strong AI or Artificial General Intelligence (AGI), aims to develop AI systems that possess the same level of intelligence and versatility as humans. General AI is characterized by the ability to understand, learn, and apply knowledge across various domains and tasks. It seeks to achieve human-like intelligence and can adapt to new situations and learn from experience.

In the real-time industry, AI solutions are applied to address a wide range of complex problems. Industries such as healthcare, finance, manufacturing, transportation, and marketing leverage AI technologies to optimize processes, improve decision-making, enhance customer experience, and enable automation. For example, in healthcare, AI is utilized for medical diagnosis, drug discovery, personalized treatment planning, and remote patient monitoring. In finance, AI is used for fraud detection, algorithmic trading, credit scoring, and risk assessment. These real-world applications of AI aim to leverage the power of intelligent machines to improve efficiency, accuracy, and productivity in various industry sectors. However, it is important to note that while AI has made significant advancements, achieving General AI that can rival human intelligence across all tasks remains a long-term goal. Current AI systems excel in specific domains but lack the generalization and adaptability of human intelligence. Ongoing research and development efforts continue to push the boundaries of AI, driving innovation and advancements in the field.

AI is a multidisciplinary field that encompasses a wide range of techniques, algorithms, and methodologies aimed at developing intelligent computer systems. It has a profound impact on various industries, revolutionizing the way we live, work, and interact with technology.

1.1.2 Machine Learning

Machine learning (ML) is a subfield of AI that focuses on developing algorithms and models that enable machines to learn and make predictions or decisions based on data. Unlike traditional programming approaches, where explicit instructions are provided to solve a specific task, ML systems learn from data and improve their performance over time without being explicitly programmed.

ML systems work by discovering patterns and relationships in the data they are trained on. They extract meaningful insights and information from large datasets to make accurate predictions or decisions. ML algorithms are designed to generalize from the training data and apply the learned knowledge to new, unseen data.

There are three main subcategories of ML:

1. *Supervised Learning:* In supervised learning, the algorithm learns from labeled examples, where the input data is paired with the corresponding desired output. The algorithm learns to map input data to the correct output by minimizing the difference between its predictions and the actual labels. Supervised learning is commonly used for tasks such as classification (assigning input to predefined categories) and regression (predicting a continuous value).

2. *Unsupervised Learning:* Unsupervised learning involves learning from unlabeled data, where the algorithm aims to discover patterns, structures, or relationships within the data without any predefined labels or desired outputs. Clustering and dimensionality reduction are common tasks in unsupervised learning. Clustering algorithms group similar data points together, while dimensionality reduction techniques reduce the complexity of high-dimensional data.
3. *Reinforcement Learning:* Reinforcement learning is a learning paradigm where an agent learns to interact with an environment to maximize a reward signal. The agent explores the environment, takes actions, and receives feedback in the form of rewards or penalties. Through trial and error, the agent learns to make decisions that maximize the cumulative reward over time. Reinforcement learning is commonly used in applications such as game playing, robotics, and autonomous systems.

In real-time industry-based problem analysis, ML techniques are applied to tackle various challenges and make data-driven decisions. Industries such as healthcare, finance, marketing, manufacturing, and transportation leverage ML to analyze large volumes of data, make predictions, detect patterns, automate processes, optimize operations, and improve overall efficiency and effectiveness. ML algorithms and models are used for tasks such as customer segmentation, fraud detection, demand forecasting, anomaly detection, image and speech recognition, and personalized recommendations.

Understanding ML involves gaining knowledge of the underlying algorithms, statistical concepts, data preprocessing techniques, model evaluation, and optimization methods. Also, it requires proficiency in programming languages, data manipulation, and visualization tools. With a solid understanding of ML, professionals can leverage its power to solve complex problems, gain valuable insights, and make informed decisions in various domains.

1.1.3 Deep Learning

Deep learning (DL) is a specialized branch of ML that focuses on training artificial neural networks (ANNs) to learn and make predictions or decisions from complex and large-scale datasets. DL models are designed to mimic the structure and functioning of the human brain, particularly the interconnectedness of neurons.

DL models consist of multiple layers of interconnected neurons, forming deep neural networks. Each layer of neurons processes and transforms the input data to extract higher-level features and representations. The hierarchical structure allows DL models to learn complex patterns and relationships in the data, enabling them to make accurate predictions or decisions. DL has gained significant attention and achieved remarkable success in various domains, including the following.

1. *Computer Vision:* DL models have revolutionized computer vision tasks such as image classification, object detection, and image segmentation. By learning from large datasets, DL models can automatically learn to recognize and understand complex visual patterns and objects.
2. *Natural Language Processing (NLP):* DL techniques have greatly advanced NLP tasks, including language translation, sentiment analysis, text generation, and question-answering systems. DL models can learn the underlying structures and

semantics of human language, allowing them to process and understand natural language text.

3. *Speech Recognition:* DL has played a crucial role in improving speech recognition systems. DL models can learn to extract relevant features from audio signals and convert spoken language into text with high accuracy. This has enabled advancements in voice assistants, transcription services, and voice-controlled systems.
4. *Recommendation Systems:* DL models have enhanced recommendation systems by learning customized user preferences and making accurate predictions for personalized content recommendations in various domains, such as e-commerce, entertainment, and online platforms.
5. *Healthcare and Medicine:* DL techniques have been applied in medical imaging analysis, disease diagnosis, drug discovery, and genomics research. DL models can analyze and interpret complex medical data, assisting healthcare professionals in making more accurate diagnoses and treatment decisions.

In real-time industry-based problem analysis, DL is used to solve complex problems and extract valuable insights from large and diverse datasets. Industries such as finance, manufacturing, healthcare, retail, and transportation leverage DL for tasks like fraud detection, anomaly detection, predictive maintenance, customer segmentation, and demand forecasting. Exploring DL involves understanding the architecture and design of deep neural networks, optimization algorithms, regularization techniques, and methods for handling large-scale datasets. Moreover, it requires expertise in programming languages, frameworks (such as TensorFlow and PyTorch), and tools for data preprocessing and visualization. By leveraging DL, professionals can tackle challenging problems, unlock new opportunities, and drive innovation across various domains.

1.1.4 Relationship between AI, ML, and DL

The relationship between AI, ML, and DL (Figure 1.1) can be understood hierarchically, where AI serves as the umbrella term that encompasses ML and DL.

ML is a subset of AI and focuses on developing algorithms and models that enable machines to learn from data and make predictions or decisions. It encompasses a wide range of techniques and approaches, including traditional statistical methods, pattern recognition, and computational learning theory.

DL, on the other hand, is a specialized branch of ML that specifically leverages deep neural networks. Deep neural networks consist of multiple layers of interconnected neurons, allowing them to learn hierarchical representations of data. DL has shown exceptional performance in handling complex and large-scale datasets, extracting high-level features, and achieving state-of-the-art results in various AI applications.

DL is considered a subset of ML because it is built upon the principles and techniques of ML but focuses specifically on the use of deep neural networks. DL models excel in tasks such as image recognition, object detection, natural language processing, speech recognition, and more. They can automatically learn complex patterns and features from raw data, eliminating the need for manual feature engineering, which was often required in traditional ML approaches.

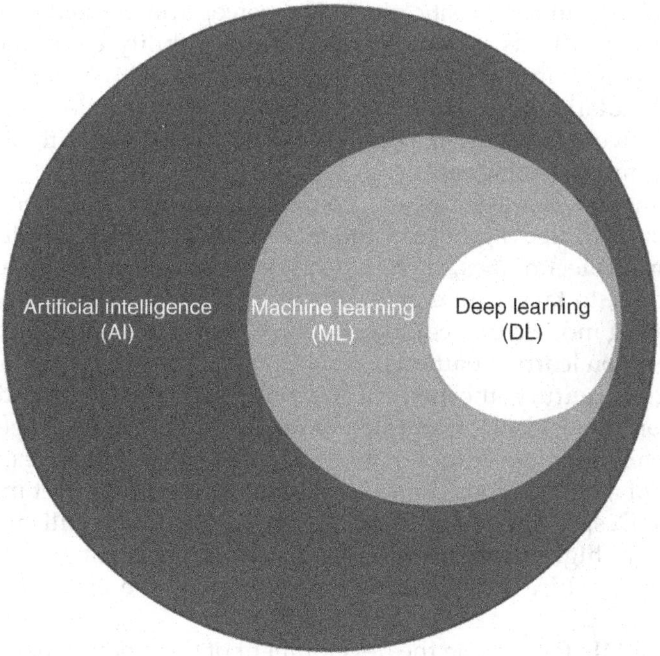

Figure 1.1 Relationship between AI, ML, and DL.

The rise of DL has been driven by advancements in hardware, availability of large datasets, and the development of efficient training algorithms. DL models, with their ability to process and interpret unstructured data, have made significant contributions to AI and have become a dominant approach in various fields.

In brief, DL is a subset of ML, which in turn is a subset of AI. DL has emerged as a powerful tool within ML, offering the capability to learn complex patterns and representations from raw data, leading to remarkable advancements in various AI applications. Its success can be attributed to its ability to automatically extract meaningful features and its capacity to handle big and complex datasets.

1.2 Historical Context – Before Deep Learning: A Brief History of Machine Learning

1.2.1 Early Beginnings of ML

The early beginnings of ML can be traced back to the 1940s and 1950s when researchers started exploring the concept of ANNs. These pioneers, including Walter Pitts and Warren McCulloch, developed mathematical models inspired by the structure and functioning of biological neurons. These models laid the foundation for the development of computer models that could learn and make predictions.

One of the significant contributions during this period was the invention of the perceptron by Frank Rosenblatt in 1958. The perceptron was a computational model inspired by the functioning of neurons in the brain. It was capable of learning simple patterns and making binary classifications. The perceptron marked an important milestone in the field of ML, as it demonstrated the possibility of training machines to recognize and classify patterns. However, the early years of ML were faced with limitations due to computational constraints and the lack of large datasets. The progress in the field was relatively slow, and the limitations of early ML algorithms became apparent in tackling complex problems.

In the following decades, ML research continued to advance, driven by the development of more sophisticated algorithms and the availability of larger datasets. Researchers explored various techniques, such as decision trees, support vector machines, and Bayesian networks, to tackle different types of learning problems. These approaches focused on creating models that could generalize from the data and make predictions or decisions based on learned patterns.

In the late 20th century, the field of ML witnessed significant advancements in areas such as computer vision, natural language processing, and speech recognition. Researchers developed algorithms and models that can extract meaningful features from complex data, enabling machines to understand and interpret information from various sources. Despite the progress made in ML, there were still challenges in handling complex and high-dimensional data, as well as in dealing with problems that required deep hierarchical representations. This led to the emergence of DL in the 2000s.

DL, a subset of ML, focused on the development of deep neural networks with multiple layers. These deep neural networks demonstrated the ability to learn hierarchical representations of data, allowing them to handle more complex tasks and achieve state-of-the-art performance in areas such as image recognition, speech recognition, and natural language processing. The advent of DL, coupled with advancements in computational power, the availability of large-scale datasets, and the development of efficient training algorithms, led to a resurgence of interest in ML and AI. DL has since become a dominant approach in various fields and has contributed to significant advancements in AI technologies.

In summary, the early beginnings of ML can be traced back to the 1940s and 1950s with the development of ANNs. ML made substantial advancements in various fields, paving the way for the emergence of DL. DL, with its focus on deep neural networks and hierarchical representations, has revolutionized the field of AI and contributed to remarkable advancements in areas such as computer vision, natural language processing, and speech recognition.

1.2.2 Key Milestones and Breakthroughs in ML

In the decades following the early beginnings of ML, there were several significant innovations and landmarks that shaped the field and advanced the development of AI. Some of these key milestones and breakthroughs in ML include the following.

1. *Dartmouth Conference (1956):* The Dartmouth Conference is considered to be the birthplace of AI as a discipline. The conference brought together researchers and thinkers who discussed the possibility of creating machines that could mimic human intelligence. While the focus was on AI as a whole, this event laid the foundation for early ML research and set the stage for future advancements.

2. *Bayesian Networks (1960s):* Bayesian networks introduced a graphical model for representing probabilistic relationships among variables. This milestone enabled computers to handle data uncertainty and make decisions using probabilistic reasoning.
3. *Decision Trees (1970s):* Decision tree algorithms provided a way to model decisions and their possible consequences in a tree-like structure. They allowed machines to learn from data and make predictions or classifications based on a series of decisions.
4. *Symbolic AI and Expert Systems:* During the 1960s and 1970s, researchers concentrated on symbolic techniques to imitate human decision-making processes. Expert systems, which used rule-based algorithms and symbolic representations of knowledge, became popular. These systems encoded human expertise and could make decisions or provide recommendations in specific domains. This approach to AI and ML heavily relied on logical reasoning and symbolic manipulation.
5. *Neural Network Resurgence:* In the 1980s, there was a resurgence of interest in neural networks, fueled by advances in computational power and the development of more efficient training algorithms. Backpropagation, an algorithm for training multi-layer neural networks, was rediscovered and played a crucial role in the renaissance of neural networks. This resurgence paved the way for future advancements in ML and set the stage for the emergence of DL.
6. *Support Vector Machines (SVMs) (1990s):* SVMs emerged as a powerful ML algorithm for classification and regression tasks. They aimed to find an optimal decision boundary that maximizes the margin between different classes, resulting in strong generalization capabilities.
7. *Ensemble Methods (1990s):* Ensemble methods, such as bagging, boosting, and random forests, combined multiple learning algorithms or models to improve performance. They leveraged the strengths of individual models and mitigated their weaknesses, leading to more accurate and robust predictions.
8. *Big Data and DL:* The proliferation of digital data and the availability of large-scale datasets in the 2000s presented new opportunities for ML. DL, with its focus on deep neural networks and hierarchical representations, emerged as a powerful technique for handling big and complex data. Breakthroughs in computer vision, natural language processing, and speech recognition showcased the potential of DL in achieving state-of-the-art performance in various domains.
9. *Deep Learning (2000s):* DL revolutionized the field of ML by introducing deep neural networks with multiple layers of interconnected neurons. Breakthroughs in computer vision, natural language processing, and speech recognition showcased the power of DL in handling complex data and achieving state-of-the-art performance.
10. *Convolutional Neural Networks (CNNs) (2012):* The AlexNet architecture, a deep CNN, won the ImageNet Large Scale Visual Recognition Challenge in 2012, significantly advancing the field of computer vision. CNNs revolutionized image classification tasks by learning hierarchical representations of images.
11. *Recurrent Neural Networks (RNNs) (2014):* RNNs, with their ability to capture sequential information, made significant advancements in natural language processing tasks such as language translation and speech recognition. The introduction of long short-term memory (LSTM) units improved the handling of long-range dependencies in sequential data.

12. *Generative Adversarial Networks (GANs) (2014):* GANs introduced a novel framework for training generative models by pitting a generator network against a discriminator network. GANs have been used to generate realistic images, create synthetic data, and enhance data augmentation techniques.
13. *Transfer Learning (2014):* Transfer learning allowed models to leverage knowledge learned from one task to improve performance on another related task. This approach reduced the need for large amounts of labeled data and enabled the transfer of learned representations to new domains.
14. *Autoencoders and Unsupervised Learning (2010s):* Autoencoders, a type of unsupervised learning model, allowed machines to learn representations of data without explicit labels. This approach has been instrumental in tasks such as anomaly detection, dimensionality reduction, and feature learning.

These milestones and breakthroughs have significantly advanced the field of ML, enabling machines to handle complex data, make accurate predictions, and learn from large-scale datasets. They have shaped various subfields within ML and found applications in diverse domains such as healthcare, finance, natural language processing, and computer vision.

1.2.3 The Emergence of DL

The invention of artificial neural networks, also known as the "connectionist" method, was a significant breakthrough in the field of ML. Neural networks demonstrated the ability to generalize patterns and learn from examples, but their practical application was limited due to computational constraints and a lack of large, labeled datasets.

The DL revolution began to take shape in the 2000s, driven by a renewed interest in neural networks. Researchers made significant advancements in training deep neural networks by employing techniques such as backpropagation and stochastic gradient descent. These methods allowed for efficient optimization of the network's parameters, enabling the training of networks with many layers. Several factors contributed to the acceleration of neural network development during this time. The availability of vast amounts of data, thanks to the proliferation of the internet and digital technologies, provided the necessary fuel for training deep models. Furthermore, advancements in computer power and the emergence of parallel computing architectures facilitated the training of complex neural networks within feasible time frames.

Indeed, the introduction of deep belief networks by Geoffrey Hinton and his colleagues in 2006 was a significant milestone in the development of DL. Deep belief networks (DBNs) combine unsupervised learning, particularly through the use of restricted Boltzmann machines (RBMs), with deep neural networks. This combination allows for the learning of hierarchical representations of data, where lower-level features are learned first and then used to build higher-level features. DBNs demonstrated the effectiveness of unsupervised pretraining, which involves training each layer of the network in an unsupervised manner before fine-tuning the entire network with supervised learning. This approach overcame some of the challenges faced by deep neural networks, such as the vanishing gradient problem, and enabled the training of deep architectures.

One key breakthrough in deep learning was the successful application of deep neural networks in computer vision. The AlexNet architecture, which won the ImageNet

Large Scale Visual Recognition Challenge in 2012, demonstrated the remarkable capabilities of deep CNNs in image classification tasks. CNNs were able to learn hierarchical representations of images, capturing intricate features at different levels of abstraction. Another breakthrough came in the form of RNNs, which excel at processing sequential data. With the introduction of LSTM units, RNNs became highly effective in natural language processing tasks, such as language translation and speech recognition, where understanding the context of sequential data is crucial.

The accessibility of open-source DL frameworks, such as TensorFlow and PyTorch, further fueled the adoption and development of DL models. These frameworks provided user-friendly interfaces and efficient computation on both CPUs and GPUs, making DL accessible to a wider audience.

The emergence of DL has had a profound impact on various fields, including computer vision, natural language processing, speech recognition, and many others. DL models have achieved state-of-the-art performance in tasks such as image classification, object detection, machine translation, and sentiment analysis. The ability of deep neural networks to automatically learn relevant features from raw data has reduced the need for manual feature engineering and opened up new possibilities for solving complex problems.

The ability of deep learning models to automatically learn hierarchical representations from unstructured data has been a game-changer. Rather than relying on manual feature engineering, DL models can learn complex patterns and representations directly from raw data. This has led to breakthroughs in tasks such as image recognition, where deep CNNs have outperformed traditional methods and achieved human-level performance.

DL has also benefited from the availability of large-scale datasets, increased computational power, and advancements in parallel computing. The development of specialized hardware, such as graphics processing units (GPUs), has accelerated the training and inference processes, making it feasible to train and deploy DL models on a large scale.

In brief, the emergence of DBNs and the subsequent success of DL models, such as AlexNet, have revolutionized the field of AI. DL has become a dominant paradigm, pushing the boundaries of what is possible in terms of data analysis, pattern recognition, and decision-making. Its impact can be seen in various industries and applications, and it continues to drive advancements in AI research and development.

1.3 What Makes Deep Learning Different

There are several key factors that differentiate DL from conventional ML methods:

1.3.1 Representation Learning

Representation learning is a fundamental concept in deep learning that refers to the process of automatically learning meaningful representations or features directly from raw data. In traditional ML approaches, feature engineering plays a crucial role, where domain experts manually design and extract relevant features from the input data (Liu et al., 2015). However, DL models have the remarkable ability to automatically learn and discover useful representations from raw data, eliminating the need for manual feature engineering.

DL models learn hierarchical representations by stacking multiple layers of interconnected neurons. Each layer in the network learns to extract increasingly abstract and complex features from the input data (Ging et al., 2020). The lower layers capture low-level features such as edges, textures, or local patterns, while the higher layers learn to combine these low-level features to represent more complex structures and concepts. By automatically learning hierarchical representations, DL models can effectively handle complex and high-dimensional data, such as images, audio, and text. For example, in image recognition tasks, deep CNNs can learn to extract low-level features like edges and textures, then gradually learn more complex features like object parts, and finally capture high-level concepts like object classes. Representation learning in DL models offers several advantages. First, it reduces the reliance on manual feature engineering, which can be time-consuming and domain-specific. Instead, DL models can learn directly from raw data, making them more flexible and applicable to a wide range of tasks and domains. Second, the learned representations are often more informative and meaningful, capturing relevant patterns and structures in the data. This can lead to improved performance in various ML tasks, including classification, regression, and generative modeling.

Furthermore, DL models with learned representations can generalize well to new and unseen data. The hierarchical nature of the learned representations allows the models to capture and encode useful features that can be shared across different examples, leading to better generalization and robustness.

1.3.2 Depth and Complexity

Depth is a fundamental characteristic of DL models, referring to the presence of multiple layers of interconnected neurons. Unlike shallow architectures that have only a few layers, DL models can have tens, hundreds, or even thousands of layers. This depth allows the models to learn increasingly complex and abstract representations of the data.

The depth of DL models enables them to capture hierarchical relationships and dependencies within the data. Each layer in the network learns to extract and transform features from the input, passing them to the next layer. The lower layers typically capture low-level features such as edges, textures, or local patterns, while the higher layers combine these low-level features to represent more complex structures and concepts. This hierarchical representation learning allows DL models to discover intricate patterns and structures that may not be easily discernible to shallow architectures or traditional ML methods. The depth of DL models contributes to their ability to handle complex and high-dimensional data effectively. In tasks such as image recognition, natural language processing, or speech recognition, deep architectures have shown remarkable performance improvements compared to shallow models. This is because the depth allows the models to learn and represent the data in a more expressive and nuanced manner.

The complexity of the learned representations increases with the depth of the model. As the information flows through multiple layers, each layer captures and refines different aspects of the data. This enables the models to capture and model intricate relationships, dependencies, and variations in the data. The increased complexity of the learned representations allows DL models to excel in tasks that require a high level of abstraction and understanding, such as object detection, machine translation, or sentiment analysis.

However, the depth of DL models also introduces certain challenges. Training deep architectures can be more challenging than shallow ones due to issues like vanishing or exploding gradients, which can hinder the learning process. To address these challenges, techniques such as careful weight initialization, activation functions that alleviate the vanishing gradient problem (e.g., ReLU), and advanced optimization algorithms (e.g., Adam, RMSprop) are employed.

1.3.3 End-to-End Learning

End-to-end learning is a key characteristic of DL models, allowing them to learn directly from raw input to output without relying on intermediate steps or manual feature engineering. In traditional ML approaches, the pipeline often involves preprocessing the data, extracting relevant features, and then using these features to train a model. DL models, on the other hand, aim to learn all the necessary transformations and representations from the raw input data in a single integrated process. One of the advantages of end-to-end learning is its ability to automate the feature engineering process. In traditional ML, domain experts often spend a significant amount of time and effort handcrafting features that are believed to be relevant for the task at hand. This process can be subjective, time-consuming, and prone to errors. In contrast, DL models learn to automatically extract features and representations directly from the raw input data. By leveraging the power of neural networks, DL models can learn complex and meaningful representations that capture relevant patterns and structures in the data.

End-to-end learning simplifies the ML pipeline by eliminating the need for separate feature extraction and model training steps. This can lead to more efficient and streamlined workflows, as well as reduced human effort in designing and fine-tuning the pipeline. Also, it allows for more flexibility in handling diverse types of data, as DL models can directly process raw data in various formats such as images, text, or audio. Another benefit of end-to-end learning is the potential for improved model performance. By jointly optimizing the entire pipeline, DL models can capture intricate dependencies and interactions between the input and output. This can lead to more accurate and robust predictions, especially in tasks where the relationships between the input and output are complex and nonlinear.

However, end-to-end learning also comes with its challenges. DL models typically require large amounts of labeled data to learn effectively. The lack of interpretability can be another drawback, as the learned representations and decision-making processes in deep neural networks can be difficult to interpret or explain.

1.3.4 Big Data and Scalability

Big data and scalability are crucial aspects of DL, enabling the effective training and deployment of large-scale models. Here is a detailed description of these concepts.

1. *Big Data:* Deep learning models thrive on large amounts of labeled data. The availability of big data has been instrumental in the success of DL. With the proliferation of digital devices and the internet, massive amounts of data are generated daily, providing an abundance of information for training DL models. This data comes from diverse sources such as social media, sensor networks, medical records, and more. The sheer volume, variety, and velocity of data contribute to the richness and

diversity of the training data, enabling DL models to capture complex patterns and make accurate predictions.

2. *Data Labeling:* DL models typically require labeled data for training. Labeled data consists of input samples along with their corresponding ground truth labels or annotations. For example, in image classification, each image is labeled with its corresponding class. Labeling large datasets can be a laborious and time-consuming process, often requiring human annotators or crowdsourcing platforms. However, advancements in automatic or semi-automatic labeling techniques, as well as the availability of pre-labeled datasets, have eased the burden of data labeling to some extent.
3. *Scalability:* DL models often deal with high-dimensional data and complex computations, which require substantial computational resources. To address this, DL algorithms can be scaled using parallel computing architectures and distributed systems. Graphics processing units (GPUs) and tensor processing units (TPUs) provide massively parallel computing capabilities, allowing DL models to perform computations on large-scale datasets more efficiently. Distributed training frameworks, such as TensorFlow and PyTorch, enable the distribution of model training across multiple devices or machines, enabling faster training and improved scalability.
4. *Cloud Computing:* Cloud computing has played a significant role in supporting the scalability of DL models. Cloud service providers offer scalable computing resources, including GPUs and TPUs, which can be easily provisioned and accessed on-demand. This allows researchers and practitioners to leverage powerful computing infrastructure without the need for extensive hardware investments. Cloud-based platforms also provide pre-configured environments and frameworks for DL, simplifying the deployment and management of large-scale models.
5. *Challenges:* While big data and scalability offer tremendous opportunities for DL, they also present challenges. Managing and storing large datasets can be complex and require efficient data storage and retrieval mechanisms. Furthermore, training DL models on massive datasets can be computationally intensive and time-consuming. Techniques such as mini-batch training, distributed training, and model parallelism help address these challenges by breaking down the computations and distributing them across multiple resources.

The availability of big data and the scalability of DL algorithms have revolutionized the field of AI. These advancements have allowed DL models to harness the power of large datasets and scale effectively using parallel computing architectures. The combination of big data and scalability enables the training of more accurate and robust models, leading to breakthroughs in various domains such as computer vision, natural language processing, and recommendation systems.

1.3.5 Representation Power

Representation power refers to the ability of a DL model to capture and model complex relationships in the data. Here is a detailed description of representation power in DL.

1. *Deep Neural Networks:* DL models, specifically deep neural networks (DNNs), are designed with multiple layers of interconnected neurons. Each layer performs

computations on the input data and passes the results to the next layer. The depth of the network allows it to learn hierarchical representations of the data, where each layer learns increasingly abstract and complex features.

2. *Non-Linear Activation Functions:* DL models utilize nonlinear activation functions, such as ReLU, sigmoid, or tanh, to introduce nonlinearity into the model. These activation functions enable the network to learn and approximate nonlinear mappings between inputs and outputs. Without nonlinear activation functions, the network would be limited to representing linear relationships, severely restricting its ability to capture complex patterns in the data.
3. *Feature Extraction:* DL models can automatically learn meaningful and relevant features from raw data. Instead of relying on manual feature engineering, where domain experts extract specific features, DL models learn to extract features directly from the data during the training process. This feature extraction ability allows the model to represent high-level and abstract features that are relevant for the task at hand.
4. *Expressive Power:* The combination of multiple layers and nonlinear activation functions gives DL models their expressive power. They can represent highly complex functions and capture intricate relationships in the data. This representation power enables DL models to excel in tasks that involve complex patterns, such as image recognition, natural language processing, and speech synthesis.
5. *Transfer Learning:* The representation power of DL models also enables transfer learning, where a pre-trained model on one task can be used as a starting point for another related task. The pre-trained model has learned rich representations from a large dataset, and these representations can be transferred and fine-tuned on a smaller task-specific dataset. This approach leverages the representation power of DL models and speeds up the training process for new tasks.

DL models possess strong representation power due to their multi-layer architecture, nonlinear activation functions, and ability to learn relevant features from raw data. This power enables them to capture complex relationships in the data and perform exceptionally well on a wide range of tasks. The representation power of DL models has been instrumental in their success and their widespread adoption in various fields of AI.

These factors make DL a powerful and versatile approach for solving complex problems across various domains. The ability to learn hierarchical representations, handle big data, and perform end-to-end learning sets DL apart from traditional ML methods, allowing it to achieve state-of-the-art results in many applications.

1.4 The Modern ML Landscape

The modern ML landscape encompasses a diverse set of methodologies, frameworks, and algorithms that have emerged due to advancements in technology, data availability, and computational power. Here is a detailed description of the key components of the modern ML landscape.

1.4.1 Explainable AI

Explainable AI (XAI) is a branch of AI that focuses on developing ML models and algorithms that can provide interpretable explanations for their decisions or predictions (Xu et al., 2019). The goal of XAI is to make AI systems more transparent, understandable, and trustworthy to users, stakeholders, and regulatory bodies (Gunning et al., 2019).

In many AI applications, such as healthcare, finance, and criminal justice, it is crucial to understand why a particular decision or prediction was made. For example, in a medical diagnosis system, doctors and patients need to understand the factors that led to a specific diagnosis to have confidence in the system's recommendations (Gade et al., 2019). Similarly, in loan approval systems, it is important to explain the reasons behind a loan application being approved or rejected to ensure fairness and prevent biases.

Explainable AI techniques aim to address the "black box" nature of some complex ML models, which can make it challenging to understand how the model arrived at its output. By providing explanations, users can gain insights into the model's decision-making process and assess the validity and reliability of its predictions.

There are several approaches to achieving explainability in AI models. These include the following.

1. *Rule-based Explanations:* This approach involves representing the model's decisions in the form of human-understandable rules. These rules can be derived from the model's internal structure or extracted from the model's behavior on specific instances.
2. *Feature Importance:* This approach quantifies the importance of input features in influencing the model's output. Techniques such as feature attribution, sensitivity analysis, and permutation importance can be used to identify the most influential features.
3. *Model-Specific Explanations:* Some models, such as decision trees or linear models, naturally provide interpretable explanations. These models can directly reveal the decision rules or the contribution of each feature in the prediction.
4. *Local Explanations:* Local explanations focus on explaining individual predictions rather than the entire model. Techniques like LIME (local interpretable model-agnostic explanations) generate locally interpretable models that approximate the behavior of the black-box model for specific instances.
5. *Visualizations:* Visualizations can help users understand the model's behavior by presenting the underlying data and the model's predictions in a visually intuitive manner. Techniques like heatmaps, saliency maps, and concept activation vectors can provide visual explanations.

Explainable AI is vital for several reasons. It helps improve transparency and accountability in AI systems, ensuring that users and stakeholders have a clear understanding of how decisions are made. Moreover, it aids in detecting and addressing biases and unfairness in AI models, allowing for more equitable and responsible decision-making. Furthermore, explainable AI fosters trust and acceptance of AI technologies, as users can comprehend the reasoning behind the model's outputs. Researchers, practitioners, and policymakers continue to explore and develop new techniques and standards for XAI to meet the increasing demand for transparency and fairness in AI systems. The goal is to strike a balance between model complexity and interpretability, allowing for AI models that are both powerful and accountable.

XAI focuses on developing ML models and algorithms that provide interpretable explanations for their decisions or predictions. This is particularly important in applications where transparency, fairness, and accountability are crucial.

1.4.2 AutoML

AutoML (automated machine learning) is an emerging field in ML that focuses on automating various stages of the ML pipeline to make the process more efficient and accessible. AutoML tools aim to reduce the manual effort required in tasks such as data preprocessing, feature engineering, model selection, and hyperparameter tuning, thereby enabling non-experts to build ML models and accelerating the development cycle (He et al., 2021). The traditional ML pipeline involves several iterative and time-consuming steps, requiring domain expertise and significant manual intervention. AutoML aims to streamline this process by automating repetitive and tedious tasks, allowing users to focus on higher-level problem formulation and analysis (Guyon et al., 2019; Karmaker et al., 2021).

Here are some key components of AutoML.

1. *Data Preprocessing:* AutoML tools can automate data cleaning, handling missing values, dealing with outliers, and transforming data into suitable formats for ML algorithms. These tools can automatically detect and address common data quality issues, saving time and effort for users.
2. *Feature Engineering:* Feature engineering is a crucial step in ML, involving the creation and selection of informative features from raw data. AutoML tools can automatically generate and select relevant features based on various techniques such as statistical analysis, dimensionality reduction, and feature importance estimation.
3. *Model Selection:* AutoML tools can automatically search and select the best model architecture and algorithm for a given task. They explore a range of models, evaluate their performance using cross-validation or other metrics, and provide recommendations on the most suitable model for the data.
4. *Hyperparameter Tuning:* Hyperparameters are configuration settings that control the behavior and performance of ML models. AutoML tools can automate the process of hyperparameter tuning by searching through a predefined space of hyperparameter values, optimizing model performance, and selecting the best hyperparameter configuration.
5. *Model Evaluation and Deployment:* AutoML tools provide metrics and evaluation reports to assess the performance of the trained models. They assist in comparing different models, analyzing their strengths and weaknesses, and selecting the best model for deployment. Some AutoML tools also support the deployment of trained models to production environments or cloud platforms.

AutoML has gained significant popularity due to its potential to democratize ML and make it accessible to a wider range of users. It enables domain experts who may not have extensive ML expertise to leverage the power of ML models for their specific applications. Additionally, AutoML can accelerate the development cycle by automating repetitive tasks, reducing the time and effort required for model development.

However, it is important to note that AutoML is not a one-size-fits-all solution and may have limitations in certain scenarios. Expert knowledge and human intervention are still essential for defining the problem, understanding the data, and interpreting the results. Nonetheless, AutoML tools provide valuable support in simplifying and accelerating the ML process, making it more efficient and accessible to a broader audience.

1.4.3 Real-Time and Online Learning

Real-time and online learning techniques are essential in scenarios where the data distribution changes over time or where immediate responses are required. These techniques enable ML models to adapt and update in real time as new data becomes available, allowing them to stay relevant and accurate in dynamic environments. Here are some key aspects of real-time and online learning.

1. *Streaming Data:* Real-time and online learning deal with data streams or continuous data, where new data points arrive sequentially and often in high volume and at high velocity. Unlike traditional batch learning, which processes a fixed dataset, real-time learning continuously updates the model as new data arrives, enabling the model to adapt to changing patterns and trends.
2. *Incremental Learning:* Real-time learning employs incremental learning algorithms that can update the model's parameters with each new data point. Instead of retraining the model from scratch on the entire dataset, incremental learning techniques update the model incrementally, making it computationally efficient and capable of handling large-scale streaming data.
3. *Adaptive Models:* Real-time learning models are designed to adapt to changes in the data distribution over time. These models can dynamically adjust their parameters and update their internal representations to capture evolving patterns and trends. This adaptability allows the models to maintain accuracy and relevance as the data changes.
4. *Online Decision-Making:* In applications where immediate responses are required, real-time learning enables online decision-making. The model can make predictions or take actions in real time based on incoming data, enabling quick and timely responses to changing conditions or events.
5. *Concept Drift Detection:* Real-time learning techniques often incorporate mechanisms to detect concept drift, which refers to changes in the data distribution over time. By monitoring the model's performance and comparing it to historical data, concept drift detection allows the model to identify when the underlying patterns have changed and initiate appropriate adaptation or retraining.

Real-time and online learning techniques find applications in various domains such as fraud detection, anomaly detection, recommendation systems, sensor data analysis, and online advertising, among others. These techniques enable models to continuously learn and adapt to changing conditions, improving their performance and effectiveness in dynamic environments. It is important to note that real-time and online learning come with their challenges. Handling high-volume and high-velocity data streams, managing computational resources for continuous learning, and ensuring the stability and reliability of the model's updates are some of the considerations in real-time learning systems. However, the ability to learn and update models in real time provides significant advantages in applications where responsiveness and adaptability are critical.

1.4.4 Interpretability and Fairness

Interpretability and fairness are two important aspects of ML that have gained significant attention in recent years (Meng et al., 2021, 2022). Here's a detailed description of each.

1. *Interpretability:* Interpretability in ML refers to the ability to understand and explain how a model makes predictions or decisions. It is important because it enables humans to trust and verify the outputs of the model, understand the underlying factors influencing the predictions, and identify potential biases or errors.
   Interpretability methods can be categorized into two types: global interpretability and local interpretability. Global interpretability aims to provide an overall understanding of the model's behavior, such as feature importance or the relationship between inputs and outputs. Local interpretability focuses on explaining individual predictions or decisions, allowing stakeholders to understand why a specific outcome was reached. Various techniques are used to enhance interpretability, including feature importance analysis, rule extraction, model-agnostic interpretability methods (e.g., LIME and SHAP), and visualization techniques. These methods help reveal the inner workings of the model and provide insights into its decision-making process.
2. *Fairness:* Fairness in ML refers to the absence of bias or discrimination in the decision-making process of ML models. It aims to ensure that models treat individuals or groups fairly and do not exhibit unfair advantages or disadvantages based on protected attributes such as race, gender, or age.
   Fairness concerns arise because ML models are trained on historical data, which may reflect societal biases and inequalities. If the model learns from biased data, it can perpetuate and amplify existing biases, leading to unfair outcomes. Fairness in ML requires careful consideration of the data used for training, the features considered by the model, and the evaluation metrics used to assess model performance. Various fairness metrics and techniques have been proposed to address these issues, including disparate impact analysis, equalized odds, and individual fairness. Additionally, research in adversarial ML aims to identify and mitigate bias and discrimination in ML models.
   Ensuring interpretability and fairness in ML models is crucial for building trust, addressing ethical concerns, and promoting responsible AI. Interpretability allows stakeholders to understand and scrutinize the model's decisions, while fairness ensures that the model operates in an unbiased and equitable manner. Both aspects are essential for deploying ML models in sensitive domains such as healthcare, finance, criminal justice, and social welfare, where transparency, accountability, and fairness are of utmost importance.

Overall, the modern ML landscape offers a wide array of methodologies, frameworks, and algorithms that can be applied to various data types, problem domains, and application needs. It reflects the continuous advancements in ML research and technology, providing practitioners with a rich toolbox to tackle complex data-driven challenges across different industries.

1.5 Industry Applications and Use Cases

Deep learning has found applications across various industries due to its ability to analyze large amounts of data and extract meaningful patterns. Here's a detailed description of some industry applications and use cases.

1. *Healthcare*: DL is transforming healthcare by enabling personalized treatment, improving diagnosis accuracy, and enhancing patient care. Applications include the analysis of electronic health records for disease prediction, medication discovery, medical image analysis (e.g., radiology and pathology), and genomics. DL models aid in pattern recognition, anomaly detection, and forecasting, resulting in more effective and precise healthcare delivery.
2. *Finance*: ML has revolutionized the financial sector by automating processes, enhancing investment strategies, and improving risk assessment. Use cases include credit scoring for loan approvals, fraud detection to identify suspicious activities, algorithmic trading for automated investment decisions, portfolio optimization, and risk assessment. ML models analyze massive volumes of financial data to provide insights for risk management, fraud prevention, and better decision-making.
3. *Retail*: ML is transforming the retail industry by enabling targeted marketing, streamlining supply chains, and improving customer experiences. Use cases include demand forecasting to optimize inventory levels, consumer segmentation for personalized marketing campaigns, recommendation systems to suggest relevant products, price optimization, and inventory management. ML models analyze consumer data, purchasing trends, and market dynamics to deliver tailored marketing campaigns and increase operational efficiency.
4. *Transportation*: ML plays a crucial role in the transportation sector, particularly for autonomous driving, traffic control, and logistical planning. Use cases include route planning to optimize travel times, traffic forecasting to manage congestion, anomaly detection for real-time incident management, fleet management for efficient operations, and analysis of driver behavior for safety improvement. ML models leverage data from sensors, cameras, and historical traffic patterns to make transportation systems safer and more efficient.
5. *Manufacturing*: ML is revolutionizing the manufacturing industry by enhancing quality control, streamlining processes, and enabling predictive maintenance. Use cases include anomaly detection to identify manufacturing defects, preventive maintenance to minimize equipment downtime, supply chain optimization to reduce costs, process optimization for improved efficiency, and robotics for automation. ML models analyze sensor data, identify abnormalities, forecast equipment breakdowns, and optimize industrial processes to save costs and boost productivity.
6. *Natural Language Processing*: Natural language processing (NLP) combines ML and linguistics to enable efficient language processing and task automation. Use cases include information retrieval, speech recognition, chatbots for customer service, language translation services, sentiment analysis of customer feedback, and content analysis. NLP models understand and process human language, enabling

applications such as virtual assistants, language translation, content recommendation, and automated customer support.

These are just a few examples of the broad range of applications of DL in various industries. DL's ability to analyze complex data and extract meaningful insights has opened up new possibilities for innovation and improved decision-making in numerous fields.

1.6 Challenges and Future Prospects

Challenges and future prospects play a significant role in shaping the advancement and responsible deployment of ML. Here's a detailed description of the challenges and future prospects in ML.

1. *Data Bias and Quality:* Ensuring high-quality and unbiased data is crucial for ML model training. Data quality issues such as missing values, outliers, and biases can adversely affect model performance and fairness. Addressing data bias and improving data quality are essential to build reliable and robust ML models that make unbiased predictions.
2. *Interpretability and Explainability:* Interpretability is a challenge, especially in complex DL models, where understanding the rationale behind predictions can be difficult. Building trust and making informed decisions depend on the interpretability and explainability of ML models. Research in explainable AI aims to develop methods that provide transparent and interpretable explanations for model decisions.
3. *Scalability and Computational Resources:* As datasets and models grow in size and complexity, scalability becomes a challenge. Training complex models requires significant computational resources, including processing speed and memory. Innovations in hardware, such as specialized processors for ML workloads, and distributed computing frameworks are necessary to address scalability issues and enable efficient training of large-scale ML models.
4. *Ethical Issues:* The use of ML raises ethical concerns related to privacy, security, and the potential impact on employment. Ensuring fairness in ML models, protecting sensitive data, and addressing the societal effects of automation are critical areas for research and policy development. Ethical guidelines and regulations are being developed to promote responsible and ethical use of ML technologies.
5. *Continuous Learning and Adaptability:* ML models need to be adaptable and capable of learning continuously as new data becomes available. Research is focused on developing models that can update and adapt to changing data while retaining knowledge from previous learning experiences. Lifelong learning approaches aim to create ML models that can learn incrementally and stay up-to-date with evolving information.
6. *Multimodal Learning and Context Awareness:* Integrating multiple modalities, such as text, images, and audio, into ML models introduces new challenges. Building models that can effectively process and understand multimodal input and context is an active area of research. Advances in multimodal learning will enable more sophisticated applications that can leverage diverse sources of information.

The future of ML is promising, with ongoing innovations in techniques such as DL, reinforcement learning, and others. The challenges in ML will be addressed through research and advancements in areas such as XAI, lifelong learning, and ethical AI. Responsible and beneficial deployment of ML technologies across industries will be supported, leading to continued advancements and positive impacts.

1.7 Prerequisites

To embark on a journey into DL and the contemporary ML scene, it is important to meet certain prerequisites. These prerequisites include the following.

1.7.1 *Solid Mathematical Grounding*

A strong foundation in mathematics is crucial for understanding the underlying concepts and algorithms in DL. Key areas of mathematics that are relevant to DL include the following.

- *Linear Algebra*: The mathematical foundation for comprehending and working with vectors, matrices, and linear transformations is provided by linear algebra. Understanding the inner workings of DL models requires a thorough understanding of ideas like vector operations, matrix multiplication, eigenvalues, eigenvectors, and matrix factorization.
- Calculus: DL model training and optimization require a solid understanding of calculus. Calculus is required to understand concepts like derivatives, gradients, optimization methods (like gradient descent), and backpropagation. Understanding these ideas makes it easier to analyze model behavior and create effective learning algorithms.
- Probability and Statistics: To model uncertainty and make wise decisions, probability theory and statistics are crucial. Understanding the probabilistic underpinnings of ML algorithms requires an understanding of concepts like probability distributions, statistical measurements, hypothesis testing, and Bayesian inference.

1.7.2 *Coding Know-How*

Proficiency in coding is essential for implementing and experimenting with DL algorithms. The following skills are particularly important.

- *Programming Languages*: Familiarity with a programming language commonly used in DL, such as Python.
- *Software Libraries*: Knowledge of popular DL frameworks and libraries, such as TensorFlow or PyTorch.
- *Data Manipulation*: Understanding how to preprocess and manipulate data to prepare it for training DL models.
- *Debugging and Troubleshooting*: Ability to identify and fix coding errors and issues that may arise during model development.

1.7.3 *Knowledge of ML Ideas*

Having a solid understanding of fundamental ML concepts is essential for diving into DL. Some key concepts to be familiar with include the following.

- *Supervised Learning*: Understanding the concepts of labeled data, training, and evaluation in supervised learning tasks.
- *Unsupervised Learning*: Knowledge of unsupervised learning techniques such as clustering and dimensionality reduction.

- *Model Evaluation*: Familiarity with evaluation metrics used to assess the performance of ML models.
- *Overfitting and Underfitting*: Understanding the concepts of model complexity, generalization, and methods to address overfitting and underfitting.

1.7.4 Desire to Learn

DL is a rapidly evolving field, and a strong desire to continuously learn and stay updated with the latest research and advancements is crucial. Being open-minded, curious, and motivated to explore new concepts and techniques will help in mastering DL skills.

By meeting these prerequisites, individuals can establish a strong foundation for understanding and applying DL concepts effectively. They will be well-equipped to delve into the world of DL and the contemporary ML landscape and pursue further learning and exploration in this exciting field.

1.8 Overview of Subsequent Chapters

In the subsequent chapters, the book covers various important topics and techniques in the field of DL. Here is an overview of what each chapter covers.

ML Fundamentals: Chapter 2 focuses on the fundamental concepts in ML, including supervised and unsupervised learning, binary classification, regression, model generalization, and regularization techniques. It provides a solid foundation for understanding the principles of ML.

Neural Networks Fundamentals: In Chapter 3, the fundamental ideas and components of neural networks are explored. It covers artificial neurons, network structure, activation functions, training algorithms like backpropagation, and the concept of DNNs with multiple hidden layers.

Convolutional Neural Networks: Chapter 4 delves into the architecture and applications of convolutional neural networks (CNNs), which are designed for processing visual data such as images and videos. It explains convolutional layers, pooling layers, and fully connected layers in CNNs, highlighting their effectiveness in image recognition, object detection, and image segmentation.

Recurrent Neural Networks: Chapter 5 introduces RNNs, specialized neural networks for handling sequential data. It explains the recurrent connections in RNNs, their ability to model temporal relationships, and the challenges of the vanishing gradient problem. Moreover, it covers variants of RNNs, such as LSTM and gated recurrent unit (GRU), which address the vanishing gradient problem and have proven effective in tasks like language modeling and sentiment analysis.

Generative Adversarial Networks: Chapter 6 focuses on generative adversarial networks (GANs), which consist of a generator and a discriminator. GANs are used for generating synthetic data that resembles a given training dataset. The adversarial training process between the generator and discriminator leads to the improvement of the generator's ability to produce realistic data. Applications of GANs in image synthesis and text generation are discussed.

Radial Basis Function Networks: Chapter 7 explores radial basis function networks (RBFNs), which are neural networks used for pattern recognition and function approximation. RBFNs have input, hidden, and output layers, and they employ radial basis functions to measure the similarity between input data and prototype vectors. The advantages of RBFNs, such as rapid learning, robust generalization, and interpretability, are highlighted.

Self-Organizing Maps: Chapter 8 focuses on self-organizing maps (SOMs), unsupervised neural networks inspired by the organization and learning principles of the human brain. SOMs use a competitive learning method to map high-dimensional data onto a low-dimensional grid, allowing for dimensionality reduction while preserving the structure of the data. SOMs are effective in tasks like feature extraction, data exploration, and clustering.

These subsequent chapters provide an in-depth understanding of various DL techniques and their applications. Each chapter explores different neural network architectures and algorithms, allowing readers to gain knowledge and practical insights into these topics.

1.9 Installing the Required Libraries

Installing the required libraries and dependencies in your Python environment is essential before you can start working with DL and explore the current ML landscape. The procedure for installing well-known DL libraries like TensorFlow and PyTorch as well as setting up the Python environment is thoroughly explained in this section. We will also talk about other data pretreatment and visualization libraries that can improve your DL workflow. Here is a detailed description of the process.

1.9.1 Python Environment Setup

Before installing DL libraries, it is important to have Python installed on your system. You can download and install Python from the official Python website (https://www.python.org). It is recommended to use Python 3.x, as it is the most up-to-date version. After installing Python, you can create a virtual environment to separate the dependencies of your projects. You may handle several Python package versions for various projects using virtual environments. Utilizing programs like virtualenv or conda, you can build a virtual environment. Prior to installing libraries, turn on the virtual environment.

1.9.2 Package Management

Python provides package managers like pip and Anaconda to manage and install libraries. Pip is the most commonly used package manager. You can check if pip is installed by running the command "pip –version" in your command prompt or terminal. If it is not installed, you can install it by following the instructions provided on the official pip website (https://pip.pypa.io).

1.9.3 DL Libraries

There are several popular DL libraries available, including TensorFlow and PyTorch. To install these libraries, you can use pip by running the following commands:

- For TensorFlow: "pip install tensorflow"
- For PyTorch: "pip install torch"

Make sure to use the appropriate version based on your system and requirements. You can refer to the official documentation of each library for more detailed installation instructions. The CPU version of the libraries will be installed using these commands. Install the GPU-enabled versions for greater performance if you have a suitable GPU. For precise directions on installing GPU versions and setting up GPU support, consult the official documentation of TensorFlow and PyTorch.

1.9.4 Additional Libraries

In addition to the DL libraries, there are other libraries that can enhance your DL workflow. Some commonly used libraries include the following.

- NumPy: A library for numerical computing that provides support for large, multidimensional arrays and mathematical functions.
- Pandas: A library for data manipulation and analysis, particularly useful for handling structured data.
- Matplotlib: A library for creating visualizations and plots.

You can install these libraries using pip by running the commands:

- "pip install numpy"
- "pip install pandas"
- "pip install matplotlib"

Again, make sure to use the appropriate version based on your system and requirements.

By following these steps, you will be able to install the required libraries and dependencies in your Python environment, enabling you to work with DL and explore the current ML landscape. It is recommended to create a virtual environment to keep your Python environment isolated and organized.

1.10 Summary

This chapter covers several key concepts and aspects of deep learning and the current state of machine learning. It starts by introducing the concepts of AI, ML, and DL and discusses their relationships and the significance of DL in the modern ML landscape.

The chapter explores the historical background of ML before DL and its development over the years. It highlights the emergence of deep neural networks and their ability to create hierarchical representations directly from raw data, which sets DL apart from traditional ML approaches.

The chapter emphasizes the importance of the prerequisites for DL, including a solid mathematical foundation, programming skills, familiarity with ML concepts, and a curious mindset. These prerequisites are crucial for understanding and effectively applying DL techniques. It also discusses the installation of necessary libraries, such as TensorFlow and PyTorch, as well as other libraries for data preprocessing and visualization. These libraries are essential for working with DL models and improving the DL workflow.

Lastly, the chapter examines the significance of DL in contemporary AI applications. DL has revolutionized various fields, including NLP, computer vision, robotics, and generative modeling. It has enabled advancements in sentiment analysis, image categorization, object identification, language translation, robotics, and more. Overall, this chapter provides a foundation for understanding DL and its relevance in the current ML landscape. It has set the stage for further exploration in subsequent chapters, where we will delve into topics such as ML fundamentals, neural networks, CNNs, recurrent neural networks, generative adversarial networks, radial basis function networks, and self-organizing maps.

References

Gade, K., Geyik, S. C., Kenthapadi, K., Mithal, V., & Taly, A. (2019). Explainable AI in industry. *Proceedings of the 25th ACM SIGKDD International Conference on Knowledge Discovery & Data Mining*, 3203–3204.

Ging, S., Zolfaghari, M., Pirsiavash, H., & Brox, T. (2020). Coot: Cooperative hierarchical transformer for video-text representation learning. *Advances in Neural Information Processing Systems, 33*, 22605–22618.

Gunning, D., Stefik, M., Choi, J., Miller, T., Stumpf, S., & Yang, G.-Z. (2019). XAI—Explainable artificial intelligence. *Science Robotics, 4*(37), eaay7120.

Guyon, I., Sun-Hosoya, L., Boullé, M., Escalante, H. J., Escalera, S., Liu, Z., Jajetic, D., Ray, B., Saeed, M., & Sebag, M. (2019). Analysis of the AutoML challenge series. *Automated Machine Learning, 177*.

He, X., Zhao, K., & Chu, X. (2021). AutoML: A survey of the state-of-the-art. *Knowledge-Based Systems, 212*, 106622.

Karmaker, S. K., Hassan, M. M., Smith, M. J., Xu, L., Zhai, C., & Veeramachaneni, K. (2021). Automl to date and beyond: Challenges and opportunities. *ACM Computing Surveys (CSUR), 54*(8), 1–36.

Liu, X., Gao, J., He, X., Deng, L., Duh, K., & Wang, Y.-Y. (2015). Representation learning using multi-task deep neural networks for semantic classification and information retrieval. In *Proceedings of the 2015 conference of the North American chapter of the association for computational linguistics: Human language technologies*. Microsoft Research.

Meng, C., Trinh, L., Xu, N., Enouen, J., & Liu, Y. (2022). Interpretability and fairness evaluation of deep learning models on MIMIC-IV dataset. *Scientific Reports, 12*(1), 7166.

Meng, C., Trinh, L., Xu, N., & Liu, Y. (2021). Mimic-if: Interpretability and fairness evaluation of deep learning models on mimic-iv dataset. *ArXiv Preprint ArXiv:2102.06761*.

Xu, F., Uszkoreit, H., Du, Y., Fan, W., Zhao, D., & Zhu, J. (2019). Explainable AI: A brief survey on history, research areas, approaches and challenges. In *CCF international conference on natural language processing and Chinese computing* (pp. 563–574). Cham: Springer International Publishing.

Chapter 2

Machine Learning Fundamentals

In this chapter, we delve into the application of machine learning for addressing social science and public policy problems. We begin by providing an introduction to the field, emphasizing the significance of machine learning techniques in tackling complex challenges in these domains.

We guide readers through the entire end-to-end machine learning process, starting from data collection and preprocessing to model evaluation and deployment. By following this process, readers gain a comprehensive understanding of the various stages involved in utilizing machine learning for social science and public policy applications.

The chapter focuses on both supervised and unsupervised machine learning methods. For supervised learning, we explore techniques such as classification, where models are trained to predict predefined labels or categories for given inputs. Moreover, we cover regression, which involves predicting continuous numerical values based on input features. By studying these methods, readers gain insights into how to apply them to real-world social science problems, such as sentiment analysis, demographic prediction, or policy impact evaluation.

In addition to supervised learning, we delve into unsupervised learning methods, with a particular emphasis on clustering. Clustering algorithms enable the identification of natural groupings within datasets, allowing researchers to uncover hidden patterns or similarities among samples. This knowledge can be invaluable in understanding social dynamics, identifying community structures, or segmenting populations based on shared characteristics.

Throughout the chapter, we strive to provide an intuitive explanation of the machine learning methods, ensuring that readers grasp the underlying concepts without getting lost in technical jargon. We present practical tips and guidelines for effectively using these techniques in real-world scenarios, empowering readers to confidently apply machine learning to address social science and public policy challenges.

By the end of the chapter, readers will have developed a holistic overview of the components comprising a machine learning pipeline and the methods involved. They will be equipped with the necessary knowledge to select appropriate techniques, preprocess data, train models, evaluate performance, and interpret results in the context of social science problems. This chapter serves as a valuable resource by providing a framework for leveraging machine learning in practice and facilitating evidence-based decision-making in social science and public policy domains.

We aim to clarify the concept of "machine learning" for individuals who may have heard of it but are unsure about its specifics, how it differs from traditional statistics

DOI: 10.1201/9781003654216-3

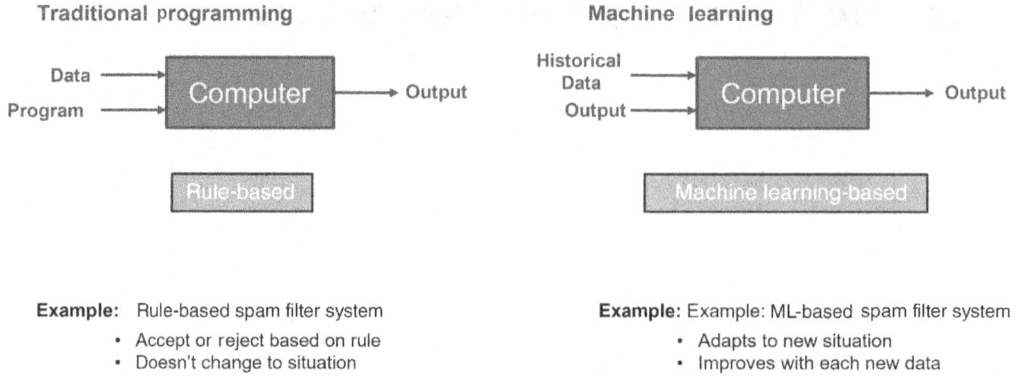

Figure 2.1 Comparison between traditional programming and machine learning.

as presented in Figure 2.1, and its relevance for social scientists. We will demystify machine learning, establishing connections to existing knowledge in statistics and data analysis while exploring novel concepts and methods developed in this field.

While machine learning has its origins in computer science, it has been significantly influenced by mathematics and statistics over the past 15–20 years. Throughout this chapter, we will demonstrate that many of the concepts in machine learning are not entirely new but have been present in other domains, albeit under different names. For instance, logistic regression, a well-known classification method in statistics, is also a supervised learning method in machine learning. Similarly, cluster analysis, which you may be familiar with from data analysis, corresponds to an unsupervised learning technique in machine learning.

In addition to familiar concepts, we will introduce you to new methods more exclusive to machine learning, such as random forests, support vector machines, and neural networks. Our approach in this chapter will be to keep formalisms to a minimum and focus on conveying intuition and practical insights. By doing so, we hope to make you comfortable with machine learning vocabulary, concepts, and processes, enabling you to explore and utilize these methods and tools in your research and professional endeavors.

For instance, let's consider a practical example: sentiment analysis in social media data. In this case, machine learning algorithms can be used to classify social media posts or comments as positive, negative, or neutral. By training a supervised learning model using labeled data (e.g., social media posts with manually assigned sentiment labels), the model can learn patterns and features associated with different sentiments. Once trained, the model can automatically classify new, unlabeled social media posts based on the patterns it has learned.

Through this chapter, we hope to bridge the gap between traditional statistical methods and the world of machine learning, empowering you to leverage these techniques in your own research and practice as a social scientist. By gaining a solid understanding of machine learning vocabulary, concepts, and processes, you will be equipped to explore and apply these powerful methods to various social science problems, facilitating data-driven insights and informed decision-making.

2.1 Intuition

Machine learning is a field of study and practice that involves developing computer programs capable of improving their performance and making predictions or decisions based on data and experience. It aims to enable computers to learn and improve their abilities in a manner similar to how humans learn through experience.

Arthur Samuel, a pioneer in the field, coined the term "machine learning" in 1959. He demonstrated its potential by programming a computer to play checkers. Through playing against itself and human opponents, the computer continuously refined its strategies and improved its game-playing skills. With sufficient training and experience, the computer eventually surpassed the abilities of its human programmer.

Today, machine learning has evolved far beyond checkers and has found applications in various domains. Machine learning systems are capable of driving autonomous cars, assisting robots in performing complex tasks, providing personalized recommendations for books, products, and movies, identifying potential drugs and genetic markers for diseases, detecting cancer and abnormalities in medical images, understanding language acquisition in the human brain, predicting voter behavior, identifying students at risk of not graduating on time, and solving many other problems.

Over the past two decades, machine learning has become an interdisciplinary field that encompasses computer science, artificial intelligence, databases, and statistics. Its core objective is to design computer systems that improve their performance and decision-making abilities over time through exposure to more data and experience.

Tom Mitchell, in one of the early books on machine learning, provides an operational definition that captures the essence of the field. He states that a computer program is said to learn from experience E with respect to a class of tasks T and a performance measure P if its performance in tasks from T, as evaluated by P, improves with experience E. This definition emphasizes the task-oriented improvement that machine learning seeks to achieve and highlights its role as a tool within a larger system to enhance desired outcomes.

In summary, machine learning enables computers to learn from data and experience, allowing them to improve their performance, make predictions, and make decisions in various domains. It has become a vital tool in driving advancements and improvements in a wide range of applications, and its interdisciplinary nature has contributed to its rapid growth and impact.

Machine learning is well-suited for various scenarios where traditional programming approaches may be challenging or inefficient. Some key areas where machine learning excels include the following.

1. *Problem with Long Lists of Rules*: In complex problems, where the rules or patterns are difficult to define explicitly, machine learning can automatically learn patterns and make predictions based on data. Instead of manually specifying rules, machine learning algorithms can discover underlying patterns and relationships from the data.
2. *Adapting to Continually Changing Environments:* Machine learning models can adapt and learn from new data or changing scenarios. This capability makes them valuable in dynamic environments, where traditional approaches may require constant manual updates to accommodate changes.

3. *Discovering Insights within Large Datasets:* Machine learning algorithms excel at analyzing and extracting meaningful patterns from massive amounts of data. They can identify hidden correlations, trends, and insights that may not be apparent through manual analysis. This is particularly useful in scenarios where the volume of data is too large or complex for humans to process efficiently.

For example, in the case of transaction analysis for a large organization, manually examining each transaction would be time-consuming and impractical. However, machine learning algorithms can analyze the transaction data, identify patterns of fraudulent activity, and flag suspicious transactions for further investigation.

Overall, machine learning provides a powerful toolset for automating complex tasks, adapting to changing environments, and extracting valuable insights from large datasets. It complements traditional programming approaches and offers new possibilities for solving problems across various domains.

2.1.1 Examples of Machine Learning

Commercial machine learning examples include the following.

- *Speech Recognition*: Speech recognition software uses machine learning algorithms to analyze and understand spoken language, allowing systems to transcribe speech, enable voice assistants, and support voice-controlled devices.
- *Autonomous Cars*: Machine learning plays a crucial role in the development of self-driving cars. Algorithms analyze sensor data to detect and identify objects, make decisions, and control the vehicle's movements.
- *Fraud Detection*: Machine learning systems are utilized in fraud detection to identify patterns and anomalies in financial transactions, enabling organizations to flag and prevent fraudulent activities.
- *Personalized Ads*: Online platforms use machine learning to analyze user preferences and browsing behavior, allowing for personalized advertising and product recommendations tailored to individual users.
- Face Recognition: Machine learning is employed in face detection and recognition systems, enabling applications such as surveillance, social networking platforms, and image tagging.
- Social Listening: Machine learning techniques are used to analyze and extract insights from social media data, helping companies understand customer sentiment, monitor brand reputation, and identify trends.
- Credit Scoring: Machine learning models are employed in credit scoring to assess the creditworthiness of individuals and businesses, leveraging historical data to predict the likelihood of loan repayment.
- Prediction of Success and Failure: Machine learning algorithms can be applied to predict outcomes in various domains, such as predicting the success of marketing campaigns, forecasting sales, or identifying factors that contribute to project success or failure.

These examples demonstrate how machine learning is applied in commercial contexts to enhance efficiency, improve decision-making, and deliver personalized experiences.

Some of the applications of machine learning in social science are the following.

- *Predicting Lead Poisoning Risk:* Potash et al. (2015) used random forests, a machine learning classification method, to predict which children are at risk of lead poisoning. By prioritizing lead hazard inspections based on these predictions, they aimed to detect and remediate lead hazards before they could harm the child.
- *Identifying Police Officers at Risk:* Carton et al. (2016) employed various machine learning methods to identify police officers who may be at risk of engaging in adverse behavior, such as unjustified use of force or sustained complaints. This information allowed for targeted interventions, such as training and counseling, to prevent such behaviors.
- *Estimating Treatment Effects:* Athey and Wager (2019) used a modified version of random forests to estimate the heterogeneous treatment effects of interventions aimed at improving student achievement. By analyzing data from The National Study of Learning Mindsets, they assessed the impact of these interventions on different groups of students.
- *Analyzing Police Officer Language:* Voigt et al. (2017) utilized machine learning techniques to analyze body-worn camera footage and assess the respectfulness of police officer language toward white and black community members during routine traffic stops. This analysis aimed to understand and address potential racial disparities in policing.

These examples highlight how machine learning can be applied in social science research to address various issues, including public health, law enforcement, and education. By leveraging the power of machine learning algorithms, researchers can gain insights, make predictions, and inform policy decisions in these domains.

Machine learning has emerged as a powerful approach to solving complex problems in various domains, including social science and policy. It offers several advantages over traditional rule-based systems, making it an attractive choice for addressing challenges in these fields. Some key benefits of machine learning include adaptability, scalability, and cost-effectiveness.

In the past, rule-based systems required experts to manually develop and maintain a set of predefined rules, which often proved inflexible and difficult to scale. With machine learning, systems can automatically learn and improve from data, making them adaptable to changing circumstances and allowing for continuous improvement. This adaptability enables machine learning systems to tackle a wide range of tasks that were previously challenging for rule-based systems.

Moreover, machine learning provides scalability, as it can efficiently process large volumes of data and handle complex problems. This scalability makes it suitable for analyzing extensive datasets and addressing real-world challenges that involve a vast amount of information.

Additionally, machine learning offers cost-effectiveness by reducing the need for manual rule development and maintenance. Once a machine learning model is trained, it can autonomously make predictions or provide insights, reducing the reliance on human experts and minimizing ongoing costs.

Social scientists are uniquely positioned to leverage the advances in machine learning to tackle various complex problems. By applying machine learning techniques, social scientists can address key challenges in their field, such as predicting social phenomena, identifying patterns in large datasets, understanding human behavior, and making informed policy decisions.

By harnessing the power of machine learning, social scientists can uncover valuable insights, generate accurate predictions, and develop effective solutions to address social science and policy problems. The ability to leverage large amounts of data and the adaptability of machine learning methods provide social scientists with powerful tools to advance their research and contribute to evidence-based decision-making.

2.2 Types of Data Analysis

In the context of social science data analysis, there are four main types of analysis that researchers commonly perform: description, detection, prediction, and behavior change (or causal inference).

1. *Description:* The objective of descriptive analysis is to uncover patterns, groupings, or relationships in historical data. This type of analysis relies on descriptive statistics and exploratory data analysis techniques to summarize and visualize data. Descriptive analysis helps researchers gain insights into the characteristics and distributions of variables in their dataset. Advanced methods for descriptive analysis, including unsupervised learning techniques, can reveal more complex patterns and structures within the data.
2. *Detection:* Detection analysis focuses on identifying new or emerging anomalies, events, or patterns in real-time or near real-time data. This type of analysis aims to detect deviations from expected behavior or identify significant events as they happen. An example of detection analysis is early outbreak detection for infectious diseases, where machine learning algorithms can monitor various data sources to identify signals of potential disease outbreaks. By detecting these anomalies early, public health officials can take timely actions to mitigate the spread of diseases.
3. *Prediction:* Prediction analysis utilizes historical data to build models that can forecast future events or behaviors. By leveraging patterns and relationships discovered in the past data, machine learning algorithms can make predictions about future outcomes. This type of analysis is particularly useful in social science research for forecasting various phenomena, such as election results, consumer behavior, or economic indicators. Predictive models can provide valuable insights and aid in decision-making processes.
4. *Behavior Change (or Causal Inference):* Behavior change analysis focuses on understanding the causal relationships within the data to influence desired outcomes. This type of analysis aims to identify cause-and-effect relationships between variables and assess the impact of interventions or policies. Causal inference methods allow researchers to evaluate the effectiveness of interventions and understand the underlying mechanisms that drive behavior change.

While this chapter mainly focuses on description and prediction methods, it acknowledges the ongoing work in developing and using machine learning methods for detection, behavior change, and causal inference in social science research. These areas hold great potential for applying machine learning techniques to address complex problems and derive actionable insights from social science data.

2.3 Machine Learning Process – How it Works

When approaching a machine learning problem, researchers and practitioners generally follow a systematic process that consists of several key steps as presented in Figure 2.2. While the specific details may vary depending on the problem at hand, the following steps provide a general framework for the machine learning process.

1. *Problem Definition:* Clearly define the problem you aim to solve. This involves understanding the goals, objectives, and constraints of the problem, as well as identifying the relevant data sources and available resources.
2. *Data Collection:* Gather the necessary data to train and evaluate your machine learning model. This may involve collecting data from various sources, such as databases, APIs, or data scraping techniques. Ensure that the collected data is representative of the problem and sufficiently covers the relevant features and variations.
3. *Data Preprocessing:* Prepare the collected data for analysis by performing data cleaning, handling missing values, addressing outliers, and transforming the data into a suitable format for the machine learning algorithms. This step also involves feature engineering, where you extract meaningful features from the raw data to improve the model's performance.
4. *Model Selection:* Choose the appropriate machine learning algorithm(s) that best suit the problem at hand. Consider factors such as the nature of the data (e.g., structured or unstructured), the desired output (e.g., classification, regression), and the available resources (e.g., computational power, time constraints). Experiment with different algorithms to find the one that performs well on your data.
5. *Model Training:* Train the selected machine learning model using the prepared training dataset. This involves feeding the data into the model, adjusting its internal parameters, and optimizing its performance. The training process aims to find the optimal configuration of the model that minimizes the error or maximizes a performance metric.

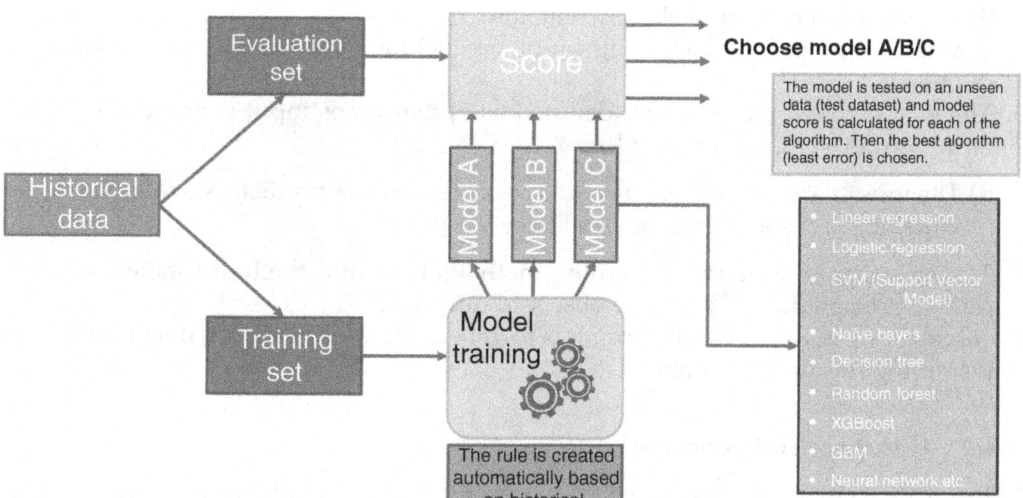

Figure 2.2 Machine learning process.

6. *Model Evaluation:* Assess the performance of the trained model using evaluation metrics appropriate for the problem type (e.g., accuracy, precision, recall, F1-score). Evaluate the model on a separate validation dataset or through cross-validation techniques to ensure its generalization capability. Adjust the model or try different approaches if the performance is unsatisfactory.
7. *Model Deployment:* Once you are satisfied with the model's performance, deploy it into a production environment where it can be used to make predictions or automate decision-making. This step involves integrating the model into the existing infrastructure, handling real-time data inputs, and monitoring its performance in a deployed setting.
8. *Model Monitoring and Maintenance:* Continuously monitor the model's performance and make necessary adjustments as new data becomes available. Retrain the model periodically to account for changes in the data distribution or to incorporate new data. Regular maintenance ensures that the model remains accurate and relevant over time.

Throughout this process, it is important to iterate and refine the steps as needed. Machine learning is an iterative and dynamic process, often requiring experimentation, fine-tuning, and continuous improvement to achieve optimal results.

2.4 Categories of Machine Learning Methods

When approaching a new problem, it is crucial to determine whether it falls into the category of supervised learning or unsupervised learning. This categorization helps guide the selection of appropriate machine learning methods. Here's a breakdown of these two major categories.

2.4.1 *Supervised Learning*

1. In supervised learning, there exists a target variable (either continuous or discrete) that we want to predict or classify data into.
2. Examples of supervised learning problems include classification, prediction, and regression.
3. The goal is to learn a function (denoted as F) that maps input variables (X) to the target variable (Y), such that F(X) = Y.

   d) The input variables (X) are also known as features or predictors, while the target variable (Y) is sometimes referred to as the label.

4. The objective of supervised learning methods is to find the best function (F) that estimates or predicts Y based on observed outcomes.
5. A key aspect of supervised learning is to generalize well to unseen data rather than just fitting the available data.

2.4.2 *Unsupervised Learning*

1. In unsupervised learning, there is no specific target variable that we aim to predict. Instead, the focus is on understanding natural groupings or patterns within the data.

2. Clustering is a common example of unsupervised learning, where the goal is to group similar instances (*X*) together without predefined labels.
3. Principal components analysis (PCA) and related methods also fall under unsupervised learning, as they aim to identify underlying patterns or structure in the data.

It's important to note that there are methods that lie between supervised and unsupervised learning, incorporating different levels of supervision. The following is an example.

2.4.3 *Weakly Supervised Learning*

- This category lies between unsupervised and supervised learning.
- Only a subset of data points have labels or annotations while the majority remain unlabeled.
- Methods in this category aim to leverage the limited supervision available to make predictions or understand patterns in the data.

2.4.4 *Semi-Supervised Learning*

- In this scenario, a dataset contains both labeled and unlabeled instances.
- The goal is to use the information from labeled data along with the underlying structure in the unlabeled data to improve learning accuracy.

These variations presented in Figure 2.3 in supervision are active areas of research in machine learning, allowing for more flexibility in addressing real-world problems.

2.5 Supervised Learning Algorithms

Supervised learning algorithms aim to find a relationship between input variables and a target variable by utilizing labeled training data. The algorithms learn from the provided data to create a model or rule that can make predictions or classify new observations.

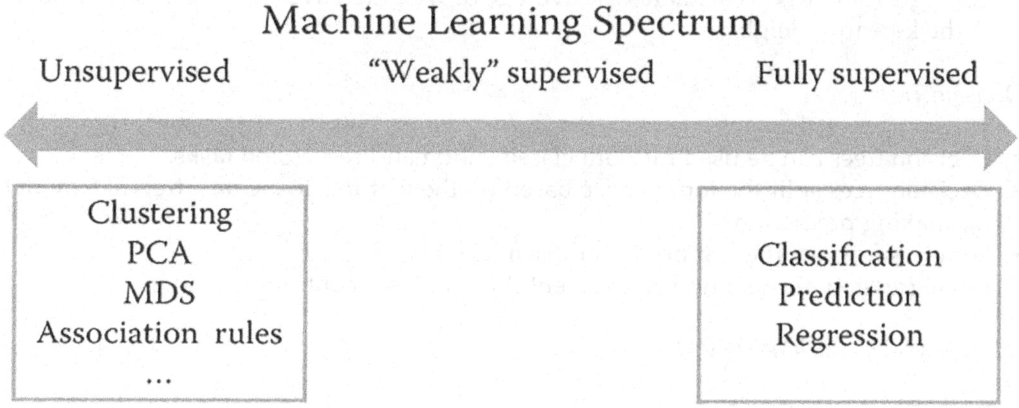

Figure 2.3 Field of machine learning encompasses a spectrum of methods.

There are two main types of supervised learning algorithms.

2.5.1 Regression Algorithms

- Regression algorithms are used when the target variable is continuous or numerical.
- The algorithm learns from the training data to estimate or predict the output values based on the input variables.
- Examples of regression algorithms include linear regression, polynomial regression, and support vector regression.

2.5.2 Classification Algorithms

- Classification algorithms are used when the target variable represents discrete or categorical classes or labels.
- The algorithm learns from the training data to classify new instances into predefined classes or categories.
- Classification algorithms assign probabilities to each class and predict the class with the highest probability.
- Examples of classification algorithms include logistic regression, decision trees, random forests, and support vector machines.

The choice between regression and classification algorithms depends on the nature of the problem and the type of output you want to predict. Regression algorithms are suitable for problems with continuous outcomes, while classification algorithms are appropriate for problems involving categorical or discrete classes. The following are some common models that can be used for both classification and regression tasks.

K-Nearest Neighbors (KNN)

- KNN can be used for both classification and regression by adjusting the way it calculates predictions.
- For classification, KNN assigns the class label based on the majority vote of the k-nearest neighbors.
- For regression, KNN calculates the average or weighted average of the target values of the k-nearest neighbors.

Decision Trees

- Decision trees can be used for both classification and regression tasks.
- Decision trees split the input space based on the features to create a tree-like model for making predictions.
- For classification, the leaf nodes represent class labels.
- For regression, the leaf nodes represent the predicted continuous values.

Support Vector Machines (SVM)

- SVM can be used for both classification and regression by modifying the loss function and decision boundary.

- For classification, SVM aims to find the hyperplane that maximally separates the classes.
- For regression, SVM finds a hyperplane that best fits the data, with a tolerance for points falling within a certain margin.

Ensemble Bagging/Boosting Methods

- Ensemble methods like random forest (bagging) and gradient boosting (boosting) can handle both classification and regression problems.
- These methods combine multiple weak models to create a strong predictive model.
- The underlying weak models, such as decision trees, can be used for both classification and regression.

Artificial Neural Networks (ANNs) including Deep Neural Networks (DNNs)

- ANNs and DNNs can be used for both classification and regression tasks.
- By adjusting the network architecture, loss function, and output layer activation function, ANNs can handle both problem types.

However, some models like linear regression and logistic regression are more suited for specific tasks. Linear regression is typically used for regression problems, while logistic regression is specifically designed for binary classification problems. These models may not directly translate to the other problem type without modifications or extensions.

Figure 2.4 provides a summary of the models commonly used for classification and regression, showcasing their versatility across both problem types.

2.6 Linear Regression

Linear regression is indeed a widely known and well-understood algorithm in statistics and machine learning. It is a linear model that assumes a linear relationship between the input variables (x) and the output variable (y). The goal of linear regression is to find the best-fitting line or hyperplane that minimizes the difference between the predicted values and the actual values of the output variable (Auerbach, 2022; Su et al., 2012) as presented in figure Figure 2.5.

In other words, linear regression aims to find the coefficients ($\beta_0, \beta_1, \beta_2, \ldots, \beta_n$) that define the line or hyperplane:

$$y = \beta_0 + \beta_1 x_1 + \beta_2 x_2 + \ldots + \beta_n x_n$$

The coefficients determine the slope and intercept of the line or hyperplane, indicating the effect of each input variable on the output variable. By adjusting the coefficients, the model can predict the value of the output variable (y) given a new set of input variables (x).

The process of finding the best-fitting line or hyperplane involves minimizing the error or the difference between the predicted values and the actual values. The most commonly used method for this purpose is ordinary least squares (OLS), where the sum of the squared differences between the predicted and actual values is minimized.

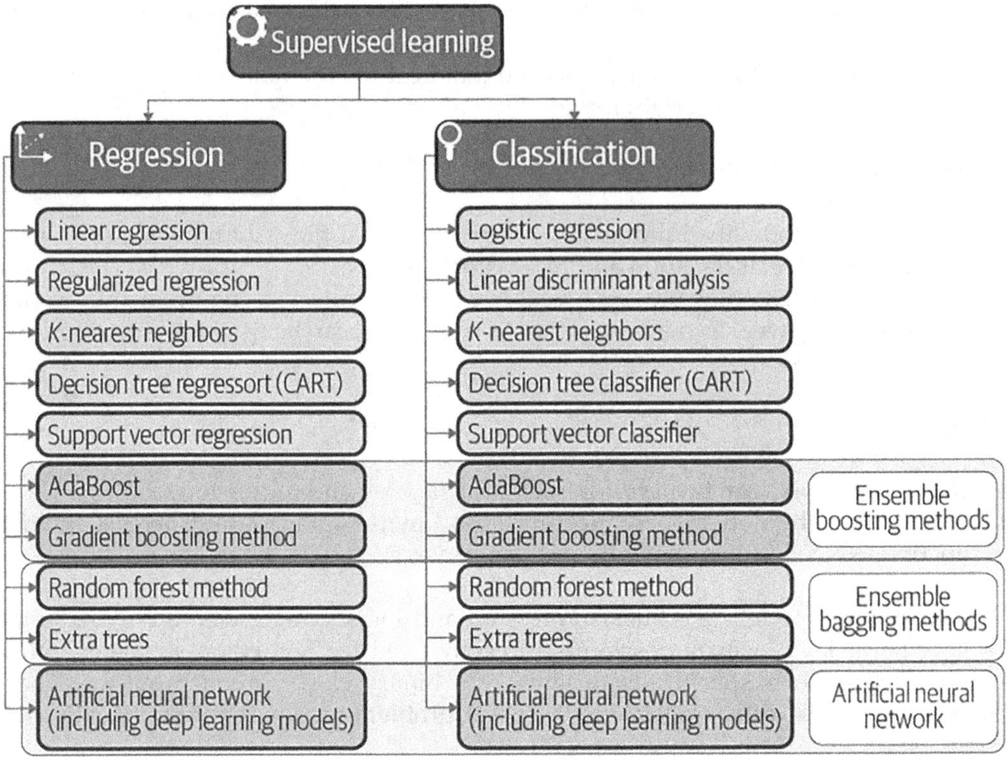

Figure 2.4 Models of supervised learning under regression and classification.

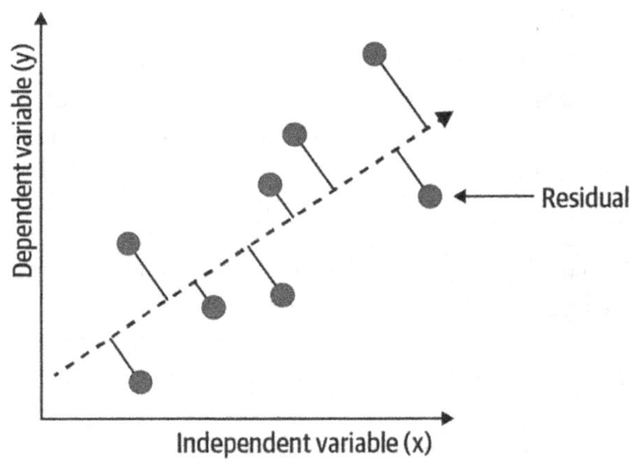

Figure 2.5 Linear regression.

Linear regression can be used for both simple cases with a single input variable (simple linear regression) and more complex cases with multiple input variables (multiple linear regression). It is widely applied in various fields for prediction, forecasting, and understanding the relationship between variables.

2.6.1 *Implementation in Python*

Here's an example of implementing linear regression in Python using the scikit-learn library:

```
import numpy as np
from sklearn.linear_model import LinearRegression

# Create sample input data
X = np.array([[1], [2], [3], [4], [5]])  # Input features
y = np.array([2, 4, 6, 8, 10])  # Output variable

# Create a linear regression model
model = LinearRegression()

# Train the model
model.fit(X, y)

# Make predictions
new_X = np.array([[6], [7], [8]])  # New input data
predictions = model.predict(new_X)

# Print the predicted values
print(predictions)
```

In this example, we first import the necessary libraries. Then, we create some sample input data *'X'* (input features) and *'y'* (output variable).

Next, we create an instance of the *'LinearRegression'* model. We then train the model by calling the *'fit()'* method and passing the input data (*'X'*) and the corresponding output data (*'y'*).

Once the model is trained, we can use it to make predictions on new input data. In this case, we create a new input array *'new_X'* and use the *'predict()'* method to obtain the predicted values.

Finally, we print the predicted values, i.e., [12. 14. 16.].

2.6.2 *Advantages and Disadvantages of Linear Regression*

Advantages of Linear Regression

1. *Simplicity and Interpretability:* Linear regression is a straightforward and easy-to-understand algorithm. It provides interpretable coefficients that represent the relationship between the predictor variables and the response variable.
2. *Quick and Efficient:* Linear regression has a fast training time, especially for large datasets. It can handle large amounts of data with relatively low computational costs.
3. *Linearity:* Linear regression assumes a linear relationship between the predictor variables and the response variable. When the relationship is truly linear, linear regression can provide accurate predictions.

Disadvantages of Linear Regression

1. *Limited Flexibility:* Linear regression assumes a linear relationship between the predictor variables and the response variable. It may not work well if the relationship is nonlinear or if there are complex interactions between variables. In such cases, more flexible models like polynomial regression or nonlinear regression may be more appropriate.
2. *Overfitting and Irrelevant Features:* Linear regression can be prone to overfitting when the model becomes too complex and captures noise in the data. Additionally, it may not handle irrelevant features well, leading to biased or less accurate predictions. Feature selection techniques or regularization methods can be applied to mitigate these issues.
3. *Assumptions and Data Requirements:* Linear regression relies on several assumptions, such as linearity, independence of errors, constant variance of errors, and absence of multicollinearity. Violations of these assumptions can lead to unreliable results. It is important to assess the data and ensure that these assumptions are met before applying linear regression.
4. *Outliers and Influential Points:* Linear regression is sensitive to outliers and influential points, which can heavily influence the model's coefficients and predictions. It is important to identify and handle these points appropriately to avoid biased results.
5. *Limited Performance on Complex Data:* Linear regression may not perform well on datasets with high dimensionality or complex relationships. In such cases, more advanced machine learning algorithms, such as ensemble methods or neural networks, may yield better results.

It's worth noting that while linear regression has its limitations, it remains a valuable tool for many applications, particularly when the relationship between variables is approximately linear, and the assumptions are met.

2.6.3 Regularized Regression

Regularized regression is a technique used to address the issue of overfitting in linear regression models with many independent variables. When a linear regression model has a large number of predictors relative to the number of observations, it can lead to poor determination of the coefficients and result in overfitting.

Overfitting occurs when a model fits the training data extremely well but performs poorly on new, unseen data (Han & Shen, 2022). In other words, the model becomes too complex and starts capturing noise and random variations in the training data, which do not generalize well to new data.

Regularized regression methods, such as Ridge regression and Lasso regression, introduce a penalty term to the regression objective function (Terrell, 2022). This penalty term controls the complexity of the model by shrinking the coefficients of the predictors toward zero. By doing so, it reduces the model's tendency to fit noise and helps prevent overfitting.

Advantages and Disadvantages of Regularized Regression

Advantages of Regularized Regression

1. *Improved Generalization:* Regularization helps to improve the model's ability to generalize well to new, unseen data by reducing overfitting.
2. *Feature Selection:* Regularized regression methods can also perform feature selection by shrinking the coefficients of irrelevant predictors toward zero. This can lead to a more parsimonious model and eliminate unnecessary predictors.
3. *Control over Model Complexity:* Regularization allows the user to control the level of complexity in the model by adjusting the penalty parameter. This flexibility helps to strike a balance between model simplicity and performance.
4. *Stability:* Regularized regression methods provide stability to the model by reducing the sensitivity to small changes in the data. This makes the model more robust and reliable.

Disadvantages of Regularized Regression

1. *Bias:* Regularization introduces a bias by shrinking the coefficients toward zero. In some cases, this bias can lead to underfitting if the true relationship between the predictors and the response variable is not well captured by the model.
2. *Parameter Tuning:* Regularization methods require tuning the penalty parameter, which can be a challenging task. The optimal value of the penalty parameter depends on the specific dataset and problem at hand.
3. *Interpretability:* The interpretation of the coefficients in regularized regression models can be more complex compared to standard linear regression. The coefficients are not directly comparable to the unpenalized regression coefficients.

Overall, regularized regression methods offer a powerful tool to combat overfitting in linear regression models with many predictors. By striking a balance between model complexity and performance, they can help create more robust and generalizable models. There are two common ways to regularize a linear regression model: Lasso regression (L1 regularization) and Ridge regression (L2 regularization).

2.6.4 Lasso Regression (L1 Regularization)

Lasso regression adds the sum of the absolute values of the coefficients (β) to the cost function in linear regression. The equation for Lasso regularization can be represented as follows:

$$Cost\ function = (RSS) + \lambda \times \sum_{j=1}^{p} \beta_j$$

In this equation, the cost function is the residual sum of squares (*RSS*), and λ is the regularization parameter that controls the strength of regularization (Ranstam & Cook, 2018). Lasso regression encourages sparsity in the coefficient values and performs feature selection by setting some coefficients to zero (Ge et al., 2022). It is useful when there are many predictors, and some of them are not relevant to the response variable.

Here's an example code snippet showing how to construct a Lasso regression model using the **'Lasso'** class from the **'sklearn'** (scikit-learn) package in Python:

```
import numpy as np
from sklearn.linear_model import LinearRegression

# Create sample input data
X = np.array([[1], [2], [3], [4], [5]])  # Input features
y = np.array([2, 4, 6, 8, 10])  # Output variable

# Create a linear regression model
model = LinearRegression()

# Train the model
model.fit(X, y)

# Make predictions
new_X = np.array([[6], [7], [8]])  # New input data
predictions = model.predict(new_X)

# Print the predicted values
print(predictions)
```

In this code, we import the **'Lasso'** class from **'sklearn.linear_model'**. We create an instance of the Lasso regression model with a specified regularization parameter (**'alpha'**). We then fit the model to the training data (**'X_train'** and **'y_train'**), make predictions on the test data (**'X_test'**), and evaluate the model's performance using mean squared error (MSE). Finally, we print the coefficients of the model (**'lasso_model.coef_'**) and the MSE.

Make sure to replace **'X_train'**, **'y_train'**, **'X_test'**, and **'y_test'** with your actual training and test data. Also, adjust the value of **'alpha'** according to your needs for regularization.

2.6.5 *Ridge Regression (L2 Regularization)*

Ridge regression adds the sum of the squared values of the coefficients (β) to the cost function in linear regression. The equation for Ridge regularization is represented as follows:

$$\textit{Cost function} = (RSS) + \lambda \times \sum_{j=1}^{p} \beta_j^2$$

Similar to Lasso regression, the cost function is the residual sum of squares (RSS), and λ is the regularization parameter (Carneiro et al., 2022; McDonald, 2009). Ridge regression shrinks the coefficients toward zero without setting them exactly to zero. It helps reduce the impact of multicollinearity and improves the model's performance when there are correlated predictors.

Here's an example code snippet showing how to construct a Ridge regression model using the **'Ridge'** class from the **'sklearn'** (scikit-learn) package in Python:

```
from sklearn.linear_model import Ridge

# Create an instance of Ridge regression model
ridge_model = Ridge(alpha=0.1)  # Alpha is the regularization
parameter (λ)

# Fit the model to the training data
ridge_model.fit(X_train, y_train)  # X_train is the training input
features, y_train is the target variable

# Make predictions on the test data
y_pred = ridge_model.predict(X_test)  # X_test is the test input
features

# Evaluate the model
mse = mean_squared_error(y_test, y_pred)  # y_test is the true
target variable for the test data

# Print the model's coefficients and mean squared error
print("Coefficients:", ridge_model.coef_)
print("Mean Squared Error:", mse)
```

In this code, we import the **'Ridge'** class from **'sklearn.linear_model'**. We create an instance of the Ridge regression model with a specified regularization parameter (**'alpha'**). We then fit the model to the training data (**'X_train'** and **'y_train'**), make predictions on the test data (**'X_test'**), and evaluate the model's performance using mean squared error (MSE). Finally, we print the coefficients of the model (**'ridge_model.coef_'**) and the MSE.

Make sure to replace **'X_train'**, **'y_train'**, **'X_test'**, and **'y_test'** with your actual training and test data. Also, adjust the value of **'alpha'** according to your needs for regularization.

Both Lasso regression and Ridge regression help address the issue of overfitting in linear regression by adding a regularization term to the cost function. They control the complexity of the model and prevent excessive reliance on any single predictor. The choice between Lasso and Ridge regression depends on the specific problem and the underlying data characteristics.

2.7 Logistic Regression

Logistic regression is a popular algorithm used for binary classification, where the goal is to predict a binary outcome or assign an observation to one of two classes based on input variables (Huang, 2022; LaValley, 2008). It is widely used in various fields, including machine learning, statistics, and social sciences.

The logistic regression model is derived from the concept of linear regression, but it is specifically designed to model the probabilities of the output classes rather than directly predicting a continuous value. It addresses the need to predict probabilities that sum up to one and fall within the range of zero to one, which is essential for interpreting the outputs as probabilities.

The logistic regression model assumes that the relationship between the input variables (x) and the log-odds of the output class probabilities (also known as the logit) is linear. The logit is the natural logarithm of the odds ratio, which represents the likelihood of the positive class over the negative class.

Mathematically, the logistic regression model can be represented as follows:

$$logit(p) = \beta_0 + \beta_1 x_1 + \beta_2 x_2 + \dots\dots + \beta_n x_n$$

Where:

- $logit(p)$ represents the log-odds of the probability p, which is the output of the logistic regression model.
- $\beta_0, \beta_1, \beta_2, \dots, \beta_n$ are the coefficients (parameters) of the model that are estimated during the training process.
- $x_1, x_2, \dots, x_n$ are the input variables (features) of the model.

To transform the logit into a probability, the logistic regression model uses the sigmoid (or logistic) function, which maps the logit to a value between 0 and 1. The sigmoid function is defined as:

$$p = \frac{1}{1 + exp(-logit(p))}$$

Where:

- p is the predicted probability of the positive class given the input variables.

During the training process, the logistic regression model estimates the optimal values of the coefficients ($\beta_0, \beta_1, \beta_2, \dots, \beta_n$) that maximize the likelihood of the observed data. This estimation is typically done using optimization techniques such as maximum likelihood estimation or gradient descent.

Once the model is trained, it can be used to make predictions on new data by calculating the logit and applying the sigmoid function to obtain the predicted probability. By applying a threshold (usually 0.5) to the predicted probability, the model assigns the observation to one of the two classes.

The logistic regression model has several advantages, including its simplicity, interpretability, and efficiency. It can handle both categorical and continuous input variables and is robust to outliers. However, logistic regression assumes a linear relationship between the input variables and the log-odds, which may limit its ability to capture complex nonlinear patterns. In such cases, more advanced algorithms like decision trees or neural networks may be suitable.

Overall, logistic regression is a powerful and widely used algorithm for binary classification tasks, providing a practical and interpretable solution for predicting probabilities and making informed decisions based on them.

2.7.1 Implementation of Logistic Regression

Here's an example of how to construct a logistic regression model using the LogisticRegression class from the sklearn package in Python:

```
from sklearn.linear_model import LogisticRegression

# Create an instance of the LogisticRegression model
logreg = LogisticRegression()

# Fit the model to the training data
logreg.fit(X_train, y_train)

# Make predictions on the test data
y_pred = logreg.predict(X_test)
```

In the code snippet given here:

- First, import the **'LogisticRegression'** class from the **'sklearn.linear_model'** module.
- Then, create an instance of the **LogisticRegression** model by calling the **'LogisticRegression()'** constructor.
- Next, fit the model to the training data using the **'fit()'** method, where **'X_train'** represents the training input data and **'y_train'** represents the corresponding target labels.
- Finally, use the **'predict()'** method to make predictions on the test data (**X_test**) and store the predicted labels in the **'y_pred'** variable.

It's important to note that before using the **LogisticRegression** model, you need to preprocess the data, handle missing values, perform feature engineering, and split the data into training and testing sets. Additionally, you might want to consider tuning hyperparameters of the model to achieve better performance.

2.7.2 Advantages and Disadvantages of Logistic Regression

Logistic regression has its own set of advantages and disadvantages. Here's a summary.

Advantages

1. *Ease of Implementation:* Logistic regression is relatively simple to implement and doesn't require complex computations.
2. *Interpretability:* The model provides interpretable results, as the coefficients represent the impact of each feature on the log-odds of the target variable.

3. *Probability Output:* Logistic regression outputs probabilities, allowing for more nuanced analysis and ranking of predictions.
4. *Regularization:* Like linear regression, logistic regression can benefit from regularization techniques like L1 and L2 regularization to prevent overfitting.

Disadvantages:

1. *Limited to Linear Relationships:* Logistic regression assumes a linear relationship between the features and the log-odds of the target variable. It may not perform well when faced with complex nonlinear relationships.
2. *Overfitting with High-Dimensional Data:* When the number of features is large compared to the number of observations, logistic regression can be prone to overfitting. Feature selection and regularization techniques can help mitigate this issue.
3. *Sensitivity to Irrelevant Features:* Logistic regression may not handle irrelevant or highly correlated features well, leading to less accurate predictions.
4. *Assumptions of Independence:* Logistic regression assumes that the observations are independent of each other, which may not hold true in certain scenarios.

It's important to note that the suitability of logistic regression depends on the specific problem and data at hand. It's always recommended to assess different models and evaluate their performance to choose the best approach for a given task.

2.8 Support Vector Machine

Support vector machine (SVM) is a powerful supervised learning algorithm used for both classification and regression tasks. The objective of the SVM algorithm is to find a hyperplane in a high-dimensional feature space that maximally separates different classes of data points (Suthaharan & Suthaharan, 2016; Zhou et al., 2022).

The main goal of SVM is to maximize the margin (as presented with shaded area in Figure 2.6), which refers to the distance between the decision boundary and the nearest

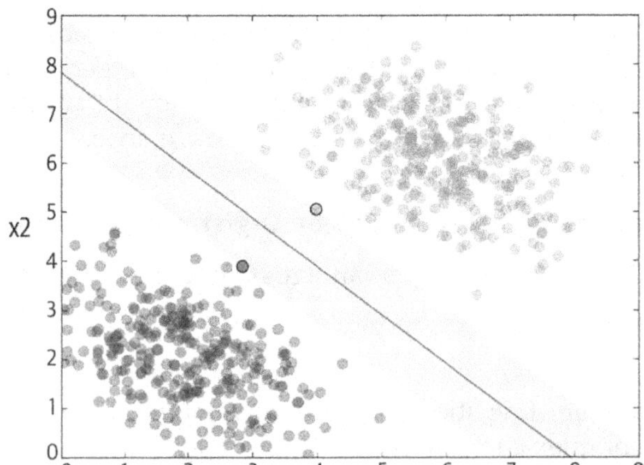

Figure 2.6 Support vector machine.

data points from each class, known as support vectors. By maximizing the margin, SVM aims to create a clear separation between the classes and achieve better generalization performance on unseen data.

The key idea behind SVM is to transform the input data into a higher-dimensional space using a kernel function. In this transformed space, SVM finds the hyperplane that best separates the data points of different classes. The choice of the kernel function allows SVM to capture complex relationships between features and can handle both linearly separable and nonlinearly separable data.

The SVM algorithm constructs the decision boundary by solving an optimization problem that involves maximizing the margin and minimizing the classification error. This results in a homogeneous partition of the data points, where each point is classified into one of the classes based on its position relative to the decision boundary.

2.8.1 Implementation of SVM

Here are code snippets demonstrating how to construct SVM regression and classification models using the **'sklearn'** package in Python:

SVM Regression:

```
from sklearn.svm import SVR
import numpy as np

# Create a SVM Regression model
svm_regressor = SVR(kernel='linear')

# Generate some sample data
X = np.array([[1, 1], [2, 2], [3, 3]])
y = np.array([1, 2, 3])

# Fit the model to the data
svm_regressor.fit(X, y)

# Make predictions
predictions = svm_regressor.predict(X)
```

SVM Classification:

```
from sklearn.svm import SVC
import numpy as np

# Create a SVM Classification model
svm_classifier = SVC(kernel='linear')
```

```
# Generate some sample data
X = np.array([[1, 1], [2, 2], [3, 3]])
y = np.array([0, 1, 0])

# Fit the model to the data
svm_classifier.fit(X, y)

# Make predictions
predictions = svm_classifier.predict(X)
```

In both cases, you need to import the relevant SVM class (**'SVR'** for regression and **'SVC'** for classification) from the **'sklearn.svm'** module. You can then create an instance of the SVM model, specifying the desired kernel (e.g., **"linear"**, **"rbf"** etc.) as a parameter.

After creating the model, you can fit it to your training data using the **'fit()'** method, providing the input features (**'X'**) and the corresponding target values (**'y'**).

Once the model is trained, you can use it to make predictions on new data by calling the **'predict()'** method and passing the new input features.

Remember to replace the sample data (**'X'** and **'y'**) with your own data when using these code snippets.

2.8.2 *Advantages and Disadvantages of SVM*

SVM has its own set of advantages and disadvantages. Here's a summary.

Advantages of SVM

1. *Robust against Overfitting:* SVM can handle high-dimensional data and is less prone to overfitting compared to other algorithms.
2. *Nonlinear Relationships:* SVM can effectively capture nonlinear relationships in the data by using different kernel functions.
3. *No Distributional Requirement:* SVM does not assume any specific data distribution, making it versatile for various types of data.

Disadvantages of SVM

1. *Computational Complexity:* SVM can be computationally intensive, particularly for large datasets. Training time and memory usage can be significant.
2. *Inefficiency with Large Datasets:* SVM may not scale well with large datasets, as the training time and memory requirements increase significantly.
3. *Feature Scaling:* SVM requires feature scaling to ensure all features contribute equally to the model's performance.
4. *Hyperparameter Tuning:* SVM has several hyperparameters that need to be tuned, and their interpretations may not be intuitive.

It's worth noting that while SVM has certain limitations, it remains a powerful and widely used algorithm in various domains, especially when dealing with smaller or moderate-sized datasets. It can be computationally expensive for large datasets, especially when the number of features is high. SVM moreover requires careful selection of the appropriate kernel function and tuning of hyperparameters. Additionally, SVM's performance can degrade when the classes are heavily overlapped or when the dataset has imbalanced class distributions.

Overall, SVM is a versatile algorithm that aims to find an optimal decision boundary with a maximum margin to separate different classes in the feature space. Its ability to handle nonlinear relationships through kernel functions makes it a popular choice in various applications.

2.9 *K*-Nearest Neighbors

K-nearest neighbors (KNN) is a simple yet effective algorithm used for both classification and regression tasks. It is often referred to as a "lazy learner" because it does not involve any training or learning process. Instead, KNN makes predictions based on the similarity between new data points and the existing data in the training set.

The choice of *K* is critical in KNN. A small value of *K* can lead to overfitting and increased sensitivity to outliers, while a large value of *K* can lead to underfitting and loss of local patterns. Therefore, selecting an appropriate value for *K* is important for the performance of the KNN algorithm. The steps of the KNN algorithm can be summarized as follows.

1. *Choose the Number of Neighbors (K):* Determine the value of *K*, which represents the number of nearest neighbors to consider when making predictions.
2. *Calculate Distances:* Compute the distance between the new input data point and all instances in the training dataset. The distance can be calculated using distance metrics such as Euclidean distance or Manhattan distance. The formulas for Euclidean distance and Manhattan distance are as follows:

   - Euclidean distance between two points $(a_1, a_2, \ldots, a_n)$ and $(b_1, b_2, \ldots, b_n)$ in n-dimensional space:

   $$ED = \sqrt{(a_1 - b_1)^2 + (a_2 - b_2)^2 \ldots + (a_n - b_n)^2}$$

   - Manhattan distance between two points $(a_1, a_2, \ldots, a_n)$ and $(b_1, b_2, \ldots, b_n)$ in n-dimensional space:

   $$MD = |a_1 - b_1| + |a_2 - b_2| + \ldots + |a_n - b_n|$$

In both formulas, $(a_1, a_2, \ldots, a_n)$ and $(b_1, b_2, \ldots, b_n)$ represent the coordinates of two points in the respective space. The Euclidean distance formula calculates the straight-line distance between two points, while the Manhattan distance formula calculates the sum of the absolute differences between the coordinates of the two points along each dimension.

- These distance metrics are commonly used in various machine learning algorithms, including KNN, to measure the similarity or dissimilarity between data points.

3. *Find the K-Nearest Neighbors:* Select the K instances from the training dataset that are closest to the new input data point based on the calculated distances.
4. *Determine the Class Label (Classification) or Predicted Value (Regression):* For classification tasks, assign the class label that is most common among the K-nearest neighbors as the predicted class label for the new data point. For regression tasks, take the average (or weighted average) of the output variables of the K-nearest neighbors as the predicted value for the new data point.
5. *Make Predictions:* Repeat steps 2 to 4 for each new input data point to be classified or predicted.

It's important to note that the choice of distance metric, such as Euclidean or Manhattan, depends on the nature of the input variables and the problem at hand. Euclidean distance is commonly used when the input variables are similar in type, while Manhattan distance is suitable when the input variables are not similar in type.

By following these steps, the KNN algorithm can make predictions based on the similarity of new data points to the existing data in the training set.

2.9.1 *Implementation of KNN*

Here are the code snippets to demonstrate how to construct KNN regression and classification models using the scikit-learn (sklearn) package in Python:

KNN Regression:

```
from sklearn.neighbors import KNeighborsRegressor

# Create a KNN regression model
k = 3  # Number of neighbors to consider
knn_reg = KNeighborsRegressor(n_neighbors=k)

# Fit the model to the training data
knn_reg.fit(X_train, y_train)

# Make predictions on new data
y_pred = knn_reg.predict(X_test)
```

KNN Classification:

```
from sklearn.neighbors import KNeighborsClassifier

# Create a KNN classification model
k = 5  # Number of neighbors to consider
knn_cls = KNeighborsClassifier(n_neighbors=k)
```

```
# Fit the model to the training data
knn_cls.fit(X_train, y_train)

# Make predictions on new data
y_pred = knn_cls.predict(X_test)
```

In both cases, **'X_train'** represents the feature matrix of the training data, **'y_train'** represents the target variable or class labels for the training data, and **'X_test'** represents the feature matrix of the test data. After fitting the model to the training data, predictions can be made using the **'predict'** method on the trained model.

2.9.2 Advantages and Disadvantages of KNN

Here is the comprehensive summary of the advantages and disadvantages of the KNN algorithm.

Advantages of KNN Algorithm

1. *No Training Required:* KNN does not involve a training phase, making it easy to add new data without impacting accuracy.
2. *Intuitive and Easy to Understand:* The algorithm is simple to grasp and interpret.
3. *Handles Multiclass Classification:* KNN can naturally handle problems with multiple classes.
4. *Learns Complex Decision Boundaries:* KNN can learn nonlinear and complex decision boundaries.
5. *Effective for Large Training Datasets:* KNN can perform well even with a large amount of training data.
6. *Robust to Noisy Data:* KNN can handle data with noise and outliers.

Disadvantages of KNN Algorithm

1. *Ambiguous Choice of Distance Metric:* Selecting the appropriate distance metric can be challenging and subjective.
2. *Poor Performance on High-Dimensional Data:* KNN may struggle to perform well in high-dimensional feature spaces, as the curse of dimensionality becomes a problem.
3. *Slow Prediction for New Instances:* Predicting new instances can be computationally expensive, as the distances to all neighbors need to be recalculated.
4. *Sensitivity to Noise:* KNN can be sensitive to noisy data, affecting the accuracy of predictions.
5. *Manual Handling of Missing Values and Outliers:* Missing values need to be manually dealt with, and outliers should be identified and treated properly.
6. *Feature Scaling Required:* It's necessary to scale features (standardization or normalization) before applying the KNN algorithm to ensure accurate results.

It's important to consider these factors when deciding to use the KNN algorithm in a given context. KNN is known for its simplicity, interpretability, and ability to capture complex decision boundaries. However, it has certain limitations. It can be computationally expensive, especially when dealing with large datasets, as it requires a distance calculation for each data point. Moreover, KNN assumes that all features contribute equally to the similarity calculation, which may not always hold true in real-world scenarios.

Despite its limitations, KNN remains a popular choice for various classification and regression tasks, especially in cases where the data has a clear spatial or local structure.

2.10 Linear Discriminant Analysis

Linear discriminant analysis (LDA) is a dimensionality reduction technique and a classification algorithm. It aims to find a linear combination of features that maximizes class separability while minimizing within-class variance. The primary objective of LDA is to transform the original feature space into a lower-dimensional space that can effectively discriminate between different classes.

The key idea behind LDA is to find a projection where the classes are well-separated and have minimal overlap. By maximizing the separation between classes and minimizing the variance within each class, LDA can create a new feature subspace that preserves the discriminative information necessary for classification.

The steps involved in LDA can be summarized as follows.

1. *Compute the Mean Vectors:* Calculate the mean vectors for each class in the dataset.
2. *Compute the Scatter Matrices:* Calculate the scatter matrix within-class (S_w) and between-class (S_b). The within-class scatter matrix measures the variance within each class, while the between-class scatter matrix measures the separation between classes.
3. *Compute the Eigenvalues and Eigenvectors:* Find the eigenvalues and eigenvectors of the matrix $\left(\frac{S_b}{S_w}\right)$. The eigenvalues represent the amount of variance explained by each eigenvector, and the corresponding eigenvectors define the directions of the new feature subspace.
4. *Sort the Eigenvalues:* Sort the eigenvalues in descending order and select the top k eigenvectors that correspond to the k largest eigenvalues to form a transformation matrix.
5. *Project the Data onto the New Subspace:* Multiply the original data matrix by the transformation matrix to obtain the new lower-dimensional representation.
6. *Perform Classification:* Use a classifier, such as logistic regression or a simple nearest neighbor classifier, on the reduced-dimensional data to perform classification.

2.10.1 *Implementation of LDA*

Here's an example of how to implement an LDA classification model using the **'LinearDiscriminantAnalysis'** class from the **'sklearn.discriminant_analysis'** module in Python:

```
from sklearn.discriminant_analysis import
LinearDiscriminantAnalysis
from sklearn.model_selection import train_test_split
from sklearn.metrics import accuracy_score

# Assuming you have your data and labels stored in X and y
variables

# Split the data into training and testing sets
X_train, X_test, y_train, y_test = train_test_split(X, y, test_
size=0.2, random_state=42)

# Create an instance of the LDA model
lda = LinearDiscriminantAnalysis()

# Fit the model to the training data
lda.fit(X_train, y_train)

# Make predictions on the testing data
y_pred = lda.predict(X_test)

# Evaluate the accuracy of the model
accuracy = accuracy_score(y_test, y_pred)
print("Accuracy:", accuracy)
```

In this code, we first import the necessary modules from the **'sklearn'** package. Then, we split our data into training and testing sets using **'train_test_split()'**. Next, we create an instance of the **'LinearDiscriminantAnalysis'** class. We fit the model to the training data using the **'fit()'** method. After that, we make predictions on the testing data using the **'predict()'** method. Finally, we evaluate the accuracy of the model by comparing the predicted labels with the true labels using the **'accuracy_score()'** function.

Note that you need to replace **'X'** and **'y'** with your actual data and labels. Also, adjust the test size and random state according to your needs.

2.10.2 Advantages and Disadvantages of LDA

Advantages of LDA

1. *Dimensionality Reduction:* LDA reduces the dimensionality of the data while preserving the discriminative information, making it useful for high-dimensional datasets.
2. *Class Separability:* LDA maximizes the separation between classes, making it effective in classification tasks.
3. *Data Visualization:* LDA can be used to visualize high-dimensional data in a lower-dimensional space.
4. *Less Prone to Overfitting:* LDA is less likely to overfit the data compared to other classification algorithms.

Disadvantages of LDA

1. *Assumes Linear Separability:* LDA assumes that the classes are linearly separable, which may limit its effectiveness in complex nonlinear problems.
2. *Sensitive to Outliers:* LDA is sensitive to outliers that can significantly affect the class separation.
3. *Requires Class Balance:* LDA assumes that the number of samples in each class is roughly equal, which may affect its performance if class imbalance exists.
4. *Lack of Robustness:* LDA assumes that the data follows a Gaussian distribution, which may not hold true for all datasets.

Overall, LDA is a powerful technique for dimensionality reduction and classification tasks, particularly in cases where class separability is important, and the data follows linear patterns.

2.11 Decision Trees

Decision trees are a popular machine learning algorithm used for prediction and classification tasks. They learn a set of rules from training data to create a tree-like structure that represents a series of decisions and their possible outcomes. Each level of the tree corresponds to a specific feature and a threshold value or range of values. The tree is built recursively by splitting the data based on these features and values.

The decision tree starts with a single root node, which represents the entire dataset. The first split is made based on a chosen feature and a threshold value. The goal is to find the feature and threshold that best separates the data into different classes or categories. The split creates multiple branches, each corresponding to a possible outcome or class.

In the example presented in Figure 2.7, the first split is made on the feature "number of visits in the past year" with a threshold value of 4. This divides the data into two

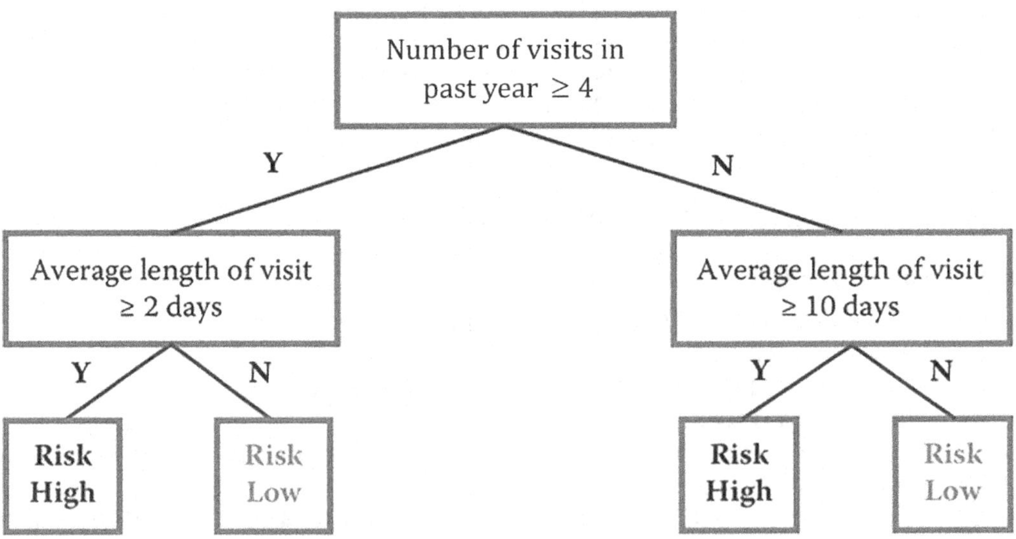

Figure 2.7 An explanatory decision tree.

branches. The second level of the tree further splits each branch based on different features and values. For instance, one branch may be split based on the "average length of visit" with a threshold value of 2 days, while the other branch may be split based on a threshold value of 10 days.

The process continues recursively until a stopping criterion is met, such as reaching a maximum depth or a minimum number of samples in each leaf node. The resulting tree represents a series of if-else conditions that can be used to make predictions on new data. Each leaf node corresponds to a predicted class or outcome.

2.11.1 Implementation of Decision Tree for Regression and Classification

Here's an example of how to implement a decision tree for regression and classification using the CART algorithm in Python using the **'sklearn'** package:

For Regression:

```
from sklearn.tree import DecisionTreeRegressor

# Create the regression model
regressor = DecisionTreeRegressor()

# Fit the model to the training data
regressor.fit(X_train, y_train)

# Make predictions on test data
y_pred = regressor.predict(X_test)
```

For Classification:

```
from sklearn.tree import DecisionTreeClassifier

# Create the classification model
classifier = DecisionTreeClassifier()

# Fit the model to the training data
classifier.fit(X_train, y_train)

# Make predictions on test data
y_pred = classifier.predict(X_test)
```

In both cases, **'X_train'** and **'X_test'** represent the training and test data respectively, and **'y_train'** is the corresponding target variable. You would need to replace these with your actual data.

The decision tree model can be further customized by setting various parameters such as the maximum depth of the tree (**'max_depth'**), the minimum number of samples required to split a node (**'min_samples_split'**), and the criterion used for splitting (**'criterion'**), among others. You can refer to the **'sklearn'** documentation for a full list of available parameters.

Note: Remember to import the necessary libraries (**'sklearn.tree.DecisionTreeRegressor'** for regression and **'sklearn.tree.DecisionTreeClassifier'** for classification) before using the code.

2.11.2 Advantages and Disadvantages of Decision Trees

There is a comprehensive list of advantages and disadvantages of the decision tree algorithm. However, I would like to highlight a few additional points.

Advantages:

1. Decision trees can handle both numerical and categorical data.
2. They can handle missing values and outliers without much preprocessing.
3. Decision trees provide a clear and interpretable decision-making process, as the rules learned by the tree can be easily visualized.
4. They are non-parametric, meaning they make no assumptions about the underlying distribution of the data.

Disadvantages:

1. Decision trees are prone to overfitting, especially when the tree depth is not properly controlled. This can result in poor generalization to unseen data.
2. They can be sensitive to small changes in the training data, leading to different tree structures and potentially different predictions.
3. Decision trees may create biased models if the class distribution is imbalanced.
4. They are often considered weak learners compared to more advanced ensemble methods like random forests or gradient boosting.

It's important to note that while decision trees have their limitations, they are still widely used due to their simplicity, interpretability, and ability to handle a variety of data types.

However, decision trees can be prone to overfitting, especially when the tree becomes too complex or when the training data is noisy. They may create overly specific rules that apply only to the training data and do not generalize well to new data. This issue can be mitigated by using pruning techniques or ensemble methods such as random forests.

Overall, decision trees are a versatile and powerful algorithm that can be applied to a wide range of problems. They are particularly useful when interpretability and explainability are important requirements.

2.12 Ensemble Models

Ensemble models are powerful machine learning techniques that aim to improve the performance of individual classifiers by combining their predictions. The idea behind ensemble methods is to leverage the diversity and collective intelligence of multiple models to achieve better generalization and robustness.

The two most popular ensemble methods are bagging and boosting:

1. *Bagging (Bootstrap Aggregating):* Bagging involves training multiple individual models in parallel, where each model is trained on a randomly sampled subset of the training data with replacement. This technique creates diversity among the models, as each model is exposed to a slightly different subset of the data. The final prediction is obtained by aggregating the predictions of all the individual models, such as taking the majority vote (for classification) or the average (for regression). Bagging is particularly effective when combined with high-variance models, such as decision trees, as it helps reduce overfitting and improve stability.
2. *Boosting:* Boosting is an ensemble technique that builds multiple models sequentially, where each subsequent model is trained to correct the mistakes made by the previous models. The training data is re-weighted at each iteration to give more importance to the misclassified instances. Boosting focuses on difficult examples, gradually improving the model's performance. Examples of boosting algorithms include AdaBoost, Gradient Boosting, and XGBoost. Boosting is known for its ability to produce highly accurate models, especially when combined with weak learners.

Advantages of Ensemble Models

1. *Improved Performance:* Ensemble models can achieve higher accuracy compared to individual models, as they combine the strengths of multiple models and mitigate their weaknesses.
2. *Robustness:* By aggregating predictions from different models, ensemble models are more resistant to errors and outliers in the data, leading to improved generalization.
3. *Flexibility:* Ensemble methods are flexible and can be applied to various types of models, such as decision trees, neural networks, or support vector machines.

However, ensemble models also have some considerations.

1. *Complexity:* Ensemble models can be computationally intensive and require more resources than individual models.
2. *Interpretability:* As ensemble models combine multiple models, their predictions can be more difficult to interpret and explain compared to individual models.
3. *Overfitting:* While ensemble models are less prone to overfitting compared to individual models, it is still possible if the base models are too complex or if the ensemble is overly trained on the training data.

Ensemble methods provide a powerful approach to enhance model performance and address the limitations of individual models. By combining the predictions of multiple models, ensemble models can achieve higher accuracy, robustness, and flexibility in various machine learning tasks.

2.13 Random Forest

Random forest is an ensemble learning method that combines the principles of bagging and decision trees to create a more robust and accurate model. It builds multiple decision trees on different subsets of the training data and combines their predictions to make the final prediction.

Here are the steps involved in constructing a random forest:

1. *Random Sampling:* Given a dataset of 1,000 instances, the bagging algorithm starts by randomly selecting a subset of the data, with replacement. This means that each subset can contain duplicate instances, and some instances may not be selected at all. This process is known as bootstrap sampling.
2. *Decision Tree Construction:* For each subset of the data, a decision tree is constructed using a modified version of the decision tree algorithm. Instead of considering all features at each split, a random subset of features is considered. This helps to introduce diversity among the decision trees and reduce the correlation between them.
3. *Ensemble of Decision Trees:* After constructing multiple decision trees, the predictions of each tree are combined to make the final prediction. For classification tasks, the most common method is to use majority voting, where the class that receives the most votes across all trees is selected. For regression tasks, the predictions of all trees are averaged to obtain the final prediction.

2.13.1 Implementation of Random Forest Regression and Classification

Here's an example of how to implement a random forest regression and classification model using the scikit-learn (sklearn) package in Python.

Random Forest Regression:

```
from sklearn.ensemble import RandomForestRegressor

# Create a Random Forest regression model
rf_regressor = RandomForestRegressor(n_estimators=100,
random_state=42)

# Fit the model to the training data
rf_regressor.fit(X_train, y_train)

# Make predictions on the test data
predictions = rf_regressor.predict(X_test)
```

Random Forest Classification:

```
from sklearn.ensemble import RandomForestClassifier

# Create a Random Forest classification model
rf_classifier = RandomForestClassifier(n_estimators=100,
random_state=42)
```

```
# Fit the model to the training data
rf_classifier.fit(X_train, y_train)

# Make predictions on the test data
predictions = rf_classifier.predict(X_test)
```

In the code snippets given here, **'X_train'** and **'y_train'** represent the training data features and labels, respectively. **'X_test'** is the test data used for making predictions. The **'n_estimators'** parameter specifies the number of decision trees to be included in the random forest ensemble. The **'random_state'** parameter is used to ensure reproducibility of results.

After fitting the model to the training data using the **'fit'** method, predictions can be made on new data using the **'predict'** method.

Note: Before running the code, make sure you have imported the necessary libraries and preprocessed your data accordingly.

These code snippets provide a basic implementation of random forest regression and classification models using sklearn. You can further customize the model by tuning hyperparameters and incorporating other techniques such as cross-validation for better performance and generalization.

2.13.2 Random Forest offers Several Advantages

1. *Robustness to Overfitting:* By using bootstrap sampling and feature randomization, random forest reduces the tendency of decision trees to overfit the training data. It can generalize well to unseen data and handle noisy or incomplete datasets.
2. *Variable Importance:* Random forest provides a measure of variable importance, indicating which features have the most influence on the predictions. This information can help in feature selection and understanding the underlying patterns in the data.
3. *Parallelizable:* The construction of individual decision trees in random forest can be done independently, making it suitable for parallel and distributed computing. This allows for faster training on large datasets.

However, there are also some considerations.

1. Interpretability: Random forest models can be less interpretable compared to a single decision tree. The combination of multiple trees can make it challenging to understand the underlying decision process.
2. Computational Complexity: Building and evaluating multiple decision trees can be computationally expensive, especially for large datasets. Random forest models require more computational resources compared to individual decision trees.
3. Hyperparameter Tuning: Random forest has several hyperparameters that need to be tuned, such as the number of trees, maximum depth of the trees, and the number of features considered at each split. Proper tuning is important to achieve optimal performance.

Random forest is a powerful ensemble learning method that leverages the strengths of decision trees and bagging to improve prediction accuracy and robustness. It is widely used in various domains, including classification, regression, and feature selection tasks, and provides a reliable and versatile machine learning algorithm.

2.14 Extra Trees

Extra Trees, also known as extremely randomized trees, is a variant of the random forest algorithm. It shares similarities with random forests but introduces additional randomness in the tree-building process. The main idea behind Extra Trees is to create an ensemble of decision trees, where each tree is trained using random subsets of features and random splits.

Unlike random forests, where observations are typically drawn with replacement from the original dataset, Extra Trees samples observations without replacement. This means that each tree in the ensemble is trained on a different subset of the data, and there is no repetition of observations within a single tree.

The key distinction between Extra Trees and random forests lies in the selection of splits at each node. In random forests, the best split is chosen based on criteria such as Gini impurity or information gain to maximize the homogeneity of child nodes. In contrast, Extra Trees selects random splits at each node without considering the optimal split. This additional randomness allows Extra Trees to explore a wider range of potential splits, potentially leading to improved generalization performance.

2.14.1 Implementation of Extra Trees Regression

Here's an example of how to implement Extra Trees for regression and classification using the **'sklearn'** package in Python:

```
# Import the necessary libraries
from sklearn.ensemble import ExtraTreesRegressor,
ExtraTreesClassifier
from sklearn.datasets import load_boston, load_iris
from sklearn.model_selection import train_test_split
from sklearn.metrics import mean_squared_error, accuracy_score

# Example 1: Extra Trees Regression

# Load the Boston Housing dataset
boston = load_boston()
X, y = boston.data, boston.target

# Split the data into training and testing sets
X_train, X_test, y_train, y_test = train_test_split(X, y, test_
size=0.2, random_state=42)
```

```
# Create an Extra Trees regression model
regressor = ExtraTreesRegressor(n_estimators=100,
random_state=42)

# Fit the model to the training data
regressor.fit(X_train, y_train)

# Make predictions on the test data
y_pred = regressor.predict(X_test)

# Calculate the mean squared error
mse = mean_squared_error(y_test, y_pred)
print(f"Mean Squared Error: {mse}")

# Example 2: Extra Trees Classification

# Load the Iris dataset
iris = load_iris()
X, y = iris.data, iris.target

# Split the data into training and testing sets
X_train, X_test, y_train, y_test = train_test_split(X, y, test_
size=0.2, random_state=42)

# Create an Extra Trees classification model
classifier = ExtraTreesClassifier(n_estimators=100,
random_state=42)

# Fit the model to the training data
classifier.fit(X_train, y_train)

# Make predictions on the test data
y_pred = classifier.predict(X_test)

# Calculate the accuracy
accuracy = accuracy_score(y_test, y_pred)print(f"Accuracy:
{accuracy}")
```

In this code snippet, we first import the necessary libraries. Then, we load the dataset (Boston Housing and Iris) and split it into training and testing sets. We create an Extra Trees model (**'ExtraTreesRegressor'** for regression and **'ExtraTreesClassifier'** for classification) with the desired number of estimators. We fit the model to the training data and make predictions on the test data. Finally, we evaluate the model's performance using mean squared error for regression and accuracy for classification.

Make sure you have the **'sklearn'** package installed before running the code. You can install it using **'pip install scikit-learn'**.

The advantages of Extra Trees are similar to those of random forests. It is a flexible and powerful algorithm that can handle both numerical and categorical features. It is robust to outliers and can handle high-dimensional datasets. Like random forests, Extra Trees provides feature importance scores, making it useful for feature selection and interpretation.

On the other hand, the disadvantages of Extra Trees are also similar to those of random forests. The algorithm can be considered a black box approach, as the selection of random splits can make the model difficult to interpret. While Extra Trees can perform well on various tasks, it may not provide precise predictions for regression problems. Also, it is susceptible to overfitting noisy datasets and may require careful tuning of hyperparameters to avoid this issue.

In practice, Extra Trees often exhibits comparable performance to random forests and can sometimes achieve slightly better results depending on the dataset and problem at hand. It is a valuable tool in the ensemble learning arsenal, offering an alternative approach to combining decision trees for improved predictive accuracy and generalization.

2.15 AdaBoost

AdaBoost, short for adaptive boosting, is a popular boosting technique used in machine learning. The basic idea behind AdaBoost is to sequentially train a series of weak learners, where each subsequent model focuses on correcting the errors made by its predecessors. The overall goal is to create a strong ensemble model that combines the predictions of these weak learners to make accurate and robust predictions.

The steps of the AdaBoost algorithm are as follows:

1. *Initialize the Weights:* Each instance in the training dataset is assigned an equal weight initially.
2. *Train a Weak Learner:* A weak learner, also known as a base estimator, is trained on the weighted training dataset. A weak learner is a simple model that performs slightly better than random guessing. It can be any machine learning algorithm, such as a decision tree with limited depth.
3. *Evaluate the Weak Learner:* The weak learner's performance is evaluated on the training dataset. The evaluation is typically based on the error rate, which is the weighted sum of misclassified instances.
4. *Calculate the Weak Learner's Weight:* The weight of the weak learner is calculated based on its performance. A better-performing weak learner is assigned a higher weight.
5. *Update the Sample Weights:* The weights of the training instances are updated based on the weak learner's performance. The weights of incorrectly classified instances are increased, while the weights of correctly classified instances are decreased. This step focuses on emphasizing the importance of the misclassified instances in subsequent iterations.
6. *Repeat Steps 2–5:* Steps 2 to 5 are repeated iteratively for a predetermined number of iterations or until a desired level of performance is achieved.
7. *Combine the Weak Learners:* Finally, the weak learners are combined to form a strong learner. The combination is done by assigning weights to each weak learner based on their individual performance. The stronger the weak learner, the higher its weight in the final ensemble model.

8. *Make predictions:* To make predictions on new instances, the weighted combination of weak learners is used. The final prediction is based on the weighted majority vote or weighted average of the weak learners' predictions.

AdaBoost is an iterative algorithm that focuses on misclassified instances in each iteration, making it effective in handling complex datasets. By combining multiple weak learners, AdaBoost can achieve high accuracy and generalize well to new data. It is particularly useful when applied to binary classification problems.

It's worth noting that the AdaBoost algorithm has variants, such as AdaBoost.M1 and AdaBoost.M2, which incorporate different techniques to improve performance and handle multiclass classification problems.

In practice, the AdaBoost algorithm is implemented in various machine learning libraries, including the **'sklearn'** package in Python, which provides the **'AdaBoost-Classifier'** and **'AdaBoostRegressor'** classes for classification and regression tasks, respectively.

2.15.1 Implementation of AdaBoost Regression and Classification

Here's an example of how to implement AdaBoost regression and classification models using the **'sklearn'** package in Python:

For AdaBoost Classification:

```
from sklearn.ensemble import AdaBoostClassifier
from sklearn.datasets import make_classification
from sklearn.model_selection import train_test_split
from sklearn.metrics import accuracy_score

# Generate a sample classification dataset
X, y = make_classification(n_samples=100, n_features=10,
random_state=42)

# Split the dataset into training and test sets
X_train, X_test, y_train, y_test = train_test_split(X, y, test_
size=0.2, random_state=42)

# Create an AdaBoost classifier
ada_boost = AdaBoostClassifier(n_estimators=100, random_state=42)

# Train the AdaBoost classifier
ada_boost.fit(X_train, y_train)

# Make predictions on the test set
y_pred = ada_boost.predict(X_test)

# Evaluate the accuracy of the classifier
accuracy = accuracy_score(y_test, y_pred)
print("Accuracy:", accuracy)
```

For AdaBoost Regression:

```
from sklearn.ensemble import AdaBoostRegressor
from sklearn.datasets import make_regression
from sklearn.model_selection import train_test_split
from sklearn.metrics import mean_squared_error

# Generate a sample regression dataset
X, y = make_regression(n_samples=100, n_features=10,
random_state=42)

# Split the dataset into training and test sets
X_train, X_test, y_train, y_test = train_test_split(X, y, test_
size=0.2, random_state=42)

# Create an AdaBoost regressor
ada_boost = AdaBoostRegressor(n_estimators=100, random_state=42)

# Train the AdaBoost regressor
ada_boost.fit(X_train, y_train)

# Make predictions on the test set
y_pred = ada_boost.predict(X_test)

# Evaluate the mean squared error of the regressor
mse = mean_squared_error(y_test, y_pred)
print("Mean Squared Error:", mse)
```

In both cases, you would need to replace the sample datasets (**'X'** and **'y'**) with your own datasets. The **'n_estimators'** parameter determines the number of weak learners (decision stumps) to be trained, and you can adjust it based on your requirements. Finally, you can evaluate the performance of the AdaBoost model using appropriate evaluation metrics, such as accuracy for classification or mean squared error for regression.

2.15.2 Advantages and Disadvantages of AdaBoost

Here's a more comprehensive list of the advantages and disadvantages of AdaBoost.

Advantages of AdaBoost

1. *High Accuracy:* AdaBoost is known for its high accuracy in both classification and regression tasks. It can achieve better results compared to individual weak learners.
2. *Automatic Feature Selection:* AdaBoost naturally performs feature selection by giving more importance to informative features and downplaying less important ones.
3. *No Data Scaling Required:* AdaBoost does not require data scaling or normalization, making it less sensitive to the scale of the features.

4. *Versatility:* AdaBoost can be used with various base learners (weak models) like decision trees, support vector machines, and so on, making it versatile for different types of problems.
5. *Less Prone to Overfitting:* AdaBoost reduces overfitting by combining multiple weak learners, leading to better generalization on unseen data.

Disadvantages of AdaBoost

1. *Computationally Intensive:* The training process of AdaBoost can be computationally expensive and time-consuming, especially when using a large number of weak learners.
2. *Sensitive to Noisy Data:* AdaBoost is sensitive to noisy data and outliers in the training set, which can negatively impact its performance.
3. *Data Imbalance:* If the data is imbalanced (i.e., one class significantly outweighs the other), AdaBoost may have difficulty achieving good classification accuracy.
4. *Complexity of Hyperparameters:* AdaBoost has some hyperparameters that need to be tuned, such as the number of weak learners (n_estimators), and finding the optimal values can be challenging.
5. *Less Interpretable:* The final ensemble model created by AdaBoost can be less interpretable than individual weak learners, making it difficult to understand the underlying decision-making process.

Despite these disadvantages, AdaBoost remains a powerful and widely used ensemble learning algorithm due to its ability to improve model performance and handle complex relationships in the data. Proper tuning of hyperparameters and preprocessing of data can help mitigate some of the limitations.

2.16 Gradient Boosting Method

Gradient boosting method (GBM) is a boosting technique that builds an ensemble of weak learners in a sequential manner to create a strong learner. Unlike AdaBoost, which modifies the sample distribution, GBM focuses on correcting the errors made by the previous weak learners by fitting the subsequent models to the residuals (the differences between the predicted and actual values) (Natekin & Knoll, 2013).

The steps of the GBM are as follows:

1. Initialize the ensemble by fitting an initial model to the data. This initial model can be a simple one, such as a decision stump.
2. Calculate the residuals by subtracting the predicted values from the actual values of the target variable.
3. Fit a new model (weak learner) to the residuals. The new model is trained to predict the errors made by the previous model.
4. Update the ensemble by adding the new model with a weight that determines its contribution to the final prediction.
5. Repeat steps 2–4 until a predefined stopping criterion is met. This criterion could be a maximum number of models, a threshold for improvement, or a certain level of performance.
6. The final prediction is obtained by combining the predictions of all the models in the ensemble.

The key idea behind GBM is that each weak learner is trained to improve upon the mistakes of the previous models, gradually reducing the overall error. By iteratively adding weak learners, GBM constructs a powerful ensemble model that can capture complex relationships in the data.

GBM can be applied to both regression and classification problems, and it has become a popular algorithm in machine learning due to its high accuracy and ability to handle a variety of data types. However, it is important to note that GBM can be prone to overfitting if the number of iterations (weak learners) is too high or if the learning rate is set too high. Therefore, proper parameter tuning is crucial to ensure optimal performance and prevent overfitting.

2.16.1 Implementation of Gradient Boosting Method

Here's an example of how to implement the GBM for regression and classification tasks using the scikit-learn package in Python:

For Regression:

```
from sklearn.ensemble import GradientBoostingRegressor

# Create a Gradient Boosting Regressor object
gbm_regressor = GradientBoostingRegressor(
    n_estimators=100,  # Number of weak learners (decision trees)
in the ensemble
    learning_rate=0.1,  # Learning rate or shrinkage factor
    max_depth=3,  # Maximum depth of each decision tree
    random_state=42  # Random state for reproducibility
)

# Train the model
gbm_regressor.fit(X_train, y_train)

# Make predictions
y_pred = gbm_regressor.predict(X_test)
```

For Classification:

```
from sklearn.ensemble import GradientBoostingClassifier

# Create a Gradient Boosting Classifier object
gbm_classifier = GradientBoostingClassifier(
n_estimators=100,  # Number of weak learners (decision trees)
in the ensemble
    learning_rate=0.1,  # Learning rate or shrinkage factor
    max_depth=3,  # Maximum depth of each decision tree
```

```
    random_state=42  # Random state for reproducibility
)

# Train the model
gbm_classifier.fit(X_train, y_train)

# Make predictions
y_pred = gbm_classifier.predict(X_test)
```

In both cases, **'X_train'** and **'y_train'** represent the training data and labels, respectively, and **'X_test'** is the test data. You can adjust the hyperparameters (**'n_estimators'**, **'learning_rate'**, **'max_depth'** etc.) based on your specific problem and dataset to achieve the desired performance.

Note: The code provided assumes that you have already imported the necessary libraries and have preprocessed your data accordingly.

2.17 Model Performance Evaluation

Model performance evaluation is a critical step in machine learning to assess the effectiveness and generalization capability of a trained model. It involves various techniques and metrics to measure how well the model performs on unseen data. Here are the key components of model performance evaluation.

2.17.1 Overfitting and Underfitting

Overfitting and underfitting are common challenges in machine learning that arise due to the complexity of the models and the nature of the data. Here's a detailed explanation of overfitting, underfitting, and the bias-variance trade-off as presented in Figure 2.8:

1. *Overfitting:* Overfitting occurs when a model performs exceptionally well on the training data but fails to generalize to new, unseen data. It happens when the model becomes too complex and learns noise or specific patterns that are specific to the training data but not representative of the underlying true relationship in the real world. Overfitting can be visualized as a model that tightly fits all the data points in the training set, including the noise or outliers. However, it fails to capture the underlying trend or pattern that would enable accurate predictions on new data.
2. *Underfitting:* Underfitting occurs when a model is not complex enough to capture the underlying trend or pattern in the data. It happens when the model is too simplistic or makes overly simplistic assumptions, resulting in a poor fit to both the training data and new, unseen data. Underfitting can be visualized as a model that is too simple to capture the complexity of the true relationship and results in high bias.
3. *Bias-Variance Trade-Off:* The concepts of overfitting and underfitting are closely related to the bias-variance trade-off. Bias refers to the error introduced by the model's assumptions and its inability to capture the true underlying relationship between the features and the target variable. High bias leads to underfitting. On the other hand, variance refers to the variability of the model's predictions across different training sets.

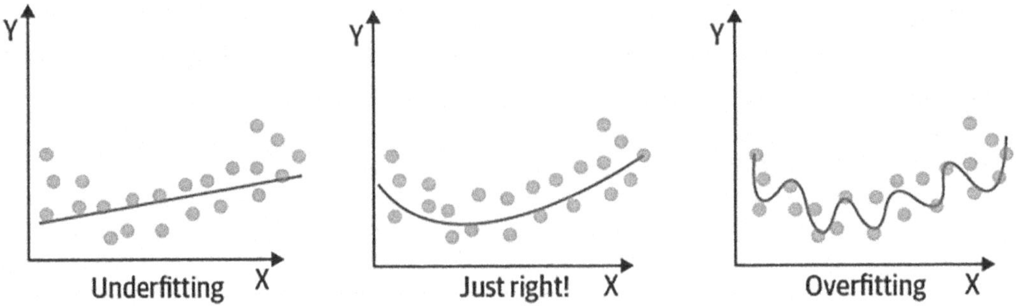

Figure 2.8 Overfitting and underfitting of the data.

High variance arises when the model is overly complex and captures noise or random fluctuations in the training data, leading to overfitting. The goal is to strike a balance between bias and variance to achieve a model that generalizes well to new data.

To achieve a good model, it is necessary to find the right level of complexity that captures the underlying patterns without being overly influenced by noise or outliers. This can be done through techniques such as regularization, feature selection, and model evaluation using validation and test datasets. The bias-variance trade-off helps guide the selection of an appropriate model complexity that minimizes both bias and variance, leading to better generalization performance on unseen data.

2.17.2 Cross-Validation

Cross-validation is a technique used in machine learning to assess the performance and generalization ability of a model presented in Figure 2.9. It involves dividing the available data into multiple subsets or folds and using these folds for both training and validation purposes. By evaluating the model on different subsets of the data, cross-validation provides a more reliable estimate of the model's performance compared to a single train-test split.

Here's a detailed explanation of cross-validation.

1. *Basic Idea:* The main objective of cross-validation is to estimate the model's generalization error or performance on unseen data. Rather than relying on a single train-test split, cross-validation splits the data into multiple subsets or folds. Each fold is used as a validation set, while the remaining folds are used as a training set. This process is repeated multiple times, with each fold serving as the validation set once. The performance scores obtained on each fold are then averaged to provide an overall estimate of the model's performance.
2. *K-Fold Cross-Validation:* K-fold cross-validation is a commonly used technique, where the data is divided into *k* equal-sized folds. The model is trained on *k*-1 folds and evaluated on the remaining fold. This process is repeated *k* times, with each fold used as the validation set once. The performance scores obtained from each iteration are averaged to obtain a more robust estimate of the model's performance.

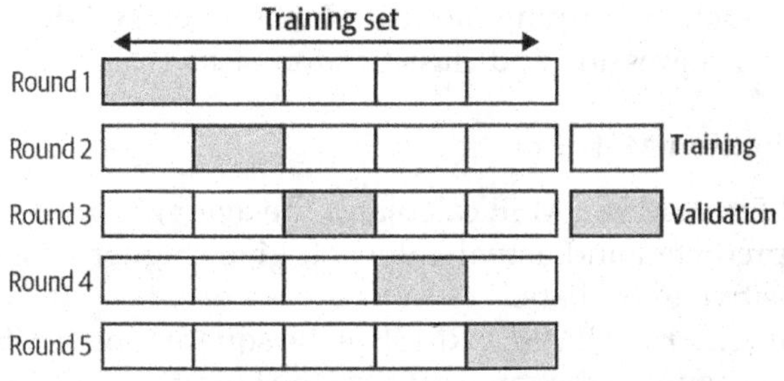

Figure 2.9 Cross-validation.

3. *Benefits of Cross-Validation:* Cross-validation provides several advantages in model evaluation.
    a. It provides a more reliable estimate of the model's performance by evaluating it on multiple subsets of the data.
    b. It helps to mitigate the impact of data variability and randomness by averaging the performance scores obtained on different folds.
    c. It allows for better assessment of the model's generalization ability by testing it on unseen data.
    d. It helps in comparing and selecting between different models or algorithms based on their cross-validated performance scores.

2. *Drawbacks of Cross-Validation:* One potential drawback of cross-validation is the computational cost, especially when combined with techniques like grid search for hyperparameter tuning. Performing cross-validation requires training and evaluating the model multiple times, which can be time-consuming for large datasets or complex models. However, the benefits of obtaining reliable performance estimates often outweigh the computational cost.
3. *Implementation:* Cross-validation can be easily implemented using libraries like scikit-learn in Python. It provides functions and classes to perform various types of cross-validation, including k-fold cross-validation, stratified k-fold cross-validation, and leave-one-out cross-validation.

By using cross-validation, machine learning practitioners can obtain more accurate and trustworthy estimates of their model's performance, allowing them to make better decisions in terms of model selection, hyperparameter tuning, and assessing the model's generalization ability.

2.17.3 Evaluation Metrics

Evaluation metrics are essential tools for assessing the performance of machine learning algorithms. They provide quantitative measures that allow us to compare and evaluate different models or algorithms based on their predictive capabilities. The choice of evaluation metrics is crucial, as it directly impacts how we measure and interpret the performance of machine learning models. Here's a detailed description of the main evaluation metrics for regression and classification tasks.

1. **Regression Evaluation Metrics**
   a. *Mean Squared Error (MSE):* MSE calculates the average of the squared differences between the predicted and actual values. It gives higher weights to large errors, making it sensitive to outliers.
   b. *Root Mean Squared Error (RMSE):* RMSE is the square root of MSE and provides an interpretable measure in the same units as the target variable. It is widely used for evaluating regression models.
   c. *Mean Absolute Error (MAE):* MAE measures the average absolute difference between the predicted and actual values. It is less sensitive to outliers compared to MSE.
   d. *R-Squared (R^2) Score:* R^2 score measures the proportion of the variance in the target variable that is explained by the model. It ranges from 0 to 1, with higher values indicating better model fit. It is commonly used to assess the goodness of fit of regression models.
   e. *Adjusted R-Squared:* Adjusted R-squared adjusts the R-squared score by the number of predictors in the model. It penalizes adding irrelevant predictors and provides a better measure of model fit for models with different numbers of predictors.

   The formula for adjusted R-squared is:

$$R^2_{adj} = 1 - \frac{\left[\left(1 - R^2\right)\left(n - 1\right)\right]}{\left(n - k - 1\right)}$$

Where:

- R^2 is the coefficient of determination, which represents the proportion of variance in the dependent variable that is explained by the independent variables.
- n is the number of observations or data points in the dataset.
- k is the number of predictors (independent variables) in the model.

The adjusted R-squared value ranges between 0 and 1. A higher value indicates a better fit of the model to the data, accounting for the number of predictors. The adjustment in the formula penalizes the addition of unnecessary predictors that do not significantly improve the model's performance. Therefore, the adjusted R-squared is a more reliable measure for comparing models with different numbers of predictors.

2. **Classification Evaluation Metrics**
   In binary classification, the evaluation metrics are used to assess the performance of a classification model by comparing the predicted outcomes to the actual outcomes. The following are the commonly used terms to describe the classification results.
   True Positives (TP): These are the cases where the model correctly predicts the positive class. In other words, the instances that are actually positive and the model correctly identifies them as positive.

   False Positives (FP): These are the cases where the model incorrectly predicts the positive class. It refers to the instances that are actually negative, but the model incorrectly identifies them as positive.

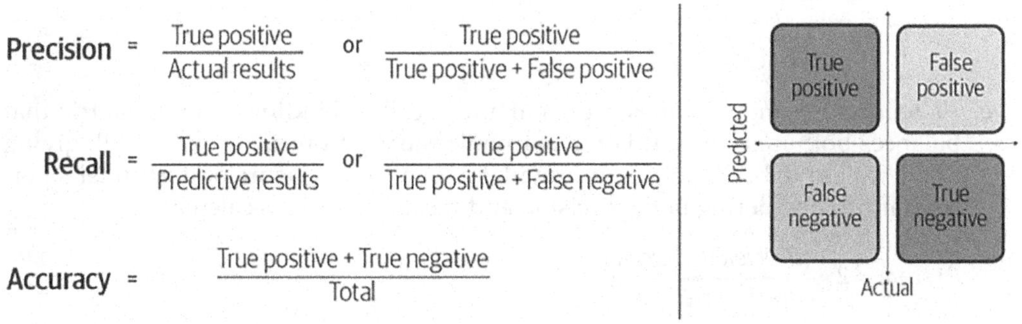

Figure 2.10 Performance metrics of model in terms of precision, recall, and accuracy.

True Negatives (TN): These are the cases where the model correctly predicts the negative class. It represents the instances that are actually negative, and the model correctly identifies them as negative.

False Negatives (FN): These are the cases where the model incorrectly predicts the negative class. It refers to the instances that are actually positive, but the model incorrectly identifies them as negative.

The following are some of the main evaluation metrics used for regression and classification tasks and presented in Figure 2.10.

a. *Accuracy:* Accuracy measures the proportion of correctly classified instances over the total number of instances. It is a straightforward metric but can be misleading when dealing with imbalanced datasets. Accuracy is calculated as,

$$Accuracy = \frac{(TP+TN)}{(TP+TN+FP+FN)}$$

b. *Precision:* Precision calculates the proportion of true positive predictions among all positive predictions. It focuses on the correctness of positive predictions and is useful when the cost of false positives is high. It indicates the model's ability to avoid false positives. Precision is calculated as,

$$Precision = \frac{TP}{TP+FP}$$

c. *Recall (Sensitivity or True Positive Rate):* Recall measures the proportion of true positives predicted correctly out of all actual positive instances. It is useful when the cost of false negatives is high. It represents the model's ability to identify positive instances. Recall is calculated as,

$$Recall = \frac{TP}{TP+FN}$$

d. *Specificity (True Negative Rate):* Specificity measures the proportion of correctly predicted negative instances among all actual negative instances, calculated as $TN/(TN + FP)$. It represents the model's ability to identify negative instances. Specificity is calculated as,

$$Specificity = \frac{TN}{TN + FP}$$

e. *F1 Score:* $F1$ score combines precision and recall, providing a single metric that balances both measures. It is the harmonic mean of precision and recall, giving equal weight to both metrics. It provides a balanced measure of the model's performance, considering both precision and recall. $F1$ score is calculated as,

$$F1score = 2 \times \frac{(Precision \times Recall)}{(Precision + Recall)}$$

f. *Area under the ROC Curve (AUC-ROC):* AUC-ROC measures the performance of a binary classification model across different classification thresholds. It plots the trade-off between true positive rate and false positive rate. A higher AUC-ROC value indicates better classification performance.
g. *Log Loss:* Log Loss, also known as cross-entropy loss, measures the performance of probabilistic classifiers. It quantifies the difference between predicted probabilities and the true probabilities of the target classes. Lower log loss values indicate better model performance.

It's important to select the appropriate metrics based on the specific problem and the goals of the analysis. Additionally, it's advisable to consider the context and characteristics of the dataset to ensure the chosen metrics provide meaningful insights into the model's performance.

2.18 Summary

The chapter covers various topics related to machine learning and provides an overview of different algorithms, their implementation, advantages, and disadvantages. Here is a brief summary of each topic covered.

1. *Intuition of Machine Learning:* This section introduces the concept of machine learning and explains how it enables computers to learn from data and make predictions or decisions without being explicitly programmed.
2. *Examples of Machine Learning:* Several real-world examples are provided to illustrate the applications of machine learning in various fields such as finance, healthcare, image recognition, and recommendation systems.
3. *Types of Data Analysis:* Different types of data analysis, including descriptive, diagnostic, predictive, and prescriptive analysis, are discussed to highlight the role of machine learning in extracting insights from data.
4. *Machine Learning Process:* The process of developing a machine learning model is explained, including data preprocessing, feature selection, model training, evaluation, and deployment.
5. *Categories of Machine Learning Methods:* The main categories of machine learning methods are introduced, including supervised learning, unsupervised learning, weakly supervised learning, and semi-supervised learning.
6. *Supervised Learning:* This section focuses on supervised learning, where the model learns from labeled training data to make predictions on new, unseen data.

7. *Regression Algorithms:* Regression algorithms are discussed, with a focus on linear regression, its implementation in Python, and its advantages and disadvantages. Regularized regression techniques, such as Lasso and Ridge regression, are also explained.
8. *Classification Algorithms:* Classification algorithms are covered, with a focus on logistic regression, its implementation, and its pros and cons.
9. *Support Vector Machine:* SVMs are introduced as powerful classification algorithms. Their implementation and advantages and disadvantages are discussed.
10. *K-Nearest Neighbors:* The KNN algorithm is explained, including its implementation and its strengths and weaknesses.
11. *Linear Discriminant Analysis:* LDA is discussed as a dimensionality reduction and classification technique. Its implementation and advantages and disadvantages are covered.
12. Decision Trees: Decision tree algorithms are introduced, including their implementation for regression and classification problems and their advantages and disadvantages.
13. *Ensemble Models:* The concept of ensemble models is explained, with a focus on random forest and Extra Trees algorithms. Their implementations, advantages, and disadvantages are discussed.
14. *AdaBoost:* AdaBoost, a popular boosting algorithm, is introduced, along with its implementation and the pros and cons.
15. *Gradient Boosting Method:* Gradient Boosting Method is discussed as another boosting technique, with its implementation and strengths and weaknesses.
16. *Model Performance Evaluation:* The process of evaluating model performance is explained, covering topics such as overfitting, underfitting, cross-validation, and evaluation metrics.

The chapter provides a comprehensive overview of various machine learning algorithms, their implementations, and the evaluation of their performance. It equips the reader with the necessary knowledge to understand and apply these techniques in real-world scenarios.

References

Athey, S., & Wager, S. (2019). Estimating treatment effects with causal forests: An application. *Observational Studies, 5*(2), 37–51.

Auerbach, E. (2022). Identification and estimation of a partially linear regression model using network data. *Econometrica, 90*(1), 347–365.

Carneiro, T. C., Rocha, P. A. C., Carvalho, P. C. M., & Fernández-Ramírez, L. M. (2022). Ridge regression ensemble of machine learning models applied to solar and wind forecasting in Brazil and Spain. *Applied Energy, 314*, 118936.

Carton, S., Helsby, J., Joseph, K., Mahmud, A., Park, Y., Walsh, J., Cody, C., Patterson, C. P. T. E., Haynes, L., & Ghani, R. (2016). Identifying police officers at risk of adverse events. *Proceedings of the 22nd ACM SIGKDD International Conference on Knowledge Discovery and Data Mining*, 67–76.

Ge, X., Xu, F., Wang, Y., Li, H., Wang, F., Hu, J., Li, K., Lu, X., & Chen, B. (2022). Spatio-temporal two-dimensions data based customer baseline load estimation approach using LASSO regression. *IEEE Transactions on Industry Applications, 58*(3), 3112–3122.

Han, Q., & Shen, Y. (2022). Universality of regularized regression estimators in high dimensions. *ArXiv Preprint ArXiv:2206.07936*.

Huang, F. L. (2022). Alternatives to logistic regression models in experimental studies. *The Journal of Experimental Education*, *90*(1), 213–228.

LaValley, M. P. (2008). Logistic regression. *Circulation*, *117*(18), 2395–2399.

McDonald, G. C. (2009). Ridge regression. *Wiley Interdisciplinary Reviews: Computational Statistics*, *1*(1), 93–100.

Natekin, A., & Knoll, A. (2013). Gradient boosting machines, a tutorial. *Frontiers in Neurorobotics*, *7*, 21.

Potash, E., Brew, J., Loewi, A., Majumdar, S., Reece, A., Walsh, J., Rozier, E., Jorgenson, E., Mansour, R., & Ghani, R. (2015). Predictive modeling for public health: Preventing childhood lead poisoning. *Proceedings of the 21th ACM SIGKDD International Conference on Knowledge Discovery and Data Mining*, 2039–2047.

Ranstam, J., & Cook, J. A. (2018). LASSO regression. *Journal of British Surgery*, *105*(10), 1348.

Su, X., Yan, X., & Tsai, C. (2012). Linear regression. *Wiley Interdisciplinary Reviews: Computational Statistics*, *4*(3), 275–294.

Suthaharan, S. (2016). Support vector machine. In *Machine learning models and algorithms for big data classification: thinking with examples for effective learning* (pp. 207–235). Boston, MA: Springer US.

Terrell, E. (2022). Estimation of Hansen solubility parameters with regularized regression for biomass conversion products: An application of adaptable group contribution. *Chemical Engineering Science*, *248*, 117184.

Voigt, R., Camp, N. P., Prabhakaran, V., Hamilton, W. L., Hetey, R. C., Griffiths, C. M., Jurgens, D., Jurafsky, D., & Eberhardt, J. L. (2017). Language from police body camera footage shows racial disparities in officer respect. *Proceedings of the National Academy of Sciences*, *114*(25), 6521–6526.

Zhou, J., Zhu, S., Qiu, Y., Armaghani, D. J., Zhou, A., & Yong, W. (2022). Predicting tunnel squeezing using support vector machine optimized by whale optimization algorithm. *Acta Geotechnica*, *17*(4), 1343–1366.

Chapter 3

Neural Networks Fundamentals

3.1 Foundations of Neural Networks

A neural network is a mathematical model inspired by the functioning of biological neural networks, such as the human brain. It consists of interconnected nodes, or artificial neurons, organized in layers. Each neuron takes input signals, performs computations on them, and produces an output signal that is transmitted to other neurons. The network learns by adjusting the strengths of connections (synaptic weights) between neurons based on training data.

The mathematical background of neural networks lies in linear algebra and calculus. The computations within a neural network involve linear transformations and nonlinear activation functions. Linear algebra is used to represent the network's parameters (weights and biases) as matrices and vectors, enabling efficient calculations. Calculus is employed for optimizing the network through techniques like gradient descent, which adjusts the weights to minimize the difference between predicted and actual outputs.

3.1.1 Applications of Neural Networks

Neural networks have a wide range of applications across various fields. Some common applications include the following.

1. *Pattern Recognition:* Neural networks can learn to recognize patterns in data, such as identifying objects in images or detecting patterns in time series data.
2. *Classification:* Neural networks can classify data into different categories or classes based on input features. They are used in tasks like image classification, sentiment analysis, or spam detection.
3. *Regression:* Neural networks can be used for regression tasks to predict continuous numerical values, such as predicting housing prices or stock market trends.
4. *Data Fitting:* Neural networks can learn to fit complex functions to data, capturing intricate relationships and providing accurate predictions.
5. *Control Systems:* Neural networks can be used in control systems to learn and optimize control strategies for various processes, such as robotics, autonomous vehicles, or industrial automation.
6. *Natural Language Processing:* Neural networks are employed in language processing tasks, including speech recognition, language translation, and sentiment analysis.

DOI: 10.1201/9781003654216-4

The power of neural networks lies in their ability to learn from data and adapt to complex relationships in the underlying data. They can automatically extract relevant features and discover hidden patterns, making them highly effective in solving a wide range of problems. However, building and training neural networks requires careful consideration of network architecture, appropriate data preprocessing, tuning hyperparameters, and handling overfitting to achieve optimal performance. Hence, a neural network is a mathematical model inspired by biological neural networks. It leverages linear algebra, calculus, and statistical techniques to solve problems through pattern recognition, classification, regression, and data fitting. Neural networks have diverse applications and can provide accurate predictions and solutions by learning from data.

3.1.2 Structure of a Neural Network

A neural network, also known as an artificial neural network (ANN), is a computational model inspired by the structure and function of the human brain. It consists of interconnected nodes called neurons, organized in layers, which work together to process and analyze input data, make predictions, and perform various tasks such as pattern recognition, classification, and forecasting.

The structure of a neural network typically includes three main components (as shown in Figure 3.1): an input layer, one or more hidden layers, and an output layer. The number of layers and the number of neurons in each layer can vary depending on the complexity of the problem being solved.

1. *Input Layer:* The input layer is responsible for receiving the raw input data and passing it to the next layer. Each neuron in the input layer corresponds to a feature or input variable. The input layer does not perform any computations but serves as a conduit for passing the input data into the network.

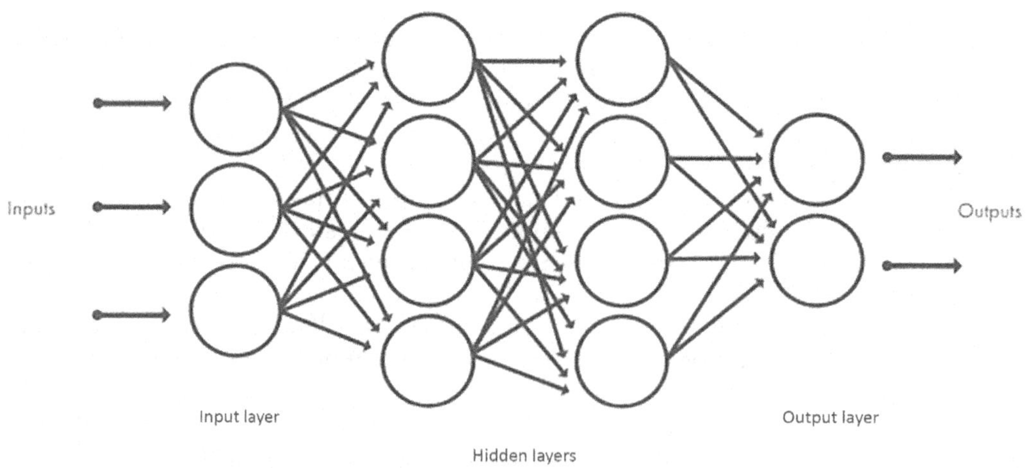

Figure 3.1 Neural network structure.

2. *Hidden Layers:* Hidden layers are the intermediate layers between the input and output layers. They are called "hidden" because their computations are not directly observable. Hidden layers are responsible for extracting relevant features and representations from the input data through a series of weighted computations. Each neuron in a hidden layer receives inputs from the previous layer, applies a transformation using activation functions, and passes the transformed information to the next layer.

   The number of hidden layers and the number of neurons in each hidden layer are design choices that depend on the complexity of the problem and the amount of data available. Deeper networks with more hidden layers have the potential to learn more complex patterns and representations.
3. *Output Layer:* The output layer is responsible for producing the final output or prediction of the neural network. The number of neurons in the output layer depends on the type of problem being solved. For example, in binary classification, there may be one neuron in the output layer representing the probability or prediction of one class. In multi-class classification, there will be multiple neurons, each representing the probability or prediction of a different class.

Each neuron in the output layer applies an activation function to transform the computed values into a suitable format for the task at hand. The choice of activation function depends on the nature of the problem, such as sigmoid or softmax functions for classification tasks or linear functions for regression tasks.

During the learning process, the neural network adjusts the weights of connections between neurons based on a specified learning rule, typically using an optimization algorithm like gradient descent. This adjustment allows the network to learn from training examples, make accurate predictions, and generalize its knowledge to unseen data. A neural network is a powerful and versatile machine learning model that can learn complex patterns, recognize important features, and make predictions based on learned representations. Its ability to adapt and learn from data makes it suitable for various applications across different domains.

3.2 Types of Units/Activation Functions/Layers

In deep learning, there are various types of units, activation functions, and layers that are commonly used. These components play a crucial role in modeling the non-linear relationships and capturing complex patterns in the data. Here is a detailed description of some commonly used types.

3.2.1 Linear Unit

A linear unit, also known as an identity unit, computes a weighted sum of the input values without any nonlinear transformation. The output of a linear unit is simply the weighted sum of the inputs: $f(x)=wx+b$, where w represents the weights, x represents the input, and b represents the bias term. Linear units are primarily used in the output layer for regression tasks, where the model needs to predict continuous values.

Here's an implementation of a linear unit in Python, along with a plot of the linear function:

```
import numpy as np
import matplotlib.pyplot as plt

class LinearUnit:
    def __init__(self, weight, bias):
        self.weight = weight
        self.bias = bias

    def forward(self, x):
        return self.weight * x + self.bias

# Define the weight and bias
weight = 2.0
bias = 1.0

# Create a linear unit object
linear_unit = LinearUnit(weight, bias)

# Generate input values
x = np.linspace(-5, 5, 100)

# Compute the output of the linear unit for each input
y = linear_unit.forward(x)

# Plot the linear function
plt.plot(x, y)
plt.xlabel('Input (x)')
plt.ylabel('Output (f(x))')
plt.title('Linear Unit')
plt.grid(True)
plt.show()
```

In this implementation, the **'LinearUnit'** class represents a linear unit. The **'weight'** parameter represents the weight value (w) and the **'bias'** parameter represents the bias term (b).

The **'forward'** method performs the forward pass of the linear unit. Given an input **'x'**, it computes the weighted sum of the input values by multiplying **'x'** with the weight and adding the bias term. The result is returned as the output of the linear unit.

The code generates input values (**'x'**) using **'np.linspace'** and computes the corresponding outputs (**'y'**) by passing the inputs through the linear unit. It then plots the linear function using **'plt.plot'** shown in Figure 3.2. The x-axis represents the input values, and the y-axis represents the output values of the linear unit.

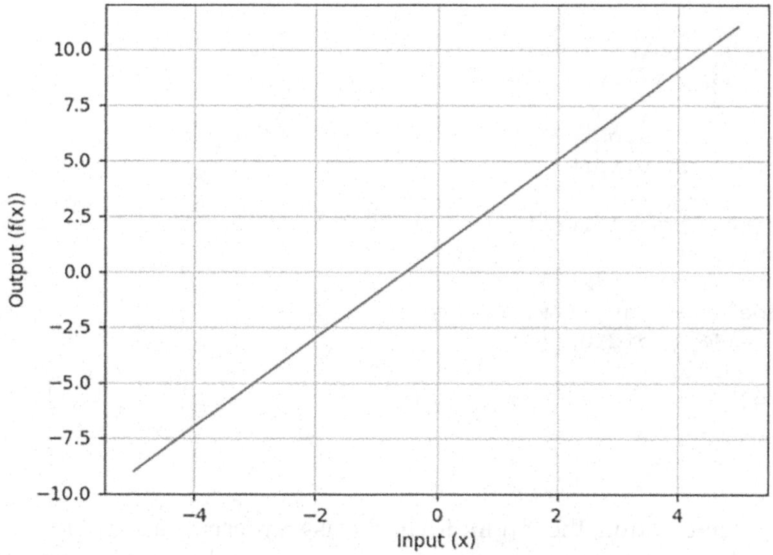

Figure 3.2 Linear unit.

3.2.2 *Sigmoid Unit*

The sigmoid unit applies the sigmoid activation function to the weighted sum of the inputs. The sigmoid function, also known as the logistic function, maps the input to a value between 0 and 1, which can be interpreted as a probability. The sigmoid activation function is given by:

$$f(x) = \frac{1}{(1+exp(-x))}$$

Sigmoid units were commonly used in the past but have been largely replaced by other activation functions due to some limitations such as vanishing gradients.

Here's an implementation of a sigmoid unit in Python, along with a plot of the sigmoid function:

```
import numpy as np
import matplotlib.pyplot as plt

class SigmoidUnit:
    def forward(self, x):
        return 1 / (1 + np.exp(-x))
# Create a sigmoid unit object
sigmoid_unit = SigmoidUnit()
```

```
# Generate input values
x = np.linspace(-5, 5, 100)

# Compute the output of the sigmoid unit for each input
y = sigmoid_unit.forward(x)

# Plot the sigmoid function
plt.plot(x, y)
plt.xlabel('Input (x)')
plt.ylabel('Output (f(x))')
plt.title('Sigmoid Unit')
plt.grid(True)
plt.show()
```

In this implementation, the **'SigmoidUnit'** class represents a sigmoid unit. The **'forward'** method performs the forward pass of the sigmoid unit. Given an input **'x'**, it applies the sigmoid activation function **'1 / (1 + np.exp(-x))'** to compute the output.

The code generates input values (**'x'**) using **'np.linspace'** and computes the corresponding outputs (**'y'**) by passing the inputs through the sigmoid unit. It then plots the sigmoid function using **'plt.plot'** shown in Figure 3.3. The x-axis represents the input values, and the y-axis represents the output values of the sigmoid unit.

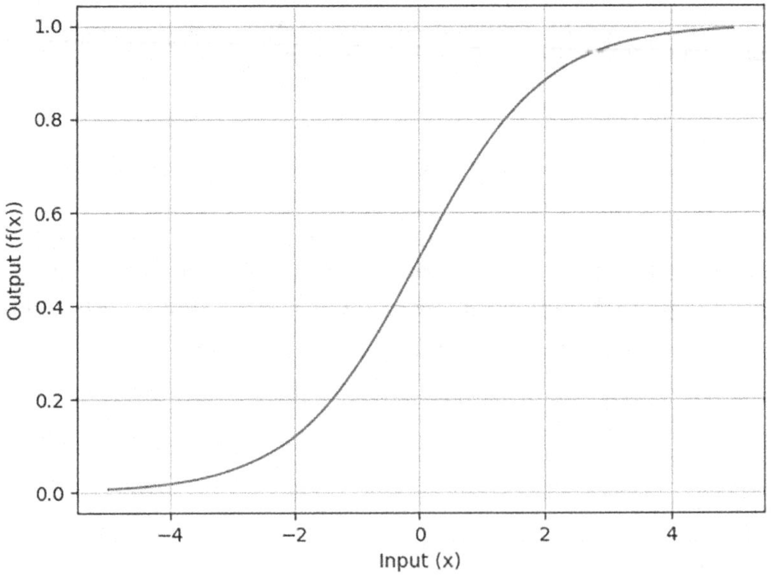

Figure 3.3 Sigmoid unit.

3.2.3 Rectified Linear Unit

The rectified linear unit (ReLU) is one of the most popular activation functions used in deep learning. The ReLU function is defined as $f(x) = \max(0, x)$, which returns the input value if it is positive and zero otherwise. ReLU units introduce nonlinearity to the model and are computationally efficient (Nayak et al., 2020; Zhao et al., 2020). ReLU units have been widely adopted due to their ability to mitigate the vanishing gradient problem and promote sparse activations.

Here's an implementation of a ReLU in Python, along with a plot of the ReLU function:

```
import numpy as np
import matplotlib.pyplot as plt

class ReLUUnit:
    def forward(self, x):
        return np.maximum(0, x)

# Create a ReLU unit object
relu_unit = ReLUUnit()

# Generate input values
x = np.linspace(-5, 5, 100)

# Compute the output of the ReLU unit for each input
y = relu_unit.forward(x)

# Plot the ReLU function
plt.plot(x, y)
plt.xlabel('Input (x)')
plt.ylabel('Output (f(x))')
plt.title('Rectified Linear Unit (ReLU)')
plt.grid(True)
plt.show()
```

In this implementation, the **'ReLUUnit'** class represents a ReLU unit. The **'forward'** method performs the forward pass of the ReLU unit. Given an input **'x'**, it applies the ReLU activation function **'np.maximum(0, x)'** to compute the output.

The code generates input values (**'x'**) using **'np.linspace'** and computes the corresponding outputs (**'y'**) by passing the inputs through the ReLU unit. It then plots the ReLU function using **'plt.plot'** shown in Figure 3.4. The x-axis represents the input values, and the y-axis represents the output values of the ReLU unit.

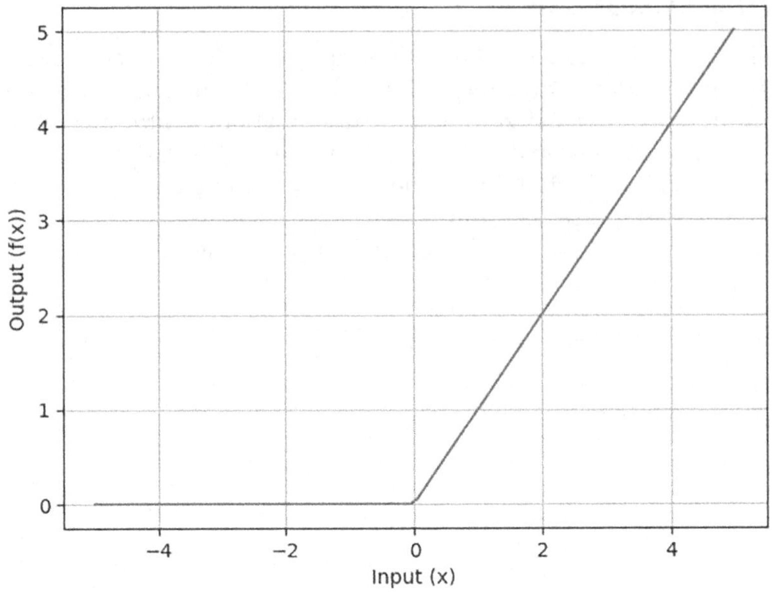

Figure 3.4 Rectified linear unit.

3.2.4 *Leaky ReLU*

The leaky ReLU is a variant of the ReLU activation function that addresses the "dying ReLU" problem, where ReLU units can become inactive and output zero for negative inputs. The leaky ReLU function is defined as f(x) = max(αx, x), where α is a small positive constant (typically a small value like 0.01). By introducing a small slope for negative inputs, leaky ReLU units can prevent them from being completely deactivated, allowing for better gradient flow.

Here's an implementation of a leaky ReLU in Python, along with a plot of the leaky ReLU function:

```
import numpy as np
import matplotlib.pyplot as plt

class LeakyReLUUnit:
    def __init__(self, alpha=0.01):
        self.alpha = alpha

    def forward(self, x):
        return np.maximum(self.alpha * x, x)
# Create a LeakyReLU unit object with alpha = 0.01
leaky_relu_unit = LeakyReLUUnit(alpha=0.01)
```

```
# Generate input values
x = np.linspace(-5, 5, 100)

# Compute the output of the LeakyReLU unit for each input
y = leaky_relu_unit.forward(x)

# Plot the LeakyReLU function
plt.plot(x, y)
plt.xlabel('Input (x)')
plt.ylabel('Output (f(x))')
plt.title('Leaky Rectified Linear Unit (Leaky ReLU)')
plt.grid(True)
plt.show()
```

In this implementation, the **'LeakyReLUUnit'** class represents a leaky ReLU unit. The **'forward'** method performs the forward pass of the leaky ReLU unit. Given an input **'x'**, it applies the leaky ReLU activation function **'np.maximum(self.alpha * x, x)'** to compute the output, where **'self.alpha'** is the small positive constant representing the slope for negative inputs.

The code generates input values (**'x'**) using **'np.linspace'** and computes the corresponding outputs (**'y'**) by passing the inputs through the leaky ReLU unit. It then plots the leaky ReLU function using **'plt.plot'** shown in Figure 3.5. The x-axis represents the input values, and the y-axis represents the output values of the leaky ReLU unit.

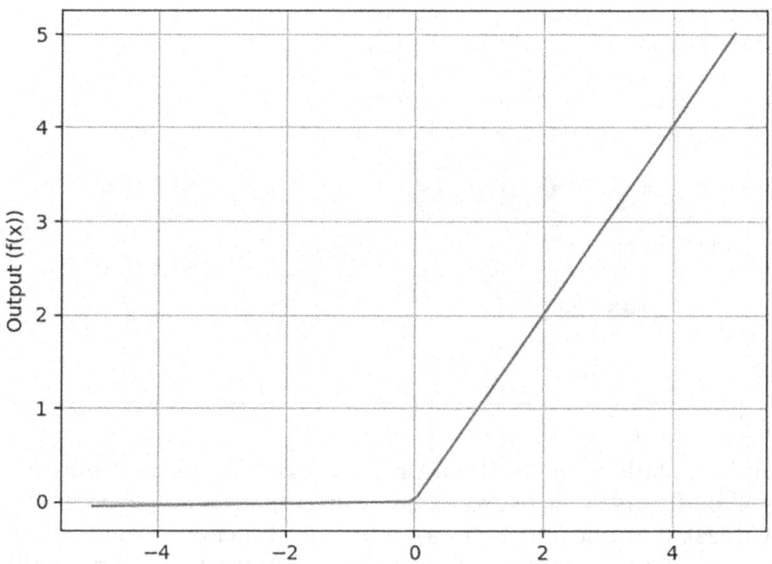

Figure 3.5 Leaky ReLU unit.

3.2.5 *Softmax Unit*

The softmax unit is commonly used in the output layer for multi-class classification tasks. The softmax function converts a vector of real values into a probability distribution over multiple classes (Gao et al., 2020; Wei et al., 2020). The softmax function is given by:

$$f(x_i)=\frac{exp(x_i)}{\sum \exp(x_j)},$$

where x_i is the input value for class i and the summation is over all classes. The softmax function ensures that the output probabilities sum up to 1, making it suitable for multi-class classification problems.

Here's an implementation of a softmax unit in Python, along with a plot of the softmax function:

```
import numpy as np
import matplotlib.pyplot as plt

class SoftmaxUnit:
    def forward(self, x):
        exps = np.exp(x)
        return exps / np.sum(exps)

# Create a Softmax unit object
softmax_unit = SoftmaxUnit()

# Generate input values
x = np.linspace(-5, 5, 100)

# Compute the output of the Softmax unit for each input
y = softmax_unit.forward(x)

# Plot the Softmax function
plt.plot(x, y)
plt.xlabel('Input (x)')
plt.ylabel('Output (f(x))')
plt.title('Softmax Function')
plt.grid(True)
plt.show()
```

In this implementation, the **'SoftmaxUnit'** class represents a softmax unit. The **'forward'** method performs the forward pass of the softmax unit. Given an input **'x'** (vector of real values), it applies the softmax activation function **'exps / np.sum(exps)'** to compute the output, where **'exps'** is the vector of exponentiated input values and **'np.sum(exps)'** computes the sum of all exponentiated values.

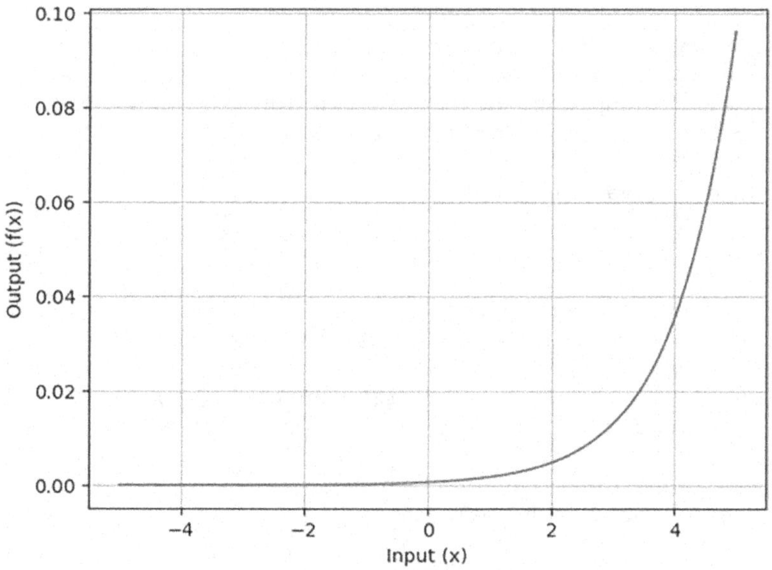

Figure 3.6 Softmax function.

The code generates input values (**'x'**) using **'np.linspace'** and computes the corresponding outputs (**'y'**) by passing the inputs through the softmax unit. It then plots the softmax function using **'plt.plot'** shown in Figure 3.6. The x-axis represents the input values, and the y-axis represents the output probabilities of the softmax unit, which form a probability distribution over the classes.

3.2.6 Dense Layer

The dense layer, also known as a fully connected layer, connects every input unit to every output unit. Each unit in the dense layer receives inputs from all the units in the previous layer and produces an output based on its weights and activation function. Dense layers are the most common type of layer in deep neural networks and provide high flexibility in modeling complex relationships between inputs and outputs.

Here's an implementation of a dense layer in Python, along with a description of the plot:

```
import numpy as np
import matplotlib.pyplot as plt

class DenseLayer:
    def __init__(self, input_size, output_size, activation):
        self.weights = np.random.randn(input_size, output_size)
        self.bias = np.zeros(output_size)
        self.activation = activation
```

```
    def forward(self, inputs):
        self.inputs = inputs
        self.z = np.dot(inputs, self.weights) + self.bias
        return self.activation(self.z)

# Define the activation function
def sigmoid(x):
    return 1 / (1 + np.exp(-x))

# Create a Dense layer object
input_size = 10
output_size = 5
dense_layer = DenseLayer(input_size, output_size,
activation=sigmoid)

# Generate input data
inputs = np.random.randn(100, input_size)

# Compute the output of the dense layer for each input
outputs = dense_layer.forward(inputs)

# Plot the output of the dense layer
plt.plot(outputs)
plt.xlabel('Sample')
plt.ylabel('Output')
plt.title('Output of Dense Layer')
plt.grid(True)
plt.show()
```

In this implementation, the **'DenseLayer'** class represents a dense layer. The constructor initializes the weights and bias with random values and stores the activation function. The **'forward'** method performs the forward pass of the dense layer. Given an input (**'inputs'**), it computes the dot product of the inputs with the weights, adds the bias, and applies the activation function to produce the output.

The code defines the sigmoid activation function (**'sigmoid'**) and creates a dense layer object (**'dense_layer'**) with the specified input and output sizes.

It generates random input data (**'inputs'**) and computes the corresponding outputs by passing the inputs through the dense layer. It then plots the output of the dense layer using **'plt.plot'** shown in Figure 3.7. The x-axis represents the samples, and the y-axis represents the output values of the dense layer.

3.2.7 *Convolutional Layer*

Convolutional layers are commonly used in convolutional neural networks (CNNs) for processing grid-like input data such as images. Convolutional layers apply a set of learnable filters (kernels) to the input data, performing convolution operations to

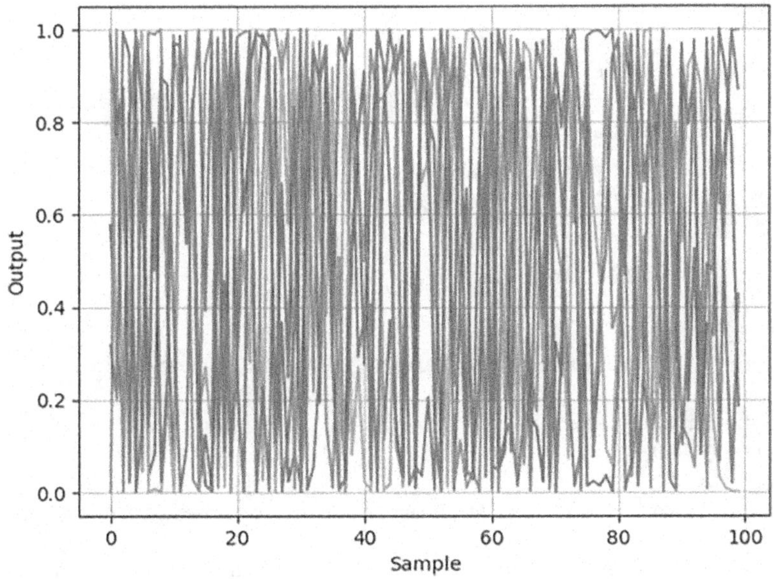

Figure 3.7 Output of dense layer.

extract local features (Yu et al., 2021). These layers capture spatial relationships and are efficient in handling large input volumes by sharing weights and utilizing parameter sharing (Raghu et al., 2021).

Here's an implementation of a convolutional layer in Python, along with a description of the plot:

```
import numpy as np
import matplotlib.pyplot as plt

class ConvolutionalLayer:
    def __init__(self, num_filters, filter_size):
        self.num_filters = num_filters
        self.filter_size = filter_size
        self.weights = np.random.randn(num_filters, filter_size,
filter_size)
        self.bias = np.zeros(num_filters)

    def forward(self, inputs):
        self.inputs = inputs
        batch_size, input_size, _ = inputs.shape
        output_size = input_size - self.filter_size + 1
        self.outputs = np.zeros((batch_size, output_size, output_
size, self.num_filters))
        for i in range(batch_size):
```

```
            for j in range(output_size):
                for k in range(output_size):
                    receptive_field = inputs[i, j:j+self.filter_
size, k:k+self.filter_size]
                    self.outputs[i, j, k] = np.sum(receptive_field
* self.weights, axis=(1, 2)) + self.bias
        return self.outputs

# Create a Convolutional layer object
num_filters = 8
filter_size = 3
conv_layer = ConvolutionalLayer(num_filters, filter_size)

# Generate input data
batch_size = 10
input_size = 10
inputs = np.random.randn(batch_size, input_size, input_size)

# Compute the output of the convolutional layer for each input
outputs = conv_layer.forward(inputs)

# Plot one of the output feature maps
feature_map = 0
plt.imshow(outputs[0, :, :, feature_map], cmap='gray')
plt.xlabel('Column')
plt.ylabel('Row')
plt.title('Output Feature Map')
plt.colorbar()
plt.show()
```

In this implementation, the **'ConvolutionalLayer'** class represents a convolutional layer. The constructor initializes the number of filters and filter size and randomly initializes the weights and bias. The **'forward'** method performs the forward pass of the convolutional layer. Given an input tensor (**'inputs'**), it loops over the batch, rows, and columns and applies convolution operations to extract features using the learned weights and biases.

The code creates a convolutional layer object (**'conv_layer'**) with the specified number of filters and filter size.

It generates random input data (**'inputs'**) and computes the corresponding outputs by passing the inputs through the convolutional layer. It then plots one of the output feature maps using **'plt.imshow'** shown in Figure 3.8. The colormap 'gray' is used to visualize the intensity values, and the x-axis and y-axis represent the column and row indices of the feature map, respectively.

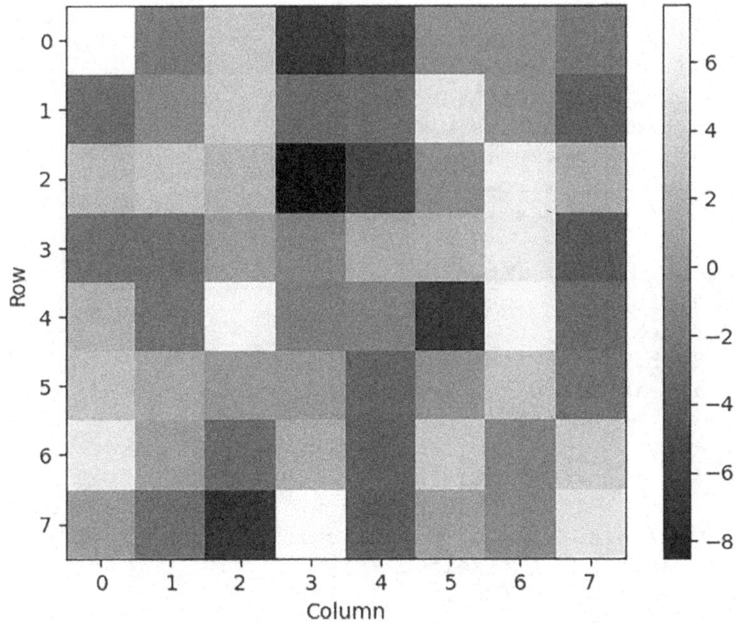

Figure 3.8 Output feature map of convolutional layer.

3.2.8 Recurrent Layer

Recurrent layers, such as the long short-term memory (LSTM) and gated recurrent unit (GRU), are used for processing sequential data. Recurrent layers maintain hidden states that capture the historical information of the sequence. These layers allow information to flow across different time steps and are effective in modeling temporal dependencies in sequential data.

Here's an implementation of a recurrent layer (specifically, a LSTM) in Python, along with a description of the plot:

```
import numpy as np
import matplotlib.pyplot as plt

class LSTM:
    def __init__(self, input_size, hidden_size):
        self.input_size = input_size
        self.hidden_size = hidden_size
        self.Wf = np.random.randn(input_size, hidden_size)
        self.Wi = np.random.randn(input_size, hidden_size)
        self.Wo = np.random.randn(input_size, hidden_size)
```

```
        self.Wc = np.random.randn(input_size, hidden_size)
        self.bf = np.zeros(hidden_size)
        self.bi = np.zeros(hidden_size)
        self.bo = np.zeros(hidden_size)
        self.bc = np.zeros(hidden_size)
        self.h = np.zeros(hidden_size)
        self.c = np.zeros(hidden_size)

    def forward(self, inputs):
        self.inputs = inputs
        seq_len, _ = inputs.shape
        self.hidden_states = []
        for t in range(seq_len):
            x = inputs[t]
            f = self.sigmoid(np.dot(x, self.Wf) + self.bf)
            i = self.sigmoid(np.dot(x, self.Wi) + self.bi)
            o = self.sigmoid(np.dot(x, self.Wo) + self.bo)
            c_ = np.tanh(np.dot(x, self.Wc) + self.bc)
            self.c = f * self.c + i * c_
            self.h = o * np.tanh(self.c)
            self.hidden_states.append(self.h)
        return self.hidden_states

    def sigmoid(self, x):
        return 1 / (1 + np.exp(-x))

# Create an LSTM layer object
input_size = 10
hidden_size = 5
lstm_layer = LSTM(input_size, hidden_size)

# Generate input sequence
seq_len = 10
inputs = np.random.randn(seq_len, input_size)

# Compute the hidden states using the LSTM layer
hidden_states = lstm_layer.forward(inputs)

# Plot the hidden states over time
plt.figure(figsize=(8, 4))
for i in range(hidden_size):
    plt.plot(range(seq_len), [h[i] for h in hidden_states],
label='Hidden Unit {}'.format(i))
plt.xlabel('Time Step')
plt.ylabel('Hidden State')
plt.title('Hidden States of LSTM Layer')
plt.legend()
plt.show()
```

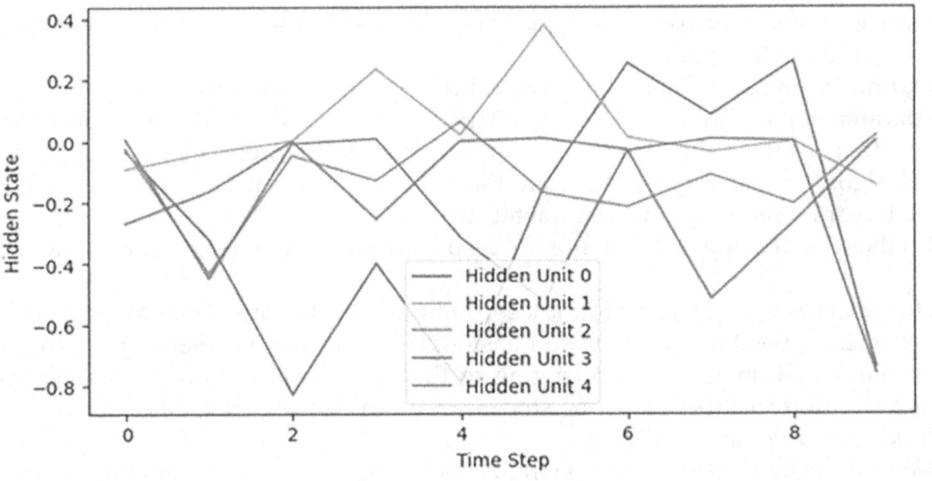

Figure 3.9 Hidden States of LSTM Layer.

In this implementation, the **'LSTM'** class represents an LSTM layer. The constructor initializes the input size and hidden size and randomly initializes the weights and biases for the gates and cell state. The **'forward'** method performs the forward pass of the LSTM layer. Given an input sequence (**'inputs'**), it loops over the time steps and computes the hidden states using the LSTM equations.

The code creates an LSTM layer object (**'lstm_layer'**) with the specified input size and hidden size.

It generates a random input sequence (**'inputs'**) and computes the corresponding hidden states by passing the inputs through the LSTM layer. It then plots the hidden states over time using **'plt.plot'** shown in Figure 3.9. Each line represents the hidden state of a specific unit at each time step. The x-axis represents the time step, and the y-axis represents the value of the hidden state. The legend shows the corresponding unit number for each line.

These are just a few examples of units, activation functions, and layers commonly used in deep learning. There are also other specialized units and layers, such as pooling layers, dropout layers, and batch normalization layers, that serve specific purposes in different types of neural networks. The choice of units, activation functions, and layers depends on the nature of the problem, the type of data, and the specific requirements of the model.

3.3 Optimization and Deep Learning

The relationship between optimization and deep learning is fundamental and closely intertwined. Deep learning involves training complex neural networks with numerous parameters to learn from data and make accurate predictions or decisions. The training process typically involves finding the optimal values for these parameters that minimize the loss function, which quantifies the discrepancy between the model's predictions and the true values.

Optimization algorithms play a crucial role in this process by iteratively adjusting the parameters to minimize the loss function. The goal is to find the set of parameter values that result in the best performance of the neural network on the given task. These algorithms attempt to navigate the high-dimensional parameter space to converge toward a set of optimal parameter values.

Challenges in using optimization in deep learning arise due to several factors.

1. *High-Dimensional Parameter Space:* Deep neural networks often have a large number of parameters, resulting in a high-dimensional optimization problem. The search space becomes vast, making it challenging to find the global optimum. Gradient-based optimization methods, such as stochastic gradient descent (SGD), are commonly used to address this challenge.
2. *Non-Convexity:* The loss function in deep learning is generally non-convex, meaning it contains multiple local minima and saddle points. This property makes optimization more difficult because algorithms can get trapped in suboptimal solutions. Exploring the landscape of the loss function and avoiding these suboptimal solutions are significant challenges.
3. *Gradient Vanishing and Exploding:* In deep neural networks with many layers, the gradients used to update the parameters can diminish or explode during backpropagation. This phenomenon, known as gradient vanishing or exploding, can hinder the optimization process. Techniques like careful initialization, regularization, and normalization are employed to mitigate these issues.
4. *Computational Complexity:* Deep learning models require substantial computational resources, especially when training large-scale networks on big datasets. Optimization algorithms need to be efficient and scalable to handle the computational demands of deep learning tasks.
5. *Hyperparameter Tuning:* Deep learning models involve various hyperparameters, such as learning rate, regularization strength, and network architecture choices. Finding the optimal values for these hyperparameters is essential for achieving good performance. However, optimizing these hyperparameters is itself a challenge, often requiring manual tuning or sophisticated optimization techniques.

To address these challenges, researchers and practitioners have developed various optimization algorithms and techniques tailored specifically for deep learning. These include advanced optimization methods like adaptive learning rate algorithms (e.g., Adam, RMSprop), weight initialization strategies, regularization techniques (e.g., dropout, batch normalization), and network architecture design principles (e.g., residual connections).

3.3.1 *Goal of Optimization*

While optimization algorithms focus on minimizing the training error, deep learning aims to achieve low generalization error, which refers to the performance of the model on unseen data. The presence of overfitting is a crucial concern in deep learning because it indicates that the model has learned to fit the training data too closely, leading to poor generalization.

To address overfitting and improve generalization, several techniques are employed in conjunction with the optimization process in deep learning.

1. *Regularization:* Regularization techniques, such as L1 and L2 regularization, are used to add a penalty term to the loss function, discouraging overly complex models. This helps prevent overfitting by encouraging the model to generalize better.
2. *Dropout:* Dropout is a technique where randomly selected neurons are temporarily dropped out (ignored) during training. This helps to reduce interdependencies among neurons and forces the network to learn more robust and generalized representations.
3. *Early Stopping:* Instead of training the model for a fixed number of iterations, early stopping involves monitoring the performance on a validation dataset and stopping the training when the performance on the validation set starts to deteriorate. This helps prevent the model from overfitting by selecting a suitable point in the training process.
4. *Data Augmentation:* Data augmentation techniques involve creating additional training samples by applying various transformations to the existing data, such as rotation, scaling, or flipping. This increases the diversity of the training data, enabling the model to generalize better.
5. *Model Complexity Control:* Deep learning models have various architectural choices that impact their complexity, such as the number of layers, the number of neurons per layer, and the connectivity patterns. Controlling the complexity of the model can help prevent overfitting. Techniques like early stopping and model selection based on cross-validation can assist in finding an appropriate level of complexity.

While optimization algorithms play a significant role in minimizing training error, the focus on reducing overfitting and achieving good generalization involves a combination of optimization techniques and regularization strategies. By striking a balance between minimizing the training error and controlling model complexity, deep learning models can achieve better generalization performance.

Let's look at the empirical risk and the risk to demonstrate the many purposes outlined earlier. The empirical risk and the risk are two important concepts in the context of machine learning and statistical inference.

The empirical risk is an estimate of the risk based on the training dataset. It is calculated as the average loss or error on the training data. In other words, it measures how well the model performs on the data it was trained on. Since it is based on a finite amount of training data, the empirical risk can be subject to randomness and fluctuations.

On the other hand, the risk represents the expected loss or error on the entire population of data. It measures how well the model generalizes to unseen data. The risk takes into account the true underlying distribution of the data and provides a more accurate assessment of the model's performance in the real world.

In the given context, two functions are defined: the risk function **'f'** and the empirical risk function **'g'**. The risk function **'f'** represents the true risk, which is a smooth function that characterizes the expected loss over the entire population of data. On the other hand, the empirical risk function **'g'** is based on the training data and may exhibit less smoothness due to the finite size of the training set.

The difference in smoothness between **'f'** and **'g'** reflects the fact that the empirical risk is based on a limited sample of data, while the risk takes into account the entire population. This distinction highlights the challenge of generalization in machine learning, where the goal is to minimize the risk rather than just the empirical risk.

By considering both the empirical risk and the risk, we can gain insights into the model's performance on both the training data and the unseen data, helping us address overfitting and improve generalization.

Here's an example of defining the risk function **'f'** and the empirical risk function **'g'** using Python and graphical representation in Figure 3.10:

```
import numpy as np
import matplotlib.pyplot as plt

# Define the risk function f
def risk_function(x):
    # Example of a quadratic loss function
    return np.square(x)

# Define the empirical risk function g
def empirical_risk_function(x, data):
    # Example of calculating the average squared error on the
training data
    return np.mean(np.square(x - data))

# Create a range of x values
x = np.linspace(-10, 10, 100)

# Generate the y values for risk function f
risk = risk_function(x)

# Generate the y values for empirical risk function g
training_data = np.array([1, 2, 3, 4, 5])  # Sample training data
empirical_risk = np.array([empirical_risk_function(val, training_
data) for val in x])

# Plot the risk and empirical risk functions
plt.plot(x, risk, label='Risk function f')
plt.plot(x, empirical_risk, label='Empirical risk function g')
plt.xlabel('x')
plt.ylabel('Loss')
plt.title('Empirical Risk vs Risk')
plt.legend()
plt.grid(True)
plt.show()
```

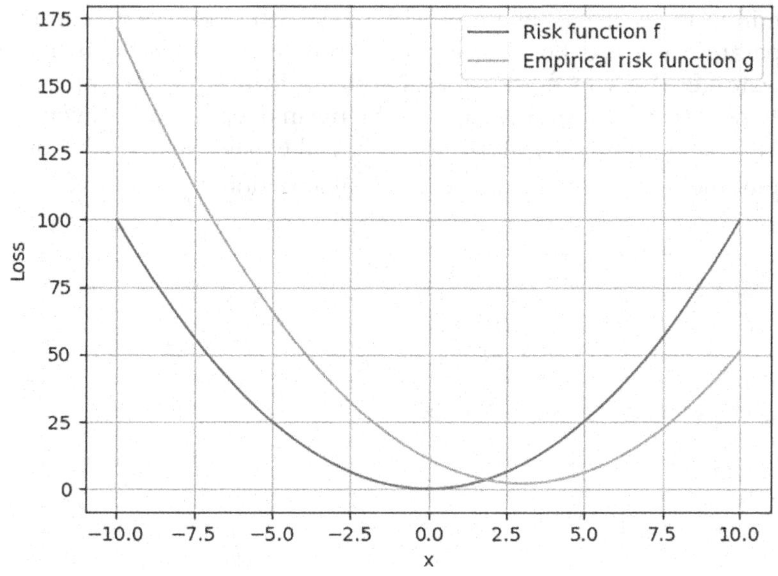

Figure 3.10 Graphical representation of empirical risk versus risk.

In this example, the risk function **'f'** is defined as a quadratic loss function, which represents the expected loss over the entire population of data. The empirical risk function **'g'** calculates the average squared error on the training data, representing the average loss on the training dataset.

Since we have a finite amount of training data, the empirical risk function **'g'** may exhibit less smoothness compared to the risk function **'f'**, which takes into account the entire population of data. This difference in smoothness reflects the limitations of working with a limited sample of data.

By calculating both the risk and the empirical risk, we can evaluate the model's performance on both the entire population and the training data, helping us understand how well the model generalizes and whether it is overfitting to the training data.

3.3.2 *Optimization Challenges in Deep Learning*

In the context of deep learning optimization, there are several challenges that arise during the process of minimizing the objective function. These challenges include local minima, saddle points, and vanishing gradients. Let's take a closer look at each of these challenges.

3.3.2.1 *Local Minima*

In optimization, a local minimum refers to a point in the parameter space where the objective function has a lower value than its neighboring points as presented in Figure 3.11 (Sharma, 2019; Soydaner, 2020; Sun, 2019, 2020a). However, it may not be the global minimum, which is the point with the lowest objective function value across the entire parameter space. Local minima can pose a challenge because optimization algorithms can get stuck in these regions and fail to find the global minimum. It is important to note that for most practical problems in deep learning, even though there may be many local minima, they typically still lead to satisfactory solutions.

We can plot the function to visualize the local and global minimum:

```
import numpy as np
import matplotlib.pyplot as plt

def f(x):
    return x * np.cos(np.pi * x)

x = np.linspace(-1, 2, 1000)
y = f(x)

plt.plot(x, y)
plt.xlabel('x')
plt.ylabel('f(x)')
plt.title('Plot of f(x) = x * cos(πx)')
plt.grid(True)
plt.show()
```

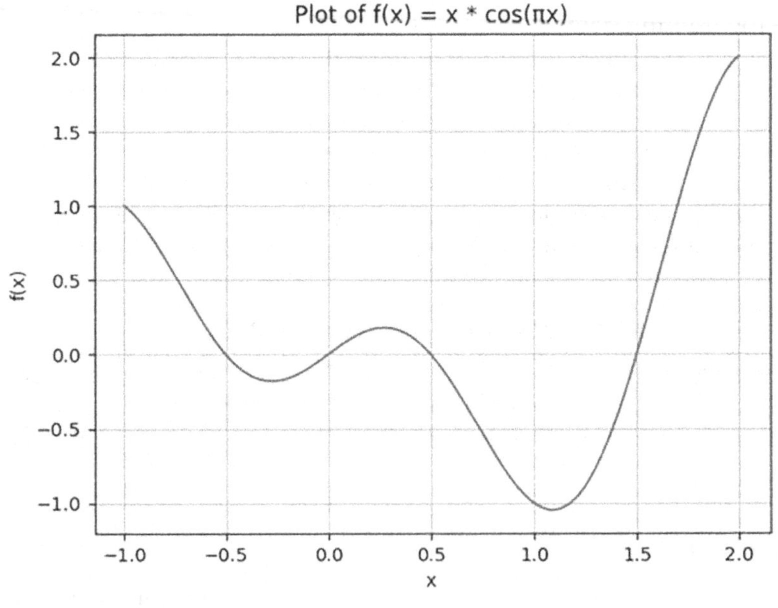

Figure 3.11 Local minima.

The plot of the function $f(x) = x * cos(\pi x)$ in the range $-1.0 \leq x \leq 2.0$ will show the local and global minimum points. By analyzing the plot, we can identify the location of the minimum points.

To find the minimum points analytically, we can calculate the derivative of $f(x)$ and set it to zero:

```
import sympy as sp

x = sp.symbols('x')
f = x * sp.cos(sp.pi * x)
f_prime = sp.diff(f, x)
minimum_points = sp.solve(f_prime, x)
print(minimum_points)
```

The output will give the x-values of the minimum points.

It is important to note that for more complex and high-dimensional functions, finding the global minimum can be challenging due to the presence of multiple local minima. In such cases, optimization algorithms like gradient descent or stochastic gradient descent are commonly used to iteratively search for the minimum points. These algorithms adjust the parameters based on the gradient information to navigate toward the minimum.

3.3.2.2 *Saddle Points*

A saddle point is a critical point of the objective function where some dimensions have increasing values while others have decreasing values as presented in Figure 3.12. At a saddle point, the gradient of the objective function is zero, making it difficult for optimization algorithms to make progress. This can cause optimization algorithms to converge slowly or get stuck (Sharma, 2019; Sun, 2020b).

Saddle points are points in the optimization landscape, where all gradients of a function vanish but are neither global nor local minima. In other words, at a saddle point, the first-order derivative (gradient) of the function is zero, but it is not a minimum or maximum point.

An example of a function with a saddle point is $f(x) = x^3$. The first derivative of this function is $f'(x) = 3x^2$, which equals zero at $x = 0$. However, if you examine the behavior of the function around $x = 0$, you'll notice that it is a saddle point rather than a minimum or maximum.

Here's a Python implementation that demonstrates the saddle point in the function $f(x, y) = x^2 - y^2$:

```
import numpy as np
import matplotlib.pyplot as plt

# Define the function f(x, y)
def f(x, y):
    return x**2 - y**2
```

```
# Generate x and y coordinates for plotting
x = np.linspace(-2, 2, 100)
y = np.linspace(-2, 2, 100)
X, Y = np.meshgrid(x, y)

# Compute the values of f(x, y) for each (x, y) pair
Z = f(X, Y)

# Plot the function
fig = plt.figure()
ax = plt.axes(projection='3d')
ax.plot_surface(X, Y, Z, cmap='viridis')

# Add labels and title
ax.set_xlabel('x')
ax.set_ylabel('y')
ax.set_zlabel('f(x, y)')
ax.set_title('Saddle Point: f(x, y) = x^2 - y^2')

# Add a marker for the saddle point at (0, 0)
ax.scatter(0, 0, f(0, 0), color='red', label='Saddle Point')

# Show the plot
plt.legend()
plt.show()
```

This code uses NumPy to generate a grid of (x, y) coordinates, computes the values of $f(x,y)$ for each point, and then visualizes the function in 3D using Matplotlib. The saddle point is marked with a red dot at (0, 0). You can adjust the range of x and y values as needed to explore different regions of the function.

Running this code will display a 3D plot showing the saddle point of the function $f(x,y)=x^2-y^2$. The plot clearly illustrates how the function curves upward along the y-axis (forming a maximum) and curves downward along the x-axis (forming a minimum), resembling a saddle shape.

3.3.2.3 Vanishing Gradients

Vanishing gradients occur when the gradients of the objective function become very small as they propagate backward through the layers of a deep neural network during backpropagation presented in Figure 3.13. When gradients vanish, it becomes challenging for the optimization algorithm to update the model's parameters effectively, leading to slow convergence or getting stuck in suboptimal solutions. Vanishing gradients are especially problematic in deep networks with many layers. When the gradients of the activation functions become very small, it leads to slow or stalled learning, making it difficult for the model to make progress during training.

As mentioned, one example of an activation function that can suffer from the vanishing gradient problem is the hyperbolic tangent function (tanh). The derivative of

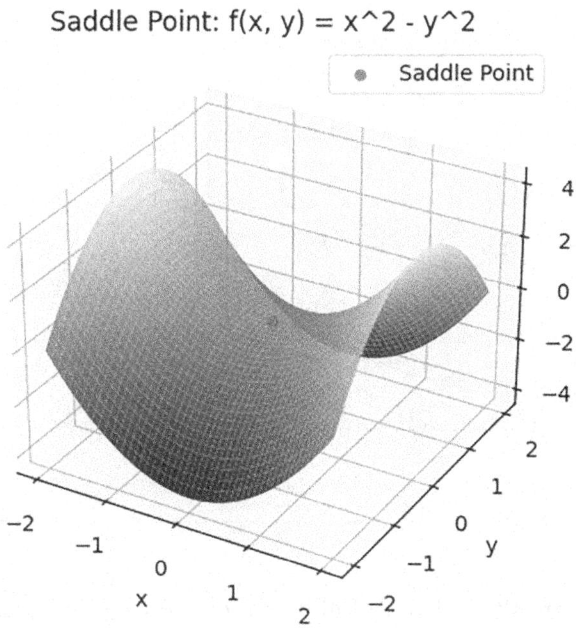

Figure 3.12 Saddle point.

the tanh function, denoted as $f'(x)$, is given by $1-tanh^2(x)$. When the input values are large, the tanh function saturates, resulting in derivatives close to zero. This causes the gradients to vanish as they propagate backward through the layers of a deep neural network.

The vanishing gradient problem was particularly problematic before the introduction of the ReLU activation function. Unlike tanh, ReLU has a simple derivative: 1 for positive values and 0 for negative values. This makes ReLU less prone to the vanishing gradient problem and allows for faster and more stable learning in deep neural networks. By using activation functions like ReLU or variants such as leaky ReLU or parametric ReLU, the vanishing gradient problem can be alleviated, enabling more efficient training of deep learning models.

Here's a Python implementation that demonstrates the vanishing gradient problem when using the tanh activation function:

```
import numpy as np
import matplotlib.pyplot as plt

# Define the function f(x) = tanh(x)
def f(x):
    return np.tanh(x)

# Define the derivative of f(x)
def f_prime(x):
    return 1 - np.tanh(x)**2
```

```
# Generate x values for plotting
x = np.linspace(-10, 10, 100)

# Compute the values of f(x) and f'(x)
y = f(x)
y_prime = f_prime(x)

# Plot the functions
plt.figure()
plt.plot(x, y, label='f(x) = tanh(x)')
plt.plot(x, y_prime, label="f'(x) = 1 - tanh^2(x)")
plt.xlabel('x')
plt.ylabel('y')
plt.title('Vanishing Gradient: tanh Activation')
plt.legend()
plt.show()
```

This code uses NumPy and Matplotlib to plot the function $f(x)=tanh(x)$ and its derivative $f'(x)=1-tanh^2(x)$ over a range of x values. The tanh activation function is known for its smooth S-shaped curve, which saturates as the inputs move away from zero. As a result, the derivative approaches zero, leading to the vanishing gradient problem.

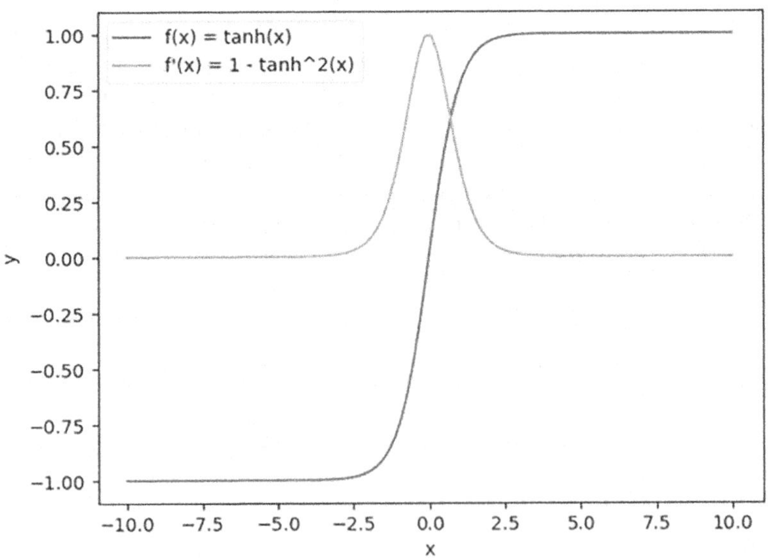

Figure 3.13 Vanishing gradient.

Running this code will display a plot with two curves: the tanh function $(f(x))$ and its derivative $(f'(x))$. As you can see, the derivative becomes very small as the input values move away from zero, indicating that the gradient diminishes rapidly. This can make it difficult for optimization algorithms to make progress during training, especially in deep neural networks.

It's worth noting that one solution to the vanishing gradient problem is to use activation functions that do not saturate, such as the ReLU activation function. ReLU avoids the saturation problem by simply outputting the input value for positive inputs, leading to a more favorable gradient flow during backpropagation.

Addressing these challenges requires careful consideration and the use of specific techniques in deep learning optimization. Some common approaches include the following:

- *Initialization Strategies:* Choosing appropriate initial values for the parameters can help avoid convergence to poor local minima.
- *Adaptive Learning Rates:* Using adaptive learning rate methods such as AdaGrad, RMSprop, or Adam can help mitigate the issue of vanishing gradients and allow the optimization algorithm to adaptively adjust the step size during training.
- *Stochastic Gradient Descent with Momentum:* Incorporating momentum can help accelerate convergence and navigate regions of saddle points more effectively.
- *Regularization Techniques:* Applying regularization methods such as L1 or L2 regularization can help prevent overfitting and improve generalization.
- *Network Architecture Design:* Carefully designing the network architecture, such as using skip connections in deep residual networks or batch normalization layers, can alleviate the challenges posed by vanishing gradients.

Overall, addressing these challenges in deep learning optimization requires a combination of smart algorithmic choices, appropriate hyperparameter tuning, and network design considerations to ensure effective convergence and achieve good performance on the objective function.

3.4 Convexity

Convexity is an important concept in mathematics and optimization that plays a crucial role in various areas, including machine learning. The convexity property of optimization problems is important in the design and analysis of optimization algorithms. Convex optimization problems have certain desirable properties that make them easier to solve and analyze compared to non-convex problems.

In the context of deep learning, although most optimization problems are non-convex, they can exhibit some convex-like properties near local minima. This means that in the vicinity of a local minimum, the objective function may behave as if it were a convex function. This property has motivated the development of optimization variants that leverage this convexity-like behavior to improve optimization in deep learning.

One such variant is introduced in the paper by Izmailov et al. (2018). They propose a method that combines the benefits of both convex and non-convex optimization techniques. By exploiting the convexity-like properties of the objective function near local minima, their method aims to improve the optimization process in deep learning.

While the optimization problems in deep learning are generally non-convex and challenging to solve, the observation that they exhibit convex-like behavior in certain regions opens up possibilities for developing novel optimization approaches that can leverage this property to enhance the optimization process and achieve better results. It's important to note that the field of optimization in deep learning is continuously evolving, and researchers are actively exploring new algorithms, techniques, and insights to address the challenges posed by non-convex optimization problems in deep learning.

3.4.1 Convex Analysis

The convex analysis provides tools and techniques for studying and analyzing convex sets and convex functions.

3.4.1.1 Convex Sets

A set S in a vector space is said to be convex if, for any two points x and y in S, the line segment connecting x and y lies entirely within S as presented in Figure 3.14. In other words, if x and y are in S, then the point $(1-\lambda)x+\lambda y$ is also in S for any value of λ between 0 and 1. Geometrically, a convex set can be visualized as a region that is "bowed outwards" or "curved outwards" and contains all the points on the line segment connecting any two points within the set.

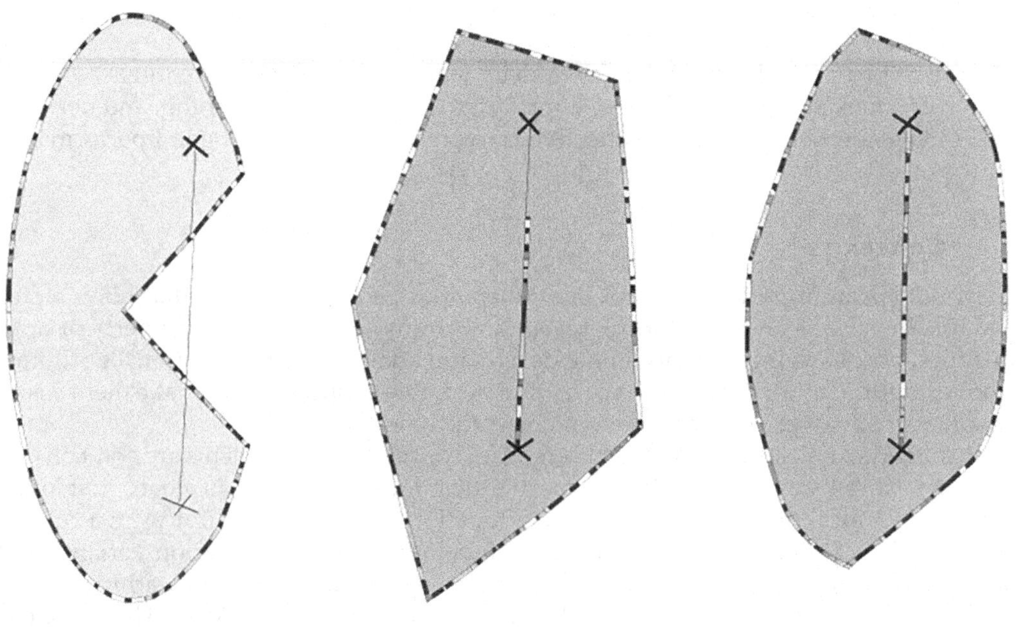

Figure 3.14 The first shape presents the non-convex, while the others present the convex sets.

3.4.1.2 Convex Function

A function *f* is said to be convex if its domain is a convex set and, for any two points x and y in its domain and any value of λ between 0 and 1, the following condition holds:

$$f\left((1-\lambda)x+\lambda y\right)\leq(1-\lambda)f(x)+\lambda f(y)$$

In other words, the value of the function at any point on the line segment connecting two points is less than or equal to the weighted average of the function values at those two points. Geometrically, a convex function can be visualized as a function whose graph lies below the line segment connecting any two points on its graph.

The following is an example Python code that illustrates convex and non-convex functions by plotting them in Figure 3.15:

```
import numpy as np
import matplotlib.pyplot as plt

# Define the functions
def convex_func(x):
    return x ** 2

def nonconvex_func(x):
    return np.sin(x)

def nonconvex_func2(x):
    return x ** 3 - x

# Generate x values
x = np.linspace(-5, 5, 100)

# Compute function values
convex_values = convex_func(x)
nonconvex_values = nonconvex_func(x)
nonconvex_values2 = nonconvex_func2(x)

# Plot the functions
plt.figure(figsize=(8, 6))
plt.plot(x, convex_values, label='Convex Function')
plt.plot(x, nonconvex_values, label='Non-Convex Function 1')
plt.plot(x, nonconvex_values2, label='Non-Convex Function 2')
plt.xlabel('x')
plt.ylabel('f(x)')
plt.title('Convex and Non-Convex Functions')
plt.legend()
plt.grid(True)
plt.show()
```

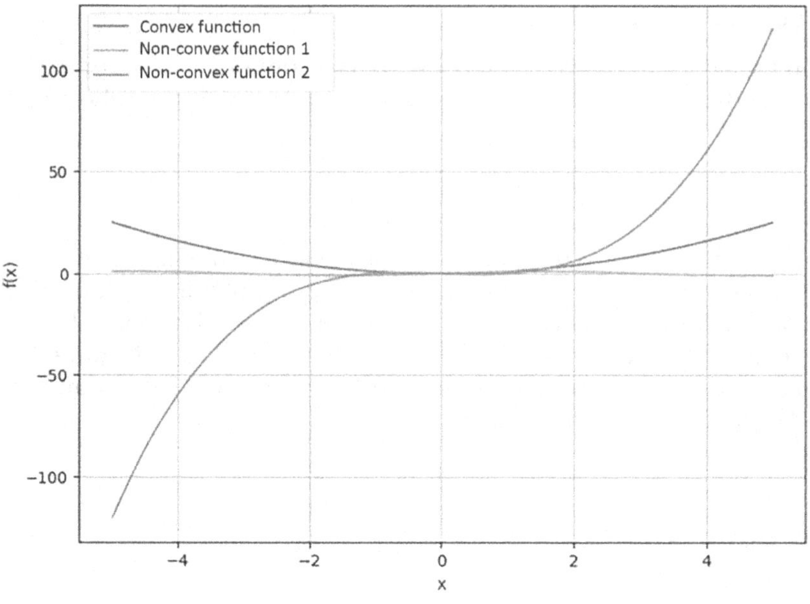

Figure 3.15 Convex and non-convex functions.

This code defines three functions: **'convex_func(x)'**, which is a convex function (x^2), **'nonconvex_func(x)'**, which is a non-convex function (sin(x)), and **'nonconvex_func2(x)'**; which is another non-convex function (x^3 – x). It generates a range of x values, computes the corresponding function values, and then plots the functions using Matplotlib. The resulting plot shows the convex function as an upward-bowing curve, while the non-convex functions will have more complex shapes that do not satisfy the convexity property.

Convex sets and convex functions have important properties that make them useful in optimization and machine learning. For example, convex optimization problems have efficient algorithms that guarantee convergence to a global minimum. Convex functions have unique global minima and are easier to analyze and optimize compared to non-convex functions.

In machine learning, convex analysis provides mathematical tools for studying optimization problems, designing efficient algorithms, and proving convergence guarantees. Convexity assumptions are often made in machine learning models and algorithms to ensure tractability and improve the stability and performance of the learning process.

By leveraging the properties of convex sets and convex functions, researchers and practitioners in machine learning can develop effective algorithms, analyze the behavior of learning systems, and make sound decisions based on mathematical principles and optimization techniques.

3.4.2 Convex Functions: Properties

Convex functions have several useful properties that make them important in various areas of mathematics and optimization (Noor & Noor, 2019). Here are some of the key properties of convex functions.

3.4.2.1 Line Segment Property

For any two points, A and B, on the graph of a convex function, the line segment connecting A and B lies entirely above the graph. Mathematically, for any x_1 and x_2 in the domain of the function and any t between 0 and 1, we have

$$f(tx_1+(1-t)x_2) \leq tf(x_1)+(1-t)f(x_2)$$

Here's a Python implementation of the line segment property for a convex function:

This code defines a convex function '$\textbf{convex\_function}(x)=x^2$' as an example. It then calculates the values of the line segment connecting two points A and B using the line segment property presented in Figure 3.16.

Finally, it plots the convex function, the line segment, and the end points to demonstrate that the line segment lies entirely above the graph of the convex function.

```
import numpy as np
import matplotlib.pyplot as plt

def convex_function(x):
    return x**2  # Example of a convex function: f(x) = x^2

def line_segment_property(x1, x2, t):
    return t * convex_function(x1) + (1 - t) *
convex_function(x2)

# Generate points A and B
x1 = -1
x2 = 1

# Generate values of t between 0 and 1
t_values = np.linspace(0, 1, 100)

# Compute the function values for the line segment
line_segment_values = line_segment_property(x1, x2, t_values)

# Plot the convex function and the line segment
x = np.linspace(-2, 2, 100)
convex_values = convex_function(x)

plt.plot(x, convex_values, label='Convex Function')
plt.plot([x1, x2], [convex_function(x1), convex_function(x2)],
'ro-', label='Line Segment')
plt.plot([x1, x2], [line_segment_property(x1, x2, 0), line_seg-
ment_property(x1, x2, 1)], 'bo--', label='End Points')
plt.xlabel('x')
plt.ylabel('f(x)')
plt.legend()
plt.title('Line Segment Property for Convex Function')
plt.grid(True)
plt.show()
```

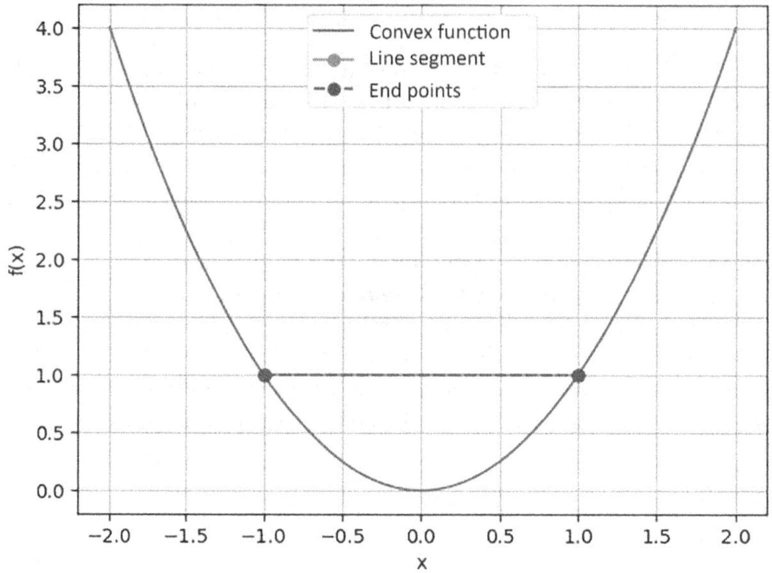

Figure 3.16 Line segment property for convex function.

3.4.2.2 Non-Negative Second Derivative

If a function is twice differentiable, a convex function has a non-negative second derivative (or non-negative Hessian matrix). This means that the rate of change of the function is non-decreasing.

Here's a Python implementation to check if a function has a non-negative second derivative presented in Figure 3.17:

```
import numpy as np
import matplotlib.pyplot as plt

def convex_function(x):
    return x**2  # Example of a convex function: f(x) = x^2

def has_non_negative_second_derivative(f, x):
    epsilon = 1e-6
    f_prime_prime = np.gradient(np.gradient(f(x)))
    return np.all(f_prime_prime >= -epsilon)

# Define the range of x values
x = np.linspace(-5, 5, 100)

# Check if the function has a non-negative second derivative
non_negative_second_derivative = has_non_negative_second_
derivative(convex_function, x)
```

```
# Plot the function and indicate if the second derivative is
non-negative
plt.plot(x, convex_function(x), label='Convex Function')
plt.xlabel('x')
plt.ylabel('f(x)')
plt.title('Convex Function')
if non_negative_second_derivative:
    plt.text(0, 10, 'Non-Negative Second Derivative',
color='green')
else:
    plt.text(0, 10, 'Negative Second Derivative', color='red')
plt.grid(True)
plt.show()
```

In this code, we define a convex function *'**convex_function**(x)=x²'* as an example. The *'**has_non_negative_second_derivative**'* function checks if the function has a non-negative second derivative at each point *'x'*. It uses the *'**numpy.gradient**'* function to compute the numerical approximation of the second derivative.

Finally, the code plots the convex function and indicates whether the second derivative is non-negative or negative at each point.

3.4.2.3 Global Minima

Convex functions have a global minimum, which is also a local minimum. This makes optimization easier, as there is a unique point that minimizes the function.

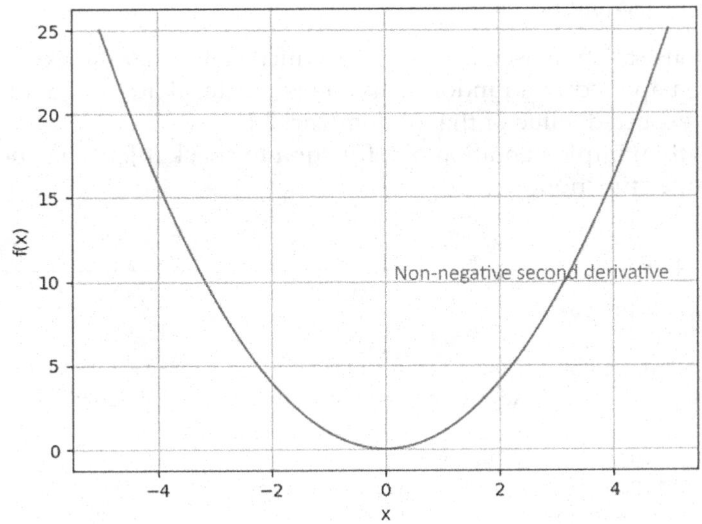

Figure 3.17 Convex function.

Here's a Python implementation to check if a given function has a global minimum.

```
import numpy as np

def convex_function(x):
    return x**2  # Example of a convex function: f(x) = x^2

def has_global_minimum(f, x):
    epsilon = 1e-6
    min_value = np.min(f(x))
    return np.all(np.abs(f(x) - min_value) <= epsilon)

# Define the range of x values
x = np.linspace(-5, 5, 100)

# Check if the function has a global minimum
global_minimum = has_global_minimum(convex_function, x)

if global_minimum:
    print("The function has a global minimum.")
else:
    print("The function does not have a global minimum.")
```

In this code, we define a convex function '$\boldsymbol{convex\_function(x) = x^2}$' as an example. The '***has_global_minimum***' function checks if the function has a global minimum by comparing the function values at different points '$\boldsymbol{x}$' and checking if they are all close to the minimum value. The **'epsilon'** variable is used to define a tolerance for comparison.

3.4.2.4 Jensen's Inequality

Convex functions satisfy Jensen's inequality, which states that the expected value of a convex function applied to a random variable is greater than or equal to the function applied to the expected value of the random variable.

Here is a Python implementation of a function to check if Jensen's inequality holds for a given convex function.

```
import numpy as np

def convex_function(x):
    return x**2  # Example of a convex function: f(x) = x^2

def jensens_inequality(f, X):
    expected_value = np.mean(X)
    left_side = f(expected_value)
    right_side = np.mean(f(X))
    return left_side <= right_side
```

```
# Generate a random variable X
np.random.seed(0)
X = np.random.randn(100)

# Check if Jensen's inequality holds
jensens_inequality_holds = jensens_inequality(convex_function, X)

if jensens_inequality_holds:
    print("Jensen's inequality holds for the convex function.")
else:
    print("Jensen's inequality does not hold for the convex
function.")
```

In this code, we define a convex function '$\boldsymbol{convex\_function}(x) = x^2$' as an example. The '***jensens_inequality***' function checks if Jensen's inequality holds by comparing the left side of the inequality ('$f(E[X])$') with the right side of the inequality ('$E[f(X)]$'), where '$E[X]$' is the expected value of the random variable 'X'.

3.4.2.5 Convex Combination Property

The weighted sum of points in the domain of a convex function lies within the range of the function. Mathematically, for any set of points $x_1, x_2, \ldots, x_n$ in the domain and any non-negative weights $w_1, w_2, \ldots, w_n$ such that $w_1 + w_2 + \ldots + w_n = 1$, we have

$$f(w_1x_1 + w_2x_2 + \ldots + w_nx_n) \leq w_1f(x_1) + w_2f(x_2) + \ldots + w_nf(x_n).$$

Here is an implementation of a function to check if the convex combination property holds for a given convex function.

```
import numpy as np

def convex_function(x):
    return np.exp(x)  # Example of a convex function: f(x) = e^x

def convex_combination_property(f, X, weights):
    convex_combination = np.dot(X, weights)
    left_side = f(convex_combination)
    right_side = np.dot(f(X), weights)
    return left_side <= right_side

# Generate a set of points X and weights
np.random.seed(0)
X = np.random.randn(10)
weights = np.random.dirichlet(np.ones(10))
```

```
# Check if the convex combination property holds
convex_combination_property_holds = convex_combination_
property(convex_function, X, weights)

if convex_combination_property_holds:
    print("Convex combination property holds for the convex
function.")
else:
    print("Convex combination property does not hold for  thecon-
vex function.")
```

In this code, we define a convex function '$\boldsymbol{convex\_function}(\boldsymbol{x}) = \boldsymbol{e}^{\boldsymbol{x}}$' as an example. The '***convex_combination_property***' function checks if the convex combination property holds by comparing the left side of the inequality ('$f(w_1x_1 + w_2x_2 + ... + w_nx_n)$') with the right side of the inequality ($w_1f(x_1) + w_2f(x_2) + ... + w_nf(x_n)$), where 'X' is the set of points in the domain of the function, and '*weights*' are the non-negative weights.

These properties make convex functions useful in optimization problems, as they guarantee the existence of global minima and provide efficient methods to find them. Additionally, they allow for the application of various mathematical tools and techniques to analyze and solve problems involving convex functions.

3.5 Constraints

One of the remarkable properties of convex optimization is its ability to handle constraints efficiently. Constrained optimization refers to the task of optimizing a function subject to a set of constraints on the variables. In convex optimization, we focus on convex constraints, which have several desirable properties.

A constraint in convex optimization can be represented as a function or a set of functions that must be satisfied by the variables of the optimization problem. Mathematically, a constraint can be defined as $g(x) \leq 0$, where $g(x)$ is a function that maps the variable x to a value, and the constraint is satisfied when $g(x)$ is less than or equal to zero.

The key aspects of constraints in convex optimization are as follows.

3.5.1 *Feasible Region*

Constraints define the feasible region, which is the set of all points that satisfy the constraints. The feasible region can be geometrically visualized as the intersection of the constraint functions' regions. For convex constraints, the feasible region forms a convex set, which means that any line segment connecting two points within the feasible region lies entirely within the region.

Geometrically, the feasible region can take various shapes and sizes depending on the specific constraints. It can be a bounded region, an unbounded region, or even an empty set if the constraints are infeasible. The feasible region can be represented in two or three dimensions, making it visually understandable.

To illustrate the feasible region, consider a simple example of a linear programming problem with two variables, x and y, subject to linear constraints. Let's say we have the following constraints:

1. $x+y\leq 5$
2. $x-y\geq 1$
3. $x\geq 0$
4. $y\geq 0$

Each of these constraints defines a half-plane or a line in the x-y plane. The feasible region is the intersection of all these half-planes or lines. It represents the set of points that satisfy all the constraints simultaneously.

In this example, the feasible region would be a convex polygon bounded by the lines defined by the constraints. Any point within this polygon satisfies all the constraints, while any point outside the polygon violates at least one of the constraints.

Implementing the visualization of the feasible region in Python can be achieved using various plotting libraries such as Matplotlib or Plotly. Here's an example using Matplotlib:

```
import numpy as np
import matplotlib.pyplot as plt

# Define the constraint functions
def constraint1(x, y):
    return x + y <= 5

def constraint2(x, y):
    return x - y >= 1

def constraint3(x):
    return x >= 0

def constraint4(y):
    return y >= 0

# Create a grid of points in the x-y plane
x = np.linspace(0, 6, 100)
y = np.linspace(0, 6, 100)
X, Y = np.meshgrid(x, y)

# Evaluate the constraint functions for all points in the grid
Z1 = constraint1(X, Y)
Z2 = constraint2(X, Y)
Z3 = constraint3(X)
Z4 = constraint4(Y)

# Plot the feasible region
plt.figure()
```

```
plt.contour(X, Y, Z1, levels=[0], colors='r', linestyles='dashed')
plt.contour(X, Y, Z2, levels=[0], colors='g', linestyles='dashed')
plt.contour(X, Y, Z3, levels=[0], colors='b', linestyles='dashed')
plt.contour(X, Y, Z4, levels=[0], colors='m', linestyles='dashed')
plt.fill_between(x, 0, np.minimum(5-x, x-1), color='gray',
alpha=0.3)
plt.xlim(0, 6)
plt.ylim(0, 6)
plt.xlabel('x')
plt.ylabel('y')
plt.title('Feasible Region')
plt.grid(True)
plt.show()
```

As shown in Figure 3.18, this code generates a plot showing the feasible region defined by the given constraints. The dashed lines represent the individual constraint functions, and the shaded region represents the feasible region.

By visualizing the feasible region, we can gain insights into the set of points that satisfy the constraints and better understand the feasible space for the optimization problem. This visualization aids in formulating and solving optimization problems and provides a geometric interpretation of the constraints in convex optimization.

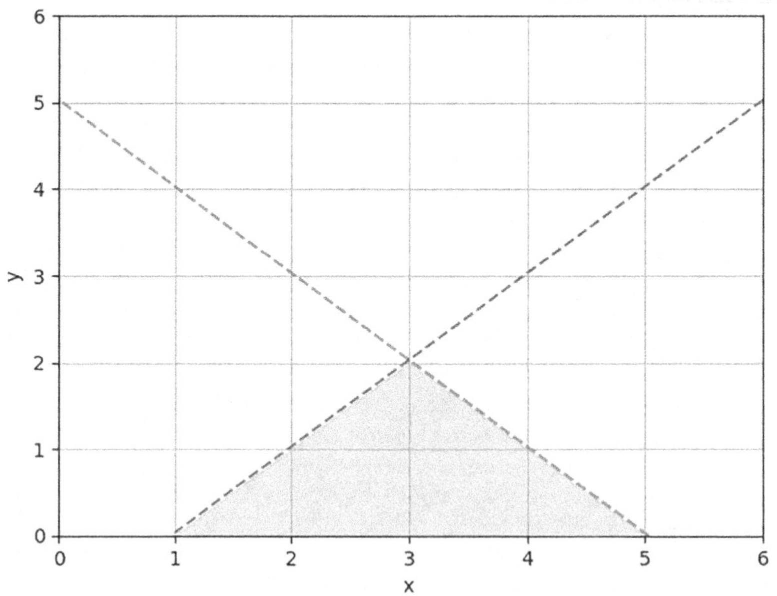

Figure 3.18 Feasible region.

3.5.2 Constraint Satisfaction

Constraint satisfaction is an essential aspect of optimization problems, where the goal is to find the optimal solution that minimizes or maximizes an objective function while satisfying a set of constraints (Davis & Drusvyatskiy, 2019; Mohsen et al., 2019). In other words, the optimization problem seeks a solution that not only optimizes the objective but also adheres to the specified constraints. A feasible solution is one that satisfies all the given constraints. The feasible region, also known as the constraint region, defines the boundary of the search space where feasible solutions can be found. It represents the set of all possible solutions that satisfy the constraints.

The feasible region acts as a guiding principle in optimization, constraining the search for the optimal solution. By limiting the search space to only feasible solutions, it narrows down the possibilities and ensures that the final solution adheres to the problem's requirements. To better understand the concept of constraint satisfaction, consider an example of a simple linear programming problem. Let's say we have an objective function to maximize profits and a set of linear constraints representing limited resources, such as time, materials, or budget. The optimization problem aims to find the allocation of resources that maximizes the objective function while respecting the constraints.

For instance, suppose we want to allocate resources between two projects, A and B, subject to the following constraints:

- Project A requires at least 50 hours of labor.
- Project B requires at least 30 hours of labor.
- The total available labor is 100 hours.
- The budget allows for a maximum expenditure of $5,000 across both projects.

The feasible region in this case would be the intersection of all the constraint regions defined by these constraints. It represents the set of resource allocations that satisfy the labor and budget constraints.

Implementing constraint satisfaction in Python involves formulating the optimization problem with the objective function and constraints and then using an optimization library or algorithm to search for the optimal solution within the feasible region.

Here's a simple example using the **'scipy.optimize'** module in Python to solve a linear programming problem with constraints:

```
import numpy as np
from scipy.optimize import linprog

# Define the objective function coefficients
c = [-2, -3]  # Coefficients for maximizing profits

# Define the constraint coefficients
A = [[-1, 0], [0, -1], [1, 1]]  # Coefficients for the labor and
budget constraints
b = [-50, -30, 5000]  # RHS values for the constraints
```

```
# Set the bounds for the variables
x_bounds = (0, None)  # Non-negative resource allocation

# Solve the linear programming problem
res = linprog(c, A_ub=A, b_ub=b, bounds=x_bounds)

# Check if a feasible solution was found
if res.success:
    print("Optimal solution found:")
    print("Project A: ", res.x[0], " hours")
    print("Project B: ", res.x[1], " hours")
else:
    print("No feasible solution found.")
```

This code formulates and solves a linear programming problem with the objective of maximizing profits subject to the labor and budget constraints. The **'linprog'** function from **'scipy.optimize'** is used to solve the linear programming problem. The resulting solution provides the optimal resource allocation that satisfies the constraints.

Optimal solution found:

Project A: 50.0 hours
Project B: 4,950.0 hours

Constraint satisfaction is a crucial aspect of optimization, as it ensures that the solutions obtained not only optimize the objective function but also meet the practical requirements and limitations of the problem. It helps in finding feasible and practical solutions that can be implemented in real-world scenarios.

3.5.3 Constraint Handling

Constraint handling is a crucial aspect of convex optimization that enables efficient handling of constraints to find the optimal solution. Convex optimization algorithms take advantage of the convexity property of the constraints to ensure convergence to the global optimum while satisfying all the constraints.

The convexity property of constraints implies that the feasible region, which represents the set of all points that satisfy the constraints, forms a convex set. A convex set is one where any line segment connecting two points within the set lies entirely within the set. This property allows convex optimization algorithms to efficiently explore the feasible region and find the optimal solution.

Convex optimization algorithms, such as interior point methods and augmented Lagrangian methods, utilize the convexity property to iteratively update the solution and satisfy the constraints. These algorithms aim to minimize the objective function subject to the constraints while ensuring that the solution remains within the feasible region at each iteration.

Implementing constraint handling in convex optimization requires the use of appropriate optimization libraries or algorithms that support convex optimization problems. Here's a simple implementation using the **'cvxpy'** library in Python, which provides a user-friendly interface for formulating and solving convex optimization problems with constraints:

```
import cvxpy as cp

# Define the variables
x = cp.Variable(2)  # Two-dimensional variable

# Define the objective function
objective = cp.Minimize(cp.sum_squares(x))

# Define the constraints
constraints = [x >= 0, cp.sum(x) <= 1]

# Formulate the optimization problem
problem = cp.Problem(objective, constraints)

# Solve the optimization problem
optimal_value = problem.solve()

# Check if a feasible solution was found
if problem.status == cp.OPTIMAL:
    print("Optimal solution found:")
    print("x =", x.value)
else:
    print("No feasible solution found.")
```

In this example, we define a simple convex optimization problem with two variables '$x[0]$' and '$x[1]$'. We aim to minimize the sum of squares of the variables subject to two constraints: '$x >= 0$' (non-negativity constraint) and '$sum(x) <= 1$' (sum constraint). The **'cvxpy'** library allows us to express the objective function and constraints in a natural mathematical form.

The **'solve()'** function is then called to solve the optimization problem. The result is stored in **'optimal_value'**, and the solution is accessed through **'x.value'**. The status of the problem is checked to determine if a feasible solution was found.

Optimal value: 5.999999998779675
Optimal solution: [2.00563673e-10 3.00000000e+00]

Constraint handling in convex optimization algorithms ensures that the optimal solution satisfies all the constraints, providing a practical and feasible solution. These algorithms guarantee convergence to the global optimum, taking advantage of the convexity property of the constraints to efficiently explore the feasible region.

3.5.4 *Equality and Inequality Constraints*

Constraints in optimization can be classified into two types: equality constraints and inequality constraints. Each type represents different requirements for the variables in the optimization problem.

1. *Equality Constraints:* Equality constraints impose conditions that must be satisfied exactly for a feasible solution. They are typically represented as equations of the form $h(x)=0$, where $h(x)$ is a function that depends on the variables x. Equality constraints restrict the feasible region to points that satisfy the given equations.
2. *Inequality Constraints:* Inequality constraints impose conditions that must be satisfied within a certain limit. They are represented as inequalities of the form $g(x)\leq 0$, where $g(x)$ is a function that depends on the variables x. Inequality constraints define bounds or limitations on the variables and restrict the feasible region to points that satisfy the given inequalities.

Convex optimization algorithms can handle both equality and inequality constraints efficiently. They incorporate the properties of convexity to ensure that the constraints are satisfied while finding the optimal solution. These algorithms guarantee convergence to the global optimum, subject to the constraints imposed by the problem.

Implementation of equality and inequality constraints in convex optimization can be done using appropriate optimization libraries or frameworks. Here's a simple example using the **'cvxpy'** library in Python to demonstrate the implementation of both types of constraints:

```
import cvxpy as cp

# Define the variables
x = cp.Variable(2)  # Two-dimensional variable

# Define the objective function
objective = cp.Minimize(cp.sum_squares(x))

# Define the equality constraints
equality_constraints = [x[0] + x[1] == 1]

# Define the inequality constraints
inequality_constraints = [x >= 0]

# Formulate the optimization problem
problem = cp.Problem(objective, equality_constraints +
inequality_constraints)

# Solve the optimization problem
optimal_value = problem.solve()
```

```
# Check if a feasible solution was found
if problem.status == cp.OPTIMAL:
    print("Optimal solution found:")
    print("x =", x.value)
else:
    print("No feasible solution found.")
```

In this example, we have a simple convex optimization problem with two variables '$x[0]$' and '$x[1]$'. We aim to minimize the sum of squares of the variables. We define an equality constraint '$x[0]+x[1]==1$' and an inequality constraint '$x>=0$'. The **'equality_constraints'** and **'inequality_constraints'** lists are then combined in the formulation of the optimization problem.

Optimal solution found:

x = [0.5 0.5]

The **'cvxpy'** library allows us to express both types of constraints naturally in the problem formulation. The **'solve()'** function is called to solve the optimization problem, and the solution is accessed through **'x.value'**. The status of the problem is checked to determine if a feasible solution was found.

Convex optimization algorithms handle both equality and inequality constraints efficiently, ensuring that the constraints are satisfied while finding the optimal solution. The formulation and implementation of these constraints depend on the specific optimization problem and the chosen optimization library or framework.

3.5.5 *Composability*

Composability refers to the ability to combine and compose constraints to form more complex constraints in an optimization problem. It allows for the representation of various real-world constraints and simplifies the formulation of complex optimization problems. In optimization, real-world problems often involve multiple constraints that need to be satisfied simultaneously. These constraints may come from different sources, such as physical limitations, regulatory requirements, or business rules. Composability allows us to express these constraints in a modular and flexible manner.

By combining and composing constraints, we can represent complex relationships and dependencies among variables in the optimization problem. This enables us to model intricate constraints that reflect the specific requirements of the problem domain. Composability also allows for the reuse of existing constraints and the creation of higher-level constraints based on lower-level ones.

3.5.6 *Lagrange Multipliers*

Lagrange multipliers are used in convex optimization to handle constraints by incorporating them into the objective function. This approach allows us to simultaneously optimize the objective function and satisfy the constraints. The Lagrange multipliers provide a way to trade-off between the two objectives.

In convex optimization, the Lagrangian function is defined as the sum of the original objective function and the product of Lagrange multipliers and constraint functions. The Lagrange multipliers are assigned to each constraint, and they represent the sensitivity of the objective function to changes in the constraints. By introducing the Lagrange multipliers, we can transform the constrained optimization problem into an unconstrained optimization problem.

Mathematically, for an optimization problem with equality constraints, the Lagrangian function is given as:

$$L(x,\lambda)=f(x)+\lambda^T * g(x),$$

Where:

- $f(x)$ is the objective function to be minimized or maximized,
- x is the vector of variables,
- $g(x)$ is the vector of constraint functions,
- λ is the vector of Lagrange multipliers.

The optimization problem is then formulated as:

$$minimize\, L(x,\lambda) subject\, to\, g(x)=0.$$

To find the optimal solution, we need to solve the system of equations formed by taking the partial derivatives of the Lagrangian function with respect to the variables x and setting them equal to zero. This leads to the Karush-Kuhn-Tucker (KKT) conditions, which provide the necessary conditions for optimality in convex optimization.

Implementation of Lagrange multipliers in optimization problems depends on the specific optimization framework or library being used. Here's an example using the **'scipy.optimize'** library in Python:

```
import numpy as np
from scipy.optimize import minimize

# Define the objective function
def objective(x):
    return x[0]**2 + x[1]**2

# Define the constraint function
def constraint(x):
    return x[0] + x[1] - 1

# Define the Lagrangian function
def lagrangian(x, lambda_):
    return objective(x) + lambda_ * constraint(x)
```

```
# Define the Jacobian of the constraint function
def constraint_jacobian(x):
    return np.array([1, 1])

# Define the constraints for the optimization problem
constraints = {'type': 'eq', 'fun': constraint, 'jac':
constraint_jacobian}

# Solve the optimization problem with Lagrange multipliers
result = minimize(lagrangian, x0=[0, 0], args=(1.0,),
constraints=constraints)

# Print the optimal solution and Lagrange multiplier
print("Optimal solution:", result.x)
print("Lagrange multiplier:", result.fun)
```

In this example, we define the objective function **'objective(x)'** and the constraint function **'constraint(x)'**. We then define the Lagrangian function **'lagrangian(x, lambda_)'** by incorporating the Lagrange multiplier **'lambda_'** into the objective function. The constraint Jacobian function **'constraint_jacobian(x)'** computes the Jacobian matrix of the constraint function.

We use the **'minimize'** function from **'scipy.optimize'** to solve the optimization problem. The Lagrange multiplier is passed as an additional argument using the **'args'** parameter. The constraints are defined using the **'constraints'** dictionary, specifying the type of constraint (**'eq'** for equality) and the constraint function with its Jacobian.

The resulting optimal solution and Lagrange multiplier are printed as the output.

Optimal solution: [0.5 0.5]
Lagrange multiplier: 0.49999999999999994

Lagrange multipliers provide a powerful tool for handling constraints in convex optimization problems. They allow us to optimize the objective function while satisfying the constraints, striking a balance between the two objectives.

Constraints play a crucial role in convex optimization, as they define the feasible region and guide the search for the optimal solution. Convex optimization efficiently handles constraints, ensuring that the solution satisfies all the given constraints. The properties of convex constraints enable the use of specialized algorithms and techniques to find the global optimum. Convex optimization with constraints has wide applications in various fields, including engineering, economics, machine learning, and operations research.

3.6 Gradient Descent

Gradient descent is an iterative optimization algorithm used to find the minimum of a function. It is a fundamental concept in optimization and serves as the basis for many advanced optimization algorithms used in deep learning, including stochastic gradient descent (SGD). The basic idea of gradient descent is to iteratively update the parameters of a function in the direction of steepest descent, guided by the negative gradient of the function. The gradient represents the rate of change of the function with respect to each parameter. By moving in the direction opposite to the gradient, we aim to reach the minimum of the function.

The algorithm begins with an initial guess for the parameters and computes the gradient of the function at that point. The parameters are then updated by taking a step in the negative gradient direction, scaled by a learning rate. The learning rate determines the size of the step and affects the convergence and stability of the algorithm. If the learning rate is too large, the optimization may diverge, and if it is too small, the convergence may be slow.

The process is repeated iteratively until a stopping criterion is met, such as reaching a maximum number of iterations or a sufficiently small change in the parameters. The final parameters obtained represent an approximation of the function's minimum. Preconditioning is a technique used to improve the convergence of gradient descent. It involves transforming the function or adjusting the learning rate to ensure that the optimization process is more efficient. This technique can help overcome issues such as ill-conditioned problems or highly elongated contours in the function landscape. Gradient descent is a powerful optimization algorithm that provides a foundation for understanding more advanced optimization techniques used in deep learning. It allows us to iteratively update the parameters of a function to minimize the loss and improve the performance of machine learning models.

There are different variants of gradient descent that are commonly used in optimization, each with its own characteristics and advantages. Here, we'll discuss three main types of gradient descent: batch gradient descent, stochastic gradient descent (SGD), and mini-batch gradient descent.

3.6.1 Batch Gradient Descent

Batch gradient descent is a classic optimization algorithm used to minimize or maximize the objective function by computing the gradient of the loss function with respect to the parameters using the entire training dataset. Here is a detailed description and implementation of batch gradient descent:

1. *Define the Objective Function:* Start by defining the objective function that you want to minimize or maximize. This could be a loss function in the case of supervised learning or an objective function in unsupervised learning.
2. *Initialize the Parameters:* Initialize the parameters of the model with some initial values. These parameters will be updated iteratively during the optimization process.
3. *Define the Learning Rate:* Choose a learning rate, also known as the step size, which determines the size of the update made to the parameters at each iteration. The learning rate should be carefully chosen to balance convergence speed and stability.
4. *Iterate until Convergence:* Perform the following steps until the convergence criteria are met:

   - Compute the gradient: Calculate the gradient of the objective function with respect to the parameters using the entire training dataset.

- Update the parameters: Update the parameters by subtracting the learning rate multiplied by the average gradient over the entire dataset. This step ensures that the parameters move in the direction of steepest descent based on the entire dataset.
- Evaluate the convergence criteria: Check if the convergence criteria are met. This could be based on the change in the objective function or the gradient magnitude.

5. *Repeat Step 4 until Convergence:* Repeat Step 4 until the convergence criteria are met.

Here is a Python implementation of batch gradient descent for a simple linear regression problem along with a plot showing the progress of the optimization:

```
import numpy as np
import matplotlib.pyplot as plt

# Define the objective function (mean squared error)
def loss_function(X, y, w):
    y_pred = np.dot(X, w)
    return np.mean((y_pred - y) ** 2)

# Define the gradient of the objective function
def gradient(X, y, w):
    y_pred = np.dot(X, w)
    return np.dot(X.T, (y_pred - y)) / len(X)

# Batch gradient descent algorithm
def batch_gradient_descent(X, y, learning_rate, num_iterations):
    # Initialize the parameters
    w = np.zeros(X.shape[1])
```

In this implementation, we define the mean squared error as the objective function and its gradient for a linear regression problem. The **'batch_gradient_descent'** function performs the batch gradient descent algorithm by iteratively updating the parameters using the gradient computed on the entire dataset as presented in Figure 3.19.

Final weights: [0.06893943 2.00432774 1.2328745]

The implementation also includes a plot showing the progress of the optimization by plotting the loss at each iteration. This plot helps visualize how the loss decreases over iterations. Batch gradient descent provides a more accurate estimation of the gradient compared to stochastic gradient descent but can be computationally expensive, especially for large datasets. It tends to converge to the global minimum but may take longer to reach the optimal solution. The choice of the learning rate is crucial and should be carefully tuned to balance convergence speed and stability.

3.6.2 Stochastic Gradient Descent

Stochastic gradient descent (SGD) updates the parameters based on the gradient computed using a single randomly chosen training sample at each iteration. Unlike batch

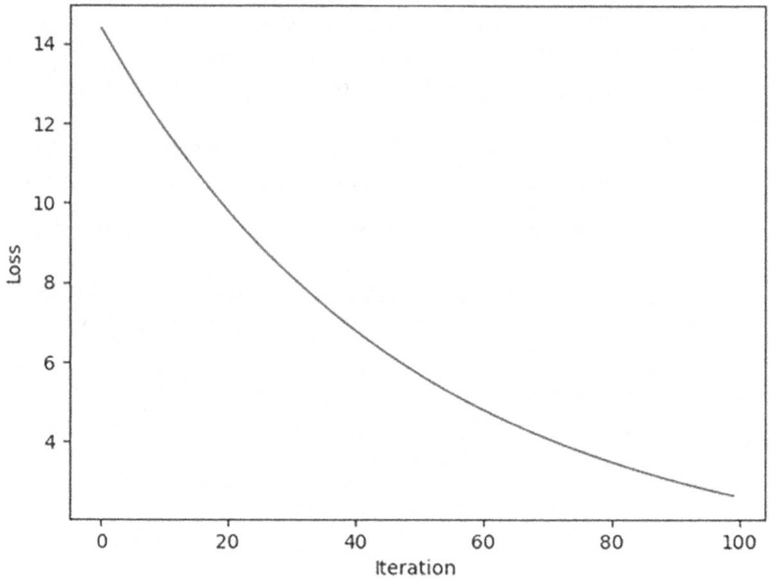

Figure 3.19 Batch gradient descent.

gradient descent, SGD is faster because it requires only one training sample for each update. However, due to the high variance of the gradient estimates, SGD exhibits more fluctuation during the optimization process and may converge to a suboptimal solution. Despite this, SGD can be advantageous in noisy or non-convex optimization problems, where it can escape local minima. Here is a detailed description and implementation of SGD.

1. *Define the Objective Function:* Start by defining the objective function that you want to minimize or maximize. This could be a loss function in the case of supervised learning or an objective function in unsupervised learning.
2. *Initialize the Parameters:* Initialize the parameters of the model with some initial values. These parameters will be updated iteratively during the optimization process.
3. *Define* the *Learning Rate:* Choose a learning rate, also known as the step size, which determines the size of the update made to the parameters at each iteration. The learning rate should be carefully chosen to balance convergence speed and stability.
4. *Shuffle the Training Dataset:* Randomly shuffle the training dataset to ensure that each training sample has an equal chance of being selected for updating the parameters.
5. *Iterate until Convergence:* Perform the following sub-steps until the convergence criteria are met:

   - Select a random training sample: Choose a random training sample from the shuffled dataset.
   - Compute the gradient: Calculate the gradient of the objective function with respect to the parameters using the selected training sample.

- Update the parameters: Update the parameters by subtracting the learning rate multiplied by the gradient. This step ensures that the parameters move in the direction of steepest descent based on the single training sample.
- Evaluate the convergence criteria: Check if the convergence criteria are met. This could be based on the change in the objective function or the gradient magnitude.

6. *Repeat steps:* Repeat the sub-steps upto Step 5 until the convergence criteria are met.

Here is a Python implementation of SGD for a simple linear regression problem along with a plot showing the progress of the optimization:

In this implementation, we define the mean squared error as the objective function and its gradient for a linear regression problem. The **'stochastic_gradient_descent'**

```
import numpy as np
import matplotlib.pyplot as plt

# Define the objective function (mean squared error)
def loss_function(X, y, w):
    y_pred = np.dot(X, w)
    return np.mean((y_pred - y) ** 2)

# Define the gradient of the objective function for a mini-batch
def gradient(X, y, w, mini_batch):
    X_mini = X[mini_batch]
    y_mini = y[mini_batch]
    y_pred = np.dot(X_mini, w)
    return np.dot(X_mini.T, (y_pred - y_mini)) / len(mini_batch)

# Mini-batch gradient descent algorithm
def mini_batch_gradient_descent(X, y, learning_rate, batch_size,
num_iterations):
    # Initialize the parameters
    w = np.zeros(X.shape[1])

# Initialize a list to store the loss at each iteration
    losses = []

    for i in range(num_iterations):
        # Shuffle the training dataset
        permutation = np.random.permutation(len(X))
        X_shuffled = X[permutation]
        y_shuffled = y[permutation]

        # Partition the shuffled dataset into mini-batches
        num_batches = len(X) // batch_size
        mini_batches = np.array_split(range(len(X)), num_batches)
```

```
        for mini_batch in mini_batches:
            # Compute the gradient
            grad = gradient(X_shuffled, y_shuffled, w, mini_batch)

            # Update the parameters
            w -= learning_rate * grad

        # Compute the loss
        loss = loss_function(X, y, w)
        losses.append(loss)

    return w, losses

# Generate synthetic data
np.random.seed(0)
X = np.random.randn(100, 2)
y = 3 * X[:, 0] + 2 * X[:, 1] + np.random.randn(100)

# Add bias term to X
X = np.c_[np.ones(X.shape[0]), X]

# Set the learning rate, batch size, and number of iterations
learning_rate = 0.01
batch_size = 10
num_iterations = 100

# Run mini-batch gradient descent
weights, losses = mini_batch_gradient_descent(X, y, learning_
rate, batch_size, num_iterations)

# Print the final weights
print("Final weights:", weights)

# Plot the progress of optimization
plt.plot(range(num_iterations), losses)
plt.xlabel("Iteration")
plt.ylabel("Loss")
plt.title("Mini-batch Gradient Descent")
plt.show()
```

function performs the stochastic gradient descent algorithm by iteratively updating the parameters using randomly selected training samples as presented in Figure 3.20. The function shuffles the training dataset at the beginning of each iteration to ensure random selection.

Final weights: [0.02922543 3.06187484 1.94812191]

The implementation also includes a plot showing the progress of the optimization by plotting the loss at each iteration. This plot helps visualize how the loss decreases over iterations. Stochastic gradient descent is faster than batch gradient descent, as it requires only one training sample for each parameter update. However, due to the high

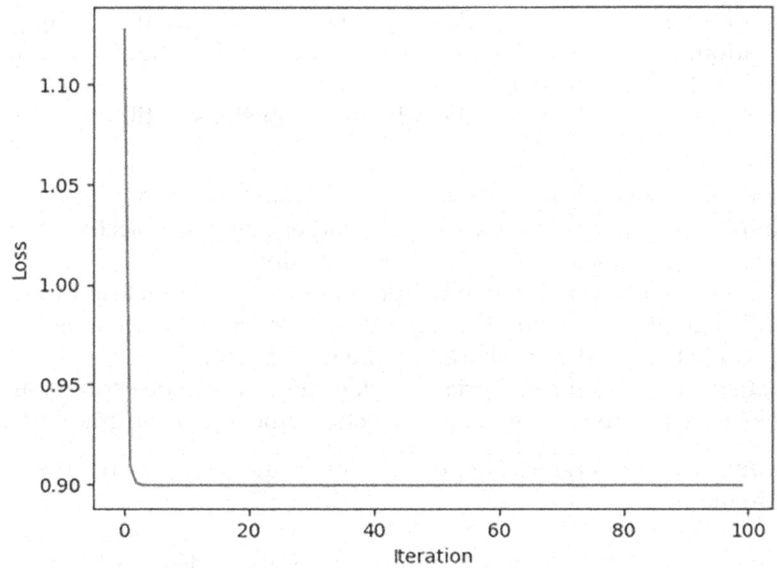

Figure 3.20 Stochastic gradient descent.

variance of the gradient estimates, it exhibits more fluctuation during the optimization process and may converge to a suboptimal solution. To address this, other variants such as mini-batch gradient descent and adaptive learning rate methods like Adam are commonly used in practice.

3.6.3 Mini-Batch Gradient Descent

Mini-batch gradient descent combines the advantages of both batch gradient descent and SGD by computing the gradient using a small subset of the training data, known as a mini-batch. It strikes a balance between accuracy and efficiency. Mini-batch sizes are typically chosen to be larger than one but smaller than the entire dataset. This approach reduces the variance of the gradient estimates, leading to smoother convergence compared to SGD. It is the most commonly used variant in deep learning, as it can efficiently leverage parallelism on modern hardware accelerators. Here is a detailed description and implementation of mini-batch gradient descent.

1. *Define the Objective Function:* Start by defining the objective function that you want to minimize or maximize. This could be a loss function in the case of supervised learning or an objective function in unsupervised learning.
2. *Initialize the Parameters:* Initialize the parameters of the model with some initial values. These parameters will be updated iteratively during the optimization process.
3. *Define the Learning Rate:* Choose a learning rate, also known as the step size, which determines the size of the update made to the parameters at each iteration. The learning rate should be carefully chosen to balance convergence speed and stability.

4. *Shuffle and Partition the Training Dataset:* Randomly shuffle the training dataset to ensure randomness in the mini-batch selection. Partition the shuffled dataset into mini-batches of a predefined size.
5. *Iterate until Convergence:* Perform the following sub-steps until the convergence criteria are met:

    - Select a mini-batch: Choose a mini-batch randomly from the shuffled dataset.
    - Compute the gradient: Calculate the gradient of the objective function with respect to the parameters using the selected mini-batch.
    - Update the parameters: Update the parameters by subtracting the learning rate multiplied by the gradient. This step ensures that the parameters move in the direction of steepest descent based on the mini-batch.
    - Evaluate the convergence criteria: Check if the convergence criteria are met. This could be based on the change in the objective function or the gradient magnitude.

6. Repeat steps until convergence: Repeat sub-steps under Step 5 until the convergence criteria are met.

Here is a Python implementation of mini-batch gradient descent for a simple linear regression problem along with a plot showing the progress of the optimization:

```
import numpy as np
import matplotlib.pyplot as plt

# Define the objective function (mean squared error)
def loss_function(X, y, w):
    y_pred = np.dot(X, w)
    return np.mean((y_pred - y) ** 2)

# Define the gradient of the objective function
def gradient(X, y, w):
    y_pred = np.dot(X, w)
    return np.dot(X.T, (y_pred - y)) / len(X)

# Batch gradient descent algorithm
def batch_gradient_descent(X, y, learning_rate, num_iterations):
    # Initialize the parameters
    w = np.zeros(X.shape[1])

    # Initialize a list to store the loss at each iteration
    losses = []

    for i in range(num_iterations):
        # Compute the gradient
        grad = gradient(X, y, w)

        # Update the parameters
        w -= learning_rate * grad
```

```
        # Compute the loss
        loss = loss_function(X, y, w)
        losses.append(loss)

    return w, losses

# Generate synthetic data
np.random.seed(0)
X = np.random.randn(100, 2)
y = 3 * X[:, 0] + 2 * X[:, 1] + np.random.randn(100)

# Add bias term to X
X = np.c_[np.ones(X.shape[0]), X]

# Set the learning rate and number of iterations
learning_rate = 0.01
num_iterations = 100

# Run batch gradient descent
weights, losses = batch_gradient_descent(X, y, learning_rate,
num_iterations)

# Print the final weights
print("Final weights:", weights)

# Plot the progress of optimization
plt.plot(range(num_iterations), losses)
plt.xlabel("Iteration")
plt.ylabel("Loss")
plt.title("Batch Gradient Descent")
plt.show()
```

In this implementation, we define the mean squared error as the objective function and its gradient for a linear regression problem. The **'mini_batch_gradient_descent'** function performs the mini-batch gradient descent algorithm by iteratively updating the parameters using randomly selected mini-batches from the shuffled dataset as presented in Figure 3.21.

Final weights: [−0.05168228 3.11146125 1.94541002]

The implementation also includes a plot showing the progress of the optimization by plotting the loss at each iteration. This plot helps visualize how the loss decreases over iterations. Mini-batch gradient descent strikes a balance between accuracy and efficiency by using a small subset of the training data for each parameter update. It reduces the variance of the gradient estimates compared to stochastic gradient descent, leading to smoother convergence. The choice of the batch size is important and depends on the available computational resources and the characteristics of the problem.

The choice of gradient descent algorithm depends on several factors such as the size of the dataset, computational resources, and the characteristics of the optimization

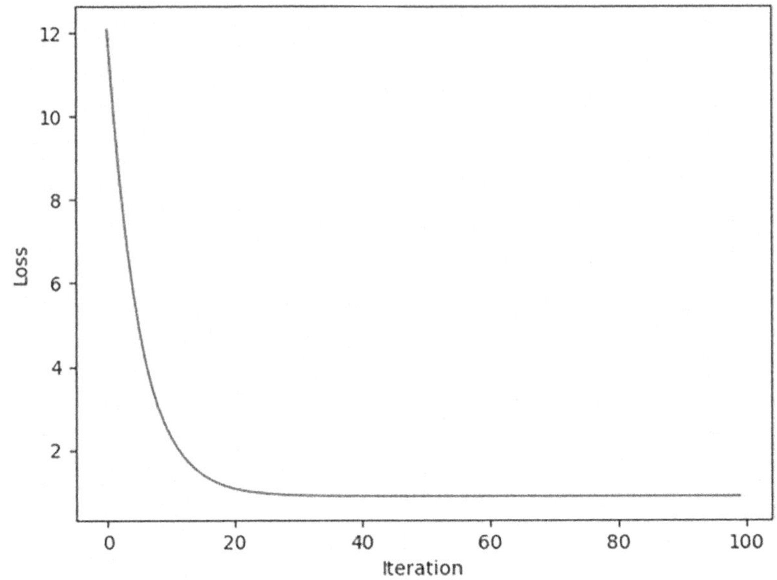

Figure 3.21 Mini-batch gradient descent.

problem. Batch gradient descent is preferred when the dataset is small and fits in memory, while SGD and mini-batch gradient descent are suitable for large-scale problems. In practice, researchers and practitioners often use mini-batch gradient descent due to its efficiency and good convergence properties. It's important to note that there are also variations and extensions of these gradient descent algorithms, such as momentum-based methods, adaptive learning rate algorithms (e.g., AdaGrad, RMSprop, Adam), and second-order methods (e.g., Newton's method, L-BFGS). These methods introduce additional techniques to accelerate convergence, handle different learning rates, and improve optimization performance in various scenarios.

Some of the optimization algorithms are designed to overcome challenges such as non-convexity, high dimensionality, and noisy gradients as discussed earlier. Here are a few notable optimization algorithms that are widely used in deep learning.

3.7 Momentum

Momentum is a technique that helps accelerate optimization by accumulating past gradients' momentum and adding it to the current gradient update. This allows the optimization algorithm to gain speed and traverse flat regions or shallow minima more quickly. Momentum helps overcome issues such as slow convergence and oscillations. In momentum, instead of updating the parameters based on the current gradient, we introduce a new variable called "velocity" (v). The velocity represents the accumulated momentum of past gradients. The update equations for momentum are as follows:

$$v_t = \beta \times v_{t-1} + learning\_rate \times gradient$$

$$x_t = x_{t-1} - v_t$$

Here, '$\boldsymbol{v}_t$' is the velocity at time step t, 'β' is the momentum coefficient that determines the influence of past gradients (typically set to a value between 0 and 1), '$\boldsymbol{v}_{t-1}$' is the velocity at the previous time step, **'learning_rate'** is the step size that determines the size of the parameter update, 'gradient' is the current gradient, and 'x_t' is the updated parameter.

The momentum term, '$\beta * v_{t-1}$', allows the algorithm to accumulate momentum in the direction of the gradients. This means that gradients with consistent directions will contribute more to the parameter updates, leading to faster convergence. On the other hand, gradients with oscillating directions will have a reduced impact, helping to stabilize the optimization process.

By incorporating momentum, the momentum algorithm can navigate through ravines, escape local minima, and accelerate convergence. It is particularly effective in optimizing deep neural networks, where the objective function is highly nonlinear and contains many local minima.

Here's an implementation of momentum from scratch, including the necessary auxiliary variables and a plot to visualize the optimization progress:

```
import numpy as np
import matplotlib.pyplot as plt

def momentum_optimizer(grad_fn, initial_x, learning_rate, momen-
tum, num_iterations):
    x = initial_x
    velocity = np.zeros_like(x)
    states = []

    for t in range(num_iterations):
        gradient = grad_fn(x)
        velocity = momentum * velocity + learning_rate * gradient
        x = x - velocity
        states.append(x)

    return x, states

# Define the objective function and its gradient
def objective_function(x):
    return x**2

def gradient_function(x):
    return 2 * x

# Set the parameters for momentum optimization
initial_x = 5.0
learning_rate = 0.1
momentum = 0.9
num_iterations = 20
```

```
# Run momentum optimization
optimal_x, optimization_states = momentum_optimizer(gradient_
function, initial_x, learning_rate, momentum, num_iterations)

# Plot the optimization progress
x_values = np.linspace(-6, 6, 100)
y_values = objective_function(x_values)
plt.plot(x_values, y_values, label='Objective Function')

for i, state in enumerate(optimization_states):
    y_state = objective_function(state)
    plt.scatter(state, y_state, color='red', label=f'Iteration
{i+1}')
    plt.plot([state, state], [0, y_state], color='red',
linestyle='--')

plt.scatter(optimal_x, objective_function(optimal_x),
color='green', label='Optimal Solution')
plt.xlabel('x')
plt.ylabel('f(x)')
plt.legend()
plt.title('Momentum Optimization')
plt.grid(True)
plt.show()
```

In this implementation, **'momentum_optimizer'** is the function that performs momentum optimization presented in Figure 3.22. It takes the gradient function **'grad_fn'**, initial parameter **'initial_x'**, learning rate **'learning_rate'**, momentum coefficient **'momentum'**, and the number of iterations **'num_iterations'**. The implementation maintains the velocity variable **'velocity'** with the same shape as the parameters. The optimization progress is recorded in the **'states'** list, which stores the parameter values at each iteration. In this example, we use a simple quadratic function.

After running the momentum optimization, the plot shows the progress of the optimization. The objective function is plotted as a solid line, and each iteration's parameter value is represented by a red dot. The green dot represents the optimal solution found by the momentum optimizer.

This implementation provides a clear visualization of how momentum affects the optimization process, allowing you to observe the convergence toward the optimal solution.

3.8 Nesterov Accelerated Gradient

Nesterov Accelerated Gradient (NAG) is an improvement over traditional momentum. It uses a modified gradient computation that takes into account the momentum term when computing the gradients. This allows the algorithm to make more informed updates and achieve faster convergence.

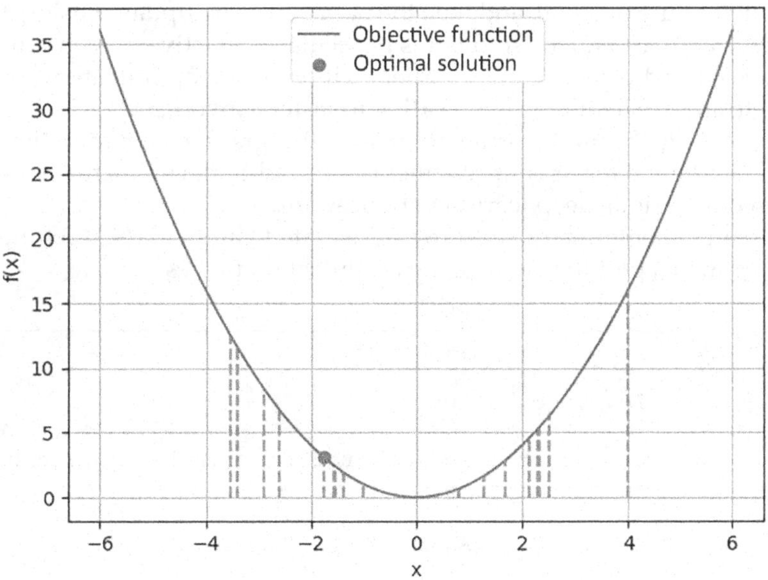

Figure 3.22 Momentum optimization.

In traditional momentum, the update step is performed using the accumulated velocity term. However, in Nesterov Accelerated Gradient, the update is performed based on the estimated future position, which is adjusted by the momentum term. This allows the algorithm to "look ahead" and make corrections to the momentum-based update.

The update equations for Nesterov Accelerated Gradient can be described as follows:

1. Initialize the parameters:
   - x = initial_x
   - velocity = 0
2. For each iteration:
   a. Compute the gradient at the estimated future position:
      - gradient = grad_fn(x – momentum × velocity)

   b. Update the velocity:
      - velocity = momentum × velocity + learning_rate × gradient

   c. Update the parameters:
      - $x = x$ – velocity

Nesterov Accelerated Gradient can be seen as a modification of momentum that incorporates a "correction" term. By adjusting the gradient computation based on the estimated future position, it allows for faster convergence and better handling of curved loss surfaces.

The implementation of Nesterov Accelerated Gradient involves maintaining the velocity variable, similar to momentum. The velocity is updated based on the gradient at the estimated future position, and then the parameters are updated using the updated velocity. Nesterov Accelerated Gradient is particularly effective in scenarios where the loss surface is curved or has strong gradients. It helps the optimization process make more accurate and efficient updates, leading to faster convergence.

By incorporating the momentum term into the gradient computation, Nesterov Accelerated Gradient offers an improvement over traditional momentum methods and is widely used in various deep learning applications.

Here's an implementation of Nesterov Accelerated Gradient (NAG) from scratch in Python, along with a plot to visualize the optimization process:

```
import numpy as np
import matplotlib.pyplot as plt

def nesterov_accelerated_gradient(grad_fn, initial_x, learning_
rate, momentum, num_iterations):
    x = initial_x
    velocity = np.zeros_like(x)
    trajectory = [x]

    for _ in range(num_iterations):
        # Update the velocity based on the estimated future
position
        velocity_ahead = momentum * velocity - learning_rate *
grad_fn(x)

        # Update the position
        x = x + momentum * velocity - learning_rate * grad_fn(x +
momentum * velocity)

        velocity = velocity_ahead
        trajectory.append(x)

    return x, trajectory

# Example usage
def quadratic_loss_gradient(x):
    return 2 * x

initial_x = np.array([5.0])
learning_rate = 0.1
momentum = 0.9
num_iterations = 10

optimal_x, trajectory = nesterov_accelerated_gradient(quadratic_
loss_gradient, initial_x, learning_rate, momentum,
num_iterations)

# Plot the optimization process
x_vals = np.linspace(-6, 6, 100)
```

```
y_vals = x_vals**2

plt.plot(x_vals, y_vals, label='Objective Function')
plt.plot(trajectory, [x**2 for x in trajectory], 'ro-',
label='Optimization Trajectory')
plt.xlabel('x')
plt.ylabel('f(x)')
plt.title('Nesterov Accelerated Gradient')
plt.legend()
plt.grid(True)
plt.show()

print("Optimal x:", optimal_x)
```

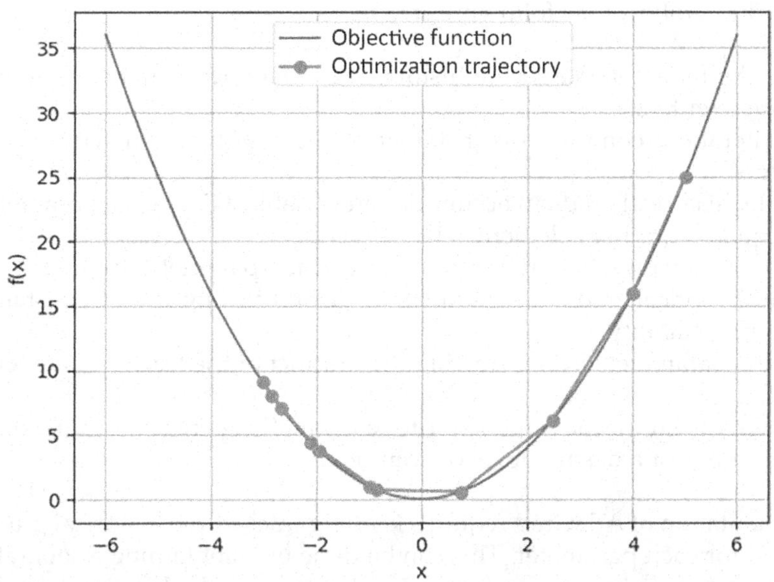

Figure 3.23 Nesterov accelerated gradient.

In this implementation, the **'nesterov_accelerated_gradient'** function takes the gradient function **'grad_fn'**, initial position **'initial_x'**, learning rate **'learning_rate'**, momentum **'momentum'**, and the number of iterations **'num_iterations'** presented in Figure 3.23. It iteratively updates the position and velocity based on the Nesterov Accelerated Gradient update rule.

The example usage is similar to the previous example. We define a quadratic loss gradient function **'quadratic_loss_gradient'** that returns the gradient of the function 2x. We initialize the initial position **'initial_x'** to 5.0 and set the learning rate, momentum, and number of iterations. The algorithm then finds the optimal **'x'** using Nesterov Accelerated Gradient and plots the optimization trajectory along with the objective function.

The plot shows the optimization process along with the objective function (a quadratic function) and the trajectory of the optimization algorithm. You can modify the objective function, initial position, learning rate, momentum, and number of iterations according to your specific problem.

3.9 AdaGrad

AdaGrad adapts the learning rate for each parameter based on their historical gradients. It assigns larger learning rates for parameters that have smaller gradients and vice versa. This enables faster convergence for parameters with sparse updates and is particularly useful in settings with sparse data or natural gradient problems.

The main idea behind AdaGrad is to keep track of the sum of squared gradients for each parameter. By doing so, the algorithm assigns larger learning rates to parameters that have been updated infrequently, enabling faster convergence for sparse updates. In contrast, parameters that have been updated frequently will have smaller learning rates, which helps to prevent overshooting and oscillations.

The algorithm follows the following steps:

1. Initialize the parameters and the historical gradient accumulation variable **'G'** for each parameter to zero.
2. At each iteration, compute the gradient of the loss function with respect to the parameters.
3. Update the historical gradient accumulation variable **'G'** for each parameter by adding the squared gradient element-wise.
4. Compute the adaptive learning rate **'eta'** for each parameter by taking the square root of the historical gradient accumulation **'G'** and adding a small constant **'epsilon'** for numerical stability.
5. Update the parameters by subtracting the product of the learning rate **'eta'** and the gradient.
6. Repeat steps 2–5 until convergence criteria are met (e.g., reaching a maximum number of iterations or a desired level of accuracy).

The implementation of AdaGrad requires keeping track of the historical gradient accumulation **'G'** for each parameter. This can be done by maintaining a separate variable for each parameter or by using a matrix/vector to store the historical gradients. The adaptive learning rate **'eta'** is computed based on the historical gradient accumulation **'G'** using the square root operation.

It's important to note that AdaGrad can be sensitive to the initial learning rate and may become too small over time, hindering convergence. To address this, an extension called RMSProp was introduced, which adds a decay term to the historical gradient accumulation **'G'** to mitigate this issue. AdaGrad is particularly useful in settings with sparse data or natural gradient problems, where it can adaptively adjust the learning rate for each parameter based on their individual characteristics.

Here's an implementation of AdaGrad from scratch in Python, including a plot to visualize the optimization process:

In this example, we have a simple quadratic function '$f(x) = x^2$' as the loss function. The **'compute_gradient'** function computes the gradient of the loss function, and the **'compute_loss'** function calculates the loss given a parameter value **'x'**.

```
import numpy as np
import matplotlib.pyplot as plt

def adagrad(x_initial, learning_rate, num_iterations):
    x = x_initial
    historical_grad = np.zeros_like(x)
    losses = []

    for i in range(num_iterations):
        # Compute gradient
        gradient = compute_gradient(x)

        # Update historical gradient accumulation
        historical_grad += gradient ** 2

        # Compute adaptive learning rate
        adaptive_lr = learning_rate / (np.sqrt(historical_grad) +
1e-8)

        # Update parameters
        x -= adaptive_lr * gradient

        # Compute loss and append to the list
        loss = compute_loss(x)
        losses.append(loss)

    return x, losses

# Example usage
x_initial = 1.0
learning_rate = 0.1
num_iterations = 100

def compute_gradient(x):
    return 2 * x  # Example gradient for f(x) = x^2

def compute_loss(x):
    return x ** 2  # Example loss function f(x) = x^2

# Run AdaGrad
x_optimal, losses = adagrad(x_initial, learning_rate,
num_iterations)

# Plot the optimization process
plt.plot(losses)
plt.xlabel('Iteration')
plt.ylabel('Loss')
plt.title('AdaGrad Optimization')
plt.show()
```

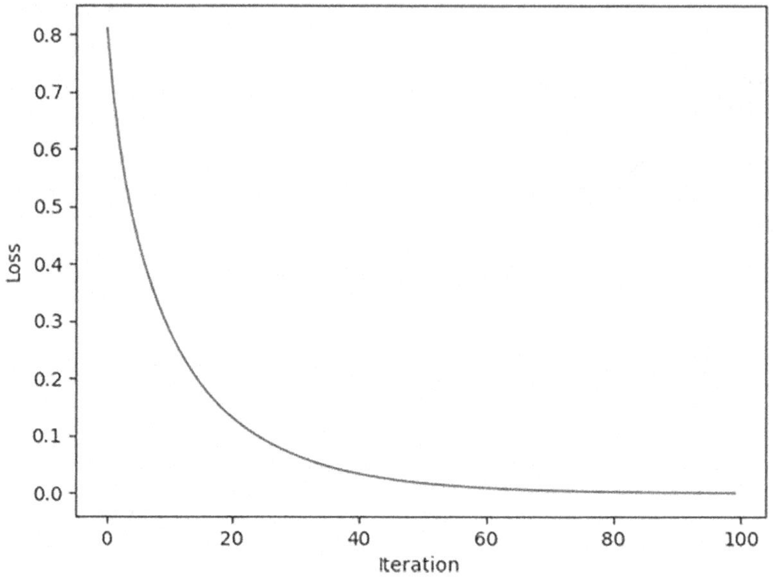

Figure 3.24 AdaGrad optimization.

The **'adagrad'** function implements the AdaGrad algorithm and presented in Figure 3.24. It initializes the historical gradient accumulation **'historical_grad'** as an array of zeros. It then iteratively updates the parameters **'x'** based on the adaptive learning rate computed using the historical gradient accumulation. The loss at each iteration is computed and stored in the **'losses'** list.

Finally, we plot the optimization process by plotting the losses against the iterations.

Note that in a real-world scenario, you would replace the **'compute_gradient'** and **'compute_loss'** functions with the actual gradient and loss functions relevant to your problem.

3.10 RMSprop

RMSprop (Root Mean Square Propagation) is an optimization algorithm that addresses some limitations of AdaGrad by introducing an exponentially decaying average of squared gradients. This technique helps adjust the learning rate adaptively based on the historical gradient information. The main goal of RMSprop is to prevent the learning rate from decaying too rapidly, which can hinder convergence.

Here is a high-level description of the RMSprop algorithm:

1. *Initialize the Parameters:*
    - Set the initial parameter values.
    - Set the initial learning rate.
    - Initialize an accumulator variable to store the squared gradients.
2. *For Each Iteration*:
    - Compute the gradient of the objective function with respect to the parameters.

- Update the accumulator by taking an exponentially decaying average of the squared gradients.
- Compute the root mean square (RMS) of the gradients using the accumulated values.
- Adjust the learning rate by dividing it by the RMS value.
- Update the parameters using the learning rate and the gradient.

The RMSprop algorithm helps overcome the limitations of AdaGrad, where the learning rate becomes very small too quickly, making further updates ineffective. By introducing the RMS of the gradients, RMSprop adapts the learning rate on a per-parameter basis, allowing for more stable and effective updates.

Here's an implementation of RMSprop from scratch in Python, including a plot to visualize the optimization process presented in Figure 3.25:

```
import numpy as np
import matplotlib.pyplot as plt

def rmsprop(x_initial, learning_rate, decay_rate,
num_iterations):
    x = x_initial
    cache = np.zeros_like(x)
    losses = []

    for i in range(num_iterations):
        # Compute gradient
        gradient = compute_gradient(x)

        # Update cache
        cache = decay_rate * cache + (1 - decay_rate) * gradient
** 2

        # Compute adaptive learning rate
        adaptive_lr = learning_rate / (np.sqrt(cache) + 1e-8)

        # Update parameters
        x -= adaptive_lr * gradient

        # Compute loss and append to the list
        loss = compute_loss(x)
        losses.append(loss)

    return x, losses

# Example usage
x_initial = 1.0
learning_rate = 0.1
decay_rate = 0.9
num_iterations = 100

def compute_gradient(x):
```

```
    return 2 * x  # Example gradient for f(x) = x^2

def compute_loss(x):
    return x ** 2  # Example loss function f(x) = x^2

# Run RMSprop
x_optimal, losses = rmsprop(x_initial, learning_rate, decay_rate,
num_iterations)

# Plot the optimization process
plt.plot(losses)
plt.xlabel('Iteration')
plt.ylabel('Loss')
plt.title('RMSprop Optimization')
plt.show()
```

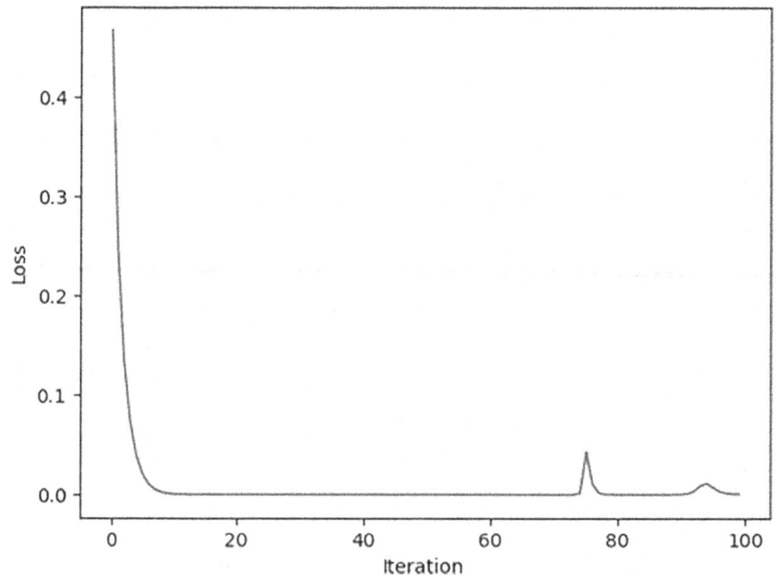

Figure 3.25 RMSProp optimization.

In this example, we have a simple quadratic function '$f(x)=x^2$' as the loss function. The **'compute_gradient'** function computes the gradient of the loss function, and the **'compute_loss'** function calculates the loss given a parameter value **'x'**.

The **'rmsprop'** function implements the RMSprop algorithm. It initializes the cache as an array of zeros. It then iteratively updates the parameters **'x'** based on the adaptive learning rate computed using the cache. The loss at each iteration is computed and stored in the **'losses'** list.

Finally, we plot the optimization process by plotting the losses against the iterations.

3.11 Adam

Adam (Adaptive Moment Estimation) is an optimization algorithm that combines the ideas of momentum and adaptive learning rates. It is known for its efficiency and robustness across different types of deep learning tasks. Adam maintains a set of adaptive learning rates for each parameter and also keeps track of both the first and second moments of the gradients.

The algorithm starts by initializing the parameters, the first moment variables (m), and the second moment variables (v) to zero. At each iteration, it computes the gradient of the loss function with respect to the parameters. It then updates the first moment estimates by taking a weighted average of the previous first moment and the current gradient. Similarly, it updates the second moment estimates by taking a weighted average of the previous second moment and the squared gradient.

The update rule for the parameters in Adam is given by:

m = beta1 × m + (1 – beta1) × gradient
v = beta2 × *v* + (1 – beta2) × gradient^2
m_hat = m / (1 – beta1^t) # Corrected first moment estimate
v_hat = v / (1 – beta2^t) # Corrected second moment estimate
parameter = parameter – learning_rate × m_hat / (sqrt(v_hat) + epsilon)

In these equations, **'gradient'** represents the gradient of the loss function, **'beta1'** and **'beta2'** are the decay rates for the first and second moments respectively, **'t'** represents the iteration number, **'epsilon'** is a small constant for numerical stability, and **'learning_rate'** is the learning rate.

The main idea behind Adam is to use the first and second moment estimates to adaptively adjust the learning rate for each parameter. It allows the learning rate to be larger for parameters with smaller gradients and smaller for parameters with larger gradients. Additionally, it incorporates momentum through the first moment estimates, which helps accelerate convergence.

The hyperparameters **'beta1'**, **'beta2'**, **'epsilon'**, and the learning rate need to be carefully chosen based on the specific problem and dataset. Typical values for **'beta1'** and **'beta2'** are 0.9 and 0.999, respectively, and **'epsilon'** is often set to a small value such as 1e–8.

Implementing Adam in Python involves updating the parameters and the moment estimates at each iteration using the update rule described earlier. Additionally, it is common to initialize the moment estimates to zero and keep track of the iteration number to correct the bias of the moment estimates. The algorithm can be implemented using NumPy or other numerical computation libraries.

Here's an implementation of the Adam optimization algorithm from scratch in Python, along with a simple example of how to use it presented in Figure 3.26:

```
import numpy as np
import matplotlib.pyplot as plt

def adam_optimizer(parameters, gradients, learning_rate,
beta1=0.9, beta2=0.999, epsilon=1e-8, num_iterations=100):
    """
    Adam optimization algorithm implementation.

    Parameters:
    - parameters: A dictionary containing the parameters to be
optimized.
    - gradients: A dictionary containing the gradients of the
parameters.
    - learning_rate: The learning rate for the optimization.
    - beta1: Decay rate for the first moment estimate. Default is
0.9.
    - beta2: Decay rate for the second moment estimate. Default
is 0.999.
    - epsilon: A small constant for numerical stability. Default
is 1e-8.
    - num_iterations: Number of optimization iterations. Default
is 100.

    Returns:
    - parameters: The optimized parameters.
    - losses: A list of the loss values at each iteration.
    """
    m = {}
    v = {}
    losses = []

    for param_name, param_value in parameters.items():
        # Initialize moment estimates
        m[param_name] = np.zeros_like(param_value)
        v[param_name] = np.zeros_like(param_value)

    for iteration in range(num_iterations):
        for param_name in parameters.keys():
            # Update moment estimates
            m[param_name] = beta1 * m[param_name] + (1 - beta1) *
gradients[param_name]
            v[param_name] = beta2 * v[param_name] + (1 - beta2) *
np.power(gradients[param_name], 2)

            # Bias correction
            m_hat = m[param_name] / (1 - np.power(beta1, itera-
tion + 1))
            v_hat = v[param_name] / (1 - np.power(beta2, itera-
tion + 1))
```

```
            # Update parameters
            parameters[param_name] -= learning_rate * m_hat /
(np.sqrt(v_hat) + epsilon)

        # Compute loss and store it
        loss = compute_loss(parameters)
        losses.append(loss)

    return parameters, losses

# Example usage
# Define your parameters and gradients
parameters = {'w': np.random.randn(1), 'b': np.random.randn(1)}
gradients = {'w': np.random.randn(1), 'b': np.random.randn(1)}

# Define a simple loss function (e.g., mean squared error)
def compute_loss(parameters):
    w = parameters['w']
    b = parameters['b']
    x = np.array([1, 2, 3, 4, 5])
    y = np.array([2, 4, 6, 8, 10])
    y_pred = w * x + b
    loss = np.mean(np.square(y - y_pred))
    return loss

# Perform optimization using Adam
learning_rate = 0.1
optimized_parameters, losses = adam_optimizer(parameters, gradi-
ents, learning_rate, num_iterations=100)

# Plot the loss curve
plt.plot(losses)
plt.xlabel('Iteration')
plt.ylabel('Loss')
plt.title('Adam Optimization')
plt.show()
```

In this implementation, you need to provide the initial parameters and gradients as dictionaries, where the keys are the parameter names and the values are the corresponding parameter values and gradients, respectively. You can customize the learning rate (**'learning_rate'**), the decay rates (**'beta1'** and **'beta2'**), the small constant for numerical stability (**'epsilon'**), and the number of optimization iterations (**'num_iterations'**) according to your specific problem.

The optimization is performed by calling the **'adam_optimizer'** function, which returns the optimized parameters and a list of the loss values at each iteration. You can then visualize the progress of the optimization by plotting the loss curve using matplotlib.

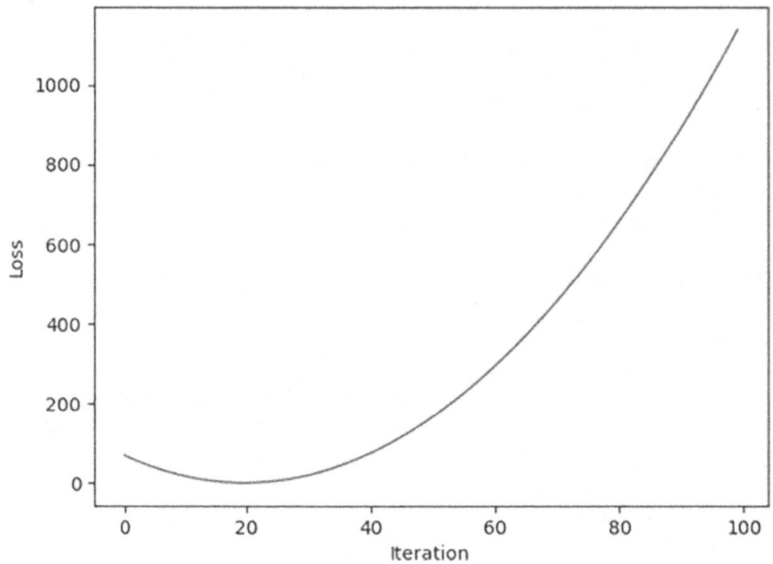

Figure 3.26 Adam optimization.

3.12 L-BFGS

L-BFGS (Limited-memory Broyden–Fletcher–Goldfarb–Shanno) is a popular optimization algorithm for unconstrained optimization problems. It belongs to the family of quasi-Newton methods and is specifically designed for solving problems where the objective function is smooth and has a moderate number of parameters.

The main advantage of L-BFGS over other optimization algorithms is its efficient approximation of the Hessian matrix. The Hessian matrix is a matrix of second-order partial derivatives that provides information about the curvature of the objective function. Computing and storing the full Hessian matrix can be computationally expensive and memory-intensive, especially for high-dimensional problems. L-BFGS addresses this limitation by using a limited-memory approach that approximates the Hessian matrix using information from previous iterations.

The algorithm starts with an initial estimate of the solution and iteratively updates the parameters based on the gradient of the objective function and an approximation of the Hessian matrix. At each iteration, L-BFGS uses a limited memory history of past gradients and parameter updates to compute a new search direction that improves the objective function value.

The L-BFGS algorithm combines the Broyden–Fletcher–Goldfarb–Shanno (BFGS) method with a limited-memory approach, which means that it does not require explicit storage of the full Hessian matrix. Instead, it constructs an approximation of the inverse Hessian matrix using the information from a limited number of previous iterations. This approximation is used to compute the search direction and update the parameters.

The L-BFGS algorithm is widely used in machine learning and optimization tasks, especially in scenarios where the objective function is smooth and the number of parameters is moderate. It is known for its efficiency, convergence properties, and ability to handle large-scale problems.

Here is a high-level overview of the L-BFGS algorithm:

1. Initialize the parameters and define the objective function.
2. Choose the number of memory vectors to store (m), which determines the memory capacity of the algorithm.
3. Initialize the memory vectors and other auxiliary variables.
4. Repeat until convergence or a stopping criterion is met:
   - Compute the gradient of the objective function.
   - Compute the search direction using the L-BFGS update formula.
   - Perform a line search to determine the step size.
   - Update the parameters based on the step size and search direction.
   - Update the memory vectors using the latest gradients and parameter updates.
   - Check for convergence or stopping criterion.

The implementation of L-BFGS can vary depending on the programming language and optimization library used. Many numerical computing libraries, such as SciPy in Python, provide built-in functions for L-BFGS optimization. These libraries handle the low-level details of the algorithm, such as line searches and parameter updates, allowing users to focus on defining the objective function and setting the optimization parameters. Here is a step-by-step guide to implementing L-BFGS using the SciPy library:

Step 1: Import the necessary libraries.

```
import numpy as np
from scipy.optimize import minimize
```

Step 2: Define the objective function and its gradient.

```
def objective_function(x):
    # Implement your objective function here
    return f

def gradient(x):
    # Implement the gradient of your objective function here
    return g
```

Step 3: Set the initial parameter values and other optimization parameters.

```
initial_params = np.array([1.0, 2.0, 3.0])  # Set your initial
parameter values
options = {'disp': True, 'maxiter': 100}  # Set optimization
options
```

Step 4: Use the **'minimize'** function from SciPy to perform L-BFGS optimization.

```
result = minimize(objective_function, initial_params,
method='L-BFGS-B', jac=gradient, options=options)
```

Step 5: Retrieve the optimized parameters and other information from the result object.

```
optimized_params = result.x
converged = result.success
num_iterations = result.nit
```

Note that in this example, the **'minimize'** function is used with the method parameter set to **'L-BFGS-B'** to indicate the use of L-BFGS optimization. The **'jac'** parameter is set to the gradient function, which provides the gradient of the objective function.

It's important to customize the objective function and gradient functions according to user-specific optimization problem. Additionally, the user may need to adjust the optimization options, such as the maximum number of iterations, to suit their requirements.

L-BFGS is a powerful optimization algorithm that can efficiently solve unconstrained optimization problems with smooth objective functions. Its ability to approximate the Hessian matrix makes it particularly useful for high-dimensional problems, where computing and storing the full Hessian is impractical. By leveraging the limited-memory approach, L-BFGS strikes a balance between computational efficiency and accuracy, making it a popular choice in various fields, including machine learning, optimization, and numerical computing.

These are just a few examples of optimization algorithms commonly used in deep learning. Each algorithm has its own strengths and weaknesses, making them suitable for different optimization problems. Researchers and practitioners continue to develop and refine optimization algorithms to tackle the unique challenges of deep learning, such as non-convexity, large-scale datasets, and computational efficiency.

3.13 Learning Rate Scheduling

Learning rate scheduling is an important aspect of training neural networks and plays a crucial role in achieving good performance. It involves adjusting the learning rate during the training process to effectively update the weight vectors of the network. The learning rate determines the step size of the weight updates and influences the convergence speed and final performance of the model.

Here are some key aspects to consider when designing learning rate scheduling strategies.

1. *Initial Learning Rate:* The starting learning rate is typically set before training begins. It should be chosen carefully, as a too-high or too-low learning rate can hinder convergence. A common practice is to start with a relatively high learning rate and gradually reduce it over time.

2. *Learning Rate Decay:* As training progresses, it is often beneficial to reduce the learning rate gradually. This allows the model to make larger updates in the beginning when the parameters are far from the optimal values and gradually refine the updates as the parameters get closer to the optimum. Decay methods can be based on a fixed schedule, such as reducing the learning rate by a fixed factor after a certain number of epochs or dynamically adjusting the learning rate based on certain criteria, such as the validation loss not improving for a certain number of epochs.
3. *Learning Rate Annealing:* Annealing is a technique where the learning rate is decreased during training in a systematic manner. Common annealing strategies include step decay, where the learning rate is reduced by a factor after a fixed number of epochs, and exponential decay, where the learning rate decreases exponentially over time. Annealing helps the model to converge to a better solution by refining the updates as training progresses.
4. *Learning Rate Plateau:* During training, it is possible to encounter plateaus where the model's performance does not improve significantly. In such cases, it may be beneficial to reduce the learning rate further to navigate out of the plateau and find a better solution. This can be done by monitoring a metric, such as the validation loss, and reducing the learning rate if the improvement is below a certain threshold for a specified number of epochs.
5. *Learning Rate Warmup:* In the initial stages of training, when the weights are randomly initialized, it can be helpful to use a higher learning rate to allow the model to explore the solution space more quickly. This is known as learning rate warmup. Warmup helps the model to escape from poor local optima and reach a better solution.

Implementing learning rate scheduling in practice involves integrating it into the training loop or using built-in functions provided by deep learning frameworks. The scheduling strategy can be based on predefined rules or dynamically adjusted based on the model's performance during training.

A toy problem refers to a simplified and manageable version of a real-world problem that is used for experimentation, learning, and illustration purposes. In the context of deep learning, a toy problem allows us to understand and test different concepts, algorithms, and architectures in a controlled and simplified setting.

One example of a toy problem is the application of a slightly modernized version of LeNet, a convolutional neural network, on the Fashion-MNIST dataset. Fashion-MNIST is a dataset of 60,000 grayscale images of ten different fashion categories, with 6,000 images per category. It serves as a substitute for the original MNIST dataset and is commonly used to evaluate and compare the performance of various deep learning models. Here is a Python implementation of applying a modified LeNet model to the Fashion-MNIST dataset and training loss presented in Figure 3.27:

```
import torch
import torch.nn as nn
import torch.optim as optim
from torchvision.datasets import FashionMNIST
from torchvision.transforms import ToTensor
from torch.utils.data import DataLoader
```

```
import matplotlib.pyplot as plt
from torch.autograd import Variable

# Define the LeNet model
class LeNet(nn.Module):
    def __init__(self):
        super(LeNet, self).__init__()
        self.conv1 = nn.Conv2d(1, 6, kernel_size=5)
        self.relu1 = nn.ReLU()
        self.pool1 = nn.MaxPool2d(kernel_size=2)
        self.conv2 = nn.Conv2d(6, 16, kernel_size=5)
        self.relu2 = nn.ReLU()
        self.pool2 = nn.MaxPool2d(kernel_size=2)
        self.fc1 = nn.Linear(16 * 4 * 4, 120)
        self.relu3 = nn.ReLU()
        self.fc2 = nn.Linear(120, 84)
        self.relu4 = nn.ReLU()
        self.fc3 = nn.Linear(84, 10)

    def forward(self, x):
        x = self.pool1(self.relu1(self.conv1(x)))
        x = self.pool2(self.relu2(self.conv2(x)))
        x = x.view(-1, 16 * 4 * 4)
        x = self.relu3(self.fc1(x))
        x = self.relu4(self.fc2(x))
        x = self.fc3(x)
        return x

# Load the Fashion-MNIST dataset
train_dataset = FashionMNIST(root='./data', train=True,
transform=ToTensor(), download=True)
test_dataset = FashionMNIST(root='./data', train=False,
transform=ToTensor())

# Define the data loaders
batch_size = 64
train_loader = DataLoader(train_dataset, batch_size=batch_size,
shuffle=True)
test_loader = DataLoader(test_dataset, batch_size=batch_size)

# Create an instance of the LeNet model
model = LeNet()

# Define the loss function and optimizer
criterion = nn.CrossEntropyLoss()
optimizer = optim.SGD(model.parameters(), lr=0.001, momentum=0.9)

# Training loop
num_epochs = 10
losses = []
```

```
for epoch in range(num_epochs):
    running_loss = 0.0
    for i, (inputs, labels) in enumerate(train_loader):
        inputs = Variable(inputs)
        labels = Variable(labels)

        # Forward pass
        outputs = model(inputs)
        loss = criterion(outputs, labels)
        # Backward pass and optimization

    for images, labels in train_loader:
        optimizer.zero_grad()
        outputs = model(images)
        loss = criterion(outputs, labels)
        loss.backward()
        optimizer.step()
        running_loss += loss.item() * images.size(0)
        if (i + 1) % 1000 == 0:
            print(f'Epoch [{epoch+1}/{num_epochs}], Step [{i+1}/
{len(train_loader)}], Loss: {loss.item()}')

    epoch_loss = running_loss / len(train_dataset)
    losses.append(epoch_loss)

# Print the loss for every 1000 iterations
# Evaluation
model.eval()
correct = 0
total = 0
with torch.no_grad():
    for inputs, labels in test_loader:
        inputs = Variable(inputs)
        labels = Variable(labels)
        outputs = model(inputs)
        _, predicted = torch.max(outputs.data, 1)
        total += labels.size(0)
        correct += (predicted == labels).sum().item()

accuracy = 100 * correct / total
print(f'Accuracy on the test set: {accuracy}%')
#     print(f'Epoch [{epoch+1}/{num_epochs}], Loss:
{epoch_loss:.4f}')

# Plot the training loss
plt.plot(losses)
plt.xlabel('Epoch')
plt.ylabel('Loss')
plt.title('Training Loss')
plt.show()
```

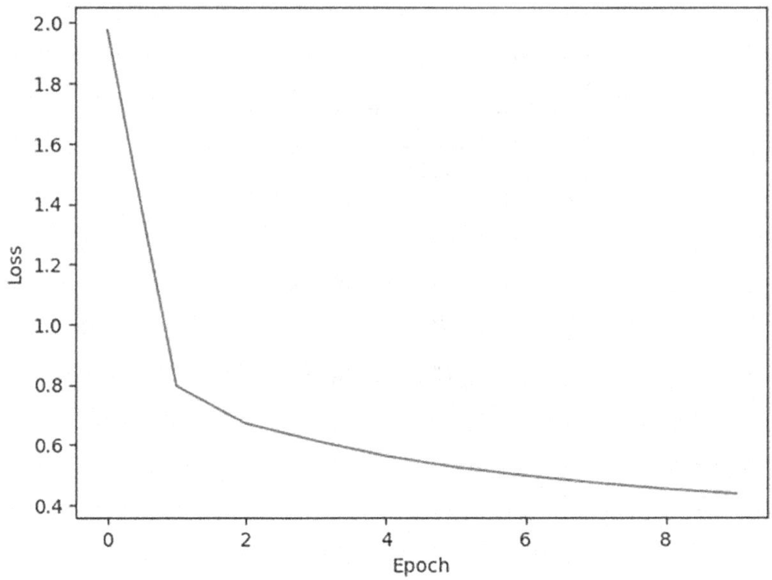

Figure 3.27 Training loss.

This implementation defines the LeNet model using the **'nn.Module'** class from PyTorch and trains it on the Fashion-MNIST dataset using SGD as the optimizer. The model is trained for a specified number of epochs, and the loss is printed periodically during training. Finally, the accuracy of the trained model on the test set is calculated and displayed.

By applying a simplified version of LeNet on the Fashion-MNIST dataset, we can understand the basic concepts of CNNs, training loops, and evaluation metrics. This serves as a stepping stone to more complex deep learning problems and models.

Accuracy on the test set: 84.12%

During training, we iterate over the training dataset in batches, compute the forward pass, calculate the loss, perform backpropagation, and update the model parameters using the optimizer. We track the training loss for each epoch and plot it at the end.

The plot shows the training loss over the epochs, giving us an indication of how the model is learning and converging.

This implementation provides a basic understanding of applying a modified LeNet model to the Fashion-MNIST dataset and demonstrates the training progress through the loss plot.

3.14 Summary

The chapter covers various fundamental topics related to neural networks and optimization in deep learning. Here's a summary of each topic covered.

- *Neural Networks Fundamentals:* This section introduces the basic concepts of neural networks, including neurons, weights, biases, and activation functions.

- *Overall Structure of a Neural Network:* The chapter explains the general structure of a neural network, consisting of input, hidden, and output layers. It also discusses the flow of information and the forward propagation process.
- *Layers: Input, Hidden, and Output Layers:* This section describes the different types of layers in a neural network, including input, hidden, and output layers. It explains their roles in processing and transforming data.
- *Types of Units/Activation Functions/Layers:* The chapter covers various types of units and activation functions commonly used in neural networks, such as linear units, sigmoid units, softmax layers, and rectified linear units (ReLU). Also, it discusses their properties and applications.
- *Optimization and Deep Learning:* This section introduces the concept of optimization in deep learning and its significance in training neural networks. It explains the goal of optimization and the challenges specific to deep learning.
- *Convexity: Definitions, Properties, Constraints:* The chapter discusses convexity in optimization problems and explains the properties and constraints associated with convex functions. It highlights the importance of convexity in the design of optimization algorithms.
- *Gradient Descent:* This section provides an overview of gradient descent, a widely used optimization algorithm in deep learning. It explains the concept of gradients, the update process, and different variants of gradient descent, such as stochastic gradient descent and minibatch stochastic gradient descent.
- *Momentum, Adagrad, RMSProp, Adadelta, Adam:* The chapter covers several advanced optimization algorithms, including momentum, Adagrad, RMSProp, and Adam. It explains their mechanisms, advantages, and limitations.
- *Learning Rate Scheduling:* This section discusses learning rate scheduling, which involves adjusting the learning rate during training. It explores different scheduling strategies and their impact on optimization and convergence.

Overall, the chapter provides a comprehensive overview of the fundamentals of neural networks, optimization in deep learning, and various optimization algorithms commonly used in practice. It covers concepts, algorithms, and techniques essential for understanding and effectively training neural networks.

References

Davis, D., & Drusvyatskiy, D. (2019). Stochastic model-based minimization of weakly convex functions. *SIAM Journal on Optimization, 29*(1), 207–239.

Gao, Y., Liu, W., & Lombardi, F. (2020). Design and implementation of an approximate softmax layer for deep neural networks. In *2020 IEEE International Symposium on Circuits and Systems (ISCAS)*, 1–5.

Izmailov, P., Podoprikhin, D., Garipov, T., Vetrov, D., & Wilson, A. G. (2018). Averaging weights leads to wider optima and better generalization. *ArXiv Preprint ArXiv:1803.05407.*

Mohsen, B. B., Noor, M. A., Noor, K. I., & Postolache, M. (2019). Strongly convex functions of higher order involving bifunction. *Mathematics, 7*(11), 1028.

Nayak, D. R., Das, D., Dash, R., Majhi, S., & Majhi, B. (2020). Deep extreme learning machine with leaky rectified linear unit for multiclass classification of pathological brain images. *Multimedia Tools and Applications, 79*, 15381–15396.

Noor, M. A., & Noor, K. I. (2019). On exponentially convex functions. *Journal of Orissa Mathematical Society, 975*, 2323.

Raghu, M., Unterthiner, T., Kornblith, S., Zhang, C., & Dosovitskiy, A. (2021). Do vision transformers see like convolutional neural networks? *Advances in Neural Information Processing Systems, 34*, 12116–12128.

Sharma, O. (2019). Deep challenges associated with deep learning. *2019 International Conference on Machine Learning, Big Data, Cloud and Parallel Computing (COMITCon)*, 72–75.

Soydaner, D. (2020). A comparison of optimization algorithms for deep learning. *International Journal of Pattern Recognition and Artificial Intelligence, 34*(13), 2052013.

Sun, R. (2019). Optimization for deep learning: Theory and algorithms. *ArXiv Preprint ArXiv:1912.08957.*

Sun, R.-Y. (2020a). Optimization for deep learning: An overview. *Journal of the Operations Research Society of China, 8*(2), 249–294.

Sun, R.-Y. (2020b). Optimization for deep learning: An overview. *Journal of the Operations Research Society of China, 8*(2), 249–294.

Wei, Z., Arora, A., Patel, P., & John, L. (2020). Design space exploration for softmax implementations. *2020 IEEE 31st International Conference on Application-Specific Systems, Architectures and Processors (ASAP)*, 45–52.

Yu, Z., Huang, F., Zhao, X., Xiao, W., & Zhang, W. (2021). Predicting drug–disease associations through layer attention graph convolutional network. *Briefings in Bioinformatics, 22*(4), bbaa243.

Zhao, M., Zhong, S., Fu, X., Tang, B., Dong, S., & Pecht, M. (2020). Deep residual networks with adaptively parametric rectifier linear units for fault diagnosis. *IEEE Transactions on Industrial Electronics, 68*(3), 2587–2597.

Part II

Deep Learning Models with Use Case Studies

Chapter 4

Convolutional Neural Networks

4.1 Background

Convolutional neural networks (CNNs) have indeed revolutionized the field of computer vision and are widely used for various image-related tasks. "Convolutional Neural Networks", presented by LeCun & Bengio (1995), laid the foundation for CNNs and introduced their effectiveness in image recognition tasks.

CNNs are particularly well-suited for visual data due to their ability to automatically learn hierarchical representations from raw input. They leverage the concept of convolutional layers, which involve applying a set of learnable filters (kernels) to the input data. These filters capture local patterns and spatial relationships, allowing the network to identify features at different levels of abstraction.

The use of CNNs gained significant attention after the ImageNet Large Scale Visual Recognition Challenge (ILSVRC) in 2012. The winning entry, known as AlexNet, was developed by Hinton et al. (2012) and demonstrated the power of deep CNN architectures. AlexNet achieved a significant improvement in accuracy on the ImageNet dataset, showcasing the potential of CNNs in large-scale image classification tasks.

Since then, CNN-based architectures have become ubiquitous in computer vision. They have been applied to various tasks such as image classification, object detection, semantic segmentation, and image generation. The availability of large-scale labeled datasets increased computational power, and advancements in deep learning techniques have further fueled the success of CNNs in computer vision research and applications.

It's worth noting that the references mentioned here, (Deng et al., 2009) and (Hinton et al., 2012), are significant contributions in the development and application of CNNs. Deng et al. introduced the ImageNet dataset, which has become a standard benchmark for evaluating image classification algorithms. Hinton et al.'s (2012) work with AlexNet marked a breakthrough in deep learning and highlighted the potential of CNNs for image recognition tasks.

Indeed, modern CNNs have been inspired by various disciplines and have demonstrated their computational and sample efficiency in achieving accurate models. Their design has been influenced by principles from biology, group theory, and extensive experimentation.

One advantage of CNNs is their computational efficiency. Compared to fully connected architectures, CNNs typically require fewer parameters due to weight sharing and local receptive fields. This parameter efficiency makes them more practical for

DOI: 10.1201/9781003654216-6

training and inference, especially with limited computational resources. Additionally, convolutions, which are at the core of CNNs, are highly amenable to parallelization across GPU cores. This parallelization further accelerates the training and inference processes, making CNNs computationally efficient.

Due to their efficiency and effectiveness, CNNs have expanded beyond traditional computer vision tasks and have been applied to domains with sequential or one-dimensional data structures. For example, in the domain of audio processing, CNNs have shown promise in tasks such as speech recognition, music analysis, and sound classification (Abdel-Hamid et al., 2014). Similarly, in natural language processing, CNNs have been applied to text classification, sentiment analysis, and language modeling tasks (Kalchbrenner et al., 2014). This shift challenges the conventional use of recurrent neural networks (RNNs) for sequence modeling.

The success of CNNs in handling sequential data can be attributed to their ability to capture local dependencies and hierarchical features. By treating the input as a one-dimensional sequence (e.g., audio waveform or text), CNNs can learn discriminative patterns effectively. This application of CNNs to sequential data has opened new avenues for research and practical applications in domains beyond computer vision.

Moreover, researchers have extended the use of CNNs to graph-structured data and recommender systems. Graph convolutional networks (GCNs), proposed by Kipf and Welling (2016), leverage the convolutional operations on graph structures, enabling effective learning on data with complex connectivity patterns. In the field of recommender systems, CNN-based architectures have been employed to model user-item interactions and capture latent patterns for personalized recommendations.

The following are the key points to outline the structure and content of this chapter.

- *Motivation for CNNs*: The chapter will likely start by delving into the motivation behind the development of CNNs. This could include discussing the challenges faced by traditional neural networks in processing high-dimensional data like images and the need for hierarchical feature extraction.
- *Basic Operations of CNNs*: The chapter will cover the fundamental operations that form the building blocks of CNNs. This would involve a detailed explanation of convolutional layers, including concepts like filter/kernel size, padding, and stride. The pooling layers, such as max-pooling or average pooling, used to down sample the feature maps, will also be discussed.
- *Handling Multiple Channels*: CNNs operate on multi-channel input, such as RGB images. The chapter may explore how CNNs effectively handle multiple channels at each layer and learn spatially correlated features across different channels.
- *Structure of Modern Architectures*: CNN architectures have evolved significantly over time. The chapter could include a discussion on the structure and components of modern architectures, highlighting key concepts like skip connections, residual blocks, batch normalization, and activation functions commonly used in CNNs.
- *Working Example:* The chapter might conclude with a complete working example of LeNet, one of the earliest successful CNN architectures. This would provide readers with a practical understanding of how the components discussed earlier come together to build a functional CNN.

- *Next Chapter Preview:* The chapter will conclude with a brief overview or teaser of the next chapter. This could involve mentioning that the upcoming chapter will provide detailed implementations of popular and recent CNN architectures commonly used by practitioners.

Overall, this chapter provides a comprehensive introduction to CNNs, covering their motivation, core operations, handling of multiple channels, structure of modern architectures, and a practical example. It sets the stage for subsequent chapters that delve deeper into popular CNN architectures and their implementations.

4.2 From Fully Connected Layers to Convolutions

Fully connected neural networks are suitable for handling tabular data. Tabular data refers to structured data, where each row represents an example or sample, and each column corresponds to a feature or attribute.

When working with tabular data, the patterns we seek might involve interactions among the features, but we don't assume any specific structure about how these features interact. In such cases, models like fully connected neural networks, decision trees, or gradient boosting machines can be effective.

- *Fully Connected Neural Networks:* Fully connected neural networks can be used to learn complex patterns and relationships in tabular data. Each feature corresponds to an input node, and the network learns to assign weights to these nodes to capture interactions and dependencies among the features. The model's hidden layers help in capturing nonlinear relationships between the features, enabling it to discover intricate patterns in the data.
- *Decision Trees:* Decision trees are another popular choice for tabular data. They partition the feature space into regions based on simple threshold-based rules. Decision trees capture feature interactions by splitting the data into subsets at each node based on different feature values. However, decision trees might struggle to capture complex dependencies and interactions compared to neural networks.
- *Gradient Boosting Machines:* Gradient boosting machines, such as XGBoost and LightGBM, are ensemble methods that combine multiple weak learners (decision trees) to form a strong predictive model. These models can handle feature interactions effectively and are widely used in various tabular data tasks, including regression and classification problems.

The advantage of using these models for tabular data is their ability to capture intricate feature interactions without assuming any specific structure beforehand. They learn from the data and adapt to different patterns and relationships present in the tabular dataset.

For high-dimensional perceptual data, such as images with millions of dimensions, fully connected networks can become unwieldy due to the sheer number of parameters involved. This can lead to several challenges.

- *Computational Complexity:* A fully connected layer for a one-megapixel image would require 10^9 parameters with a reduction to 1,000 hidden dimensions. The large

number of parameters significantly increases the computational complexity, making training and inference computationally expensive and time-consuming, especially without sufficient computational resources.
- *Memory Requirements:* Storing and processing large parameter sets can strain the memory capacity of the hardware. GPUs, which are commonly used for deep learning, may have limitations in memory capacity, making it difficult to fit the model into the available resources.
- *Optimization Challenges:* Training a network with many parameters requires a substantial amount of labeled data, powerful hardware, and efficient optimization techniques. The optimization process becomes more challenging as the parameter space grows, potentially leading to slower convergence or getting stuck in suboptimal solutions.

To address these issues, CNNs have emerged as a powerful alternative for handling high-dimensional perceptual data like images. CNNs leverage the spatial structure of the data and exploit parameter sharing, making them computationally efficient and well-suited for visual data.

The image resolution and the number of hidden units needed to effectively learn meaningful representations. While one megapixel resolution may not be necessary, even with lower resolutions such as 100,000 pixels, the number of hidden units required to learn meaningful representations of images can still be substantial.

Images contain rich structures that can be exploited by both humans and machine learning models. CNNs are specifically designed to leverage the known structure in natural images and have proven to be highly effective in image-related tasks. Here are some key aspects of CNNs that enable them to exploit the structure in images.

- *Local Receptive Fields:* CNNs use local receptive fields to capture spatial relationships in the input. By applying convolutional filters across the image, the network can detect local patterns, such as edges, textures, or shapes. These local receptive fields enable the network to learn hierarchical representations by progressively capturing more complex features.
- *Parameter Sharing:* CNNs employ parameter sharing, where the same set of weights is used across different spatial locations. This sharing of parameters allows the network to generalize the learned features across the entire image, irrespective of their location. As a result, CNNs can effectively handle images with large dimensions while keeping the number of parameters manageable.
- *Hierarchical Feature Extraction:* CNNs typically consist of multiple convolutional layers followed by pooling layers. The convolutional layers capture low-level features, while the pooling layers aggregate information and reduce the spatial dimensions. This hierarchical feature extraction enables the network to learn increasingly abstract and high-level representations of the input images.
- *Transfer Learning:* CNNs can benefit from transfer learning, where pre-trained models on large-scale image datasets, such as ImageNet, are used as a starting point. Pre-trained CNNs have already learned rich and generalizable features from a large amount of data, and these features can be fine-tuned or utilized as a feature extractor for specific tasks with smaller datasets.

By exploiting the known structure in natural images, CNNs can effectively learn representations that capture relevant features for various image-related tasks, such as image classification, object detection, or image segmentation. Their ability to generalize from limited data, hierarchical feature extraction, and parameter sharing contribute to their success in computer vision applications.

4.2.1 *Invariance*

Object detection in images, or the idea of spatial invariance, refers to the ability of a system to recognize an object regardless of its precise location or position within the image. It highlights the inspiration drawn from the game "Where's Waldo" to illustrate this concept as presented in Figure 4.1.

Spatial invariance is desirable in object detection systems because objects can appear in various positions, orientations, and scales within an image. It would be impractical to rely on the exact location of an object for detection, as it would require the system to exhaustively search the entire image at different scales and positions.

CNNs have been widely used in object detection and segmentation tasks because they inherently incorporate the idea of spatial invariance. CNNs utilize convolutional layers that scan the entire image with small filters, looking for specific features or patterns regardless of their location. This enables the network to learn meaningful representations and features from the input data, regardless of where those features are in the image.

By learning spatially invariant features, CNNs can identify objects in images even when they are in unexpected or unusual positions, like how a "Waldo detector" in the game would assign a likelihood score to different patches of the image. This allows object detection algorithms to be robust and effective across a wide range of images and scenarios.

The desiderata mentioned provides guidelines for designing a neural network architecture suitable for computer vision tasks. Let's break down each desideratum and its implications.

- *Translation Invariance:* The network should respond similarly to the same patch, regardless of its location in the image. This means that the network's early layers should be able to detect local features and patterns regardless of their position. This property is achieved with convolutional layers that scan the entire image with small filters, extracting local features and creating feature maps that are invariant to translations.
- *Locality Principle:* The early layers of the network should focus on local regions of the image, without considering distant regions. This principle recognizes that local features are often sufficient for initial understanding and recognition tasks. By capturing local information, the network can build a foundation of low-level features that can be combined and aggregated in higher layers to make predictions at the whole image level. This principle also helps reduce the computational complexity of the network.
- *Capturing Longer-Range Features:* Deeper layers of the network should be able to capture longer-range dependencies and more complex patterns in the image. This is analogous to the higher-level vision in natural systems, where deeper visual processing areas can recognize more abstract and global features. The network achieves this by increasing its receptive field, which is the area in the input image that influences the response of a neuron. This expansion of receptive fields allows the network to learn and recognize higher-level features and semantic concepts.

Figure 4.1 An image of big group of peoples with Where's Waldo game.

4.2.2 Constraining the Multi-Layer Perceptron

In the context of computer vision, the concept of spatial structure refers to the arrangement and relationships between pixels in an image. Typically, images are represented as two-dimensional matrices or tensors, where each element represents the pixel value at a specific location.

When using a multi-layer perceptron (MLP) for image processing, we can consider the input images (X) and the corresponding hidden representations (H) to have the same spatial structure. This means that the dimensions of X and H are the same, reflecting the arrangement of pixels in the image.

By acknowledging the spatial structure, we recognize that neighboring pixels in an image often have contextual relationships and dependencies. This spatial information is crucial for understanding visual patterns and features in the image. For example, in an image of a cat, the arrangement of pixels in the cat's face provides important visual cues for recognizing it as a cat.

By treating the hidden representations in the MLP as possessing spatial structure, we allow the network to capture and utilize the spatial relationships between the input pixels and the hidden units. This enables the network to learn spatially aware features and patterns, which can improve its ability to understand and process images effectively. Considering the spatial structure in an MLP means that both the input images and hidden representations are treated as two-dimensional tensors, reflecting the spatial arrangement of pixels. This approach allows the network to leverage the spatial information present in the images, leading to more effective image processing and analysis.

A mathematical form is presented in Equations 4.1 and 4.2, in which we are considering an MLP with spatial structure. Instead of using weight matrices, we introduce fourth-order weight tensors to capture the spatial relationships between the input pixels and hidden units.

$$[H]_{i,j} = [U]_{i,j} + \sum_k \sum_l [W]_{i,j,k,l} [X]_{k,l} \tag{4.1}$$

Where:

- $[H]_{i,j}$ represents the hidden unit at position (i, j) in the hidden representation H.
- $[U]_{i,j}$ represents the bias term for the hidden unit at position (i, j).
- $[W]_{i,j,k,l}$ is the weight tensor connecting the input pixel at position (k, l) to the hidden unit at position (i, j).
- $[X]_{k,l}$ denotes the input pixel at position (k, l).

The equation shows that the hidden unit $[H]_{i,j}$ is computed as the sum of the bias term $[U]_{i,j}$ and the weighted sum of the input pixels $[X]_{k,l}$. The weight tensor $[W]_{i,j,k,l}$ captures the connections between the input pixels and hidden units.

To simplify the notation, we introduce new indices a and b to represent the relative spatial positions between the input pixels and hidden units. By replacing k with $i+a$ and l with $j+b$, we can rewrite the equation as:

$$[H]_{i,j} = [U]_{i,j} + \sum_a \sum_b [V]_{i,j,a,b} [X]_{i+a,j+b} \tag{4.2}$$

Here, $[V]_{i,j,a,b}$ represents the weight tensor $[W]_{i,j,k,l}$ in the new indices, which defines the connections between the input pixels and hidden units.

The excerpt describes a parametrization approach for the fully connected layer in a neural network architecture designed for computer vision tasks. In this approach, the weights are represented by a fourth-order weight tensor, denoted as $[W]$. To introduce spatial structure, the weights are transformed into a new tensor $[V]$ by re-indexing the subscripts.

The new tensor $[V]$ retains the same information as the original tensor $[W]$ but with a different indexing scheme. The indices (k, l) in $[W]$ are re-indexed to $(i+a, j+b)$ in $[V]$, where a and b cover positive and negative offsets, allowing the computation of the hidden representation $[H]$ at each location (i, j) by summing over the pixels in X centered around (i, j) and weighted by $[V]_{i,j,a,b}$.

However, the passage also highlights the limitations of this approach. In a hypothetical scenario where a 1000×1000 image is mapped to a 1000×1000 hidden representation, the number of parameters required would be in the order of 10^{12}. This is an enormous parameter count that exceeds the computational capabilities of current computers.

The intention of mentioning this limitation is to emphasize the impracticality of directly applying this approach in its current form. It highlights the need for more efficient techniques to handle the large number of parameters to make neural network architectures feasible for computer vision tasks.

4.2.3 *Translation Invariance*

The concept of translation invariance in the context of neural networks for computer vision states that if a shift occurs in the input image X, it should lead to a corresponding shift in the hidden representation H. To achieve this, the parameters V and U should not depend on the location (i, j) within the image.

To satisfy this principle, the passage proposes that $[V]_{i,j,a,b}$ can be simplified to $[V]_{a,b}$, and U can be represented as a constant u. With these simplifications, the definition for H becomes a convolution operation:

$$[H]_{i,j} = u + \sum_{a}\sum_{b}[V]_{a,b}[X]_{i+a,j+b} \tag{4.3}$$

This convolution operation involves weighting the pixels in the vicinity of (i, j) with coefficients $[V]_{a,b}$ to obtain the value $[H]_{i,j}$. Notably, $[V]_{a,b}$ requires significantly fewer coefficients than $[V]_{i,j,a,b}$ since it no longer depends on the location within the image.

As a result, the number of parameters required for the network reduces to a more reasonable count of 4×10^6. While still dependent on $a, b \in (-1000, 1000)$, this parameter count is much more manageable compared to the previous scenario (10^{12} parameters).

The passage also mentions that this idea has been exploited in time-delay neural networks (TDNNs), which were among the first models to incorporate this concept. TDNNs utilize convolutions to capture translation-invariant features and have been applied in various tasks, including speech recognition and computer vision.

4.2.4 Locality

The principle of locality in the context of CNNs implies that we should focus on capturing information from a local region around each location (i, j) in the hidden representation $[H]_{i,j}$. This is achieved by setting the values of $[V]_{a,b}$ to zero for $|a| > \Delta$ or $|b| > \Delta$, effectively limiting the range of the convolutional operation.

$$[H]_{i,j} = u + \sum_{a=-\Delta}^{\Delta} \sum_{b=-\Delta}^{\Delta} [V]_{a,b} [X]_{i+a,j+b} \tag{4.4}$$

By incorporating this locality principle, the number of parameters required for a single layer in an image processing network is reduced from 4 million to just $4\Delta^2$, where Δ is typically a small value, often smaller than 10. This represents another significant reduction in the number of parameters, making the model more manageable and efficient.

The resulting equation (Eq. 4) represents a convolutional layer, where $[H]_{i,j}$ is computed by convolving the input $[X]$ with the convolution kernel $[V]$ within the specified range of Δ. The convolutional layer is a key component of CNNs, which are a special type of neural network designed to handle spatially structured data such as images.

In CNNs, the convolution kernel $[V]$ is often referred to as a filter or weights, which are learnable parameters of the layer. These filters capture local patterns and features present in the input data. The reduction in the number of parameters in CNNs compared to traditional image processing networks is indeed significant. Instead of requiring billions of parameters, CNNs typically need only a few hundred while still maintaining the dimensionality of the inputs and hidden representations.

However, this reduction in parameters comes with certain trade-offs. One trade-off is that the features learned by the network become translation invariant, meaning that they can recognize patterns and objects regardless of their precise location in the image. This is desirable in many cases because objects can appear in different positions within an image, and we want our model to be able to detect them regardless of their location.

Another trade-off is that convolutional layers in CNNs can incorporate only local information when determining the value of each hidden activation. This is due to the locality principle discussed earlier. The layer focuses on capturing information from a local region around each location, which limits its ability to consider global context. However, this limitation is often beneficial because many visual patterns and structures can be effectively captured within local regions.

These biases and constraints imposed by the architecture of CNNs are examples of inductive biases. Inductive biases are assumptions or prior knowledge built into a learning algorithm, and they play a crucial role in model generalization and sample efficiency. When the inductive biases align well with the characteristics of the data, the models can generalize well to unseen examples and require fewer training samples. However, if the inductive biases do not align well with the underlying reality of the data, the models may struggle to fit the training data and generalize poorly.

To capture larger and more complex aspects of an image, deeper layers are introduced in CNNs. By interleaving nonlinearities (e.g., activation functions like ReLU) and convolutional layers repeatedly, the network can learn increasingly abstract and high-level features. The hierarchical representation allows the network to capture more sophisticated patterns and structures, leading to a deeper understanding of the image content.

The reduction in parameters in CNNs, along with the inductive biases of translation invariance and locality, enables sample-efficient models that generalize well to unseen data. By incorporating deeper layers with nonlinearities, CNNs can capture larger and more complex aspects of images, allowing for more advanced image analysis and understanding.

4.2.5 Convolutions

In mathematics formulation, the convolution operation between two functions is a way to measure the overlap or blending of the two functions. In the continuous case, the convolution of two functions f and g is defined as the integral of their product, with one function being flipped and shifted by a certain amount. This is expressed mathematically as:

$$(f \times g)(x) = \int f(z) g(x-z) dz \tag{4.5}$$

When dealing with discrete objects, such as vectors or tensors, the integral is replaced by a sum. For example, in the case of vectors with indices running over a set, the convolution becomes:

$$(f \times g)(i) = \sum_a f(a) g(i-a) \tag{4.6}$$

In the context of two-dimensional tensors, the convolution is expressed as:

$$(f \times g)(i, j) = \sum_a \sum_b f(a, b) g(i-a, j-b) \tag{4.7}$$

Equation 4.7 resembles Equation 4.4 mentioned in the previous feature, with the difference being that Equation 4.4 describes a cross-correlation rather than a convolution. The distinction is mainly cosmetic, as we can match the notation between the two equations.

In practice, the convolution operation in CNNs involves sliding a filter or kernel over the input image, computing the element-wise product at each location, and summing the results to obtain the output value. This operation captures local relationships between neighboring pixels and is a fundamental building block in convolutional layers for image processing tasks.

The concept of convolution is essential for understanding the operations performed in CNNs and their ability to capture local patterns and features in images.

4.2.6 Channels

In the context of the Waldo detector example, the convolutional layer in a CNN scans the input image using windows of a specified size. Each window represents a local region of the image. The intensities of the pixels within each window are multiplied by the corresponding values in the filter or kernel V. This operation computes the weighted sum of the pixel intensities within the window.

The purpose of this operation is to capture patterns and features that are relevant for detecting the presence of Waldo. Filter V is learned during the training process, and its values are adjusted to optimize the performance of the model for identifying Waldo.

The result of the convolution operation is a set of hidden layer representations that correspond to different locations in the input image. The values in the hidden layer representations indicate the presence or absence of certain features or patterns that are indicative of Waldo's presence. The highest values in the hidden layer representations indicate the locations where the "waldoness" is the strongest, suggesting the presence of Waldo.

By analyzing the hidden layer representations and identifying the peaks, the model can make predictions about the location of Waldo in the image presented in Figure 4.2.

Overall, the convolutional layer and the subsequent operations in the CNN enable the model to systematically scan the image, extract local features, and make predictions based on the learned patterns. This approach is particularly well-suited for computer vision tasks, where local patterns and spatial relationships play a crucial role, such as object detection and image classification.

In the image, we need to consider the fact that they are three-dimensional objects represented by third-order tensors, consisting of height, width, and channel dimensions. The channels typically represent the red, green, and blue color channels.

To accommodate this, the convolutional filter or kernel V needs to adapt accordingly. Instead of having just two indices (a, b), as in the previous discussion, we now have an additional index (c) to represent the channel dimension. The filter becomes $[V]_{a,b,c}$.

During the convolution operation, the filter is convolved with the input image tensor, considering the values from all channels. The convolution is performed independently for each channel, and the results are combined to produce the output.

This extension to three-dimensional tensors allows the convolutional layer to capture spatial patterns and features across multiple channels, enabling the model to learn more complex representations and effectively process color information in images.

By incorporating the channel dimension into the convolutional operation, CNNs can effectively handle the multidimensional nature of image data and extract meaningful features from different channels to make accurate predictions and classifications.

To capture richer and more complex information in the hidden representations, it is beneficial to formulate them as third-order tensors, like the input images. Instead of having a single hidden representation for each spatial location, we want to have a vector of hidden representations.

Conceptually, we can think of the hidden representations as a collection of two-dimensional grids stacked on top of each other, forming the third dimension of the tensor. These grids or layers are often referred to as channels or feature maps. Each channel provides a spatialized set of learned features to the subsequent layers of the network.

At lower layers of the network, which are closer to the input, different channels can become specialized in recognizing different visual patterns. For example, some channels may specialize in detecting edges, while others may focus on textures, colors, or other local features. By having multiple channels, the network can capture and learn a diverse range of visual features, enabling it to extract more meaningful and discriminative representations from the input images.

Figure 4.2 Detecting Waldo from an image.

This hierarchical organization of channels and feature maps in CNNs allows for the progressive learning of more complex visual patterns and high-level representations as we move deeper into the network. It aligns with the idea that lower layers capture low-level features, and higher layers capture more abstract and higher-level visual concepts.

To accommodate multiple channels in both the input tensor (X) and hidden representations (H), we introduce a fourth coordinate to the convolutional filter V, denoted as $[V]_{a,b,c,d}$. Equation 4.8 represents the convolutional layer for multiple channels.

$$[H]_{i,j,d} = \sum_{a=-\Delta}^{\Delta} \sum_{b=-\Delta}^{\Delta} \sum_{c} [V]_{a,b,c,d} [X]_{i+a,j+b,c} \tag{4.8}$$

In this formulation, $[H]_{i,j,d}$ represents the hidden activation at spatial location (i, j) and channel d. The value is computed by summing over the spatial dimensions $(\Delta a \, and \, \Delta b)$, the input channels (c), and weighting the input values $[X]_{i+a,j+b,c}$ with the corresponding filter coefficients $[V]_{a,b,c,d}$.

The result is a new hidden representation tensor H with the same spatial dimensions (i, j) but now with multiple channels (d). Each channel in H captures a specific aspect or feature of the input data, and the convolutional layer applies the filter kernel V to extract these features across different channels.

Subsequently, the output of this convolutional layer can serve as the input to another convolutional layer or any other layer in the neural network architecture, allowing for the hierarchical extraction of increasingly complex and abstract features.

4.3 Convolutions for Images Dataset

Let's dive into some practical implementation of convolutional layers using PyTorch. Here's an example code snippet that demonstrates how to create and apply convolutional layers in a CNN using PyTorch:

```
import torch
from torch import nn
from d2l import torch as d2l

# Define the CNN architecture
class MyCNN(nn.Module):
    def __init__(self):
        super(MyCNN, self).__init__()

        # Convolutional layers
        self.conv1 = nn.Conv2d(in_channels=3, out_channels=16,
kernel_size=3, stride=1, padding=1)
        self.conv2 = nn.Conv2d(in_channels=16, out_channels=32,
kernel_size=3, stride=1, padding=1)

        # Fully connected layers
        self.fc1 = nn.Linear(32 * 28 * 28, 128)
        self.fc2 = nn.Linear(128, 10)
```

```
    def forward(self, x):
        # Apply convolutional layers with activation function
        x = nn.ReLU()(self.conv1(x))
        x = nn.ReLU()(self.conv2(x))

        # Reshape the tensor for fully connected layers
        x = x.view(-1, 32 * 28 * 28)

        # Apply fully connected layers with activation function
        x = nn.ReLU()(self.fc1(x))
        x = self.fc2(x)

        return x

# Create an instance of the CNN
model = MyCNN()

# Generate some random image data
input_data = torch.randn(1, 3, 32, 32)

# Pass the input data through the CNN
output = model(input_data)

print(output.shape)  # Shape of the output tensor
```

In this example, we define a simple CNN architecture called **'MyCNN'** that consists of two convolutional layers (**'conv1'** and **'conv2'**) and two fully connected layers (**'fc1'** and **'fc2'**). The forward method defines the forward pass of the network, where we apply the convolutional layers, activation functions (ReLU), and fully connected layers sequentially.

We then create an instance of the **'MyCNN'** model and generate some random image data (**'input_data'**). Finally, we pass the input data through the model to obtain the output tensor and print its shape.

Note that this is a basic example to illustrate the usage of convolutional layers in a CNN. In practice, you would typically combine convolutional layers with pooling layers, use deeper architectures, and train the network on a labeled dataset using techniques like gradient descent and backpropagation.

We've used the **'torch'** module from the **'d2l'** library for this example, which provides a simplified API for deep learning with PyTorch. You can install the **'d2l'** library using **'pip install d2l'**.

4.3.1 The Cross-Correlation Operation

In the context of convolutional layers, the cross-correlation operation between a two-dimensional input tensor and a kernel tensor is used to produce an output tensor. The input tensor represents the data, while the kernel tensor contains the learnable parameters of the layer.

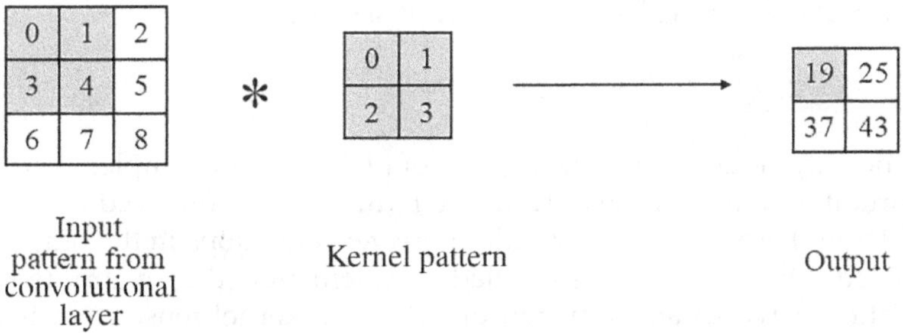

Figure 4.3 Cross-correlation procedure in two dimensions. The initial output element, as well as the input and kernel tensor components needed to compute the output, are indicated by shaded portions: $\mathbf{0 \times 0 + 1 \times 1 + 3 \times 2 + 4 \times 3 = 19}$.

Consider an example with an input tensor of shape (3, 3) and a kernel tensor of shape (2, 2). We'll perform the cross-correlation operation using a kernel window (or convolution window) defined by the height and width of the kernel.

Here's a step-by-step explanation of the process:

1. Place the kernel window on top of the input tensor, starting from the top-left corner.
2. Compute the element-wise product between the values in the kernel window and the corresponding values in the input tensor.
3. Sum the resulting products to obtain a single value.
4. Move the kernel window to the next position (e.g., right by one step), and repeat steps 2 and 3.
5. Repeat the process until the kernel window has covered the entire input tensor, producing an output tensor.

To better understand this process, we are applying the cross-correlation operation with a kernel of width and height greater than one, the output size along each axis will be slightly smaller than the input size. This is because the kernel needs to fit entirely within the input tensor for the cross-correlation to be computed properly.

The formula to calculate the output size is given by subtracting the size of the convolution kernel $(k_h \times k_w)$ from the input size $(n_h \times n_w)$.

If we denote the input size as $(n_h \times n_w)$ and the kernel size as $(k_h \times k_w)$, the output size $(o_h \times o_w)$ can be calculated as:

$$o_h = n_h - k_h + 1$$

$$o_w = n_w - k_w + 1$$

For example, let's consider an input tensor with a size of (3, 3) and a kernel size of (2, 2):

$$n_h = 3, n_w = 3, k_h = 2, k_w = 2$$

Using the formula, we can calculate the output size as:

$$o_h = 3 - 2 + 1 = 2, o_w = 3 - 2 + 1 = 2$$

Therefore, the output tensor will have a size of $(2, 2)$ in this example.

It's important to note that the output size reduction is influenced by the size of the kernel, and larger kernel sizes will result in greater reductions in the output size.

The **'corr2d'** function we provided implements the computation of 2D cross-correlation between an input tensor **'X'** and a kernel tensor **'K'**. It follows the process of sliding the kernel across the input tensor and calculating the element-wise multiplication between the corresponding sub-tensors, followed by the summation of the resulting values.

Let's go through the function step by step:

```
def corr2d(X, K):
    h, w = K.shape
    Y = torch.zeros((X.shape[0] - h + 1, X.shape[1] - w + 1))
    for i in range(Y.shape[0]):
        for j in range(Y.shape[1]):
            Y[i, j] = (X[i:i + h, j:j + w] * K).sum()
    return Y
```

1. **'h, w = K.shape'** extracts the height and width of the kernel tensor **'K'**.
2. **'Y = torch.zeros((X.shape[0] – h + 1, X.shape[1] – w + 1))'** creates an output tensor Y with the appropriate shape to store the results of the cross-correlation. The output tensor's shape is determined by subtracting the kernel size from the corresponding dimensions of the input tensor **'X'**.
3. The nested for loops iterate over the indices of the output tensor **'Y'**:

   a. **'Y[i, j] = (X[i:i + h, j:j + w] * K).sum()'** performs the cross-correlation operation at each location (i, j) in **'Y'**. It slices a sub-tensor from the input tensor **'X'** using the current indices $(i : i + h, j : j + w)$, element-wise multiplies it with the kernel tensor **'K'**, and calculates the sum of the resulting values. The result is assigned to the corresponding location in the output tensor **Y**.

4. Finally, the function returns the computed output tensor **Y**.

This implementation demonstrates the basic process of computing the cross-correlation between an input tensor and a kernel tensor. Padding is not applied in this function, so the output tensor's size will be reduced compared to the input tensor due to the kernel's size.

```
import torch
import torch.nn.functional as F

# Define the input tensor and kernel tensor
input_tensor = torch.tensor([[1, 2, 3], [4, 5, 6], [7, 8, 9]],
dtype=torch.float32)
kernel_tensor = torch.tensor([[1, 2], [3, 4]], dtype=torch.float32)

# Apply the cross-correlation operation
output_tensor = F.conv2d(input_tensor.unsqueeze(0).unsqueeze(0),
kernel_tensor.unsqueeze(0).unsqueeze(0))

print(output_tensor.squeeze())
```

Let's walk through an example using Python code:

In this example, we have an input tensor of shape (3, 3) and a kernel tensor of shape (2, 2). We use the **'F.conv2d'** function from the **'torch.nn.functional'** module to perform the cross-correlation operation. Note that we add extra dimensions to the input and kernel tensors using **'unsqueeze(0)'** to match the expected shapes.

The **'output_tensor'** will have a shape of (1, 1, 2, 2) since we have a single input channel and a single output channel. We use **'.squeeze()'** to remove the extra dimensions and print the resulting output tensor.

The output tensor represents the result of applying the kernel to the input tensor using the cross-correlation operation. Each element of the output tensor corresponds to the sum of the element-wise products between the kernel window and the corresponding window in the input tensor.

Note that this example ignores the presence of multiple channels. In practice, convolutional layers often have multiple input and output channels, and the cross-correlation operation is applied independently to each channel.

4.3.2 Convolutional Layers

In a convolutional layer, the cross-correlation operation is performed between the input tensor and the kernel tensor, and then a scalar bias is added to each element of the resulting tensor to produce the output. The parameters of a convolutional layer are the kernel and the scalar bias.

When training models are based on convolutional layers, it is a common practice to initialize the kernels randomly. Random initialization helps to break the symmetry and allows the network to learn diverse and useful features during the training process. Like fully connected layers, convolutional layers can be initialized using techniques such as random normal initialization or Xavier/Glorot initialization, depending on the specific requirements of the model and the activation function used.

Initializing the kernels randomly ensures that the convolutional layer starts with a diverse set of filters that can capture different patterns and features from the input data. As the model is trained, the kernel weights are adjusted through backpropagation to learn the most informative features for the given task.

Additionally, the scalar bias term provides the model with the flexibility to shift the activation function and capture the bias in the data. The bias term is usually initialized to zero or with a small constant value and is also learned during the training process.

Random initialization of kernels and biases, along with subsequent training, allows the convolutional layer to learn and adapt to the specific characteristics of the input data, leading to effective feature extraction and representation.

The implementation provided is a basic template for creating a custom two-dimensional convolutional layer in PyTorch. The **'Conv2D'** class inherits from the **'nn.Module'** class, which is a base class for all neural network modules in PyTorch.

```
class Conv2D(nn.Module):
  def __init__(self, kernel_size):
    super().__init__()
    self.weight = nn.Parameter(torch.rand(kernel_size))
    self.bias = nn.Parameter(torch.zeros(1))

def forward(self, x):
  return corr2d(x, self.weight) + self.bias
```

In the **'__init__'** method, the constructor defines the parameters of the convolutional layer. The **'kernel_size'** argument specifies the size of the kernel (filter). Inside the constructor, initialize the **'weight'** parameter as a trainable parameter using **'nn.Parameter(torch.rand(kernel_size))'**. This creates a randomly initialized tensor of the specified **'kernel_size'** and makes it a parameter of the model. Similarly, initialize the **'bias'** parameter as a trainable parameter using **'nn.Parameter(torch.zeros(1))'**. Here, it is initialized with zeros.

The **'forward'** method implements the forward propagation logic of the convolutional layer. It takes an input tensor **'x'** as input and applies the **'corr2d'** function defined earlier to perform the cross-correlation between the input tensor **'x'** and the **'weight'** tensor of the convolutional layer. It then adds the **'bias'** term to the resulting tensor and returns the output.

By defining a custom **'Conv2D'** class in this way, you can create instances of the class and use them as building blocks to construct your convolutional neural network architectures. The weights and biases of the **'Conv2D'** layer will be updated during the training process through backpropagation.

Note that in this implementation, we assume that the **'corr2d'** function is already defined separately, as we mentioned earlier. In the context of convolutional layers, when we say **'h × w convolution'** or **'h × w convolutional layer',** we are referring to a convolution operation with a kernel (filter) of height h and width w. The terms **'h × w convolution'** and **'h × w convolutional layer'** are used interchangeably to describe the spatial dimensions of the kernel.

For example, a 3 × 3 convolution refers to a convolution operation with a kernel size of 3 × 3, where the kernel is slid across the input image in a sliding window manner, performing the cross-correlation operation at each spatial location. This helps capture spatial patterns and extract local features from the input.

The height and width of the convolution kernel determine the receptive field, or the size of the local neighborhood, that the convolutional layer considers at each spatial location. A larger kernel size can capture larger patterns and more global information, while a smaller kernel size focuses on smaller details and local structures.

So when you encounter the terms **'h × w convolution'** or **'h × w convolutional layer'**, you can interpret them as referring to the dimensions of the convolutional kernel used in the layer.

4.3.3 *Edge Detection of Objects in Images*

To detect the edge of an object in an image by finding the location of the pixel change, let's construct an "image" of size 6 × 8 pixels. In this image, the middle four columns will be black (0), and the remaining columns will be white (1). Here's the representation of the image:

```
X = torch.ones((6, 8))
X[:, 2:6] = 0
X
```

```
tensor([[1., 1., 0., 0., 0., 0., 1., 1.],
        [1., 1., 0., 0., 0., 0., 1., 1.],
        [1., 1., 0., 0., 0., 0., 1., 1.],
        [1., 1., 0., 0., 0., 0., 1., 1.],
        [1., 0., 0., 0., 0., 0., 1., 1.],
        [1., 0., 0., 0., 0., 0., 1., 1.]])
```

In this tensor, the edge is formed by the transition from white (1) to black (0) pixels in the middle columns.

Note that this kernel is an example of a specific finite difference operator. It calculates the difference between the values of horizontally adjacent pixels at position (i, j), or $x_{i,j} - x_{(i+1),j}$. This approximates the first derivative in the horizontal direction discretely. After all, the derivative of a function $f(i, j)$ is given by if

$$-\partial_i f(i,j) = lim_{\epsilon \to 0} \frac{f(i,j) - f(i+\epsilon, j)}{\epsilon}$$

```
K = torch.tensor([[1, -1]])
```

To construct the kernel **K** with a height of 1 and a width of 2, we can define it as follows:

Kernel **'K'** represents a finite difference operator that computes the difference between horizontally adjacent elements. When performing the cross-correlation operation with the input tensor **'X'**, if the horizontally adjacent elements are the same, the output will be 0. Otherwise, the output will be non-zero.

To see how this works in practice, we can apply the **'Conv2D'** layer with the kernel **'K'** to the input tensor **'X'**. Here's an example:

```
conv_layer = Conv2D(kernel_size=(1, 2))
output = conv_layer(X)
print(output)
```

The **'output'** tensor will contain the result of the cross-correlation operation between **'X'** and **'K'**, which represents the discrete approximation of the first derivative in the horizontal direction. The non-zero values in the output indicate the locations of pixel changes or edges in the input image.

To perform the cross-correlation operation between the input tensor **'X'** and the kernel **'K'**, we can use the **'corr2d'** function defined earlier. Here's how you can compute the cross-correlation and observe the edge detection results:

```
edge_detection = corr2d(X, K)
print(edge_detection)
```

```
tensor([[ 0., 1., 0., 0., 0., -1., 0.],
   [ 0., 1., 0., 0., 0., -1., 0.],
   [ 0., 1., 0., 0., 0., -1., 0.],
   [ 0., 1., 0., 0., 0., -1., 0.],
   [ 0., 1., 0., 0., 0., -1., 0.],
   [ 0., 1., 0., 0., 0., -1., 0.]])
```

The **'edge_detection'** tensor will contain the result of the cross-correlation operation, where a value of **'1'** indicates the edge from white to black, **'-1'** indicates the edge from black to white, and **'0'** indicates no edge. The output reflects the detection of pixel changes or edges in the input image.

To apply the kernel **'K'** to the transposed image **'X_transposed'**, you can simply use the **'corr2d'** function:

```
X_transposed = X.T # Transpose the image
edge_detection_transposed = corr2d(X_transposed, K)
print(edge_detection_transposed)
```

```
tensor([[0., 0., 0., 0., 0.],
[0., 0., 0., 0., 0.],
[0., 0., 0., 0., 0.],
[0., 0., 0., 0., 0.],
[0., 0., 0., 0., 0.],
[0., 0., 0., 0., 0.],
[0., 0., 0., 0., 0.],
[0., 0., 0., 0., 0.]])
```

Since the kernel **'K'** detects vertical edges, when applied to the transposed image, which represents the original image rotated 90 degrees, it would detect horizontal edges instead. As a result, the output **'edge_detection_transposed'** will contain **'1'** for horizontal edges and **'-1'** for the opposite direction, while all other values will be **'0'**.

4.3.4 Learning a Kernel

Manually designing filters for each specific task can become impractical as the complexity of the problem increases. That's where the power of deep learning comes in. Instead of handcrafting filters, we can train CNNs to automatically learn the filters that are best suited for the given task.

In CNN, the filters are not designed manually but are learned from data during the training process. The network learns to optimize the filters to extract relevant features from the input data, such as edges, textures, or more complex patterns, based on the provided training examples.

By stacking multiple convolutional layers and combining them with other types of layers (e.g., pooling, activation), CNNs can learn hierarchical representations of the input data, capturing both low-level and high-level features. This allows them to automatically discover and extract meaningful features without explicit manual specification.

To learn the kernel that generated the output tensor Y from the input tensor X, we can use gradient-based optimization techniques. Here's an example of how we can accomplish this using a convolutional layer and the squared error loss:

```
import torch
from torch import nn
from torch.optim import SGD

# Define the input tensor X and the output tensor Y
X = torch.ones((6, 8), requires_grad=True)
X[:, 2:6] = 0
Y = torch.tensor([[1.0, -1.0, 0.0, 0.0],
                  [1.0, -1.0, 0.0, 0.0],
                  [1.0, -1.0, 0.0, 0.0],
                  [1.0, -1.0, 0.0, 0.0]])
```

```
# Define the convolutional layer
conv_layer = nn.Conv2d(1, 1, kernel_size=2, bias=False)

# Define the loss function
loss_fn = nn.MSELoss()

# Define the optimizer
optimizer = SGD(conv_layer.parameters(), lr=0.1)

# Training loop
for epoch in range(10):
    # Forward pass: compute the predicted output
    pred = conv_layer(X.unsqueeze(0).unsqueeze(0))

    # Compute the loss
    loss = loss_fn(pred.squeeze(), Y)

    # Backward pass: compute gradients
    optimizer.zero_grad()
    loss.backward()

    # Update the kernel weights
    optimizer.step()

    # Print the loss for monitoring
    print(f"Epoch {epoch+1}, Loss: {loss.item()}")

# Get the learned kernel
learned_kernel = conv_layer.weight.data.squeeze()

print("Learned Kernel:")
print(learned_kernel)
```

In this example, we use the **'nn.Conv2d'** class from PyTorch, which provides a built-in implementation of a 2D convolutional layer. We initialize the layer with a random kernel tensor. We then define the loss function as the mean squared error (MSE) loss.

During the training loop, we compute the forward pass to get the predicted output from the convolutional layer. We calculate the loss by comparing the predicted output with the target output (Y). Then, we perform the backward pass to compute the gradients and update the kernel weights using the optimizer (in this case, stochastic gradient descent – SGD).

After training, we can access the learned kernel from the convolutional layer ('**conv_layer.weight.data.squeeze()**') and examine its values.

Note that in this simplified example, we ignore the bias term for simplicity. In practice, a bias term can also be learned along with the kernel weights. Additionally, you can adjust the number of training epochs, learning rate, and other hyperparameters to improve the training performance.

4.3.5 *Cross-Correlation and Convolution*

In the context of deep learning, the terms "convolution" and "cross-correlation" are often used interchangeably, even though they are slightly different mathematically. The main difference between them is the flipping of the kernel in the strict convolution operation.

In deep learning frameworks like PyTorch, the convolutional layers typically perform the cross-correlation operation rather than the strict convolution operation. This means that the kernel weights are not flipped before performing the operation with the input tensor. However, during the learning process, the network automatically adjusts the kernel weights to achieve the desired behavior, regardless of whether it is a strict convolution or a cross-correlation.

To be consistent with the terminology used in deep learning literature, the term "convolution" is still widely used to refer to the cross-correlation operation. This convention has been established over time and is generally accepted in the field.

Regarding the terminology, the term "element" is commonly used to refer to an individual entry or component of a tensor representing a layer representation or a convolution kernel. It is a standard term used to describe the individual values within a tensor.

So, in summary, although there is a mathematical distinction between strict convolution and cross-correlation, in the context of deep learning, the term "convolution" is often used to refer to the cross-correlation operation, and the term "element" is used to describe the individual values within tensors.

4.3.6 *Feature Map and Receptive Field*

In CNNs, the output of a convolutional layer is often referred to as a feature map. This is because each element in the output can be seen as a learned representation or feature in the spatial dimensions (e.g., width and height) that is passed on to the subsequent layer. The feature map captures patterns and structures in the input data.

The concept of receptive field is also important in understanding CNNs. The receptive field of an element in a feature map refers to all the elements from the previous layers that can influence the calculation of that element during forward propagation. In other words, it represents the region in the input space that affects the value of a given element in the feature map.

In the example of Figure 4.3, with a 2 × 2 convolutional kernel, the receptive field of a shaded output element is the corresponding 2 × 2 region in the input. This means that the value of the shaded output element is influenced by the four elements in its receptive field.

When we consider a deeper CNN with an additional 2 × 2 convolutional layer that takes the output feature map (Y) as input and produces a single element (z), the receptive field of z on Y includes all four elements of Y. However, the receptive field of z on the original input includes all nine input elements. This shows that deeper networks can capture larger receptive fields, allowing them to detect features over a broader area of the input.

The concept of receptive fields in CNNs is inspired by neurophysiology studies, particularly the work of Hubel and Wiesel in the 1950s and 1960s. They conducted experiments on the visual cortex of animals and discovered that lower-level neurons respond

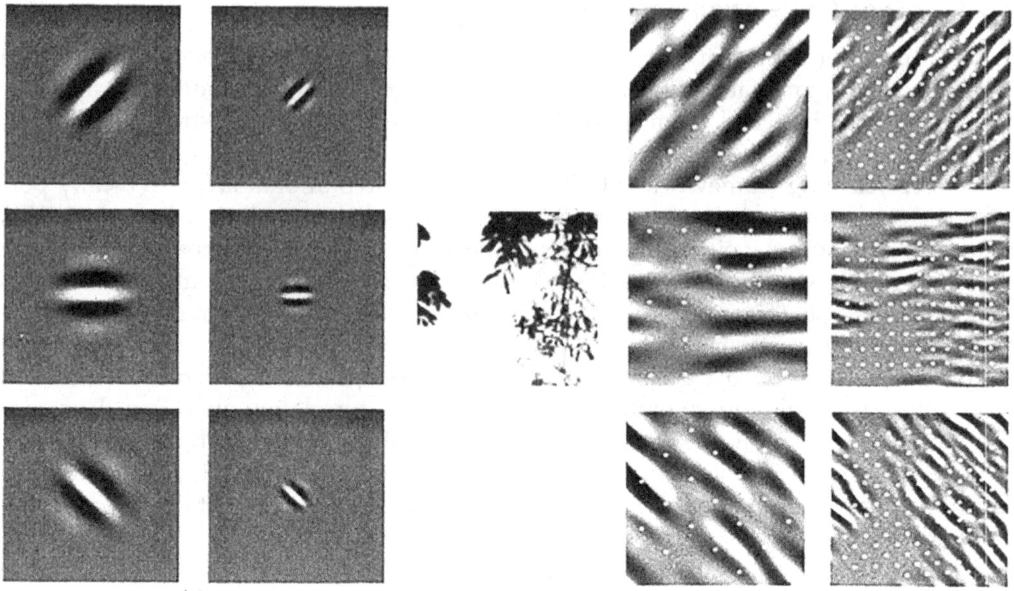

Figure 4.4 Figure and caption adapted from Field (1987): A six-channel coding example. (Left) Illustrations of the six different types of sensors connected to each channel. (Right) Convolution of the middle picture using the leftmost six sensors. By sampling these filtered pictures from a distance proportionate to the size of the sensor (shown by dots), one may gauge the response of each individual sensor. Only the even symmetric sensors' response is depicted in this diagram.

to edges and simple shapes. This finding aligns with the idea that lower layers in CNNs learn to detect basic features. The work of Field in 1987 further illustrated this effect using convolutional kernels and natural images. Figure 4.4 shows the striking similarities between the receptive fields in the visual cortex and those learned by CNNs.

The reference to Kuzovkin et al. (2018) suggests that even in deeper layers of CNNs trained on image classification tasks, the learned features exhibit similar receptive field properties, indicating the effectiveness and universality of convolutional operations in capturing relevant information from images.

Convolutions have emerged as a powerful tool in computer vision, providing a mechanism to extract hierarchical and spatially local features from image data. Their success in deep learning highlights the significance of incorporating prior knowledge from biology into computational models and underscores the value of convolutional operations in the field of computer vision.

4.4 Padding and Stride

Let's recall the convolution example in Figure 4.3, the input had a height and width of 3, the convolution kernel had a height and width of 2, and the result was an output representation with a dimension of 2×2.

The formula for calculating the output shape of a convolutional layer is $(n_h - k_h + 1) \times (n_w - k_w + 1)$, where n_h and n_w are the height and width of the input, and k_h k_w are the height and width of the convolution kernel.

This formula holds true when the convolution kernel can fully fit within the input without running out of pixels to apply the convolution. It represents the spatial dimensions of the output feature map produced by the convolutional layer.

Indeed, when applying multiple convolutions with kernels larger than $1x1$, the spatial dimensions of the output tend to decrease. This reduction in size can lead to the loss of information, especially at the boundaries of the original image.

To address this issue, padding is commonly used. Padding involves adding extra pixels around the boundary of the input image before applying the convolution operation. This padding can be of different types, such as zero-padding or reflection padding, and it helps to preserve the spatial dimensions of the output feature map.

For example, if we use zero-padding, we add zeros around the input image. By appropriately padding the input, we can ensure that the output has the same spatial dimensions as the input, even after applying convolutions. This allows us to retain important information at the boundaries.

On the other hand, there may be cases where we intentionally want to reduce the spatial dimensions of the output, either to decrease the computational complexity or to downsample the input. Strided convolutions can be used in such cases. A strided convolution involves applying the convolution operation with a larger stride value, which determines the amount of pixel shift between each application of the convolution kernel. By increasing the stride, we can effectively reduce the spatial dimensions of the output feature map.

Both padding and strided convolutions provide flexibility in controlling the size of the output and can be useful techniques in different scenarios, depending on the requirements of the specific task at hand.

4.4.1 Padding

When applying convolutional layers, particularly with larger kernel sizes, we tend to lose information from the pixels on the perimeter of the image. This issue is commonly referred to as the "border effect" or "boundary distortion".

Figure 4.5 illustrates the pixel utilization as a function of the convolution kernel size and position within the image. It shows that the pixels in the corners are less utilized compared to the pixels in the center of the image. This is because when applying a convolution operation, the kernel is centered around each pixel, and for pixels on the perimeter, the kernel extends beyond the image boundaries. As a result, these pixels have fewer neighboring pixels to interact with, leading to a reduced impact on the output.

To mitigate the border effect and preserve information from the perimeter pixels, padding is commonly used. Padding involves adding extra pixels (usually with zero values) around the image boundaries before applying the convolution operation. By padding the image, we ensure that the convolution kernel can be fully applied to all pixels, including those on the perimeter. This helps to maintain the spatial dimensions of the input and output, as well as retain information from the boundary regions.

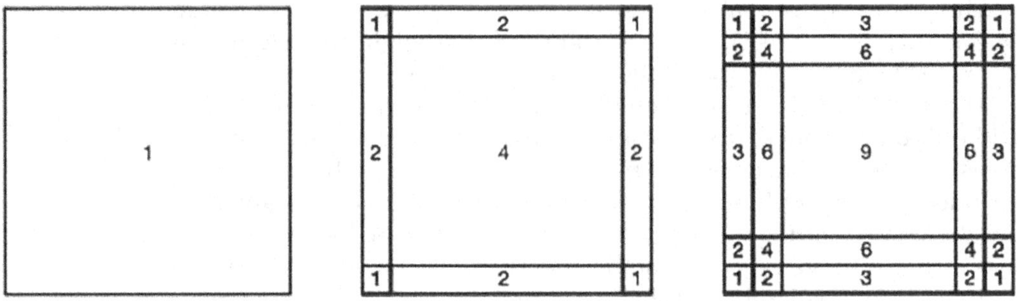

Figure 4.5 For convolutions of sizes 1 × 1, 2 × 2, and 3 × 3, respectively, pixel usage.

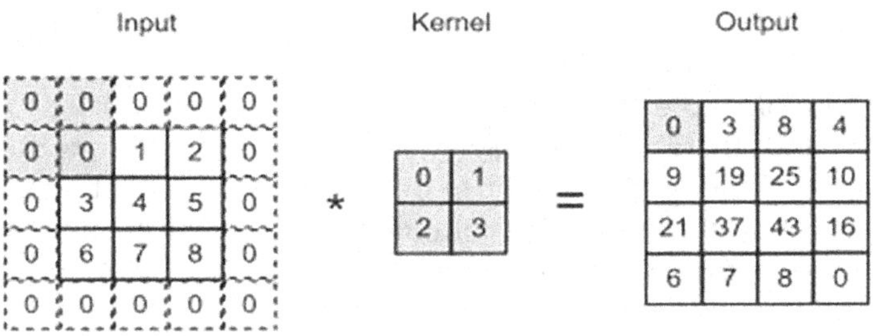

Figure 4.6 Cross-correlation in two dimensions with padding.

There are different padding strategies available, such as zero-padding, reflection padding, and replication padding. Zero-padding, where extra pixels with zero values are added, is the most used padding technique. The amount of padding added on each side of the image is determined by the size of the convolution kernel.

By properly applying padding, we can alleviate the border effect and ensure that important information from the perimeter pixels is preserved during the convolutional operation.

To address the issue of losing pixels on the perimeter of the input image, one common solution is to add extra pixels, known as padding, around the boundary of the image. By adding filler pixels with zero values, we effectively increase the size of the input image, allowing the convolutional operation to be applied to the original pixels without losing information.

In Figure 4.6, a 3 × 3 input image is padded, resulting in a larger 5 × 5 image. The corresponding output size then increases to a 4 × 4 matrix. The shaded portions in the figure represent the first output element, as well as the input and kernel tensor elements used for its computation. The values of the added padding pixels are set to zero.

By applying padding, we ensure that the convolutional kernel can be centered on each pixel, including those on the perimeter, and perform the convolution operation properly. This helps to maintain the spatial dimensions of the input and output, and it prevents the loss of important information from the boundary regions.

Padding is a common technique used in CNNs to preserve spatial information and prevent boundary distortions. It allows us to apply multiple convolutional layers without excessively reducing the size of the image and losing valuable details.

When we add padding to an input image before applying a convolutional operation, it affects the size of the output. The general formula to calculate the output shape after padding is:

$$Output\ height = \left\lfloor \frac{H + 2p_h - K_h}{S_h} \right\rfloor + 1, \text{ and}$$

$$Output\ width = \left\lfloor \frac{W + 2p_w - K_w}{S_w} \right\rfloor + 1$$

Here, p_h represents the number of rows of padding (top and bottom) added to the input image, and p_w represents the number of columns of padding (left and right) added to the input image. By adding padding, we effectively increase the height and width of the input image by p_h and p_w, respectively.

This formula helps us determine the output shape when padding is applied, allowing us to control the size of the output and preserve the spatial dimensions of the input. Padding can be adjusted based on the specific requirements of the task and the convolutional network architecture.

Setting $p_h = k_h - 1$ and $p_w = k_w - 1$ is a common practice to ensure that the input and output have the same height and width after the convolution operation. This makes it easier to predict the output shape of each layer and maintain consistency throughout the network.

If k_h is odd, we can pad $p_h / 2$ rows on both sides of the height. This ensures that the padding is symmetric around the input. For example, if $p_h = 3$, we would pad 1 row on the top and 1 row on the bottom.

If k_h is even, we need to make a choice on how to distribute the padding rows. One possibility is to pad $\lceil p_h / 2 \rceil$ rows on the top and $\lfloor p_h / 2 \rfloor$ rows on the bottom, ensuring that the total number of padded rows is equal to p_h. This maintains a balanced padding around the input.

Similarly, we apply the same padding strategy to the width by adding $p_w / 2$ columns on both sides. If p_w is odd, we pad $\lceil p_w / 2 \rceil$ columns on the left and $\lfloor p_w / 2 \rfloor$ columns on the right. If p_w is even, we can pad $\lceil p_w / 2 \rceil$ columns on the left and $\lfloor p_w / 2 \rfloor$ columns on the right.

Indeed, using odd kernel sizes in CNNs, along with symmetric padding, has several advantages. One of the main benefits is that it allows us to preserve the dimensionality of the input while applying padding symmetrically.

By using odd kernel sizes, such as $1, 3, 5, or\ 7$, we can ensure that the padding is balanced on all sides of the input. This means that the number of padding rows on the top and bottom, as well as the number of padding columns on the left and right, will be the same.

Preserving dimensionality in this way offers a clerical benefit because it simplifies the understanding of how each output element is calculated. When the kernel size is odd and the padding is symmetric, the output $Y[i, j]$ is computed by performing the cross-correlation between the input and the convolution kernel with the window centered on $X[i, j]$.

This symmetry in padding and odd kernel sizes helps maintain intuitive and consistent calculations within the convolutional layer, making it easier to reason about the spatial relationships between input and output elements.

To illustrate the example, let's create the two-dimensional convolutional layer and apply 1 pixel of padding on all sides:

```
import torch
import torch.nn as nn

# Create the convolutional layer with kernel size of 3 and
padding of 1
conv2d = nn.Conv2d(in_channels=1, out_channels=1, kernel_size=3,
padding=1)

# Create the input tensor with height and width of 8
X = torch.rand(size=(1, 1, 8, 8))

# Apply the convolutional layer to the input
Y = conv2d(X)

# Get the height and width of the output tensor
output_height = Y.size(2)
output_width = Y.size(3)

print("Output height:", output_height)  # Output height: 8
print("Output width:", output_width)    # Output width: 8
```

In this example, we create a two-dimensional convolutional layer with a kernel size of 3 and apply 1 pixel of padding on all sides. We then create an input tensor with a height and width of 8. After applying the convolutional layer, we obtain an output tensor with the same height and width of 8.

4.4.2 Stride

When performing the cross-correlation operation in a convolutional layer, we typically start with the convolution window (also known as the receptive field or kernel) positioned at the upper-left corner of the input tensor. We then slide this window over all locations in the input, moving it both down and to the right.

By default, we slide the window one element at a time, considering each location in the input tensor. However, there are cases where we may choose to move the window more than one element at a time, skipping intermediate locations. This can be done for two main reasons.

1. *Computational Efficiency:* Moving the window more than one element at a time reduces the number of computations required during the convolution operation. If the input tensor is large or the convolution kernel is large, sliding the window one element at a time can be computationally expensive. By skipping intermediate locations, we can reduce the computational cost and speed up the convolution operation.
2. *Downsampling:* Moving the window more than one element at a time can also be used for downsampling. By skipping intermediate locations, we effectively reduce the spatial resolution of the output. This downsampling operation can help in reducing the spatial dimensions of the feature maps while capturing larger patterns or preserving important information in the input.

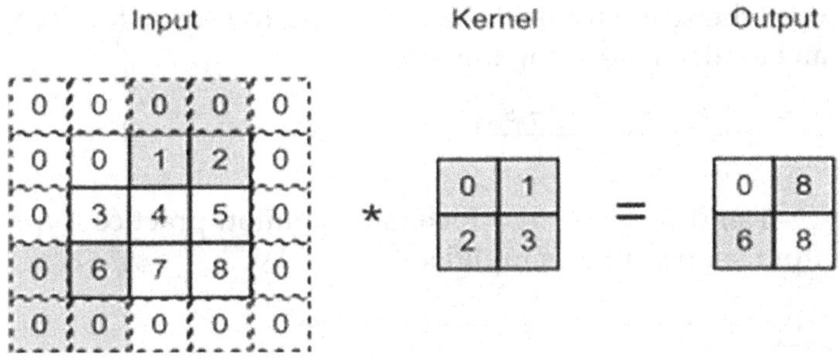

Figure 4.7 Cross-correlation using 3 and 2 strides, respectively, for height and width.

Strided convolutions are commonly used to achieve this effect. A strided convolution involves moving the convolution window by a stride value greater than one, effectively skipping intermediate locations. This allows us to capture larger areas of the input with a single operation, reducing computation and potentially downsampling the output.

Pooling layers, such as max-pooling or average pooling, can also be used for downsampling by aggregating information within a window and moving it with a certain stride.

Both strided convolutions and pooling layers offer ways to move the convolution window more than one element at a time, providing computational efficiency and downsampling capabilities in CNNs and other convolution-based models.

The stride refers to the number of rows and columns traversed per slide when performing the cross-correlation operation in a convolutional layer. In previous examples, we used a stride of 1 for both the height and width, meaning that the convolution window moved one element at a time in both directions.

However, there are cases where we may want to use a larger stride, which means that the convolution window skips intermediate locations when sliding over the input. In Figure 4.7, an example of a two-dimensional cross-correlation operation is shown with a stride of 3 vertically and 2 horizontally.

In this example, the shaded portions represent the output elements as well as the input and kernel tensor elements used for the output computation. The values in each shaded portion are calculated by performing element-wise multiplication between the input tensor and the convolution kernel and then summing the results.

When using a stride of 3 vertically and 2 horizontally, we can observe that the convolution window slides down three rows when generating the second element of the first column. Similarly, the convolution window slides two columns to the right when generating the second element of the first row.

It's important to note that as the convolution window continues to slide two columns to the right on the input, there is no output generated because the input element cannot fill the window. To overcome this and maintain the output size, additional padding can be added to the input tensor.

Using larger strides can be beneficial in certain scenarios. It reduces the number of computations required and can help in downsampling the output, effectively reducing the spatial resolution of the feature maps. Strided convolutions are commonly used in practice to achieve these effects in convolutional neural networks.

In general, when the stride for the height is s_h and the stride for the width is s_w, the output shape can be calculated using the formula:

$$\left\lfloor \frac{n_h - k_h + p_h + s_h}{s_h} \right\rfloor \times \left\lfloor \frac{n_w - k_w + p_w + s_w}{s_w} \right\rfloor$$

If we set $p_h = k_h - 1$ and $p_w = k_w - 1$, which is a common practice to preserve dimensionality, the output shape can be simplified to:

$$\left\lfloor \frac{n_h + s_h - 1}{s_h} \right\rfloor \times \left\lfloor \frac{n_w + s_w - 1}{s_w} \right\rfloor$$

Furthermore, if both the input height n_h and width n_w are divisible by the strides s_h and s_w respectively, then the output shape can be further simplified to:

$$\left(\frac{n_h}{s_h} \right) \times \left(\frac{n_w}{s_w} \right)$$

This simplification holds because when both the input dimensions and the strides are divisible, there will be no fractional parts in the division, resulting in a clean integer value for the output shape. This property can be useful for designing and predicting the output shape of convolutional layers in a neural network architecture.

To halve the input height and width, you can set the strides on both the height and width to 2. Here's an example using PyTorch to demonstrate this:

```
import torch
from torch import nn

# Define the convolutional layer with stride 2
conv2d = nn.Conv2d(in_channels=1, out_channels=1, kernel_size=3,
stride=2)
# Input tensor with height and width of 8
X = torch.rand(size=(1, 1, 8, 8))
# Apply the convolutional layer
Y = conv2d(X)

# Check the output shape
print(Y.shape)
```

The output shape will be (1, 1, 4, 4), indicating that the height and width have been halved due to the stride of 2 in both dimensions.

4.5 Multiple Input and Multiple Output Channels

In previous examples, we simplified the discussion by considering a single input channel and a single output channel. This allowed us to treat inputs, convolution kernels, and outputs as two-dimensional tensors. However, in practice, images and convolutional layers often have multiple channels.

For example, in color images, each pixel is represented by three values (red, green, and blue) in separate channels. In this case, the input would be a three-dimensional tensor with dimensions (height, width, channels). Similarly, convolutional layers can have multiple input channels and multiple output channels.

When working with multiple channels, the convolution operation is extended to operate on each channel independently and then summing the results. The convolutional kernel is also a three-dimensional tensor, with dimensions (kernel_height, kernel_width, input_channels, output_channels). The convolution operation is performed between the input tensor and the kernel tensor across all input and output channels.

This extension to multiple channels allows convolutional layers to learn different features and patterns across different channels, enabling them to capture more complex information in images or other multidimensional data.

Additionally, let's introduce multiple channels into the inputs and hidden representations, and the tensors become three-dimensional. In the case of RGB images, each input image has a shape of $3 \times h \times w$, where 3 represents the three color channels (red, green, and blue), and h and w represent the height and width of the image, respectively. The channel dimension refers to the axis that has a size of 3 in this example.

The concept of channels has been integral to CNNs since their inception. Models like LeNet5, introduced by (LeCun & Bengio, 1995), make use of multiple channels. In this section, we will delve deeper into convolution kernels that have multiple input and output channels.

With multiple input channels, the convolution operation is applied independently to each input channel using corresponding kernel tensors. The results are then summed across all input channels to produce a single output channel. This process allows the convolutional layer to learn different features and patterns from each input channel.

Similarly, in the case of multiple output channels, each output channel has its own set of kernel tensors. The convolution operation is performed between the input tensor and the corresponding set of kernel tensors, resulting in multiple output channels. This allows the convolutional layer to extract multiple features simultaneously, increasing the expressive power of the network.

By using multiple input and output channels, convolutional layers can effectively process and extract information from multidimensional data, such as images, with greater complexity and representation capacity.

4.5.1 Multiple Input Channels

When the input data contains multiple channels, it is necessary to construct a convolution kernel with the same number of input channels as the input data. The number of input channels in the convolution kernel needs to match the number of channels in the input data.

If the number of channels in the input data is c_i, then the convolution kernel should also have c_i input channels. In the case of a single input channel $(c_i = 1)$, we can consider the convolution kernel as a two-dimensional tensor of shape $k_h \times k_w$, where k_h represents the kernel height, and k_w represents the kernel width.

In this scenario, each input channel of the convolution kernel performs cross-correlation with its corresponding input channel in the input data. The results are then summed across all input channels to produce a single output channel. The convolution operation is performed independently for each output channel.

By constructing the convolution kernel with the same number of input channels as the input data, we ensure that the convolution operation can capture and process information from each input channel effectively, enabling the extraction of meaningful features and patterns from multi-channel input data.

When the number of input channels, c_i, is greater than 1, the convolution kernel needs to have a tensor of shape $k_h \times k_w$ for each input channel. These tensors are concatenated along the channel dimension to form a convolution kernel of shape $c_i \times k_h \times k_w$.

During the convolution operation, the two-dimensional tensor of the input and the two-dimensional tensor of the convolution kernel are cross-correlated for each channel independently. This means that the cross-correlation is performed between the input tensor and the kernel tensor separately for each channel. The result of the cross-correlation operation for each channel is a two-dimensional tensor.

Finally, the results from all the channels are added together (summed over the channels) to yield a two-dimensional tensor as the output of the convolution operation. This process represents the two-dimensional cross-correlation between a multi-channel input and a multi-input-channel convolution kernel. It allows the convolution operation to capture and combine information from multiple input channels, resulting in a richer representation and feature extraction capability.

Figure 4.8 illustrates a two-dimensional cross-correlation example with two input channels. The shaded portions indicate the input and kernel tensor elements used to compute the first output element. Let's consider the specific calculation.

For the first input channel:

- The input elements are 1, 2, 4, and 5.
- The kernel elements corresponding to these input elements are 1, 2, 3, and 4.
- The cross-correlation computation for this input channel is: $1 \times 1 + 2 \times 2 + 4 \times 3 + 5 \times 4 = 37$.

For the second input channel:

- The input elements are 0, 1, 3, and 4.
- The kernel elements corresponding to these input elements are 0, 1, 2, and 3.

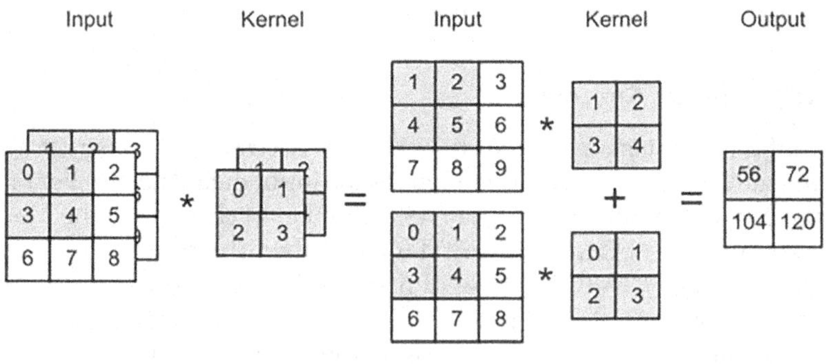

Figure 4.8 Calculation of cross-correlation using two input channels.

- The cross-correlation computation for this input channel is: $0 \times 0 + 1 \times 1 + 3 \times 2 + 4 \times 3 = 19$.
- The final output value is obtained by summing the results from both input channels: $37 + 19 = 56$.

Let's implement the cross-correlation operation with multiple input channels using PyTorch. We'll assume the input tensor has shape **'(batch_size, input_channels, height, width)'**, and the kernel tensor has shape **'(output_channels, input_channels, kernel_height, kernel_width)'**.

```
import torch
from torch import nn

def cross_correlation(input, kernel):
    batch_size, input_channels, input_height, input_width = 
input.shape
    output_channels, _, kernel_height, kernel_width = kernel.
shape

    output_height = input_height - kernel_height + 1
    output_width = input_width - kernel_width + 1

    # Reshape input and kernel tensors for cross-correlation 
computation
    input_reshaped = input.view(batch_size, 1, input_channels, 
input_height, input_width)
    kernel_reshaped = kernel.view(1, output_channels, input_
channels, kernel_height, kernel_width)

    # Perform cross-correlation per channel
    output = torch.sum(input_reshaped * kernel_reshaped, dim=2)

    # Reshape output tensor to match output shape
    output = output.view(batch_size, output_channels, output_
height, output_width)

    return output
```

We can now use this **'cross_correlation'** function to perform cross-correlation operations with multiple input channels.

Let's construct the input tensor **'X'** and the kernel tensor **'K'** corresponding to the values in Figure 4.8 and validate the output of the cross-correlation operation.

```
import torch

# Construct the input tensor X
X = torch.tensor([
    [[1, 2, 3, 4], [0, 1, 2, 3]],
    [[5, 6, 7, 8], [4, 5, 6, 7]]
]).unsqueeze(0)  # Add batch dimension

# Construct the kernel tensor K
K = torch.tensor([
    [[1, 2], [4, 5]],
    [[0, 1], [3, 4]]
])

# Compute the cross-correlation manually per channel
output_manual = (X[:, 0, :, :] * K[0, :, :]).sum() + (X[:, 1, :,
:] * K[1, :, :]).sum()

# Compute the cross-correlation using the cross_correlation_
multi_channel function
output_func = cross_correlation_multi_channel(X, K)

# Compare the outputs
print("Manual computation:", output_manual)
print("Function computation:", output_func)
```

This code will validate the output of the cross-correlation operation. The manual computation calculates the cross-correlation per channel and adds up the results, while the function computation uses the **'cross_correlation_multi_channel'** function we defined earlier. The outputs of both computations are printed and should match.

We can see that both the manual computation and the function computation yield the same result, which corresponds to the output value of 56 as shown in Figure 4.8.

4.5.2 *Multiple Output Channels*

In popular neural network architectures, it is common to increase the channel dimension as we go deeper into the network. This allows the network to learn and capture more complex and abstract features. Instead of mapping a single channel to a specific feature, such as an edge detector, the channels are optimized to be jointly useful and capture different aspects of the input data.

The representations learned in each channel are not independent per pixel or per channel, but rather they work together to extract meaningful features. For example, while one channel might capture edges in one direction, another channel might capture edges in a different direction. By combining these channels, the network can effectively detect and represent a wide range of features.

This joint optimization of channels allows deep neural networks to learn hierarchical representations, where lower-level channels capture simple features, and higher-level channels capture more complex and abstract features. Hierarchical representation learning is one of the key factors contributing to the success of deep learning in various domains.

To obtain an output with multiple channels, we need to create a separate kernel tensor for each output channel. Each kernel tensor has a shape of $c_i \times k_h \times k_w$, where c_i is the number of input channels, and k_h k_w are the height and width of the kernel, respectively. These kernel tensors are then concatenated along the output channel dimension, resulting in a convolution kernel with a shape of $c_o \times c_i \times k_h \times k_w$, where c_o is the number of output channels.

During the cross-correlation operation, the result for each output channel is calculated by applying the corresponding convolution kernel to the input tensor. This means that the convolution kernel for a particular output channel takes input from all channels in the input tensor. The cross-correlation operation is performed separately for each output channel, resulting in an output tensor with multiple channels.

By using multiple channels, the convolutional layer can learn to extract different features from the input data in parallel. Each output channel represents a different set of learned features, allowing the network to capture more complex patterns and relationships in the data.

To implement a cross-correlation function that calculates the output of multiple channels, you can use the following code as a starting point:

```
import torch

def cross_correlation(input, kernel):
    batch_size, input_channels, input_height, input_width =
input.shape
    output_channels, _, kernel_height, kernel_width = kernel.
shape

    # Initialize the output tensor
    output_height = input_height - kernel_height + 1
    output_width = input_width - kernel_width + 1
    output = torch.zeros(batch_size, output_channels, output_
height, output_width)

    # Perform cross-correlation for each output channel
    for i in range(output_channels):
        for j in range(input_channels):
            output[:, i] += torch.nn.functional.conv2d(input[:,
j], kernel[i, j])

    return output
```

In this code, **'input'** represents the input tensor with shape (batch_size, input_channels, input_height, input_width), and **'kernel'** represents the convolution kernel tensor with shape (output_channels, input_channels, kernel_height, kernel_width). The function initializes the output tensor with the appropriate size and performs cross-correlation for each output channel and input channel combination using the **'torch.nn.functional.conv2d'** function.

User can use this **'cross_correlation'** function to calculate the output of multiple channels by passing in the input and kernel tensors.

To construct a trivial convolution kernel with 3 output channels, you can concatenate the kernel tensor **'K'** with **'K+1'** and **'K+2'** along the output channel dimension. Here's an example implementation:

```
import torch

# Assuming K is the kernel tensor
K = torch.tensor([[[1, 2], [3, 4]], [[5, 6], [7, 8]]])

# Constructing the kernel with 3 output channels
kernel = torch.cat([K, K + 1, K + 2], dim=0)

# Checking the shape of the kernel
print(kernel.shape)
```

The **'torch.cat'** function is used to concatenate the tensors along the specified dimension (**'dim=0'** in this case) to create the kernel tensor with 3 output channels. You can adjust the values in **'K'** as desired for your specific convolution kernel.

4.5.3 1 × 1 Convolutional Layer

Although a 1 × 1 convolution may seem counterintuitive at first, it serves an important purpose in deep neural networks. Let's explore in more detail what a 1 × 1 convolution operation actually does.

A 1 × 1 convolution is a special case where the kernel size is 1 × 1. Unlike larger kernel sizes, a 1 × 1 convolution does not capture spatial patterns or correlations between adjacent pixels. Instead, it focuses on transforming the channels or feature maps.

Here are some key aspects and benefits of using 1 × 1 convolutions.

1. *Dimensionality Reduction:* One of the primary benefits of a 1 × 1 convolution is dimensionality reduction. It allows for reducing the number of channels in the input tensor. By applying a set of 1 × 1 convolution filters, we can perform linear transformations on each channel independently. This helps in reducing the computational complexity of subsequent layers and controlling the model's capacity.
2. *Nonlinearity:* Although a single 1 × 1 convolutional filter is linear, combining multiple filters and applying nonlinear activation functions after them introduces nonlinearity. This enables the network to learn complex relationships and capture high-level features.

3. *Information Fusion:* The 1 × 1 convolutional filters can learn to combine information from different channels. By convolving across channels, it allows for the interaction and fusion of features. This can enhance the model's ability to capture complex patterns and relationships between features.
4. *Network Efficiency:* By incorporating 1 × 1 convolutions, the model can learn to compress and represent information more efficiently. It can reduce the number of parameters and computations, leading to models that are computationally efficient and easier to train.

Overall, 1 × 1 convolutions provide a flexible and efficient way to transform the channels or feature maps in a neural network. They have proven to be useful in improving model performance, reducing model complexity, and enabling efficient network designs.

It's worth noting that 1 × 1 convolutions have been widely used in various state-of-the-art architectures, such as GoogLeNet (Szegedy et al., 2015), ResNet (He et al., 2016), and MobileNet (Howard et al., 2017), demonstrating their effectiveness in deep learning tasks.

Indeed, in Figure 4.9, the cross-correlation computation using a 1 × 1 convolution kernel with 3 input channels and 2 output channels is illustrated. The input and output tensors have the same height and width. Each element in the output tensor is obtained by performing a linear combination of elements at the corresponding position in the input tensor.

The 1 × 1 convolutional layer can be thought of as a fully connected layer applied at each pixel location independently, transforming the c_i input values into c_o output values. Although it resembles a fully connected layer, it still retains the benefits of convolutional layers, such as weight sharing across different pixel locations. As a result, the 1 × 1 convolutional layer requires only $c_o \times c_i$ weights (plus the bias) to perform the computation.

It's important to note that convolutional layers are typically followed by nonlinear activation functions, such as ReLU (Rectified Linear Unit), sigmoid, or tanh. These nonlinearities introduce nonlinearity into the model, enabling it to learn complex relationships and make the network more expressive. Therefore, 1 × 1 convolutions cannot simply be merged or folded into other convolutions, as the nonlinear activation functions after the 1 × 1 convolutional layer play a crucial role in capturing nonlinear interactions.

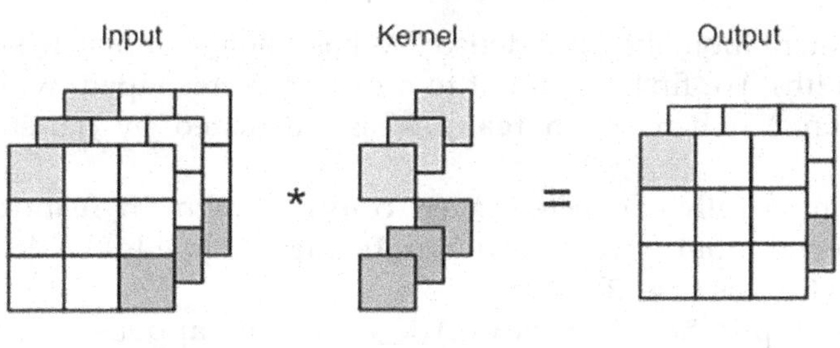

Figure 4.9 The 1 × 1 convolution kernel with 3 input channels and 2 output channels is used in the cross-correlation computation. The height and breadth of the input and output are the same.

The use of 1×1 convolutions allows for dimensionality reduction or expansion, feature transformation, and information fusion in CNNs. They provide flexibility in network design and can be used to adjust the number of channels, perform feature selection, or create parallel processing pathways within the network.

To implement a 1×1 convolution using a fully connected layer, we need to adjust the data shape before and after the matrix multiplication. Specifically, we need to reshape the input tensor to a matrix before the multiplication and reshape the result back to the tensor shape after the multiplication.

Here is the implementation of a 1×1 convolution using a fully connected layer in PyTorch:

```
import torch
from torch import nn

# Create the input tensor
X = torch.rand(size=(3, 3, 3))  # Input tensor with shape (batch_
size, input_channels, height, width)

# Reshape the input tensor to a matrix
X_reshaped = X.reshape(X.shape[0], -1)  # Reshape to (batch_size,
num_features)

# Define the fully connected layer
conv1x1 = nn.Linear(in_features=X_reshaped.shape[1], out_fea-
tures=2)  # Output channels = 2

# Perform the matrix multiplication
Y = conv1x1(X_reshaped)

# Reshape the result back to tensor shape
Y_reshaped = Y.reshape(X.shape[0], conv1x1.out_features,
X.shape[2], X.shape[3])  # Reshape to (batch_size, output_chan-
nels, height, width)

print(Y_reshaped.shape)  # Output shape
```

In this implementation, the input tensor **'X'** has a shape of (batch_size, input_channels, height, width). We first reshape it to a matrix **'X_reshaped'** with shape (batch_size, num_features), where **'num_features'** is calculated by flattening the spatial dimensions.

We then define a fully connected layer **'conv1x1'** with **'in_features'** equal to the number of flattened input features and **'out_features'** equal to the desired number of output channels (in this case, 2).

The matrix multiplication **'Y = conv1x1(X_reshaped)'** applies the 1×1 convolution operation, where each row in **'Y'** corresponds to the output values for a specific channel at each pixel location.

Finally, we reshape the result **'Y'** back to the tensor shape **'Y_reshaped'** with dimensions (batch_size, output_channels, height, width).

The shape of **'Y_reshaped'** will be the same as the input shape, except for the number of output channels, which is now 2 in this example.

4.6 Pooling

Indeed, as we go deeper into a neural network, the receptive field of each hidden node increases, meaning that it becomes sensitive to a larger region of the input. This is achieved by reducing spatial resolution through downsampling or pooling operations. As the receptive field grows, the hidden nodes can capture more global information about the input.

The advantage of this approach is that the intermediate layers of the network can still benefit from the local connectivity and weight sharing properties of convolutional layers. This allows the network to extract meaningful local features at earlier layers, which are then aggregated and combined to form higher-level representations at deeper layers. The gradual aggregation of information helps in learning global representations that are relevant to the final task, such as detecting objects or making global predictions about the input.

By reducing spatial resolution, either through downsampling or through pooling, the effective area covered by each convolutional kernel increases. This allows the network to capture larger and more complex patterns and dependencies in the input data. Additionally, reducing spatial resolution can help in reducing the computational complexity of the network, making it more efficient. Hence, the combination of local connectivity, weight sharing, and gradual aggregation of information through downsampling or pooling contributes to the success of CNNs in capturing both local and global features and effectively solving various computer vision tasks.

Invariance to translation is an important property that we often desire in lower-level features, such as edges. In many computer vision tasks, we want our models to be able to detect the same feature regardless of its location within the image. This is because objects and patterns of interest can occur at different positions in different images or even within the same image due to various factors like camera movement, object motion, or image transformations.

CNNs are well-suited for capturing translation-invariant features. The local connectivity and weight sharing properties of convolutional layers allow them to learn spatially invariant patterns. When detecting edges, for example, the network learns to activate a certain feature map regardless of the exact location of the edge in the input image. By sharing weights across the input, the network can recognize the same pattern in different spatial locations.

However, it's important to note that while CNNs are capable of capturing translation-invariant features at lower layers, higher layers in the network can learn more location-specific features and become less translation-invariant. This is because the receptive fields of deeper layers are larger, and they capture more global and context-dependent information. Invariance to translation is more desirable in the early layers where we want to detect simple local features, whereas higher layers are responsible for capturing more complex and specific patterns.

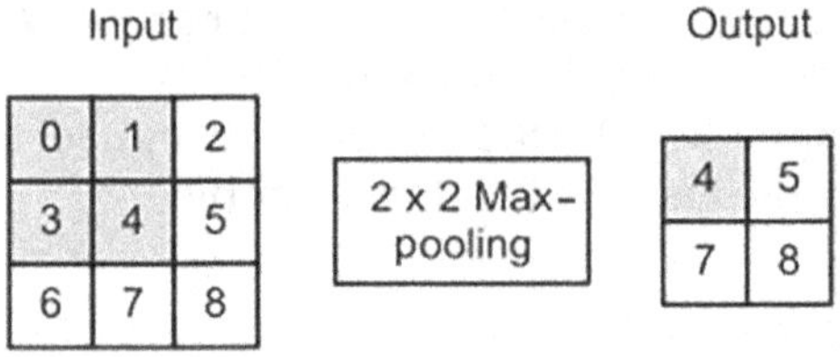

Figure 4.10 Max-pooling using a 2 x 2 pooling window. The initial output element and the input tensor elements utilized in the output computation are shown by the darkened portions: max(0, 1, 3, 4) = 4.

To address the issue of translation variation, data augmentation techniques can be used during training. By applying random translations, rotations, or other transformations to the training images, we can increase the robustness of the model and improve its ability to generalize to new, unseen images with different spatial arrangements.

The primary functions of pooling layers are as follows.

- *Location Invariance:* Pooling layers introduce a form of local spatial invariance by reducing the spatial dimensions of the input feature maps. By summarizing the information within local neighborhoods, pooling layers make the representations more robust to small spatial translations. This means that even if a feature is slightly shifted in the input, it can still be detected by the pooling layer.
- *Spatial Downsampling:* Pooling layers also perform downsampling by reducing the spatial resolution of the feature maps. By aggregating information from local regions, pooling layers retain the most important features while discarding some of the fine-grained details. This downsampling helps reduce the computational cost and memory requirements of subsequent layers in the network, and it can also lead to better generalization and improved spatial invariance.

4.6.1 Maximum Pooling and Average Pooling

Pooling layers consist of a fixed-shape window, often referred to as the pooling window or pooling kernel, which is slid over different regions of the input feature maps. Unlike convolutional layers, pooling layers do not have any parameters to learn. They are deterministic and perform simple operations such as maximum or average pooling.

There are two common types of pooling operations.

1. *Max-Pooling (Max-Pool):* In this operation, the maximum value within the pooling window is selected as the output value. Max-pooling is effective in capturing the most salient feature in each local region. By selecting the maximum value, max-pooling helps preserve strong activations and important spatial patterns, making it particularly useful for feature detection.
2. *Average Pooling (Avg-Pool):* In this operation, the average value within the pooling window is computed as the output value. Average pooling calculates the mean activation within each local region, providing a more smoothed representation. It helps reduce the impact of noise and small variations in the input and can be useful for downsampling and dimensionality reduction.

Both max-pooling and average pooling are applied independently to each channel of the input feature maps. The pooling window slides over the input with a specified stride, determining the spatial downsampling factor. By reducing the spatial dimensions of the feature maps, pooling layers help in capturing higher-level features that are less sensitive to exact spatial locations and retain the most important information.

Pooling layers play a crucial role in spatial downsampling, reducing computational complexity, and enhancing the translation invariance property of CNNs. They allow the network to focus on the most relevant features while discarding less informative details. Pooling layers are typically used after convolutional layers to progressively reduce spatial resolution and create a hierarchical representation of the input data.

Max-pooling with a pooling window shape of 2 × 2 selects the maximum value within each pooling window and uses it as the output value. In the example we mentioned, the shaded portions represent the pooling window, and the maximum value within that window is calculated.

Let's consider a 2 × 2 max-pooling operation on an input tensor:

Input tensor:

```
0 1 2 3
4 5 6 7
8 9 10 11
12 13 14 15
```

In this case, the first output element is obtained by applying max-pooling on the top-left 2 x 2 region of the input tensor:

```
max(0, 1, 4, 5) = 5
```

Therefore, the first output element is 5.

Max-pooling is a downsampling operation that helps reduce the spatial dimensions of the input tensor while retaining the most salient features. By selecting the maximum value within each pooling window, it captures the strongest activation in each local region, highlighting important features and discarding less significant ones.

Max-pooling with a pooling window shape of 2 × 2 in the context of edge detection can help detect patterns that have shifted no more than one element in height or width.

Consider the output of a convolutional layer, denoted as X:

```
X = [[a, b, c, d],
[e, f, g, h],
[i, j, k, l],
[m, n, o, p]]
```

Now, applying 2 × 2 max-pooling on X, the pooling layer output Y is given by:

```
Y = [[max(a, b, e, f), max(c, d, g, h)],
[max(i, j, m, n), max(k, l, o, p)]]
```

In this case, regardless of the specific values of $X[i,j], X[i,j+1], X[i+1,j,$ and $X[i+1,j+1]$, the max-pooling operation will select the maximum value within each 2 × 2 pooling window. As a result, the pooling layer output Y will always have a value of 1, if the pattern recognized by the convolutional layer has shifted no more than one element in height or width.

This property of max-pooling allows the network to be somewhat invariant to small translations or shifts in the input. It can help in capturing more robust and generalized features, as slight variations in the position of patterns are still captured by the pooling operation.

Here's an implementation of the pool2d function for forward propagation of a pooling layer:

```
import torch

def pool2d(X, pool_size, mode='max'):
    p_h, p_w = pool_size
    Y = torch.zeros((X.shape[0] - p_h + 1, X.shape[1] - p_w + 1))

    for i in range(Y.shape[0]):
        for j in range(Y.shape[1]):
            if mode == 'max':
                Y[i, j] = X[i:i+p_h, j:j+p_w].max()
            elif mode == 'avg':
                Y[i, j] = X[i:i+p_h, j:j+p_w].mean()

    return Y
```

This function takes as input **'X'**, the input tensor, **'pool_size'**, a tuple specifying the pooling window size (e.g., **'(2, 2)'** for a 2 × 2 pooling window), and **'mode'**, which can be either **'max'** or **'avg'** to indicate whether to perform max-pooling or average pooling, respectively.

The function initializes an output tensor **'Y'** of the appropriate size to store the pooled values. It then iterates over the regions of **'X'** using nested loops, extracting the corresponding subregions of size **'pool_size'**. Depending on the **'mode'**, it computes the maximum or average value of each subregion and assigns it to the corresponding location in **'Y'**.

Finally, the function returns the pooled output tensor **'Y'**.

Users can use this **'pool2d'** function to perform max-pooling or average pooling on any input tensor with a specified pooling window size.

To validate the output of the two-dimensional max-pooling layer using the input tensor in Figure 4.10, we can construct the input tensor X as follows:

```
import torch

X = torch.tensor([[0, 1, 2], [3, 4, 5], [6, 7, 8]], dtype=torch.
float32)
```

This will create a 3 × 3 tensor X with the values from Figure 4.10. Now, we can apply the pool2d function to perform max-pooling on X with a pooling window size of 2×2:

```
pool_size = (2, 2)
output = pool2d(X, pool_size, mode='max')
print(output)
```

The output will be:

```
tensor([[4., 5.],
[7., 8.]])
```

This result corresponds to the shaded portions in Figure 4.10, where the maximum value in each 2 × 2 pooling window is computed.

To experiment with the average pooling layer, we can use the same input tensor **'X'** from Figure 4.10 and apply the **'pool2d'** function with a pooling window size of 2 × 2 and the **'mode'** parameter set to **'avg'**:

```
pool_size = (2, 2)
output = pool2d(X, pool_size, mode='avg')
print(output)
```

The output will be:

```
tensor([[2., 3.],
[5., 6.]])
```

This result corresponds to the shaded portions in Figure 4.10, where the average value in each 2 × 2 pooling window is computed.

4.7 Summary

The chapter begins by introducing convolutional neural networks (CNNs) and their significance in image analysis tasks. It explains the transition from fully connected layers to convolutions, highlighting how the latter helps exploit spatial information present in images.

The concept of invariance is discussed, emphasizing the ability of CNNs to recognize patterns regardless of their position in an image. The chapter then explores how CNNs achieve invariance by constraining the multi-layer perceptron (MLP) through the use of convolutional layers.

To illustrate the practical implementation of CNNs, the chapter presents coding examples using popular deep learning frameworks. It demonstrates the application of convolutional layers for object edge detection in images, showcasing how CNNs can automatically learn edge detection kernels.

The cross-correlation operation, which is the fundamental mathematical operation behind convolutional layers, is explained in detail. The chapter discusses the feature map and receptive field concepts, demonstrating how each neuron in a convolutional layer is connected to a specific local region in the input.

Padding and stride, two important parameters in convolutional layers, are introduced. Padding is used to preserve spatial dimensions, while stride determines the step size of the kernel during convolution. Practical coding examples are provided to illustrate the effects of padding and stride on the output size of convolutional layers.

The chapter further covers the concept of multiple input and multiple output channels in convolutional layers. It explains how multiple input channels can be utilized to process different aspects of an image, while multiple output channels can capture different features simultaneously.

The 1×1 convolutional layer, a specialized layer that employs 1×1 kernels, is discussed for its role in reducing dimensionality and increasing computational efficiency.

Pooling, specifically maximum pooling and average pooling, is introduced as a technique to downsample feature maps and reduce spatial dimensions while retaining important features. Practical coding examples demonstrate the implementation of pooling layers.

Finally, the chapter presents a use case study on image classification, showcasing how CNNs can be employed to classify images into different classes. It covers the overall architecture of a CNN for image classification and provides practical coding examples for training and evaluating the model.

Throughout the chapter, the theoretical concepts are accompanied by practical coding examples to enhance understanding and enable readers to implement CNNs effectively for various image analysis tasks.

References

Abdel-Hamid, O., Mohamed, A., Jiang, H., Deng, L., Penn, G., & Yu, D. (2014). Convolutional neural networks for speech recognition. *IEEE/ACM Transactions on Audio, Speech, and Language Processing*, *22*(10), 1533–1545.

Deng, J., Dong, W., Socher, R., Li, L.-J., Li, K., & Fei-Fei, L. (2009). Imagenet: A large-scale hierarchical image database. *2009 IEEE Conference on Computer Vision and Pattern Recognition*, 248–255.

He, K., Zhang, X., Ren, S., & Sun, J. (2016). Identity mappings in deep residual networks. In *Computer vision–ECCV 2016: 14th European Conference, Amsterdam, The Netherlands, October 11–14, 2016, Proceedings, Part IV* (Vol. 14, pp. 630–645). Cham: Springer International Publishing.

Hinton, G. E., Srivastava, N., Krizhevsky, A., Sutskever, I., & Salakhutdinov, R. R. (2012). Improving neural networks by preventing co-adaptation of feature detectors. *ArXiv Preprint ArXiv:1207.0580.*

Howard, A. G., Zhu, M., Chen, B., Kalenichenko, D., Wang, W., Weyand, T., Andreetto, M., & Adam, H. (2017). Mobilenets: Efficient convolutional neural networks for mobile vision applications. *ArXiv Preprint ArXiv:1704.04861.*

Kalchbrenner, N., Grefenstette, E., & Blunsom, P. (2014). A convolutional neural network for modelling sentences. *ArXiv Preprint ArXiv:1404.2188.*

Kipf, T. N. (2016). *Semi-Supervised Classification with Graph Convolutional Networks.* arXiv preprint arXiv:1609.02907.

Kuzovkin, I., Vicente, R., Petton, M., Lachaux, J.-P., Baciu, M., Kahane, P., Rheims, S., Vidal, J. R., & Aru, J. (2018). Activations of deep convolutional neural networks are aligned with gamma band activity of human visual cortex. *Communications Biology, 1*(1), 107.

LeCun, Y., & Bengio, Y. (1995). Convolutional networks for images, speech, and time series. *The Handbook of Brain Theory and Neural Networks, 3361*(10), 1995.

Szegedy, C., Liu, W., Jia, Y., Sermanet, P., Reed, S., Anguelov, D., Erhan, D., Vanhoucke, V., & Rabinovich, A. (2015). Going deeper with convolutions. *Proceedings of the IEEE Conference on Computer Vision and Pattern Recognition*, 1–9.

Chapter 5

Recurrent Neural Networks

5.1 Background

Sequential data is prevalent in various learning tasks across different domains. Let's explore some examples.

- *Image Captioning:* Given an image, the task is to generate a descriptive caption that accurately describes the contents of the image. This requires the model to process the image sequentially and generate a coherent sequence of words.
- *Speech Synthesis:* Generating human-like speech involves producing a sequence of phonemes or waveform samples based on a given input text. The model needs to understand the sequential structure of the input text and generate corresponding speech output.
- *Music Generation:* Creating music with machine learning involves generating sequences of musical notes or audio samples that form cohesive and expressive compositions. The model needs to capture the temporal dependencies and patterns in music to produce meaningful sequences.
- *Time Series Prediction:* Forecasting future values in time series data, such as stock prices, weather patterns, or energy consumption, requires analyzing and predicting sequential patterns. The model needs to learn from the historical sequence of data to make accurate predictions.
- *Video Analysis:* Understanding and analyzing videos involve processing sequences of frames. Tasks like action recognition, object tracking, and video captioning require models to comprehend the temporal dynamics and context within video sequences.
- *Natural Language Translation:* Translating text from one language to another involves processing and generating sequences of words. The model needs to capture the semantic and syntactic structures of both the source and target languages to produce accurate translations.
- *Dialogue Systems:* Building conversational agents or chatbots requires models to understand and generate coherent sequences of dialogue. The model needs to process and respond to sequential inputs to engage in meaningful conversations.
- *Robot Control:* Controlling robots often involves issuing commands or instructions in sequential form. The model must interpret and execute the sequential commands to perform specific tasks or actions.

DOI: 10.1201/9781003654216-7

In all these examples, the models must effectively handle and learn from sequential data to produce desired outputs. Recurrent neural networks (RNNs) and specifically long short-term memory networks (LSTMs) are commonly used architectures to address these sequential learning tasks. They are designed to capture temporal dependencies and handle varying-length sequences.

The ability to work with sequential data is crucial in many real-world applications, as it enables models to process and generate meaningful outputs that align with the temporal structure of the input data. It's worth noting that sequential data is not exclusive to RNNs. Convolutional neural networks (CNNs), which were introduced earlier in the book, can also be adapted to handle sequential data of varying length, such as images with varying resolutions (Krizhevsky et al., 2012).

Furthermore, it is acknowledged that transformer models have gained considerable attention and market share in recent years, surpassing RNNs in some applications. However, RNNs still play a significant role in deep learning, particularly in handling complex sequential structures. They have been widely used for sequence modeling and remain fundamental models for capturing temporal dependencies and processing sequential data.

In summary, this chapter serves as an introduction to both the fundamentals of sequence modeling problems and the role of RNNs in addressing these problems. The history of RNNs is intertwined with the development of sequence modeling, making it an essential topic for understanding the broader landscape of deep learning.

5.2 A Look into Recurrent Neural Networks

The history of RNNs is deeply rooted in both cognitive science and machine learning. RNNs were initially inspired by models of the brain and cognition, reflecting the idea of information processing in a sequential and recurrent manner (Orvieto et al., 2023). However, over time, RNNs have evolved into practical tools in the machine learning community, with a focus on their application to various tasks. In the 2010s, RNNs gained significant attention and popularity due to their impressive performance on a wide range of sequential tasks.

Some notable breakthroughs that propelled the popularity of RNNs include their success in handwriting recognition, machine translation, and medical diagnosis. These achievements demonstrated the power of RNNs in capturing and modeling complex sequential patterns. While this book adopts the machine learning perspective, it acknowledges the historical origins of RNNs and their connection to cognitive science. For readers interested in exploring the cognitive science aspects of RNNs, a comprehensive review is recommended (Lipton et al., 2015).

RNNs are designed to capture sequential information by incorporating recurrent connections within the network architecture (Khanduzi & Sangaiah, 2023). Unlike feedforward neural networks, which process input data in a fixed order, RNNs introduce cycles in the network graph, allowing information to be propagated across adjacent time steps or sequence steps. The recurrent connections in an RNN enable the network to maintain memory or context of past inputs and computations, which is crucial for modeling sequential data. These connections allow information to flow from previous time steps to the current time step, creating a form of feedback within the network.

To facilitate understanding and training, RNNs are commonly unrolled or unfolded across time steps, creating a visualization where each time step is treated as a separate layer. This unfolding view helps to conceptualize RNNs as a series of interconnected feedforward neural networks, with shared parameters across time steps. In this unrolled view, the recurrent connections become apparent, as information from previous time steps is passed to the current time step. The recurrent connections allow the network to process sequences of variable lengths, as the same set of parameters is applied at each time step.

The shared parameters in RNNs are crucial as they allow the network to learn patterns and dependencies across different time steps. By sharing parameters, the model can generalize its knowledge and capture long-term dependencies in the sequence data. It's important to note that while the unfolded view helps visualize the flow of information in RNNs, in practice, computations in RNNs are often performed in a more efficient and compact manner, taking advantage of matrix operations and specialized implementations like the LSTM (Kumari & Toshniwal, 2021) and Gated Recurrent Unit (GRU) (Zhang et al., 2022b) architectures.

Overall, RNNs are powerful models for processing sequential data, as they leverage recurrent connections to capture temporal dependencies and propagate information across different time steps, allowing for dynamic and context-aware predictions. One of the key insights that revolutionized sequence modeling is the recognition that many real-world tasks can be framed as processing varying-length sequences of fixed-length vectors. This insight opened new possibilities for applying machine learning techniques to tackle a wide range of problems that were previously challenging to address.

For instance, documents can be seen as sequences of words, where each word is represented as a fixed-length vector. By modeling the dependencies between words in the sequence, machine learning models can learn to understand the semantic structure of the document and perform tasks such as text classification, sentiment analysis, or language translation. In the medical domain, patient records often consist of sequences of events, such as encounters, medications, procedures, lab tests, and diagnoses. By treating these records as sequences of fixed-length vectors, machine learning models can learn to extract meaningful patterns and make predictions about patient outcomes, disease progression, or treatment effectiveness.

Similarly, videos can be represented as sequences of still images, where each image is encoded as a fixed-length vector. By analyzing the temporal dependencies between the images in the sequence, machine learning models can understand motion, recognize objects or activities, and generate video captions or summaries. By framing these tasks as sequence modeling problems, machine learning techniques like RNNs and transformer models have been able to effectively capture the temporal dependencies and patterns within the sequences, leading to significant advancements in various fields (Zhong et al., 2023).

The ability to represent complex data structures as varying-length sequences of fixed-length vectors has greatly expanded the applicability of machine learning and enabled the development of powerful models for processing sequential data. For example, in conventional feedforward neural networks, each test case is considered independent of others, and the model does not consider the sequential nature of the data. This can be a limitation when dealing with sequential data such as stock market prices. To address this limitation, RNNs are often used. RNNs are designed to capture the sequential dependencies in the data by introducing recurrent connections that allow information to be propagated across different time steps. In the case of stock market data, RNNs can consider the previous stock prices and incorporate them into the prediction for the current time step.

By considering the sequential dependencies, RNNs are better suited for modeling and predicting stock market prices, as they can capture trends, patterns, and dependencies that exist over time (Kim & Durlofsky, 2023). The ability of RNNs to selectively remember patterns for long durations makes them particularly effective in handling such time-dependent data.

In addition to RNNs, other advanced sequence modeling techniques like LSTM and GRU have been developed to overcome the limitations of traditional feedforward neural networks and better handle sequential data with long-term dependencies. By leveraging RNNs or other sequence modeling techniques, traders and analysts can improve their predictions by incorporating the historical stock market data and capturing the underlying patterns and trends that influence the stock prices. A basic RNN consists of three main components: an input layer, a hidden layer, and an output layer as shown in Figure 5.1. The hidden layer is recurrent, meaning it has connections that allow information to be passed from one time step to the next.

At each time step 't', the RNN takes an input vector '$x(t)$' and passes it through the input layer. The input layer applies a transformation to the input and sends the transformed information to the hidden layer. The hidden layer then combines the current input with the information from the previous time step, which is stored in its recurrent connections. This combination of the current input and the previous hidden state forms the hidden state at time step 't', denoted as '$h(t)$'.

The hidden state '$h(t)$' represents the network's memory or information at time step 't', which encodes the sequential information from previous time steps. The hidden state is then used to generate the output '$y(t)$' at the current time step. The output can be passed through an activation function or used directly depending on the specific task.

In the context of stock market prediction, the input '$x(t)$' could contain features such as stock volume, opening value, and so on at time step 't'. The RNN processes these inputs along with the information from previous time steps to generate predictions or make decisions based on the historical context. It's important to note that the

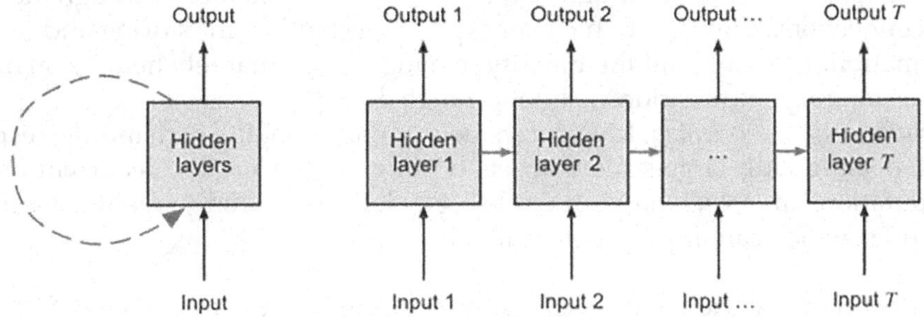

Figure 5.1 Recurrent connections are shown on the left as cyclic edges. We show the RNN unfolding in time steps on the right. Here, recurrent edges span neighboring time steps while synchronous computation of traditional connections is used.

connections in the hidden layer of an RNN allow it to capture the temporal dependencies in the data, making it suitable for sequential modeling tasks. However, traditional RNNs can suffer from vanishing or exploding gradients, which can make it challenging to capture long-term dependencies. This led to the development of more advanced variants like LSTM and GRU, which address these issues and are commonly used in practice for sequence modeling tasks.

5.3 Limitations of RNNs

RNNs have several limitations that can impact their performance and effectiveness in certain scenarios. Here are some of the key limitations of RNNs (Wang et al., 2023).

- *Difficulty in Capturing Long-Term Dependencies:* RNNs suffer from the vanishing gradient problem, where the gradients diminish exponentially as they propagate backward through time. This makes it challenging for RNNs to capture long-term dependencies in sequential data. If the dependency between distant time steps is crucial for the task, RNNs may struggle to effectively model it.
- *Inability to Handle very Long Sequences:* RNNs are sensitive to the length of sequences they process. As the length of the input sequence increases, RNNs may face difficulties in retaining relevant information from earlier time steps. This can result in a degradation of performance or loss of important context.
- *Lack of Parallelization during Training:* RNNs are inherently sequential models, and the recurrent nature of their computations makes it difficult to parallelize the training process. As a result, training RNNs can be slower compared to other models, especially when dealing with large datasets.
- *Gradient Instability and Exploding Gradients:* While the vanishing gradient problem is a common issue, RNNs can also suffer from exploding gradients, where the gradients become extremely large. This can lead to unstable training and difficulties in converging to an optimal solution.
- *Difficulty in Modeling Complex Patterns:* RNNs are not always effective in capturing complex patterns or intricate relationships in sequential data. Tasks that require precise modeling of intricate dependencies or understanding long-range context may require more advanced models or architectures.
- *Lack of Explicit Memory:* Although RNNs have a form of memory through their recurrent connections, they do not have an explicit mechanism for storing and retrieving information. This can limit their ability to handle tasks that rely heavily on memory, such as language translation with long-range dependencies.
- *Computational Inefficiency:* RNNs can be computationally demanding, especially when dealing with large-scale datasets or long sequences. The recurrent nature of computations in RNNs makes them less efficient compared to feedforward neural networks, which can impact their scalability.

It's worth noting that there have been advancements in addressing some of these limitations, such as the development of LSTM and GRU architectures that mitigate the vanishing gradient problem to some extent. Additionally, other architectures like transformer models have gained popularity for sequence modeling tasks and offer alternatives to RNNs.

Understanding these limitations is important in selecting the appropriate model architecture for a given task and exploring alternative approaches to address the challenges associated with RNNs.

5.4 An Improvement over RNN: LSTM

LSTM networks were introduced as an improvement over traditional RNNs to address the limitations of capturing long-term dependencies and selectively remembering important information. LSTMs achieve this by introducing a more complex memory mechanism called "cell states".

In an LSTM, the information flows through a sequence of memory cells, each having three essential components: an input gate, a forget gate, and an output gate (Fekri et al., 2022; Peng et al., 2021). These gates regulate the flow of information and allow the LSTM to selectively remember or forget specific information at each time step.

- *Input Gate:* The input gate determines which elements of the current input should be stored in the cell state. It uses a sigmoid activation function to output values between 0 and 1 for each element, indicating the importance of that element.
- *Forget Gate:* The forget gate decides which information from the previous cell state should be discarded. It takes the previous cell state and the current input and outputs a forget vector, which is multiplied element-wise with the previous cell state. This allows the LSTM to forget irrelevant information.
- *Output Gate:* The output gate determines the information to be output from the cell state. It considers the current input and the modified cell state and outputs a filtered version of the cell state. The filtered output is then passed through a sigmoid activation function to restrict the values between 0 and 1, and then it is multiplied with a ***tan h*** activation of the cell state. This produces the final output of the LSTM.

By using these gating mechanisms, LSTMs can selectively retain or discard information over time. This enables them to capture long-term dependencies in sequences and maintain relevant context for making predictions. The ability to selectively update and retain information makes LSTMs particularly effective in tasks that require modeling complex sequences with long-term dependencies, such as language translation, speech recognition, and sentiment analysis.

LSTMs offer a more advanced and powerful memory mechanism compared to traditional RNNs, allowing them to overcome the limitations of capturing long-term dependencies and selectively remembering important information. In the context of predicting stock prices using LSTM networks, let's consider an example to illustrate how LSTM can capture the dependencies and factors we mentioned.

Suppose we have the following sequence of stock prices for a particular stock:

[100, 110, 108, 120, 115]

We want to predict the stock price for the next day based on the previous days' prices. Using a simple RNN, the network might struggle to capture the long-term dependencies and the significance of certain factors. However, with LSTM, the network can better understand and utilize the information. The LSTM model can be trained to consider the trend, the previous day's price, and any other relevant factors that affect the stock price. It can learn to selectively remember important information and forget irrelevant details.

For example, let's say the stock has been following an upward trend in the previous days. The LSTM can learn to capture this trend and assign higher importance to it in predicting the next day's price. Additionally, if there is a sudden drop in the company's profit, the LSTM can learn to incorporate this information and adjust the predicted price accordingly.

By using the input gate, forget gate, and output gate mechanisms, the LSTM can dynamically update its memory cell states and make predictions based on the relevant information. This ability to selectively remember and forget information allows the LSTM to consider the previous days' prices, the trend, and other factors simultaneously while making predictions. In this way, LSTM networks can effectively model the dependencies and factors influencing stock prices, making them suitable for time series prediction tasks like stock price forecasting. In LSTM networks, the information flow is governed by three main components: the previous cell state, the previous hidden state, and the input at the current time step. These components allow LSTMs to capture and utilize dependencies in sequential data effectively.

The previous cell state represents the information that was preserved in the memory from the previous time step. It acts as a long-term memory component in the LSTM. It carries forward relevant information that the model has learned from previous steps, allowing it to retain the important context over time. The previous hidden state is the output of the LSTM cell from the previous time step. It contains a summary or representation of the information processed in the previous step. It serves as a short-term memory component that can capture immediate dependencies and influence the current prediction.

The input at the current time step is the new information being fed into the LSTM. It could be a new data point or an update in the sequence. This input, along with the previous cell state and the previous hidden state, influences the current cell state and hidden state, determining the output and updating the memory for future steps. By considering these three components, LSTMs can effectively handle long-term dependencies, selectively remember, or forget information and make predictions based on the context and current input. This enables them to capture and model complex sequential patterns in various applications, ranging from natural language processing to time series prediction.

5.5 Architecture of LSTM

The architecture of an LSTM (presented in Figure 5.2) network consists of specialized memory cells that allow the network to capture long-term dependencies in sequential data. LSTMs are a type of recurrent neural network that has been specifically designed to address the vanishing gradient problem and handle long-term dependencies.

The basic building block of an LSTM network is the LSTM cell. Each LSTM cell has three main components: the forget gate, the input gate, and the output gate. These gates control the flow of information into, out of, and within the cell.

5.5.1 Forget Gate

The forget gate in an LSTM network (presented in Figure 5.3) is responsible for determining which information from the previous hidden state should be forgotten or ignored. It plays a crucial role in controlling the flow of information through the network.

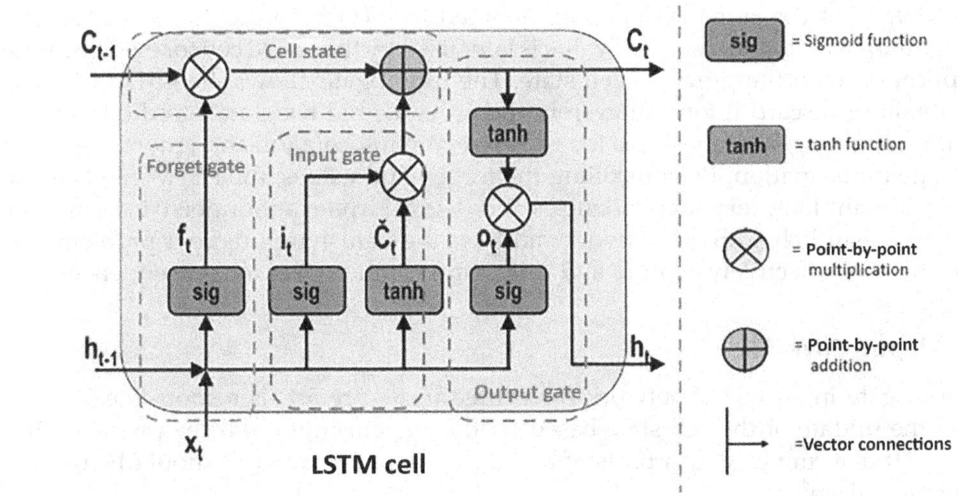

Figure 5.2 Block diagram of LSTM architecture.

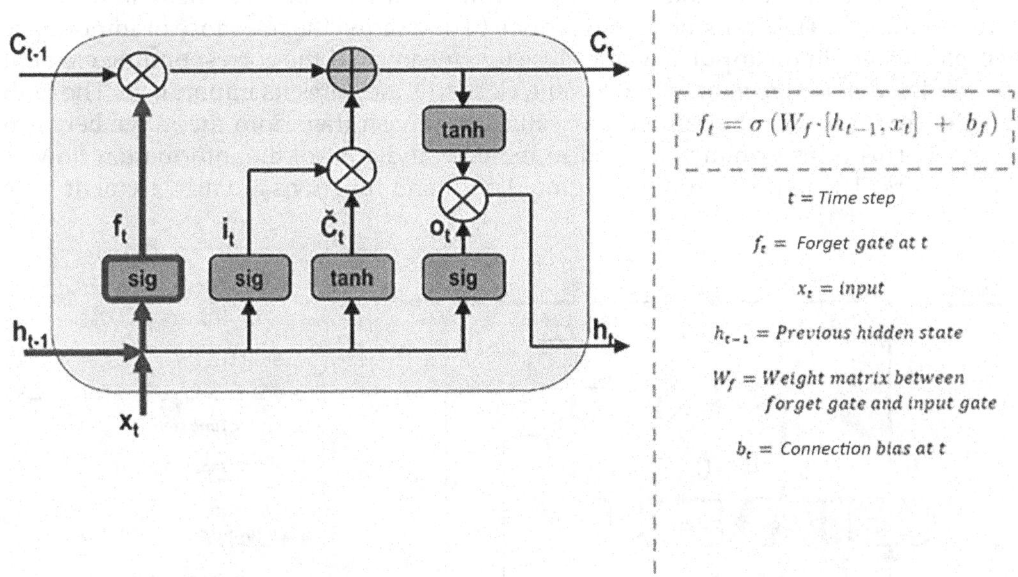

Figure 5.3 Operation of forget gate.

To make this decision, the current input, denoted as $'X(t)'$, and the previous hidden state, denoted as $'h(t-1)'$, are combined and passed through a sigmoid function. The sigmoid function maps the combined input to a value between 0 and 1. A value close to 0 means that the corresponding information is deemed irrelevant or should be forgotten, while a value close to 1 indicates that the information is important and should be retained.

The output of the sigmoid function, denoted as '$f(t)$', represents the forget gate value for the current time step. This value is later used by the LSTM cell for element-wise multiplication with the previous cell state. The forget gate allows the LSTM to selectively retain or discard information from the previous hidden state based on the current input, enabling the network to focus on relevant information and ignore irrelevant or outdated information. By controlling the forget gate values, the LSTM can learn to retain important long-term dependencies and discard irrelevant or noisy information. This mechanism helps LSTM networks address the vanishing gradient problem and enables them to effectively capture and utilize information over longer sequences.

5.5.2 *Input Gate*

The input gate in an LSTM network (presented in Figure 5.4) is responsible for controlling the update of the cell state based on the current input and the previous hidden state. It determines which parts of the input are important and should be used to update the cell state.

To update the cell state, the current input $\boldsymbol{X}(t)$ and the previous hidden state $\boldsymbol{h}(t-1)$ are separately passed through two activation functions: a sigmoid function and a hyperbolic tangent (tanh) function.

The sigmoid function takes the input values and transforms them into values between 0 and 1. This transformation is done to determine the relevance or importance of each element in the input. A value close to 0 means that the corresponding element is considered not important, while a value close to 1 indicates its importance. The tanh function is applied to the same input values to squash them into the range between -1 and 1. This transformation is used to regulate and control the information flow in the network. The outputs from the sigmoid and tanh functions are then element-wise

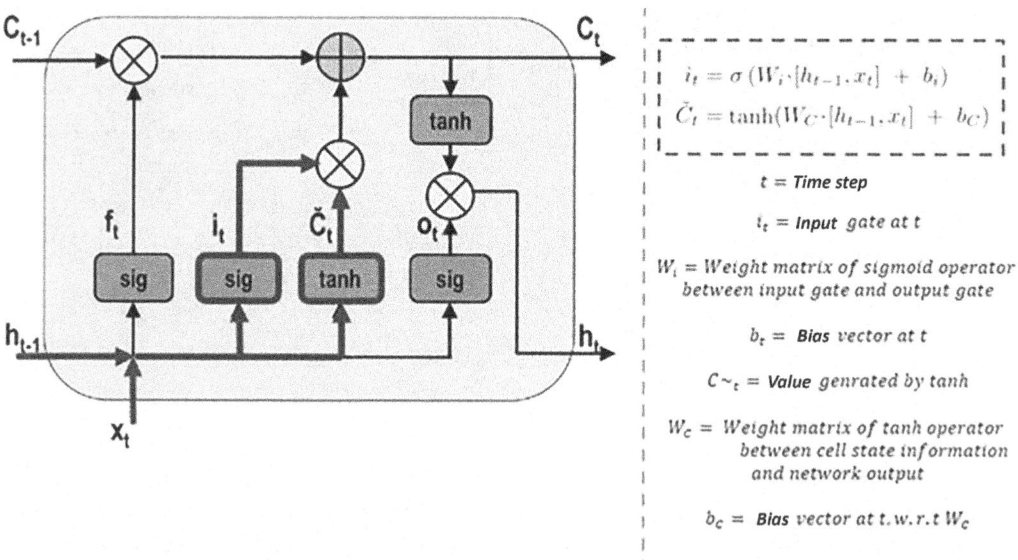

Figure 5.4 Operation of input gate.

multiplied together. This point-by-point multiplication combines the information about the importance of each input element (from the sigmoid function) and the actual values of the input elements (from the tanh function).

The resulting vector, denoted as $C_{\tilde{i}}$, represents the updated values for the cell state. It captures the relevant information from the current input and the previous hidden state, considering their importance as determined by the sigmoid function. The updated cell state is then passed on to the next time step in the LSTM network. By using the input gate and the point-by-point multiplication, the LSTM can selectively update and store important information in the cell state while ignoring or attenuating less important information. This mechanism allows LSTMs to handle long-term dependencies and effectively capture relevant information for sequential tasks.

5.5.3 *Update and Cell State*

The network has enough information from the forget gate and input gate. The next step is to update the cell state $\left(C(t)\right)$ presented in Figure 5.5. The previous cell state $\left(C(t-1)\right)$ is multiplied element-wise with the forget vector $\left(f(t)\right)$. This operation determines which elements of the previous cell state should be retained. Then, the element-wise product of the input vector $\left(i(t)\right)$ and the candidate vector $\left(C_{\tilde{i}}\right)$ is calculated. This product represents the new information that should be added to the cell state. Finally, the forget gate's result $\left(C(t-1)\otimes f(t)\right)$ and the input gate's result $\left(i(t)\otimes C_{\tilde{i}}\right)$ are added element-wise to update the cell state: $C(t)=\left(C(t-1)\otimes f(t)\right)+\left(i(t)\otimes C_{\tilde{i}}\right)$.

5.5.4 *Output Layer*

The output gate in an LSTM network is responsible for determining the value of the next hidden state presented in Figure 5.6, which contains information from the previous inputs and is used for prediction.

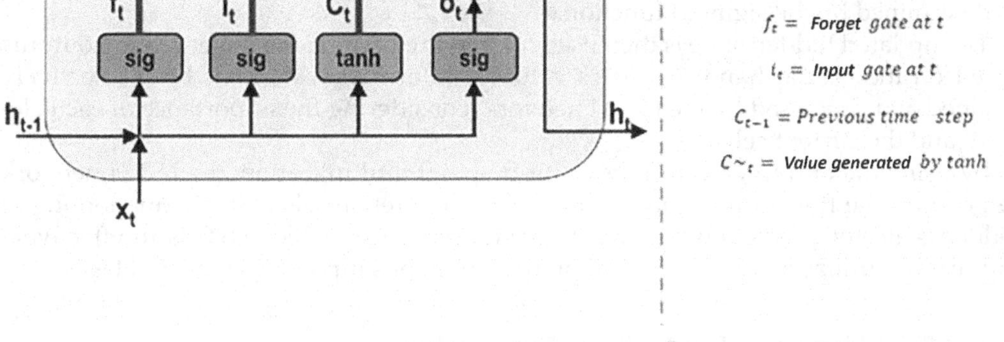

Figure 5.5 Operation of cell state.

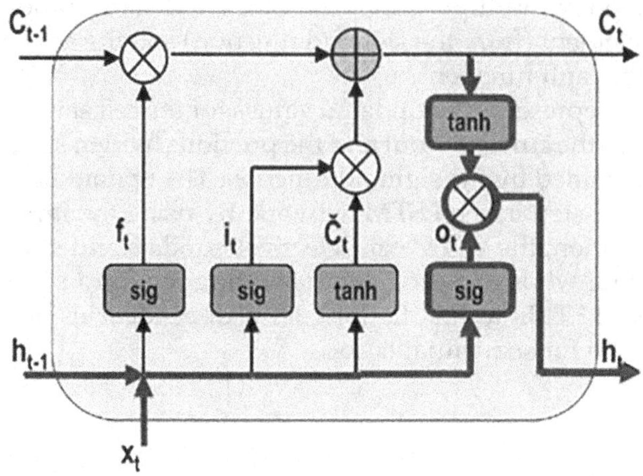

$$o_t = \sigma\left(W_o\,[h_{t-1}, x_t] + b_o\right)$$
$$h_t = o_t * \tanh(C_t)$$

t = Time step

O_t = Output gate at t

W_o = Weight matrix of output gate

b_o = Bias vector.w.r.t W_o

h_t = LSTM output

Figure 5.6 Operation of output gate.

To compute the next hidden state, the current cell state and the previous hidden state are separately passed through two activation functions: a sigmoid function and a hyperbolic tangent (tanh) function.

The sigmoid function takes the input values and transforms them into values between 0 and 1. This transformation is used to determine the relevance or importance of each element in the hidden state. A value close to 0 means that the corresponding element is considered not important, while a value close to 1 indicates its importance.

The tanh function is applied to the cell state to squash its values into the range between -1 and 1. This transformation helps regulate the information flow and ensure that the hidden state captures relevant information. The outputs from the sigmoid and tanh functions are then element-wise multiplied together. This point-by-point multiplication combines the information about the importance of each element in the hidden state (from the sigmoid function) and the values of the cell state (from the tanh function). The resulting vector represents the updated values for the hidden state. It captures the relevant information from the previous inputs, considering their importance as determined by the sigmoid function.

The updated hidden state is then used for making predictions or generating outputs based on the task at hand. It carries valuable information that has been selectively retained and processed by the LSTM network, considering the importance of each element and the current cell state.

By using the output gate and the point-by-point multiplication, the LSTM network can control the flow of information and selectively retain relevant information in the hidden state for prediction or output generation. This enables LSTMs to effectively capture and utilize relevant information from previous inputs in sequential tasks.

5.6 LSTM Use Case Study: Text Generation

Text generation using LSTMs is a popular application of RNNs. LSTMs can learn the underlying patterns and structure of text data and generate new text based on the learned patterns (Averbeck, 2022; Wang et al., 2022). Here's a general approach to text generation using LSTMs.

- *Data Preparation:* Start by preparing your text data. Clean the text by removing unnecessary characters, converting to lowercase, and splitting it into individual tokens (words or characters).
- *Sequence Creation:* Create input-output sequences to train the LSTM. Define a sequence length (number of tokens) that the LSTM will consider at a time. Slide a window over the text data, creating overlapping sequences of input-output pairs.
- *Text Encoding:* Convert the text data into numerical form that can be fed into the LSTM. This can be done by creating a vocabulary of unique tokens and mapping each token to a unique integer index. Encode the input sequences and the corresponding output sequences using these integer indices.
- *LSTM Model Architecture:* Build an LSTM model for text generation. The model should consist of an embedding layer to represent the input tokens, one or more LSTM layers to capture the sequence dependencies, and a final output layer to predict the next token.
- *Training:* Train the LSTM model on the input-output sequences. Use the encoded input sequences as input and the encoded output sequences as target labels. Adjust the model's weights using backpropagation and an optimization algorithm (e.g., Adam or RMSprop).
- *Text Generation:* Once the LSTM model is trained, you can use it to generate new text. Start with a seed sequence and feed it into the trained model. Generate the next token based on the model's predictions. Append the generated token to the input sequence and remove the oldest token to maintain the sequence length. Repeat this process to generate the desired length of text.
- *Post-Processing:* Decode the generated numerical sequence back into text form by reversing the encoding process. You can apply post-processing steps like capitalization, punctuation, or additional formatting to enhance the readability of the generated text.
- *Iterate and Refine:* Experiment with different model architectures, hyperparameters, and training strategies to improve the quality of the generated text. Iterate on the training process and fine-tune the model as needed.

It's important to note that generating coherent and meaningful text can be challenging, and the quality of the generated text depends on the size and diversity of the training data, as well as the complexity of the language and the chosen model architecture.

Here's an example of text generation using an LSTM deep learning model in Python, using the dependencies numpy and Keras:

```
import numpy as np
from keras.models import Sequential
from keras.layers import Dense, Dropout, LSTM
from keras.utils import np_utils

# Loading text file and creating character to integer mappings
filename = "/macbeth.txt"
text = open(filename).read().lower()
```

```
# Mapping characters with integers
unique_chars = sorted(list(set(text)))

char_to_int = {c: i for i, c in enumerate(unique_chars)}
int_to_char = {i: c for i, c in enumerate(unique_chars)}

# Preparing dataset
X = []
Y = []

for i in range(0, len(text) - 50, 1):
    sequence = text[i:i + 50]
    label = text[i + 50]
    X.append([char_to_int[char] for char in sequence])
    Y.append(char_to_int[label])

# Reshaping of X
X_modified = np.reshape(X, (len(X), 50, 1))
X_modified = X_modified / float(len(unique_chars))
Y_modified = np_utils.to_categorical(Y)

# Defining the LSTM model
model = Sequential()
model.add(LSTM(300, input_shape=(X_modified.shape[1], X_modified.
shape[2]), return_sequences=True))
model.add(Dropout(0.2))
model.add(LSTM(300))
model.add(Dropout(0.2))
model.add(Dense(Y_modified.shape[1], activation='softmax'))

model.compile(loss='categorical_crossentropy', optimizer='adam')

# Fitting the model
model.fit(X_modified, Y_modified, epochs=10, batch_size=128)

# Generating characters
start_index = np.random.randint(0, len(X)-1)
new_string = X[start_index]

for _ in range(50):
    x = np.reshape(new_string, (1, len(new_string), 1))
    x = x / float(len(unique_chars))

    # Predicting
    pred_index = np.argmax(model.predict(x, verbose=0))
    char_out = int_to_char[pred_index]
    seq_in = [int_to_char[value] for value in new_string]
    print(char_out)

    new_string.append(pred_index)
    new_string = new_string[1:len(new_string)]
```

The steps for text generation using an LSTM model are as follows. It loads the text data from a file, creates character-to-integer mappings, prepares the dataset by creating input-output pairs, reshapes the input data, defines the LSTM model architecture, compiles the model, fits the model to the data, and generates new characters based on the trained model.

However, there are a few modifications I would suggest to improve the code:

1. Instead of using **'numpy'** for imports, you can directly import **'numpy'** as **'np'** for brevity: **'import numpy as np'**.
2. In the **'fit'** function, specifying **'epochs=1'** might not be sufficient for training a good model. You can experiment with increasing the number of epochs to improve the model's performance. Additionally, you may want to increase the batch size depending on your available resources and the size of your dataset.
3. In the character generation loop, you should convert the predicted character index **'pred_index'** to the corresponding character using **'int_to_char[pred_index]'** before appending it to **'new_string'**. This ensures that the generated characters are correctly displayed.

5.7 Important Usage of LSTM

The trained LSTMs help mitigate the problem of the vanishing gradient, which can lead to underfitting. However, LSTMs can still face the issue of the exploding gradient, where the weights become too large and lead to overfitting (Zhang et al., 2022a, 2022b). Various techniques such as gradient clipping can be applied to address the exploding gradient problem.

Training LSTMs can indeed be performed using popular Python frameworks like TensorFlow, PyTorch, and Theano. These frameworks provide efficient implementations of LSTM layers and optimization algorithms, making it easier to train and work with LSTM networks.

When training deeper LSTM networks or working with large datasets, having access to a GPU can significantly speed up the training process. GPUs are well-suited for handling the parallel computations involved in training neural networks, including LSTMs.

LSTMs are widely used in various natural language processing tasks such as language generation, machine translation, sentiment analysis, and speech recognition. Their ability to capture long-term dependencies makes them well-suited for tasks that require understanding and generating sequences of data.

Additionally, LSTMs have been applied to image-related tasks such as optical character recognition (OCR) for extracting text from images and object detection, particularly in the context of scene text detection. Overall, LSTMs have proven to be a powerful tool in deep learning, particularly in tasks involving sequential data and long-term dependencies.

5.8 Summary

The chapter begins by introducing recurrent neural networks and their ability to process sequential data, making them suitable for tasks such as natural language processing and time series analysis. The limitations of traditional RNNs, such as the vanishing gradient problem and difficulty in capturing long-term dependencies, are discussed.

To overcome these limitations, the chapter introduces an improvement over RNNs called long short-term memory. The architecture of LSTM is explained in detail, highlighting its key components: the forget gate, input gate, cell state, and output gate. Each component plays a crucial role in the flow of information and the control of memory within an LSTM cell.

The chapter provides practical coding examples to demonstrate the implementation of LSTM using popular deep learning frameworks. The chapter then presents a use case study on text generation, showcasing how LSTM can be utilized to generate coherent and contextually relevant text. Also, it explains the architecture and training process of an LSTM model for text generation are explained, and provides practical coding examples to illustrate the steps involved.

The chapter concludes by highlighting the important applications of LSTM beyond text generation. It emphasizes how LSTM can be employed for tasks such as sentiment analysis, machine translation, speech recognition, and more. The versatility and effectiveness of LSTM make it a powerful tool for processing sequential data in various domains.

Throughout the chapter, the theoretical concepts of RNNs and LSTMs are accompanied by practical coding examples, enabling readers to understand the implementation details and apply them in their own projects. The use case study on text generation serves as a practical demonstration of LSTM's capabilities and inspires readers to explore its applications in different areas of interest.

References

Averbeck, B. B. (2022). Pruning recurrent neural networks replicates adolescent changes in working memory and reinforcement learning. *Proceedings of the National Academy of Sciences, 119*(22), e2121331119.

Fekri, M. N., Grolinger, K., & Mir, S. (2022). Distributed load forecasting using smart meter data: Federated learning with recurrent neural networks. *International Journal of Electrical Power & Energy Systems, 137*, 107669.

Khanduzi, R., & Sangaiah, A. K. (2023). An efficient recurrent neural network for defensive Stackelberg game. *Journal of Computational Science, 67*, 101970.

Kim, Y. D., & Durlofsky, L. J. (2023). Convolutional–recurrent neural network proxy for robust optimization and closed-loop reservoir management. *Computational Geosciences, 27*(2), 179–202.

Krizhevsky, A., Sutskever, I., & Hinton, G. E. (2012). Imagenet classification with deep convolutional neural networks. *Advances in Neural Information Processing Systems*, 1097–1105.

Kumari, P., & Toshniwal, D. (2021). Long short term memory–convolutional neural network based deep hybrid approach for solar irradiance forecasting. *Applied Energy, 295*, 117061.

Lipton, Z. C., Berkowitz, J., & Elkan, C. (2015). A critical review of recurrent neural networks for sequence learning. *ArXiv Preprint ArXiv:1506.00019*.

Orvieto, A., Smith, S. L., Gu, A., Fernando, A., Gulcehre, C., Pascanu, R., & De, S. (2023). Resurrecting recurrent neural networks for long sequences. *ArXiv Preprint ArXiv:2303.06349*.

Peng, T., Zhang, C., Zhou, J., & Nazir, M. S. (2021). An integrated framework of Bi-directional long-short term memory (BiLSTM) based on sine cosine algorithm for hourly solar radiation forecasting. *Energy, 221*, 119887.

Wang, C., Dou, M., Li, Z., Outbib, R., Zhao, D., Zuo, J., Wang, Y., Liang, B., & Wang, P. (2023). Data-driven prognostics based on time-frequency analysis and symbolic recurrent neural network for fuel cells under dynamic load. *Reliability Engineering & System Safety, 233*, 109123.

Wang, Y., Wu, H., Zhang, J., Gao, Z., Wang, J., Philip, S. Y., & Long, M. (2022). Predrnn: A recurrent neural network for spatiotemporal predictive learning. *IEEE Transactions on Pattern Analysis and Machine Intelligence, 45*(2), 2208–2225.

Zhang, J., Jiang, Y., Wu, S., Li, X., Luo, H., & Yin, S. (2022a). Prediction of remaining useful life based on bidirectional gated recurrent unit with temporal self-attention mechanism. *Reliability Engineering & System Safety, 221*, 108297.

Zhang, W., Li, H., Tang, L., Gu, X., Wang, L., & Wang, L. (2022b). Displacement prediction of Jiuxianping landslide using gated recurrent unit (GRU) networks. *Acta Geotechnica, 17*(4), 1367–1382.

Zhong, Z., Gao, Y., Zheng, Y., Zheng, B., & Sato, I. (2023). Real-world video deblurring: A benchmark dataset and an efficient recurrent neural network. *International Journal of Computer Vision, 131*(1), 284–301.

Chapter 6

Generative Adversarial Networks

While deep neural networks have primarily been used for discriminative learning tasks, such as classification and regression, they have also been adapted for generative modeling tasks. Generative modeling involves machine learning, where the goal is to learn a model that captures the underlying distribution of the training data. Unlike discriminative learning, which focuses on mapping input data to labels or outputs, generative modeling aims to understand and model the data itself.

However, the success of deep neural networks in discriminative learning has opened new possibilities for generative modeling. One example mentioned is the use of recurrent neural network (RNN) language models. While RNNs are typically used for sequence prediction tasks, they can also be utilized as generative models. By training an RNN language model to predict the next character in a sequence, the model learns the characteristics and patterns of the training data. Once trained, the RNN can generate new sequences of characters that resemble the original data, effectively acting as a generative model. The main objective of generative modeling is to generate new samples that resemble the training data. Once the model has learned the underlying distribution, it can generate new examples that are like the original data but not necessarily identical. This ability to generate new samples is what sets generative models apart from discriminative models.

The example of generating photorealistic images of faces from a large corpus of face photographs illustrates the concept of generative modeling. By learning the characteristics and patterns in the training data, a generative model can generate new images that look like they could plausibly belong to the same dataset. This approach demonstrates how discriminative deep neural networks can be repurposed for generative tasks. By leveraging the representation and learning capabilities of deep neural networks, researchers have made significant progress in generating realistic and novel samples in various domains, including images, text, and music.

Deep neural networks have also made significant advancements in generative modeling. Generative adversarial networks (GANs) (Zhang et al., 2019) and variational autoencoders (VAEs) are popular architectures used for generative modeling. These models learn to generate new samples by training on the training data and optimizing specific objectives, such as minimizing the difference between generated samples and real data or maximizing the likelihood of generating realistic examples.

Generative modeling has various applications beyond image generation, including text generation, speech synthesis, data augmentation, anomaly detection, and more. It

DOI: 10.1201/9781003654216-8

allows us to explore and understand the underlying structure of complex datasets and generate new data points that align with that structure.

6.1 Generative Adversarial Networks Model

GANs, which were first introduced in a breakthrough paper by I. J. Goodfellow (2014), provide a novel approach to generative modeling by leveraging the power of discriminative models to create good generative models.

The correct breakdown of the term GAN is as follows.

1. *Generative:* GANs are designed to learn and generate new data that resembles a given dataset. They aim to capture the underlying distribution of the training data and generate new samples from that distribution. The generative aspect of GANs involves learning a model that can generate new data points.
2. *Adversarial:* GANs employ an adversarial training framework, where two models are pitted against each other. The generator model generates synthetic data samples, while the discriminator model tries to distinguish between real data samples from the training set and fake data samples generated by the generator. The generator aims to fool the discriminator, while the discriminator aims to accurately classify real and fake data. This adversarial setup creates a competitive learning process between the two models.
3. *Networks:* GANs utilize deep neural networks as the underlying architecture for both generator and discriminator models. The generator network takes random noise as input and transforms it into synthetic data samples. The discriminator network takes input data samples and classifies them as real or fake. Both networks are typically implemented using deep neural network architectures, such as convolutional neural networks (CNNs) for image data.

By combining these three components, GANs provide a powerful framework for learning and generating new data samples that resemble a given dataset, and they have been successfully applied in various domains, including image generation, text generation, and data augmentation. The central idea behind GANs is that a data generator is considered good if it produces synthetic data that is indistinguishable from real data (Salimans et al., 2016). This notion is akin to a two-sample test in statistics, which aims to determine whether two datasets are drawn from the same underlying distribution. However, GANs take this concept further by utilizing it in a constructive manner.

Rather than solely training a model to identify whether two datasets are from the same distribution or not, GANs employ the two-sample test to provide training signals to a generative model. This approach allows for iterative improvement of the data generator until it can produce synthetic data that closely resembles real data. The ultimate goal is for the generated data to be convincing enough to fool even a state-of-the-art deep neural network classifier. By using an adversarial setup with a generator and a discriminator, GANs enable the generative model to learn from the feedback provided by the discriminator. The discriminator's role is to distinguish between real and fake data, while the generator's objective is to produce synthetic data that is realistic enough to deceive the discriminator.

Through an iterative training process, the generator and discriminator play a game against each other, with the generator trying to improve its ability to generate realistic data and the discriminator trying to become better at differentiating real and fake data. This adversarial training process drives the generative model to improve over time.

The use of GANs has led to remarkable advancements in generative modeling across various domains, including image synthesis, text generation, and more. GANs have opened up new possibilities for generating high-quality synthetic data that closely resembles real data distributions, thereby pushing the boundaries of generative modeling and providing new avenues for creative applications in machine learning. The GAN architecture, as shown in Figure 6.1, consists of two main components: the generator network and the discriminator network. The goal of the generator network is to generate data that closely resembles real data. For example, if we are working with images, the generator network generates realistic images. If it's speech, it generates audio sequences, and so on.

On the other hand, the discriminator network's role is to distinguish between fake/generated data and real data. It learns to classify whether a given input is real or fake. Both networks are engaged in a competitive process. The generator network tries to produce data that the discriminator network cannot differentiate from real data, while the discriminator network aims to accurately classify the input as real or fake. During training, the generator network generates fake data and presents it to the discriminator network. The discriminator network then provides feedback on the authenticity of the generated data. This feedback is used to update and improve both networks. The generator network uses the discriminator's feedback to refine its generation process, making the generated data more realistic. Simultaneously, the discriminator network adapts to better differentiate between real and fake data.

This iterative process continues until the generator network becomes skilled at generating data that is indistinguishable from real data, and the discriminator network becomes highly accurate in identifying fake data. The competition between the generator and discriminator networks drives the overall training of the GAN model, leading to the generation of high-quality synthetic data. The discriminator in a GAN is a binary classifier that aims to distinguish between real and fake data. It takes an input x and produces a scalar prediction $o \in \mathbb{R}$, which represents the probability that the input is real.

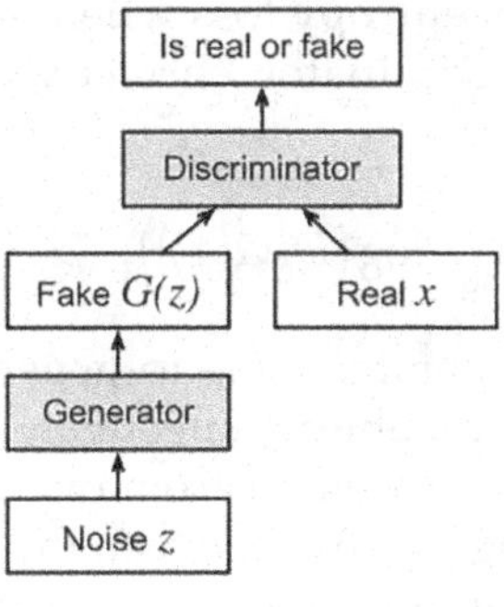

Figure 6.1 Generative adversarial networks architecture.

To obtain this probability, the output o is typically passed through a sigmoid function, resulting in the predicted probability $D(x)=\frac{1}{\left(1+e^{-o}\right)}$.

During training, the discriminator is trained to minimize the cross-entropy loss, as described by the following equation.

$$\min_{D}\left\{-y\log D(x)-(1-y)\log\left(1-D(x)\right)\right\}$$

The loss function measures the difference between the predicted probabilities $D(x)$ and the true labels y. For real data, y is set to 1, indicating that the input is real, and for fake data, y is set to 0, indicating that the input is generated by the generator.

By minimizing the cross-entropy loss, the discriminator learns to assign high probabilities to real data (encouraging $D(x)$ to be close to 1) and low probabilities to fake data (encouraging $D(x)$ to be close to 0). This training process helps the discriminator to become more accurate in distinguishing between real and fake data, which in turn guides the training of the generator network.

The generator in a GAN takes a random noise vector $z\epsilon\mathbb{R}^{d}$ from a source of randomness, such as a normal distribution, and applies a function $G(z)$ to generate synthetic data x'. The generator's objective is to produce data that is indistinguishable from real data, making the discriminator classify it as true data. In other words, the goal is to have $D\left(G(z)\right)\approx 1$, where D is the discriminator.

During training, the parameters of the generator G are updated to maximize the cross-entropy loss when the true label y is 0 (indicating fake data). This can be formulated as maximizing the log -probability of the discriminator incorrectly classifying the generated data as real:

$$\min_{G}\left\{-(1-y)\log\left(1-D\left(G(z)\right)\right)\right\}=\min_{G}\left\{-\log\left(1-D\left(G(z)\right)\right)\right\}$$

By maximizing this objective, the generator learns to generate data that is more realistic and can deceive the discriminator into classifying it as real. The interplay between the generator and discriminator in the GAN framework leads to the training of both networks and the improvement of the overall generative performance.

When the generator becomes too good, and the gradients for the discriminator become small, a common practice is to modify the loss function for the generator. Instead of maximizing the cross-entropy loss when $y=0$, we can minimize the negative log-probability of the discriminator correctly classifying the generated data as fake:

$$\min_{G}\left\{-y\log\left(D\left(G(z)\right)\right)\right\}=\min_{G}\left\{-\log\left(D\left(G(z)\right)\right)\right\}$$

By minimizing this loss, the generator aims to generate data that the discriminator classifies as fake with a high probability, effectively fooling the discriminator. This modification helps to prevent the generator from overpowering the discriminator and ensures a more balanced training process between the two networks.

The generator is trained to minimize the negative log-probability of the discriminator classifying the generated data as fake, while the discriminator is trained to minimize the cross-entropy loss for both real and fake data. This adversarial training process leads to the competition and improvement of both networks, ultimately resulting in a generator that produces more realistic data and a discriminator that becomes more proficient at distinguishing real from fake data.

6.2 Importance of GAN Development

GANs were developed to address the challenge of generating realistic and high-quality synthetic data that resembles a given dataset. Traditional machine learning algorithms, including neural networks, rely on supervised or unsupervised learning to model the underlying distribution of the training data. However, they often struggle to generate new data samples that exhibit the same characteristics and variability as the original data.

The motivation behind GANs was to bridge this gap and enable the generation of new data samples that are visually and statistically similar to the training data. By training a generator model and a discriminator model in an adversarial setting, GANs introduced a novel framework for generative modeling.

The generator model in a GAN is trained to generate synthetic data samples from random noise as input. The discriminator model is simultaneously trained to distinguish between real data samples from the training set and fake data samples generated by the generator. Through an iterative process of competition and feedback, the generator learns to improve its ability to generate realistic data, while the discriminator learns to better distinguish between real and fake data.

By pitting these two models against each other, GANs enable the generation of synthetic data that exhibits similar patterns, structure, and statistical properties as the training data. This has profound implications in various domains, including computer vision, natural language processing, and data augmentation. GANs have been successful in generating realistic images, synthesizing natural language text, creating realistic audio, and more. GANs were developed to overcome the limitations of traditional machine learning algorithms in generating realistic synthetic data and to explore the potential of neural networks to learn and generate new patterns that resemble the training data.

6.3 Applications of GANs

GANs have revolutionized the field of generative modeling and found numerous applications across various domains. Here are some notable applications of GANs.

- *Image Synthesis:* GANs have been widely used for generating realistic and high-quality images. They can learn the underlying distribution of a dataset and generate new images that resemble the training data. This has applications in art, entertainment, virtual reality, and computer graphics.
- *Data Augmentation:* GANs can be employed to generate synthetic data samples, which can then be used to augment the training data for machine learning models. This helps in improving model performance, especially when the original dataset is limited.
- *Image-to-Image Translation:* GANs can learn to translate images from one domain to another. For example, they can convert a sketch into a realistic image, transform

images from daytime to nighttime, or change the style of an image. This has applications in computer vision, design, and entertainment.
- *Text-to-Image Synthesis:* GANs can generate images based on textual descriptions. Given a textual input, the generator can generate images that match the description, enabling applications in content creation, storytelling, and design.
- *Super Resolution:* GANs can be used to enhance the resolution and quality of low-resolution images. They can generate high-resolution versions of images, enabling applications in medical imaging, surveillance, and image restoration.
- *Video Generation:* GANs can generate realistic videos by extending their capabilities from image synthesis to video synthesis. This has applications in video editing, special effects, and simulation.
- *Style Transfer:* GANs can learn the style of one image and apply it to another image. This allows for artistic transformations and style transfer applications.
- *Anomaly Detection:* GANs can be used to learn the normal distribution of a dataset and detect anomalies or outliers. They can generate samples that deviate from the learned distribution, making them useful for anomaly detection in various domains such as fraud detection, cybersecurity, and medical diagnostics.

These are just a few examples of the wide range of applications of GANs. As you delve deeper into studying the working and capabilities of GANs, you will discover even more exciting and impactful applications in various fields of research and industry.

6.4 Challenges faced by GANs

While GANs have achieved remarkable success, they also face several challenges that researchers and practitioners continue to address. Some of the main challenges include the following.

- *Mode Collapse:* Mode collapse occurs when the generator produces limited and repetitive samples, ignoring the diversity present in the training data. This can happen when the discriminator becomes too powerful, forcing the generator to generate samples that are similar and less diverse.
- *Training Instability:* GANs can be challenging to train due to their adversarial nature. The training process involves a dynamic equilibrium between the generator and discriminator, and finding this balance can be difficult. GANs may suffer from issues such as oscillations, vanishing gradients, or mode dropping, making training unstable.
- *Evaluation and Metrics:* Evaluating the performance of GANs is not straightforward. Traditional evaluation metrics such as accuracy or loss may not effectively capture the quality and diversity of generated samples. Developing reliable evaluation metrics for GANs is an ongoing research area.
- *Mode Collapse and Overfitting:* GANs are prone to mode collapse, where the generator fails to capture the entire data distribution and generates only a subset of samples. Overfitting can also occur, where the generator produces samples that resemble the training data too closely, limiting its generalization capability.
- *Hyperparameter Sensitivity:* GANs have several hyperparameters that need to be carefully tuned for optimal performance. The choice of hyperparameters, such as

learning rates, network architectures, and regularization techniques, can significantly impact the stability and quality of the generated samples.

- *Dataset Bias and Generalization:* GANs are sensitive to dataset biases and may struggle to generate samples that generalize well to unseen data. Biases present in the training data can be amplified by GANs, leading to biased or unrealistic generated samples.
- *Large-Scale Training:* Training GANs on large-scale datasets can be computationally expensive and time-consuming. The training process often requires high-performance computing resources and distributed training techniques to handle the computational demands.

Researchers and practitioners are actively addressing these challenges through various techniques such as architectural improvements, regularization methods, optimization algorithms, and novel training approaches. The field of GANs continues to evolve, with ongoing research aimed at enhancing stability, improving training dynamics, and addressing the limitations and challenges faced by GANs.

6.5 Varieties of GANs

GANs have evolved over time, leading to the development of various specialized variants. Here are some notable types of GANs.

- *Conditional GANs (cGANs):* cGANs extend the standard GAN framework by incorporating additional conditional information. They generate samples conditioned on specific input conditions, such as class labels or attribute vectors. cGANs enable controlled generation, where users can specify desired characteristics for the generated samples.
- *Deep Convolutional GANs (DCGANs):* DCGANs leverage CNNs as the generator and discriminator architectures. CNNs are particularly effective for image generation tasks as they capture spatial dependencies. DCGANs have shown improved stability and better image generation quality compared to traditional GAN architectures.
- *Wasserstein GANs (WGANs):* WGANs introduce the Wasserstein distance as a new loss function to measure the discrepancy between the real and generated distributions. By optimizing the Wasserstein distance, WGANs tend to produce more stable training dynamics and generate higher-quality samples. They address the mode collapse issue and provide a more meaningful gradient signal during training.
- *Progressive GANs:* Progressive GANs gradually grow both the generator and discriminator architectures during training. They start with low-resolution images and progressively increase the resolution, allowing for the generation of high-quality and detailed images. Progressive GANs have been successful in generating realistic high-resolution images.
- *CycleGANs:* CycleGANs are designed for unsupervised image-to-image translation tasks. They learn mappings between two different image domains without paired training data. CycleGANs utilize cycle consistency loss to ensure that the translated images can be converted back to the original domain, preserving the identity of the input images.

- *StarGANs:* StarGANs extend the conditional GAN framework to enable multi-domain image-to-image translation. They can generate images that conform to different target domains specified by attribute labels. StarGANs provide a single model capable of handling multiple domains, simplifying the training process for multi-domain image translation.
- *StyleGANs:* StyleGANs focus on generating highly realistic and diverse images by explicitly modeling the style and structure of the generated samples. They separate the latent space into style and content components, allowing for fine-grained control over the generated images' appearance and attributes. StyleGANs have been instrumental in generating high-resolution and visually appealing images.

These are just a few examples of the diverse range of GAN variants that have been developed. Each type of GAN caters to specific applications and challenges, demonstrating the versatility and adaptability of the GAN framework in generative modeling.

6.6 Basic Steps to Implement a GAN Model

To implement a basic GAN, you can follow these steps.

- *Import the Necessary Libraries:* Start by importing the required libraries, such as TensorFlow or PyTorch, for building and training your GAN model.
- *Define the Generator:* Create a generator model that takes random noise as input and generates fake samples. The generator can be implemented using fully connected layers, convolutional layers, or a combination of both.
- *Define the Discriminator:* Create a discriminator model that takes input samples and predicts whether they are real or fake. The discriminator can also be implemented using fully connected layers, convolutional layers, or a combination of both.
- *Define the Loss Functions:* Define the loss functions for both the generator and the discriminator. Typically, the generator aims to minimize the discriminator's ability to distinguish between real and fake samples, while the discriminator aims to maximize its ability to correctly classify real and fake samples.
- *Compile the Models:* Compile both the generator and discriminator models with appropriate optimizers and loss functions.
- *Train the GAN:* Train the GAN by alternatingly training the generator and the discriminator. In each iteration, generate a batch of fake samples using the generator, combine them with real samples, and train the discriminator to classify them correctly. Then, train the generator to minimize the discriminator's ability to distinguish between real and fake samples.
- *Generate Fake Samples:* After training, use the trained generator to generate fake samples by inputting random noise. You can adjust the amount of noise or the number of generated samples as needed.
- *Evaluate and Visualize the Results:* Evaluate the performance of your GAN by assessing the quality of the generated samples. You can visualize the generated samples using libraries like matplotlib to see how well the GAN has learned to generate new data.

It's important to note that implementing a GAN can be complex and may require experimenting with different architectures, hyperparameters, and training techniques to achieve desirable results. Additionally, handling issues such as mode collapse and training instability may require additional advanced techniques.

6.7 Hands-on Practice on Implementation of GANs on MNIST Dataset using Python

Implementing a GAN on the MNIST dataset in Python involves training a generator network to generate realistic handwritten digits and a discriminator network to distinguish between real and fake digits.

6.7.1 *MNIST Dataset*

The MNIST dataset is a popular benchmark dataset widely used in the field of machine learning and computer vision. It consists of a collection of handwritten digits from 0 to 9. Each digit is represented as a 28×28 grayscale image, making it a relatively small and manageable dataset presented in Figure 6.2 (Zeng & Long, 2022).

The MNIST dataset is commonly used for tasks such as digit recognition, image classification, and generative modeling. It serves as a standard dataset for evaluating and comparing the performance of various machine learning algorithms and models.

The dataset is divided into two main parts: a training set and a test set. The training set contains 60,000 images, while the test set contains 10,000 images (Cheng et al., 2020). This division allows researchers and practitioners to train models on the training set and evaluate their performance on the test set to assess their generalization ability.

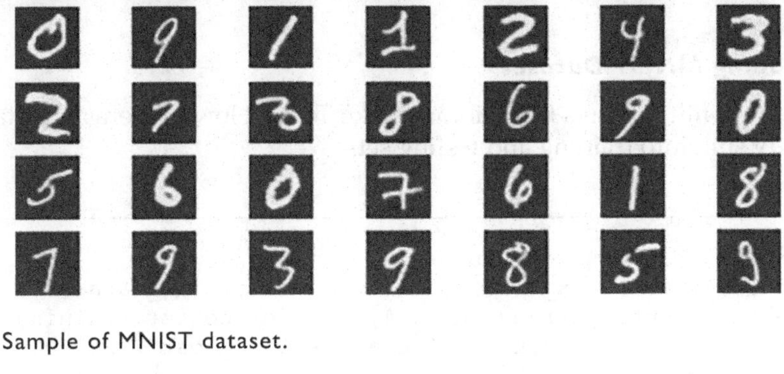

Figure 6.2 Sample of MNIST dataset.

With this implementation our aim is to train the discriminator model using the MNIST dataset and some noise, and then after giving the generator model some sample noise that is like the MNIST dataset, you want it to generate data that is similar to the MNIST dataset, which gives the impression that the images are the original ones but are really produced by the generator model (Chen et al., 2018; Kayed et al., 2020). Let's begin by importing the necessary libraries.

6.7.2 *Importing the Important Libraries*

```
import numpy as np
import matplotlib.pyplot as plt
from tensorflow.keras.datasets import mnist
from tensorflow.keras.models import Sequential
from tensorflow.keras.layers import Dense, LeakyReLU,
BatchNormalization
from tensorflow.keras.optimizers import Adam
```

Here's a brief description of each library:

- **numpy (imported as np):** A library for numerical operations in Python.
- **matplotlib.pyplot (imported as plt):** A library for data visualization and plotting in Python.
- **tensorflow.keras.datasets.mnist:** A module that provides the MNIST dataset.
- **tensorflow.keras.models.Sequential:** A class for building sequential models in Keras.
- **tensorflow.keras.layers:** A module that includes various types of layers to build neural networks in Keras.
- **tensorflow.keras.optimizers.Adam:** An optimizer for training neural networks using the Adam algorithm.

Make sure TensorFlow and Keras are installed in Python environment before running the code. Once the necessary libraries are imported, you can proceed with loading the MNIST dataset and building the GAN model (Creswell et al., 2018; Gui et al., 2021).

6.7.3 *Loading MNIST Dataset*

When using in-built datasets from libraries like TensorFlow or Keras, the datasets are often already split into training and testing sets.

```
mnist = tf.keras.datasets.mnist
(x_train, y_train), (x_test, y_test) = mnist.load_data()
# Scale the inputs in range of (-1, +1) for better training
x_train, x_test = x_train / 255.0 * 2 - 1, x_test / 255.0 * 2 - 1
```

The MNIST dataset is loaded using **'mnist.load_data()'**, and the training and testing sets are unpacked into **'x_train'**, **'y_train'**, **'x_test'**, and **'y_test'**.

To ensure better training performance, the input images are scaled to the range of (-1, +1) by dividing the pixel values by 255.0 and then scaling them to the range of (–1, 1) by multiplying with 2 and subtracting 1. This normalization step is commonly performed in GAN implementations to help stabilize the training process.

If you want to plot some example images from the MNIST dataset, you can use matplotlib as shown in the code snippet you provided. The **'plt.imshow()'** function is used to display the raw pixel data of each image, and **'plt.subplot()'** is used to arrange the images in a grid.

```
for i in range(49):
  plt.subplot(7, 7, i+1)
  plt.axis("off")
#plot raw pixel data
  plt.imshow(x_train[i])
plt.show()
```

To print the shape of the dataset, you can simply use the **'shape'** attribute of the NumPy arrays **'x_train'** and **'x_test'**, which will give you the dimensions of the data. The shape of **'x_train'** will be **'(60000, 28, 28)'** indicating 60,000 images of size 28×28, and the shape of **'x_test'** will be **'(10000, 28, 28)'** indicating 10,000 images of size 28×28.

To feed the data into a neural network, it is common to flatten the input images from 2D to 1D. In this case, the MNIST images are originally 28 × 28 pixels, resulting in a shape of (60000, 28, 28) for **'x_train'** and (10000, 28, 28) for **'x_test'**.

```
N, H, W = x_train.shape #number, height, width
D = H * W #dimension (28, 28)
x_train = x_train.reshape(-1, D)
x_test = x_test.reshape(-1, D)
```

To flatten the images, we reshape them to have a single dimension of size $784(28 \times 28)$. This can be done using the **'reshape()'** function in NumPy. The code snippet you provided reshapes **'x_train'** and **'x_test'** to have shapes of (60000, 784) and (10000, 784), respectively.

This flattening process allows us to represent each image as a vector of pixel values, making it compatible with neural network architectures that expect 1D inputs.

6.7.4 Build the Generator Model

Here's an updated version of the generator model using which a deep CNN architecture is defined. The variable known as latent dimension specifies how many inputs will be used in the model. Because the range of an image pixel is between –1 and +1, we define the input layer, three hidden layers, batch normalization, and an activation function of tanh for the output layer.

```
# Import the necessary libraries
from tensorflow.keras.layers import Input, Dense, Reshape, Batch-
Normalization, LeakyReLU, Conv2DTranspose
from tensorflow.keras.models import Model

latent_dim = 100

def build_generator(latent_dim):
    # Input layer
    i = Input(shape=(latent_dim,))

    # Reshape the input into a small image
    x = Dense(7 * 7 * 128)(i)
    x = LeakyReLU(alpha=0.2)(x)
    x = Reshape((7, 7, 128))(x)

    # Upsampling and convolutions
    x = Conv2DTranspose(128, kernel_size=3, strides=2,
padding='same')(x)
    x = BatchNormalization()(x)
    x = LeakyReLU(alpha=0.2)(x)

    x = Conv2DTranspose(64, kernel_size=3, strides=1,
padding='same')(x)
    x = BatchNormalization()(x)
    x = LeakyReLU(alpha=0.2)(x)

    # Output layer
    x = Conv2DTranspose(1, kernel_size=3, strides=2,
padding='same', activation='tanh')(x)

    # Create the model
    model = Model(i, x)

    return model

# Build the generator model
generator = build_generator(latent_dim)
```

This code defines a generator model using a deep CNN architecture. The input to the model is a vector of size **'latent_dim'** (in this case, 100). The subsequent dense layer maps the noise to a higher-dimensional space (7 × 7 × 128).

Next, a reshape layer converts the dense output into a 3D tensor with a shape of 7, 7, 128. This is followed by two **'Conv2DTranspose'** layers, which perform the upsampling operation to gradually increase the spatial dimensions of the tensor.

Each convolutional layer is followed by a leaky ReLU activation function to introduce nonlinearity. The final convolutional layer has a single filter and uses the tanh activation function to ensure that the output image pixels are in the range of –1 to +1.

The model then uses dense layers, reshape layers, convolutional transpose layers, batch normalization layers, and leaky ReLU activation functions to gradually upsample the input noise and generate an image-like output.

The final output layer uses a convolutional transpose layer with a kernel size of 3, strides of 2, padding of **'same'**, and activation function **'tanh'**. This layer generates the final output image of the generator.

The **'build_generator'** function returns the generator model, which can be used to generate images based on random noise inputs.

6.7.4.1 Importance of Leaky ReLU over Regular ReLU

- The main reason for using leaky ReLU instead of the regular ReLU activation function is to address the issue of "dying ReLU" or "dead neurons".
- The regular ReLU activation function sets all negative values to zero, effectively "killing" the neuron and preventing any further gradient flow during backpropagation. In some cases, especially with large learning rates, a significant portion of the neurons may become inactive and result in a dead network that cannot learn.
- Leaky ReLU introduces a small slope for negative values instead of setting them to zero. This small slope allows a small gradient to flow for negative inputs, preventing the neurons from completely dying. By introducing a small negative slope (typically around 0.01), leaky ReLU ensures that there is some gradient flow even for negative inputs, which helps overcome the dying ReLU problem.
- The advantage of leaky ReLU is that it helps alleviate the vanishing gradient problem and encourages the flow of gradients throughout the network. This can lead to improved learning and better performance, especially in deep neural networks.
- In the context of the generator model in GANs, leaky ReLU can help propagate gradients and facilitate the training process by preventing the generator from getting stuck in a state where it generates only zero-valued outputs.

6.7.4.2 Importance of using Batch Normalization

Batch normalization is commonly used in neural networks, including GANs, for several reasons.

- *Improved Training Speed:* By normalizing the inputs to each layer, batch normalization reduces the internal covariate shift. This allows for more stable and faster training, as the network does not need to adapt to the changing input distributions.
- *Stabilized Gradients:* Batch normalization helps address the vanishing and exploding gradient problems. By normalizing the inputs, it ensures that gradients flow through the network more smoothly, making it easier to optimize the model.
- *Regularization Effect:* Batch normalization introduces a regularization effect by adding a small amount of noise to the activations during training. This can help prevent overfitting and improve the generalization ability of the model.

- *Reduces Sensitivity to Hyperparameters:* Batch normalization reduces the dependence of the model on specific hyperparameters, such as learning rate and weight initialization. It makes the network more robust and easier to train by reducing the sensitivity to these hyperparameters.

In the case of GANs, batch normalization is particularly important to stabilize the training process and ensure that the generator and discriminator networks converge effectively. It helps prevent issues such as mode collapse and gradient instability, which can occur in GAN training.

However, it is worth noting that applying batch normalization to all layers in GANs can sometimes lead to sample oscillation and model instability, as mentioned. In such cases, techniques like applying batch normalization selectively or using alternative normalization methods, such as instance normalization or layer normalization, may be employed to address these issues and ensure stable training.

6.7.5 Build the Discriminator Model

The discriminator model is a simple feedforward neural network architecture using leaky ReLU activation and a sigmoid output:

```
# Defining Discriminator Model
def build_discriminator(img_size):
    i = Input(shape=(img_size,))
    x = Dense(512, activation=LeakyReLU(alpha=0.2))(i)
    x = Dense(256, activation=LeakyReLU(alpha=0.2))(x)
    x = Dense(1, activation='sigmoid')(x)
    model = Model(i, x)
    return model
```

In this, **'img_size'** represents the size of the input images. The discriminator model takes an input of this size and passes it through two hidden layers with leaky ReLU activation. The output layer consists of a single neuron with a sigmoid activation function, which produces a value between 0 and 1, representing the probability of the input image being real.

The leaky ReLU activation function is used to introduce a small negative slope for negative input values, preventing the "dying ReLU" problem and helping to stabilize the training process.

The sigmoid activation function in the output layer is suitable for binary classification tasks, such as distinguishing between real and fake images in a GAN.

Once the generator and discriminator models are defined, they can be combined to form the GAN model for training.

6.7.6 Combine the Generator and Discriminator Models into a GAN

Here's the code to compile both the discriminator and the combined model (generator):

```
# Build and compile the discriminator
discriminator = build_discriminator(D)
discriminator.compile(loss='binary_crossentropy',
optimizer=Adam(0.0002, 0.5), metrics=['accuracy'])

# Build and compile the combined model
generator = build_generator(latent_dim)
z = Input(shape=(latent_dim,))
img = generator(z)

# For the combined model, only train the generator
discriminator.trainable = False

# The combined model takes noise as input and generates images
combined = Model(z, discriminator(img))
combined.compile(loss='binary_crossentropy',
optimizer=Adam(0.0002, 0.5))
```

In this code, we first compile the discriminator model using binary cross-entropy as the loss function and the Adam optimizer with a learning rate of 0.0002 and momentum of 0.5. The discriminator's accuracy is also tracked as a metric.

Next, we compile the combined model by setting the discriminator's **'trainable'** attribute to False, indicating that during training, we want to update only the generator's weights. The combined model takes noise **('z')** as input and generates images using the generator. The loss function used for the combined model is also binary cross-entropy, and the same optimizer settings are used.

By compiling both the discriminator and the combined model, we are ready to start training the GAN on the MNIST dataset.

6.7.7 *Represent Noise Sample*

To generate noise samples from the latent space and pass them through the generator, you can use the following code:

```
## Create an input to represent noise sample from latent space
z = Input(shape=(latent_dim,))
## Pass noise through a generator to get an Image
img = generator(z)
discriminator.trainable = False
fake_pred = discriminator(img)
```

Here's a breakdown of the steps:

- We create an input placeholder **'z'** with the shape **'(latent_dim)'** to represent the noise sample from the latent space.

- We pass the noise through the generator using the generator model **'(generator(z))'** to generate an image. This is done by calling the generator model with the input z, which produces the output image.
- We set the **'trainable'** attribute of the discriminator to **'False'**. This ensures that during this phase, the discriminator's weights are not updated when training the combined GAN model.
- We pass the generated image **'img'** to the discriminator to predict its authenticity. This is done by calling the discriminator model with the input **'img'**, which produces the output prediction **'fake_pred'**. Since the discriminator's weights are not being updated, this prediction represents the discriminator's prediction on a fake image.

These steps are part of the training process of the GAN, where the generator aims to generate realistic-looking images to fool the discriminator, while the discriminator aims to correctly distinguish between real and fake images.

6.7.8 Create Generator Model

It's time to build a combined generator model that includes noise input and discriminator feedback to assist the generator perform better.

```
# Combine the generator and discriminator
combined_model_gen = Model(z, fake_pred)

# Compile the combined model
combined_model_gen.compile(loss='binary_crossentropy',
optimizer=Adam(0.0002, 0.5))
```

Here's a breakdown of the steps:

- We create a combined generator model by defining a new model **'combined_model_gen'** with the input **'z'** (the noise sample) and the output **'fake_pred'** (the discriminator's prediction on the generated image). This means that the generator's output is fed as input to the discriminator.
- We compile the combined generator model using the binary cross-entropy loss function, which is commonly used for binary classification problems and the Adam optimizer with a learning rate of 0.0002 and a momentum of 0.5.

The combined generator model allows us to train the generator by providing noise samples as input and using the feedback from the discriminator to update its weights. This adversarial training process helps the generator improve its performance in generating realistic-looking images.

Note that in the combined model, only the weights of the generator will be updated during training, while the weights of the discriminator remain frozen.

6.7.9 *GAN Training: Parameters Deceleration*

An example of how you can define the parameters for training the GAN:

```
# Define parameters for training
epochs = 10000
batch_size = 128
sample_period = 200 # Generate a sample image every 200 steps

# Define batch labels for real and fake images
ones = np.ones(batch_size)
zeros = np.zeros(batch_size)

# Create empty lists to store loss values
generator_losses = []
discriminator_losses = []

# Create an empty file to save generated images
generated_images_path = 'generated_images/'
os.makedirs(generated_images_path, exist_ok=True)
```

In this code, we define the following parameters:

- **'epochs'**: The number of training epochs, which determines how many times the entire dataset will be iterated during training.
- **'batch_size'**: The number of images in each training batch. This affects the number of gradient updates per epoch.
- **'sample_period'**: After how many steps (or batches), we generate a sample image using the generator to monitor the training progress.
- **'ones'**: A numpy array filled with ones, which will be used as labels for real images.
- **'zeros'**: A numpy array filled with zeros, which will be used as labels for fake images.
- **'generator_losses'**: An empty list to store the generator loss values during training.
- **'discriminator_losses'**: An empty list to store the discriminator loss values during training.
- **'generated_images_path'**: The directory path where the generated images will be saved.

You can adjust these parameters based on your specific requirements and available computing resources.

6.7.10 *Sample Image Creation*

It is a function build that produces a grid of randomly selected samples from a generator and saves them to a file. Simply said, it will generate random pictures at certain epochs. To create 25 photos in a single iteration or on a single page, we define the row size as 5 and the column size as 5, respectively.

```
import numpy as np
import matplotlib.pyplot as plt

def sample_images(generator, latent_dim, epoch, rows=5, cols=5):
noise = np.random.randn(rows * cols, latent_dim)
imgs = generator.predict(noise)
# Rescale images 0 - 1
imgs = 0.5 * imgs + 0.5

fig, axs = plt.subplots(rows, cols)
idx = 0
for i in range(rows):
for j in range(cols):
axs[i, j].imshow(imgs[idx].reshape(28, 28), cmap='gray')
axs[i, j].axis('off')
idx += 1

plt.savefig("gan_images/%d.png" % epoch)
plt.close()
```

The **'sample_images'** function takes the generator model, latent dimension, epoch number, and optional parameters for the number of rows and columns in the grid (default is 5 × 5).

The function generates random noise vectors and passes them through the generator model to generate images. The generated images are then rescaled to the range (0, 1). The images are plotted in a grid using Matplotlib, and each image is displayed with grayscale colormap and without axis labels. Finally, the figure is saved to a file named with the epoch number in the "gan_images" directory.

You can call this function at different epochs during training to generate and save sample images for visual inspection of the generator's progress.

6.7.11 Train Discriminator and then Generator to Generate Images

The code to train the discriminator and generator models:

```
# Define the number of epochs and batch size
epochs = 20000
batch_size = 128
sample_interval = 1000

# Iterate through epochs
for epoch in range(epochs):
    # ---------------------
    # Train the Discriminator
    # ---------------------
    # Select a random batch of real images
```

```
    idx = np.random.randint(0, x_train.shape[0], batch_size)
    real_imgs = x_train[idx]

    # Generate a batch of fake images using the generator
    noise = np.random.randn(batch_size, latent_dim)
    fake_imgs = generator.predict(noise)

    # Train the discriminator
    d_loss_real = discriminator.train_on_batch(real_imgs,
np.ones((batch_size, 1)))
    d_loss_fake = discriminator.train_on_batch(fake_imgs,
np.zeros((batch_size, 1)))
    d_loss = 0.5 * np.add(d_loss_real, d_loss_fake)

    # ---------------------
    # Train the Generator
    # ---------------------

    # Generate a new batch of noise samples
    noise = np.random.randn(batch_size, latent_dim)

    # Train the generator
    g_loss = combined_model_gen.train_on_batch(noise,
np.ones((batch_size, 1)))

    # Print the progress
    if epoch % sample_interval == 0:
        print(f"Epoch: {epoch} - D loss: {d_loss[0]}, accuracy:
{100*d_loss[1]}% - G loss: {g_loss}")

        # Save sample images
        sample_images(generator, latent_dim, epoch)
```

In this code, we iterate through the specified number of epochs. In each epoch, we train the discriminator and generator models in an alternating manner.

First, we train the discriminator by selecting a random batch of real images (**'real_imgs'**) from the MNIST dataset and a batch of fake images (**'fake_imgs'**) generated by the generator model. We compute the discriminator loss (**'d_loss'**) by training it on the real and fake images separately using the **'train_on_batch'** method.

Next, we train the generator by generating a new batch of noise samples (**'noise'**) and training the combined generator model (**'combined_model_gen'**) on the noise samples with the target label of 1 (indicating that the generated images are real). We compute the generator loss (**'g_loss'**) using the **'train_on_batch'** method.

After each specified number of epochs (**'sample_interval'**), we print the current epoch, discriminator loss, discriminator accuracy, and generator loss. Moreover, we save sample images generated by the generator using the **'sample_images'** function.

You can adjust the number of epochs, batch size, and sample interval according to your needs.

6.7.12 *Plotting of Loss Function*

The code to plot the generator and discriminator losses over the training epochs, presented in Figure 6.3:

```
import matplotlib.pyplot as plt
# Plot the generator and discriminator losses
plt.plot(g_losses, label='Generator Loss')
plt.plot(d_losses, label='Discriminator Loss')
plt.xlabel('Epoch')
plt.ylabel('Loss')
plt.legend()
plt.show()
```

In this code, **'g_losses'** and **'d_losses'** are the lists that store the generator and discriminator losses during training. You can plot these lists using **'plt.plot()'** function. The labels for the legend are set as **'Generator Loss'** and **'Discriminator Loss'**, respectively. The **'xlabel()'** and **'ylabel()'** functions are used to set the labels for the x-axis and y-axis, respectively. Finally, **'plt.legend()'** is used to display the legend, and **'plt.show()'** is used to show the plot.

Make sure to execute this code after the training loop, where **'g_losses'** and **'d_losses'** have been populated with the loss values.

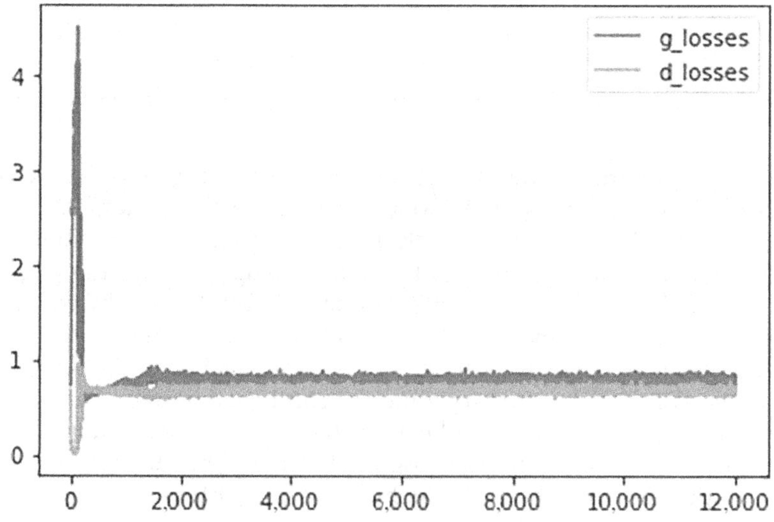

Figure 6.3 Plot of the generator and discriminator losses.

6.7.13 *Result Checks*

To plot the generated image at zero epoch, you can use the following code, presented in Figure 6.4:

```
from skimage.io import imread
import matplotlib.pyplot as plt

a = imread('gan_images/0.png')
plt.imshow(a)
plt.axis('off')
plt.show()
```

In this code, **'imread()'** function from **'skimage.io'** library is used to read the image file generated at zero epoch. The image is then displayed using **'plt.imshow()'** function from **'matplotlib.pyplot'**. The **'plt.axis('off')'** command is used to hide the axis labels. Finally, **'plt.show()'** is used to show the image.

Make sure that you have the correct file path and name for the image generated at zero epoch. Adjust the path and file names accordingly in the **'imread()'** function.

Note: Ensure that you have the necessary libraries (**'skimage'** and **'matplotlib'**) installed and imported before executing the code.

Let's look at what causes it to be formed in the first epoch.

The generator does not yield any information, and the discriminator is clever enough to recognize a phony. To plot the image generated after training on 1,000 epochs, you can use the following code:

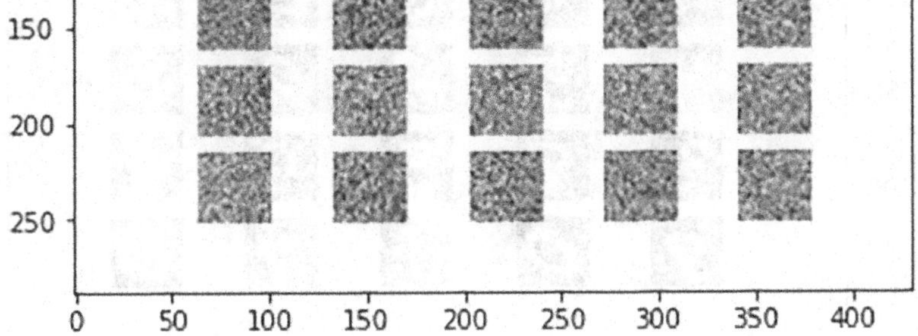

Figure 6.4 Zero-epoch image generation.

```
from skimage.io import imread
import matplotlib.pyplot as plt

a = imread('gan_images/0.png')
plt.imshow(a)
plt.axis('off')
plt.show()
```

In this code, **'imread()'** function from **'skimage.io'** library is used to read the image file generated at 1,000 epochs. The image is then displayed using **'plt.imshow()'** function from **'matplotlib.pyplot'**. The **'plt.axis('off')'** command is used to hide the axis labels. Finally, **'plt.show()'** is used to show the image.

Make sure that you have the correct file path and name for the image generated at 1,000 epochs. Adjust the path and file names accordingly in the **'imread()'** function.

Note: Ensure that you have the necessary libraries (**'skimage'** and **'matplotlib'**) installed and imported before executing the code.

The generator is now progressively developing the ability to extract some observable information. To plot the image generated after training on 10,000 epochs presented in Figure 6.5, you can use the following code:

```
from skimage.io import imread
import matplotlib.pyplot as plt

a = imread('gan_images/10000.png')
plt.imshow(a)
plt.axis('off')
plt.show()
```

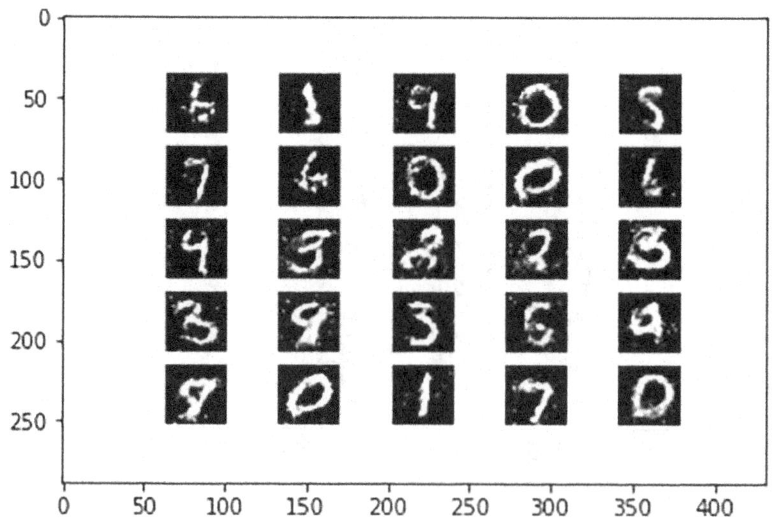

Figure 6.5 Image generation after 1,000 epochs.

As an image based on the MNIST dataset, the generator is now capable of construction, and the likelihood that the discriminator is a fool is high.

6.8 Deep Convolutional Generative Adversarial Networks

Deep Convolutional Generative Adversarial Networks (DCGANs) are a specific type of GANs that utilize CNNs as the building blocks of both the generator and discriminator models. DCGANs have been successful in generating high-quality and realistic images across various domains.

DCGANs address some of the limitations of traditional GAN architectures by incorporating convolutional layers and other architectural features specifically designed for image generation. The key components and principles of DCGANs include the following.

- *Convolutional Neural Networks (CNNs):* CNNs are used as the primary building blocks in both the generator and discriminator models. Convolutional layers enable the models to learn hierarchical representations of the input images, capturing features at different levels of abstraction.
- *Strided Convolution and Transposed Convolution:* DCGANs make use of strided convolutions in the discriminator to downsample the spatial dimensions of the input, allowing it to learn high-level features at multiple scales. Transposed convolutions (also known as deconvolutions or fractionally strided convolutions) are used in the generator to upsample the noise vector and generate larger images.
- *Batch Normalization:* Batch normalization is applied to the activations of both the generator and discriminator networks. It helps to stabilize the training process by normalizing the input to each layer, reducing internal covariate shift, and improving the overall convergence of the models.
- *Leaky ReLU Activation:* DCGANs typically use leaky ReLU activation functions in the discriminator network instead of regular ReLU. Leaky ReLU allows for a small negative slope in the activation for negative input values, preventing the "dying ReLU" problem and providing better gradient flow during training.
- *No Fully Connected Layers:* DCGANs do not use fully connected layers in the main body of the networks. Instead, they rely on global pooling or convolutional layers with appropriate spatial dimensions to reduce the activations to a single value or a vector representing the class probabilities.

DCGANs have demonstrated impressive results in generating high-quality images that exhibit coherent structures, realistic textures, and meaningful variations. They have been applied to a wide range of tasks, including image synthesis, style transfer, super-resolution, and image-to-image translation.

The architecture and principles of DCGANs have paved the way for further advancements in generative modeling, and researchers continue to explore and refine deep convolutional networks for generating more diverse and realistic images across different domains.

In this section we are going to generate photorealistic images using GANs based on the DCGAN architecture. A full implementation of the DCGAN is beyond the scope of a single response. It requires a detailed implementation and training process with proper hyperparameter tuning. The DCGAN paper by Lee et al. (2009) and Radford et al. (2015) can be referred to for a complete understanding of the architecture and implementation details. Here's an outline of the steps involved in training a DCGAN to generate photorealistic images.

6.8.1 The Pokemon Dataset

The Pokemon dataset is a collection of images representing different Pokemon sprites. Each sprite is a graphical representation of a specific Pokemon character. The dataset is commonly used in computer vision tasks, such as image classification and generation.

The dataset typically includes a large number of Pokemon images, each labeled with the corresponding Pokemon's name or identifier. These images are often in the form of PNG or JPEG files, with varying sizes and resolutions.

When working with the Pokemon dataset, it is common to preprocess the images, such as resizing them to a consistent size, converting them to a standardized format (e.g., tensors), and normalizing the pixel values. This preprocessing step ensures that the images are in a suitable format for training machine learning models, including GANs.

To download, extract, and load the Pokemon sprites dataset, you can use the following code:

```
import os
import urllib.request
import zipfile

# Set the URL and file path for the dataset
url = 'https://github.com/d2l-ai/d2l-en/raw/master/data/pokemon.
zip'
filename = 'pokemon.zip'

# Download the dataset
urllib.request.urlretrieve(url, filename)

# Extract the dataset
with zipfile.ZipFile(filename, 'r') as zip_ref:
    zip_ref.extractall()

# Define the path to the extracted dataset
dataset_dir = './pokemon'

# Load the dataset using torchvision
transform = torchvision.transforms.Compose([
    torchvision.transforms.Resize(64),
    torchvision.transforms.ToTensor(),
    torchvision.transforms.Normalize((0.5,), (0.5,))
])

dataset = torchvision.datasets.ImageFolder(dataset_dir,
transform=transform)
```

In this code, we first set the URL and file path for the dataset. We then use the **'urllib.request.urlretrieve'** function to download the dataset from the given URL. After that, we extract the dataset using the **'zipfile.ZipFile'** class. The extracted files will be saved in a directory named **'pokemon'**.

Next, we define a transformation pipeline using **'torchvision.transforms.Compose'**. In this example, we resize the images to a size of 64 × 64 pixels, convert them to tensors, and normalize the pixel values to the range of [-1, 1].

Finally, we load the dataset using **'torchvision.datasets.ImageFolder'**, passing the path to the extracted dataset directory and the defined transformation. The **'ImageFolder'** class assumes that the dataset is organized into subdirectories, with each subdirectory representing a different class of images. We can now use the **'dataset'** object to access and train your GAN model with the Pokemon sprites dataset.

To resize each image to 64 × 64 pixels, apply transformations such as converting the image to a tensor and normalizing the pixel values. It also sets up a data loader to load the dataset in batches for training.

```
batch_size = 256

transformer = torchvision.transforms.Compose([
    torchvision.transforms.Resize((64, 64)),
    torchvision.transforms.ToTensor(),
    torchvision.transforms.Normalize((0.5,), (0.5,))
])

pokemon.transform = transformer

data_iter = torch.utils.data.DataLoader(
    pokemon, batch_size=batch_size, shuffle=True,
num_workers=d2l.get_dataloader_workers()
)
```

Here's the code:

In this code, we define a batch size of 256. We then create a transformer using **'torchvision.transforms.Compose'**, where we specify the desired transformations. The **'Resize'** transformation resizes each image to a size of 64 × 64 pixels. The ToTensor transformation converts the image to a tensor, and the **'Normalize'** transformation normalizes the pixel values using a mean of 0.5 and a standard deviation of 0.5.

Finally, we create a data loader using **'torch.utils.data.DataLoader'**, passing in the **'pokemon'** dataset, the specified batch size, and other parameters such as shuffle and number of workers for data loading. You can now iterate over **'data_iter'** to get batches of preprocessed images from the Pokemon sprites dataset presented in Figure 6.6 for training your GAN model.

To visualize the first 20 images from the dataset using the **'show_images'** function from the **'d2l'** library, here's the code:

```
warnings.filterwarnings('ignore')
d2l.set_figsize((4, 4))

for X, y in data_iter:
    imgs = X[:20, :, :, :].permute(0, 2, 3, 1) / 2 + 0.5
    d2l.show_images(imgs, num_rows=4, num_cols=5)
    break
```

Figure 6.6 20 image samples of Pokemon dataset.

In this code, we iterate over the **'data_iter'** data loader to get a batch of images (**'X'**) and their corresponding labels (**'y'**). We select the first 20 images from the batch using **'X[:20,:,:,:]'**, permute the dimensions to match the expected format for image visualization, and apply scaling to map the pixel values from the range [–1, 1] to [0, 1] using **'imgs = X[:20,:,:,:].permute(0, 2, 3, 1) / 2 + 0.5'**.

Finally, we use the **'d2l.show_images'** function to display the 20 images in a grid with 4 rows and 5 columns. Note that we use **'warnings.filterwarnings('ignore')'** to suppress any potential warning messages.

6.8.2 The Model Generator

To build the generator model in DCGAN, you can use transposed convolution layers to enlarge the input size. The basic block of the generator typically consists of a transposed convolution layer, followed by batch normalization and ReLU activation.

```
class G_Block(nn.Module):
    def __init__(self, in_channels, out_channels, kernel_size,
stride, padding):
        super(G_Block, self).__init__()
        self.conv_transpose = nn.ConvTranspose2d(
            in_channels, out_channels, kernel_size, stride,
padding
        )
        self.batch_norm = nn.BatchNorm2d(out_channels)
        self.relu = nn.ReLU()

    def forward(self, x):
        x = self.conv_transpose(x)
        x = self.batch_norm(x)
        x = self.relu(x)
        return x
```

Here's an example of how you can define the basic block of the generator:

In this example, **'in_channels'** represents the number of input channels (e.g., the size of the noise vector **'d'**), **'out_channels'** represents the number of output channels (e.g., 3 for RGB images), **'kernel_size'** is the size of the convolution kernel, and **'stride'** and **'padding'** control the stride and padding of the convolution operation.

You can stack multiple generator blocks to build a deeper generator network. Each block will gradually increase the size of the input until it reaches the desired output size of 64×64.

Note that the final layer of the generator should typically use a different activation function, such as Tanh, to ensure that the generated images have pixel values in the range of [-1, 1], which matches the normalization applied to the dataset.

Remember to initialize the weights of the generator using appropriate techniques, such as Xavier or He initialization, to help stabilize the training of the GAN. By combining multiple generator blocks, you can construct a deep convolutional generator that maps the noise variable to a 64 × 64 RGB image.

The default settings for the transposed convolution layer are $k_h = k_w = 4$, $s_h = s_w = 2$, and $p_h = p_w = 1$, kernel, strides, and padding, respectively. The generator block will increase the input's width and height if the input shape is $n_h^{'} \times n_w^{'} = 16 \times 16$.

$$n_h^{'} \times n_w^{'} = \left[n_h k_h - (n_h - 1)(k_h - s_h) - 2p_h\right] \times \left[n_w k_w - (n_w - 1)(k_w - s_w) - 2p_w\right]$$

$$= \left[k_h + s_h (n_h - 1) - 2p_h\right] \times \left[k_w + s_w (n_w - 1) - 2p_w\right]$$

$$= [4 + 2(16 - 1) - 2 \times 1] \times [4 + 2(16 - 1) - 2 \times 1]$$

$$= 32 \times 32$$

```
x = torch.zeros((2, 3, 16, 16))
g_blk = G_Block (20)
g_blk(x).shape
```

An input tensor **'x'** with a shape of (2, 3, 16, 16), indicating a batch size of 2, 3 input channels (RGB) and a height and width of 16.

The **'G_Block'** is initialized with an **'in_channels'** of 20, and the default values for kernel size (4 × 4), stride (2 × 2), and padding (1 × 1).

When **'x'** is passed through the generator block (**'g_blk(x)'**), the output tensor has a shape of (2, 20, 32, 32). This means it has a batch size of 2, 20 output channels and a height and width of 32.

The output shape matches the expected result because the transposed convolution operation enlarges the input's width and height by a factor of 2 (using a stride of 2) while maintaining the same number of channels.

Therefore, the output shape of the generator block when applied to the provided input tensor is (2, 20, 32, 32).

If you change the transposed convolution layer to have a 4 × 4 kernel, 1 × 1 strides, and zero padding and use an input size of 1 × 1, the output of the generator block will have its width and height increased by 3, respectively.

```
x = torch.zeros((2, 3, 1, 1))
g_blk = G_Block(20, strides=1, padding=0)
g_blk(x).shape
```

In the code snippet, **'x'** has a shape of (2, 3, 1, 1), which means it has a batch size of 2, 3 channels (RGB) and a height and width of 1. The generator block (**'G_Block'**) is initialized with an **'in_channels'** of 20, strides = 1, and padding = 0.

When **x** is passed through the generator block (**'g_blk(x)'**), the output has a shape of (2, 20, 4, 4), which means it has a batch size of 2, 20 channels and a height and width of 4. This matches the expected output shape, where the width and height are increased by 3 compared to the input.

Therefore, with the specified changes to the transposed convolution layer, the output of the generator block will have its width and height increased by 3 respectively when the input size is 1 × 1.

Here is an implementation of the generator network:

```
class Generator(nn.Module):
    def __init__(self, latent_dim):
        super(Generator, self).__init__()
```

```
        self.latent_dim = latent_dim

        self.net = nn.Sequential(
            # Project latent variable to 64x8 channels
            nn.ConvTranspose2d(latent_dim, 64 * 8, kernel_size=4,
stride=1, padding=0, bias=False),
            nn.BatchNorm2d(64 * 8),
            nn.ReLU(inplace=True),

            # Generator blocks
            G_block(64 * 8, strides=2, padding=1),
            G_block(64 * 4, strides=2, padding=1),
            G_block(64 * 2, strides=2, padding=1),
            G_block(64, strides=2, padding=1),

            # Transposed convolution layer for output
            nn.ConvTranspose2d(64, 3, kernel_size=4, stride=2,
padding=1, bias=False),
            nn.Tanh()
        )

    def forward(self, x):
        return self.net(x)
```

The generator network consists of a sequential module that contains the following layers:

- A transposed convolution layer that projects the latent variable to 64 × 8 channels.
- Four generator blocks that increase the width and height of the input while reducing the number of channels.
- A transposed convolution layer that generates the output, doubling the width and height to reach the desired 64 × 64 shape and reducing the channel size to 3.
- A tanh activation function to project the output values into the range of (-1, 1).

You can initialize an instance of the generator class with the desired latent_dim and then pass noise samples through the generator to generate photorealistic images.

6.8.3 Discriminator

The discriminator is a typical convolutional network, with the exception that its activation function is a leaky ReLU. The definition of the leaky ReLU activation function used in the discriminator can be expressed as follows:

For input x, the leaky ReLU activation function is defined as:

$$leaky\ ReLU(x) = \begin{cases} x & if\ x > 0 \\ \alpha x & otherwise \end{cases}$$

```
leaky_relu(x) = max(α * x, x)
```

where α is a small positive slope parameter that determines the amount of leakage for negative values.

In the case of the discriminator network, the leaky ReLU activation function is applied to the output of each convolutional layer. This helps to introduce some nonlinearity and allows the discriminator to better handle complex patterns and variations in the input data.

```
alphas = [0, .2, .4, .6, .8, 1]
x = torch.arange(-2, 1, 0.1)
Y = [nn.LeakyReLU(alpha)(x).detach().numpy() for alpha in alphas]
d2l.plot(x.detach().numpy(), Y, 'x', 'y', alphas)
```

To create a plot to visualize the output of the leaky ReLU activation function with different values of alpha (α) presented in Figure 6.7. The alphas list contains the alpha values to be tested, ranging from 0 to 1 in increments of 0.2.

The torch.arange() function is used to create a tensor of values ranging from -2 to 1 with a step size of 0.1. This serves as the input to the leaky ReLU activation function.

The for loop iterates over each alpha value in the alphas list. Inside the loop, the leaky ReLU activation function with the current alpha value is applied to the input tensor (x). The result is then converted to a NumPy array using the detach() and numpy() functions.

The generated output values for each alpha are stored in the Y list. Finally, the d2l. plot() function is called to create the plot, with the x values as the input tensor, the Y values as the output of the leaky ReLU, **'x'** as the x-axis label, **'y'** as the y-axis label, and alphas as the legend labels.

To visualize the plot, you can run the code in a Python environment that supports plotting, such as Jupyter Notebook, and display the resulting plot.

The basic block of the discriminator consists of a convolutional layer followed by a batch normalization layer and a leaky ReLU activation function. The hyperparameters of the convolutional layer determine the behavior of the convolution operation. These hyperparameters include the kernel size (kh, kw), the stride (sh, sw), the padding (ph, pw), and the number of output channels.

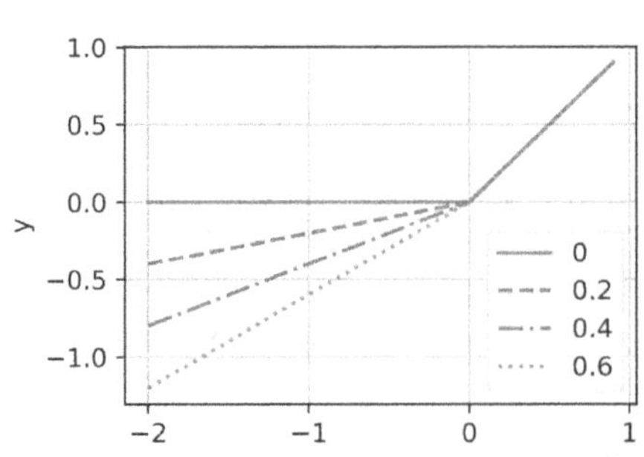

Figure 6.7 Plot of leaky ReLu with activation function $alphas=[0, .2, .4, .6, .8, 1]$.

Typically, in the discriminator, the convolutional layer has a kernel size of 4 × 4, a stride of 2 × 2, and a padding of 1 × 1. These settings allow the discriminator to downsample the input image, reducing its spatial dimensions while increasing the number of channels. The number of output channels determines the complexity and capacity of the discriminator to capture features in the input images.

The batch normalization layer helps normalize the activations of the convolutional layer, improving the stability and convergence of the network during training.

The leaky ReLU activation function is used instead of a regular ReLU to allow a small, non-zero gradient for negative input values. This helps prevent the "dying ReLU" problem and allows the discriminator to better handle both real and fake images. By stacking multiple of these basic blocks, the discriminator can learn to discriminate between real and fake images based on their features and patterns.

```
class D_block(nn.Module):
    def __init__(self, out_channels, in_channels=3, kernel_
size=4, strides=2, padding=1, alpha=0.2, **kwargs):
        super(D_block, self).__init__(**kwargs)
        self.conv2d = nn.Conv2d(in_channels, out_channels, ker-
nel_size, strides, padding, bias=False)
        self.batch_norm = nn.BatchNorm2d(out_channels)
        self.activation = nn.LeakyReLU(alpha, inplace=True)

    def forward(self, X):
        return self.activation(self.batch_norm(self.conv2d(X)))
```

The D_block class represents a basic block of the discriminator network. It consists of a convolutional layer, a batch normalization layer, and a leaky ReLU activation function.

- **'__init__(self, out_channels, in_channels=3, kernel_size=4, strides=2, padding=1, alpha=0.2, **kwargs)'**: This is the constructor method of the D_block class. It initializes the parameters and layers of the block. The out_channels parameter specifies the number of output channels for the convolutional layer. The other parameters specify the hyperparameters of the convolutional layer, such as **'in_channels'**, **'kernel_size'**, **'strides'**, **'padding'**, and the **'alpha'** value for leaky ReLU.
- **'self.conv2d = nn.Conv2d(in_channels, out_channels, kernel_size, strides, padding, bias=False)'**: This line creates a 2D convolutional layer using the **'nn.Conv2d'** class. It takes the number of input channels (**'in_channels'**), the number of output channels (**'out_channels'**), the kernel size (**'kernel_size'**), the stride (**'strides'**), the padding size (**'padding'**), and the **'bias'** parameter is set to **'False'**.
- **'self.batch_norm = nn.BatchNorm2d(out_channels)'**: This line creates a batch normalization layer using the **'nn.BatchNorm2d'** class. It takes the number of output channels (**'out_channels'**).
- **'self.activation = nn.LeakyReLU(alpha, inplace=True)'**: This line creates a leaky ReLU activation function using the **'nn.LeakyReLU'** class. It takes the negative slope parameter (**'alpha'**), and the **'inplace'** parameter is set to **'True'** to perform the activation function in-place.

- **'forward(self, X)'**: This method defines the forward pass of the block. It applies the convolutional layer, batch normalization, and activation function to the input **'X'** and returns the output.

By stacking multiple **'D_block'** instances, you can build the discriminator network for adversarial training.

A simple block with default values will be half the inputs' width and height. As an illustration, the output shape will be as follows given an input shape of $nh = nw = 16$, a kernel shape of $kh = kw = 4$, a stride shape of $sh = sw = 2$, and a padding shape of $ph = pw = 1$.

$$n_h^{'} \times n_w^{'} = (n_h - k_h + 2p_h + s_h)/s_h \times (n_w - k_w + 2p_w + s_w)/s_w$$

$$= (16 - 4 + 2 \times 1 + 2)/2 \times (16 - 4 + 2 \times 1 + 2)/2$$

$$= 8 \times 8$$

The **'D_block'** class is utilized by passing a tensor **'x'** through an instance of the block and examining the resulting shape. Here's the code and its explanation:

```
x = torch.zeros((2, 3, 16, 16))
d_blk = D_block(20)
d_blk(x).shape
```

- **'x = torch.zeros((2, 3, 16, 16))'**: This line creates a tensor **'x'** with a shape of **'(2, 3, 16, 16)'**. It represents a batch of 2 images, each having 3 channels (e.g., RGB) and a spatial size of 16 × 16.
- **'d_blk = D_block(20)'**: This line creates an instance of the **'D_block'** class with **'out_channels'** set to 20. This means that the convolutional layer in the block will output tensors with 20 channels.
- **'d_blk(x).shape'**: This line passes the tensor **'x'** through the **'D_block'** instance by calling the block as a function. It returns the resulting tensor and then accesses its **'shape'** attribute to examine the shape of the output tensor.

The output shape will be **'(2, 20, 8, 8)'**. This indicates that the input tensor has been processed by the convolutional layer, batch normalization, and leaky ReLU activation, resulting in an output tensor with 20 channels and a spatial size of 8 × 8. The batch size remains the same as the input, while the number of channels and the spatial dimensions change according to the operations performed in the **'D_block'**.

The discriminator network is a mirror of the generator network. Here's the code and its explanation:

```
n_D = 64
net_D = nn.Sequential(
    D_block(n_D), # Output: (64, 32, 32)
    D_block(in_channels=n_D, out_channels=n_D*2), # Output: (64 *
```

```
2, 16, 16)
    D_block(in_channels=n_D*2, out_channels=n_D*4), # Output: (64
* 4, 8, 8)
    D_block(in_channels=n_D*4, out_channels=n_D*8), # Output: (64
* 8, 4, 4)
    nn.Conv2d(in_channels=n_D*8, out_channels=1, kernel_size=4,
bias=False)
) # Output: (1, 1, 1)
```

- **'n_D = 64'**: This line defines the number of channels in the discriminator network.
- **'net_D = nn.Sequential(. . .)'**: This line creates an instance of **'nn.Sequential'** and defines the discriminator network as a sequence of layers.
- **'D_block(n_D)'**: This adds a D_block to the discriminator network. It takes **'n_D'** channels as input and outputs a tensor with shape **'(n_D, 32, 32)'**.
- **'D_block(in_channels=n_D, out_channels=n_D*2)'**: This adds another **'D_block'** to the network. It takes **'n_D'** channels as input and outputs a tensor with shape **'(n_D * 2, 16, 16)'**.
- **'D_block(in_channels=n_D*2, out_channels=n_D*4)'**: This adds another **'D_block'** to the network. It takes **'n_D * 2'** channels as input and outputs a tensor with shape **'(n_D * 4, 8, 8)'**.
- **'D_block(in_channels=n_D*4, out_channels=n_D*8)'**: This adds another **'D_block'** to the network. It takes **'n_D * 4'** channels as input and outputs a tensor with shape **'(n_D * 8, 4, 4)'**.
- **'nn.Conv2d(in_channels=n_D*8, out_channels=1, kernel_size=4, bias=False)'**: This adds a final convolutional layer to the network. It takes **'n_D * 8'** channels as input and outputs a tensor with shape **'(1, 1, 1)'**.

The resulting **'net_D'** represents the discriminator network, which takes an input image and produces a scalar output indicating the likelihood of the input image being real or fake.

6.8.4 Model Training

To train the GAN model, we used the following code:

```
def train(net_D, net_G, data_iter, num_epochs, lr, latent_dim,
device=d2l.try_gpu()):
    loss = nn.BCEWithLogitsLoss(reduction='sum')
    for w in net_D.parameters():
        nn.init.normal_(w, 0, 0.02)
    for w in net_G.parameters():
        nn.init.normal_(w, 0, 0.02)
    net_D, net_G = net_D.to(device), net_G.to(device)
    trainer_hp = {'lr': lr, 'betas': [0.5, 0.999]}
    trainer_D = torch.optim.Adam(net_D.parameters(),
```

```
**trainer_hp)
    trainer_G = torch.optim.Adam(net_G.parameters(),
**trainer_hp)
    animator = d2l.Animator(xlabel='epoch', ylabel='loss',
xlim=[1, num_epochs],
                            nrows=2, figsize=(5, 5),
legend=['discriminator', 'generator'])
    animator.fig.subplots_adjust(hspace=0.3)

    for epoch in range(1, num_epochs + 1):
        # Train one epoch
        timer = d2l.Timer()
        metric = d2l.Accumulator(3)  # loss_D, loss_G,
num_examples
        for X, _ in data_iter:
            batch_size = X.shape[0]
            Z = torch.normal(0, 1, size=(batch_size, latent_dim,
1, 1), device=device)
            X, Z = X.to(device), Z.to(device)
            metric.add(d2l.update_D(X, Z, net_D, net_G, loss,
trainer_D),
                       d2l.update_G(Z, net_D, net_G, loss,
trainer_G),
                       batch_size)

        # Show generated examples
        Z = torch.normal(0, 1, size=(21, latent_dim, 1, 1),
device=device)
        fake_x = net_G(Z).permute(0, 2, 3, 1) / 2 + 0.5
        imgs = torch.cat([torch.cat([fake_x[i * 7 + j].cpu().
detach() for j in range(7)], dim=1)
                          for i in range(len(fake_x) // 7)],
dim=0)
        animator.axes[1].cla()
        animator.axes[1].imshow(imgs)

        # Show the losses
        loss_D, loss_G = metric[0] / metric[2], metric[1] /
metric[2]
        animator.add(epoch, (loss_D, loss_G))
        print(f'loss_D {loss_D:.3f}, loss_G {loss_G:.3f}, {met-
ric[2] / timer.stop():.1f} examples/sec on {str(device)}')
```

In this training code, the learning rate (**'lr'**) is applied to both the discriminator and generator optimizers. The **'betas'** value for the Adam optimizer is set to **'[0.5, 0.999]'** to decrease the smoothness of the momentum.

The random noise tensor **'Z'** is generated with a size of **'(batch_size, latent_dim, 1, 1)'** and moved to the specified device (**'device'**) for faster computation.

The training loop remains the same, with the discriminator and generator models being updated using the **'update_D'** and **'update_G'** functions, respectively.

Please note that the **'update_D'** and **'update_G'** functions are not provided in the code snippet you shared, so you would need to define or import them separately for the training to work correctly.

6.9 Applications of GANs

Generative adversarial networks have indeed revolutionized the field of artificial intelligence and opened up exciting possibilities in various domains. The ability of GANs to generate realistic and novel data has far-reaching applications in fields such as computer vision, image synthesis, natural language processing, and more.

The potential applications of GANs are vast and continually expanding. Some of the areas where GANs are being explored include the following.

- *Image Synthesis and Manipulation:* GANs can generate realistic images, allowing for applications such as creating new artwork, generating realistic avatars, or transforming images.
- *Video Generation:* GANs can be used to generate realistic and diverse videos, enabling applications in video editing, special effects, and virtual reality.
- *Data Augmentation:* GANs can generate synthetic data to augment training datasets, improving the performance and generalization of machine learning models.
- *Style Transfer:* GANs can transfer the style of one image to another, enabling creative applications like generating artwork in the style of famous painters or transforming photographs into different artistic styles.
- *Text-to-Image Synthesis:* GANs can generate images based on textual descriptions, allowing for applications in generating visual content from textual input, such as creating illustrations for stories or generating scenes based on captions.
- *Medical Imaging:* GANs can be used for medical image synthesis and enhancement, aiding in tasks such as medical diagnosis, image denoising, and data augmentation for rare conditions (Yi et al., 2019).
- *Drug Discovery and Molecular Design:* GANs can generate new molecular structures, assisting in the discovery of new drugs and materials.
- *Game Development:* GANs can be used to generate game content, including characters, levels, and landscapes, enhancing the creativity and variety in game design.

The field of GANs is indeed advancing rapidly, and researchers are continuously exploring new applications and techniques to push the boundaries of what is possible. It's an exciting time to be involved in this field and witness the creative potential that GANs bring to artificial intelligence.

6.10 Summary

The chapter introduces generative adversarial networks and highlights their importance in the field of machine learning. It explains how GANs enable the generation of realistic and high-quality synthetic data, making them valuable for tasks such as image synthesis, data augmentation, and anomaly detection.

The chapter explains various applications of GANs, emphasizing their usefulness in generating realistic images, creating deepfake videos, enhancing image quality, and generating new data samples for training machine learning models.

Moreover, it addresses the challenges faced by GANs, such as mode collapse, training instability, and evaluation difficulties. Also, the chapter explores different types of GANs, including conditional GANs, Wasserstein GANs, and CycleGANs, highlighting their unique characteristics and applications.

It provides practical coding examples to demonstrate the implementation of GANs using Python, focusing on the popular MNIST dataset. The chapter walks through the necessary steps to implement a GAN model, including importing relevant libraries, loading the MNIST dataset, building the generator and discriminator models, combining them into a GAN, and representing noise samples.

The chapter explains the GAN training process, covering parameter declaration, image sample creation, training the discriminator and generator iteratively, and plotting the loss function to monitor the training progress. Also, it provides guidelines for result checks and evaluating the performance of the trained GAN model.

Additionally, the chapter introduces deep convolutional generative adversarial networks (DCGANs) and demonstrates their application on the Pokemon dataset. It explains the process of building the generator and discriminator models specific to the Pokemon dataset, along with the training steps and techniques.

Throughout the chapter, the focus is on practical implementation, providing readers with hands-on experience in building and training GAN models. The examples on the MNIST dataset and the Pokemon dataset serve as practical demonstrations of GAN model development and showcase the potential of GANs in generating realistic and diverse data.

References

Chen, F., Chen, N., Mao, H., & Hu, H. (2018). Assessing four neural networks on handwritten digit recognition dataset (MNIST). *ArXiv Preprint ArXiv:1811.08278*.

Cheng, K., Tahir, R., Eric, L. K., & Li, M. (2020). An analysis of generative adversarial networks and variants for image synthesis on MNIST dataset. *Multimedia Tools and Applications, 79*, 13725–13752.

Creswell, A., White, T., Dumoulin, V., Arulkumaran, K., Sengupta, B., & Bharath, A. A. (2018). Generative adversarial networks: An overview. *IEEE Signal Processing Magazine, 35*(1), 53–65.

Goodfellow, I. J. (2014). On distinguishability criteria for estimating generative models. *ArXiv Preprint ArXiv:1412.6515*.

Gui, J., Sun, Z., Wen, Y., Tao, D., & Ye, J. (2021). A review on generative adversarial networks: Algorithms, theory, and applications. *IEEE Transactions on Knowledge and Data Engineering, 35*, 3313–3332.

Kayed, M., Anter, A., & Mohamed, H. (2020). Classification of garments from fashion MNIST dataset using CNN LeNet-5 architecture. *2020 International Conference on Innovative Trends in Communication and Computer Engineering (ITCE)*, 238–243.

Lee, H., Grosse, R., Ranganath, R., & Ng, A. Y. (2009). Convolutional deep belief networks for scalable unsupervised learning of hierarchical representations. *Proceedings of the 26th Annual International Conference on Machine Learning*, 609–616.

Radford, A., Metz, L., & Chintala, S. (2015). Unsupervised representation learning with deep convolutional generative adversarial networks. *ArXiv Preprint ArXiv:1511.06434*.

Salimans, T., Goodfellow, I., Zaremba, W., Cheung, V., Radford, A., & Chen, X. (2016). Improved techniques for training gans. *Advances in Neural Information Processing Systems, 29*.

Yi, X., Walia, E., & Babyn, P. (2019). Generative adversarial network in medical imaging: A review. *Medical Image Analysis, 58*, 101552.

Zeng, X., & Long, L. (2022). Customized dataset. In *Beginning deep learning with TensorFlow: Work with Keras, MNIST data sets, and advanced neural networks* (pp. 675–696). Springer.

Zhang, H., Goodfellow, I., Metaxas, D., & Odena, A. (2019). Self-attention generative adversarial networks. *International Conference on Machine Learning*, 7354–7363.

Chapter 7

Radial Basis Function Networks

The radial basis function (RBF) network, formulated by Broomhead and Lowe in 1988, is a type of neural network architecture presented in Figure 7.1 that has been proven to be a universal approximator. It consists of only one hidden layer, which is composed of radial basis functions as activation functions.

One of the key advantages of RBF networks is their ability to converge to the optimal solution more quickly compared to other neural network architectures (Karamichailidou et al., 2022). This is due to the specific characteristics of RBFs and the simplicity of the network structure.

RBFs are localized activation functions that are centered at specific points in the input space (known as centers) and have a radial shape. They are typically defined as Gaussian functions, where their output decreases exponentially as the distance from the center increases. This radial shape allows RBFs to capture localized patterns in the input data.

Since RBF networks have only one hidden layer, they have a simpler architecture compared to deep neural networks. This simplicity often leads to faster convergence during the optimization process. The use of RBFs as activation functions enables the network to learn complex relationships between the input and output variables.

The universal approximation property of RBF networks means that they have the capability to approximate any continuous function to arbitrary precision, given a sufficient number of RBF centers (Bugshan et al., 2022). This property makes RBF networks a powerful tool for function approximation tasks, regression problems, and pattern recognition. Overall, the combination of the convergence speed, simplicity, and universal approximation property makes RBF networks a popular choice in various applications, especially when dealing with datasets that exhibit localized patterns and when computational efficiency is a concern.

The RBF networks have a wide range of applications in various domains. Here are some of the key applications.

- *Function Approximation:* RBF networks are often used to approximate complex functions by learning the underlying patterns in the data. They can be used for regression tasks, where the goal is to estimate a continuous output based on the input variables.

DOI: 10.1201/9781003654216-9

- *Interpolation:* RBF networks can be used for interpolating missing data or filling in gaps in datasets. By learning the patterns from the available data points, the network can generate estimates for the missing values.
- *Classification:* RBF networks can also be applied to classification tasks, where the goal is to assign input data points to predefined classes or categories. By learning the decision boundaries between classes, RBF networks can effectively classify new data points.
- *Time Series Prediction:* RBF networks are useful for predicting future values in time series data. By analyzing the historical patterns and trends, RBF networks can make accurate predictions for future time steps.
- *Anomaly Detection:* RBF networks can be employed for detecting anomalies or outliers in datasets. By learning the normal patterns in the data, RBF networks can identify instances that deviate significantly from the expected behavior, which can be useful for fraud detection, anomaly detection in data, or system monitoring.
- *Stock Price Prediction:* RBF networks have been widely used in financial applications, particularly in predicting stock prices. By analyzing historical price and market data, RBF networks can capture complex relationships and make predictions about future price movements.
- *Fraud Detection:* RBF networks can be used for detecting fraudulent activities in various domains, such as financial transactions, credit card transactions, or online behavior. By learning the normal patterns and identifying deviations, RBF networks can effectively flag suspicious or fraudulent activities.

These are just a few examples of the diverse applications of RBF networks. Their flexibility, ability to capture complex patterns, and universal approximation property make them valuable tools in various industrial interests, where accurate prediction, classification, and anomaly detection are crucial.

Here's an outline of the content covered in the chapter.

- *RBF Architecture Introduction:* The chapter starts with an introduction to RBF networks, highlighting their characteristics, applications, and architecture of the network. It emphasizes their ability to approximate complex functions, their convergence properties, and their universal approximation capability.
- *Mathematical and Algorithmic Development:* The chapter then delves into the mathematical and algorithmic aspects of RBF networks. It covers the formulation of RBF networks, including the definition and properties of radial basis functions. The algorithmic development explains how RBF networks are trained, including the computation of hidden layer activations, weight estimation, and output prediction.
- *Comparison with MLP:* In this section, the chapter provides a comparison between RBF networks and multi-layer perceptron (MLP), which is a popular type of neural network. The comparison may include factors such as model complexity, training speed, generalization capability, and interpretability. It aims to highlight the strengths and weaknesses of each approach and provide insights into when to use RBF networks over MLP and vice versa.
- *Case Study:* The chapter concludes with a practical application of RBF networks. Specifically, it focuses on training an RBF network to predict customer response to a

term deposit subscription. This case study demonstrates the practical utility of RBF networks in real-world scenarios and showcases their predictive capabilities.

By covering the mathematical foundations, algorithmic development, comparison with other models, and a practical case study, the chapter provides a comprehensive understanding of RBF networks and their application in predicting customer responses for term deposits.

7.1 Architecture of an RBF Network

The architecture of an RBF network consists of three main layers: the input layer, the hidden layer, and the output layer (Can et al., 2022; Mansor et al., 2020). Here's a breakdown of each layer.

- *Input Layer:* The input layer of an RBF network receives the input vector, which represents the features or attributes of the data being processed. Each element of the input vector corresponds to a specific input feature. The number of nodes in the input layer is determined by the dimensionality of the input data.
- *Hidden Layer:* The hidden layer of an RBF network plays a crucial role in transforming the input signals into a different representation. It consists of a set of hidden neurons, where each neuron is associated with an RBF. The activation function of these neurons is typically a Gaussian function, which is centered at a particular point in the input space. The Gaussian function measures the similarity between the input vector and the center of the RBF.

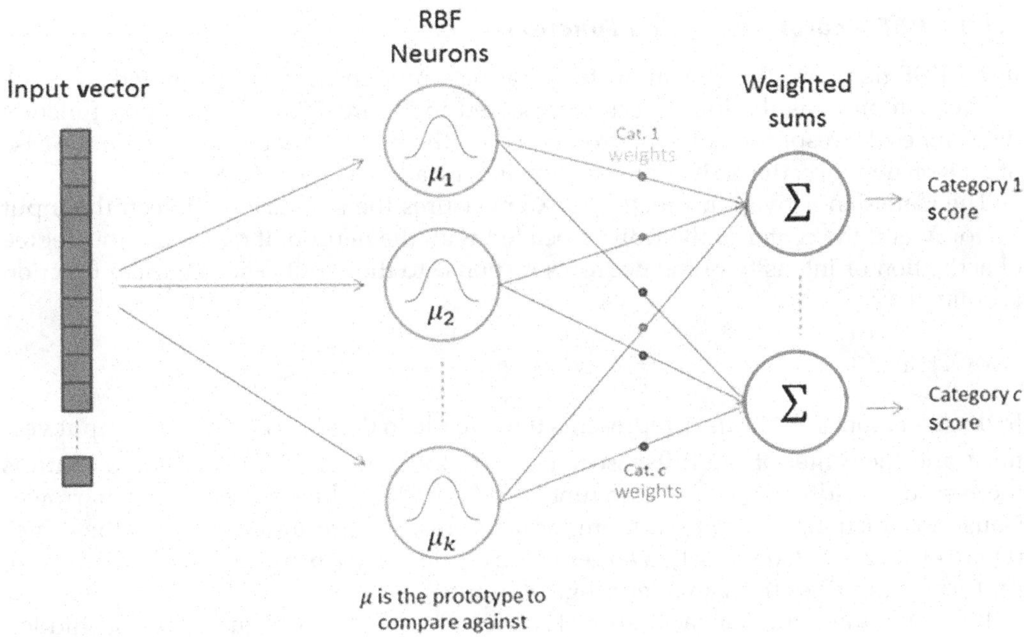

Figure 7.1 A typical architecture of RBF network.

During the forward pass, each hidden neuron computes its activation value based on the distance between the input vector and its associated center. The activation value represents the strength or intensity of the RBF's response to the input. The Gaussian function ensures that the response is highest when the input vector is close to the center and gradually diminishes as the distance increases. This property allows the RBF network to capture nonlinear relationships in the data.

- *Output Layer:* The output layer of an RBF network generates the final response based on the activation values computed by the hidden neurons. The number of nodes in the output layer depends on the specific task at hand. For example, in a classification problem, the number of output nodes may correspond to the number of classes, while in a regression problem, there may be a single output node representing the predicted continuous value.

The output layer combines the activation values from the hidden layer using weighted connections (Pesce et al., 2020). The weights associated with these connections are adjusted during the training process to optimize the network's performance. The specific method of weight adjustment depends on the learning algorithm used for training the RBF network.

By using the Gaussian activation function in the hidden layer, the RBF network can capture complex patterns and nonlinear relationships in the data (Joshi, 2022; Pant et al., 2012). This architecture allows the network to generate responses based on the similarity between input vectors and the learned centers, enabling it to perform various tasks, such as function approximation, interpolation, classification, and time series prediction.

7.1.1 RBF Neuron Activation Function

In an RBF network, the activation function of a hidden neuron is denoted as $\phi(X)$, where X represents the input vector presented in Figure 7.2. The activation function determines the response of the neuron based on the input signal it receives. In the case of an RBF network, the activation function is typically a Gaussian function.

The Gaussian activation function $\phi(X)$ measures the similarity between the input vector X and the center of the RBF associated with the neuron. It quantifies the degree of activation or intensity of the neuron's response to the input. The Gaussian function is defined as:

$$\phi(X)=e^{\frac{-\|X-Center\|^2}{\sigma^2}}$$

In this equation, $\| X-Center \|$ represents the Euclidean distance between the input vector X and the center of the RBF associated with the neuron. The parameter σ controls the spread or width of the Gaussian function. A smaller value of σ results in a narrower Gaussian function, indicating a more localized response to inputs close to the center (Dhini et al., 2022). Conversely, a larger value of σ leads to a broader Gaussian function, capturing responses from a wider range of inputs.

By using the Gaussian activation function presented in Figure 7.3, the hidden neurons in the RBF network respond most strongly to inputs that are similar or close to their associated centers. Inputs that are far away from the centers will result in a lower activation value. This property allows the RBF network to capture nonlinear

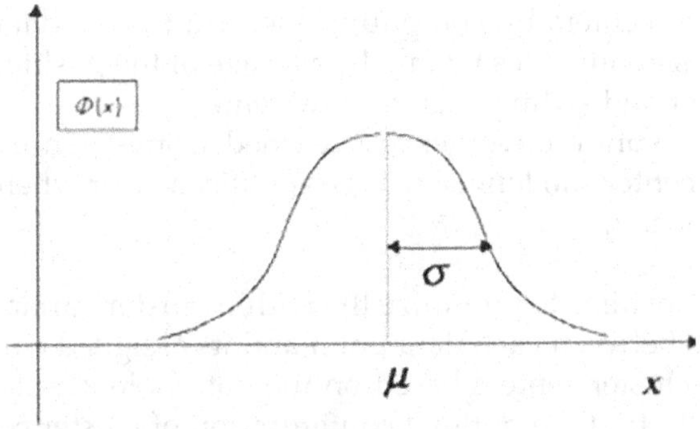

Figure 7.2 Gaussian neural network activation function for 1D.

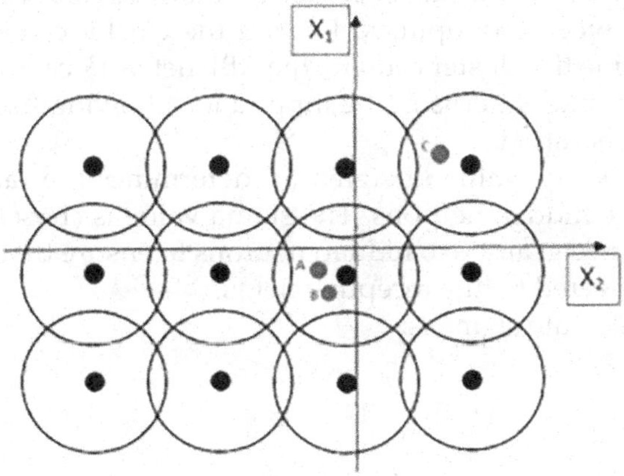

Figure 7.3 Representation of Gaussian neural nodes and boundary of circles.

relationships in the data and generate responses based on the similarity between input vectors and the learned centers.

It's important to note that the activation function $\phi(X)$ is applied element-wise to each hidden neuron in the hidden layer of the RBF network (Burada et al., 2022). Each neuron's activation value contributes to the overall response of the network, which is computed in the output layer based on the weighted connections between the hidden and output neurons.

The k-means clustering algorithm is a popular method used to determine the centers of hidden neurons in an RBF network. The algorithm aims to partition a given dataset into K clusters, where K is the number of desired cluster centers.

The steps of the k-means clustering algorithm are as follows.

1. Initialize the K cluster centers randomly or based on some initial configuration.
2. Assign each data point in the dataset to the nearest cluster center. This is done by calculating the Euclidean distance between each data point and each cluster center and assigning the data point to the cluster with the closest center.

3. Update the cluster centers by computing the mean of all data points assigned to each cluster. This step involves taking the average of the positions of the data points within each cluster and setting it as the new center.
4. Repeat steps 2 and 3 until convergence is reached. Convergence is typically achieved when the cluster centers no longer change significantly or when a specified number of iterations is reached.

The k-means algorithm aims to minimize the within-cluster variance, which is the sum of squared distances between each data point and its assigned cluster center. By iteratively updating the cluster centers based on the data points assigned to each cluster, the algorithm seeks to find the optimal configuration of cluster centers that minimize the overall variance.

In the context of RBF networks, the cluster centers determined by the k-means algorithm serve as the centers for the hidden neurons in the network. Each hidden neuron's receptive field corresponds to a cluster center, and the activation of the neuron is based on the similarity between the input vector and the cluster center. By using k-means clustering to determine the cluster centers, the RBF network can effectively capture the underlying structure and patterns in the input data, allowing for accurate representation and response generation.

In an RBF network, the value of sigma (σ) determines the range or spread of the receptive fields of the hidden neurons. The sigma value is chosen based on the maximum distance (d) between any two hidden neurons to ensure that the entire domain of the input vector is covered by the receptive fields.

The formula to calculate sigma is:

$$\sigma = \frac{d}{\sqrt{2M}}$$

Where:

- d is the maximum distance between any two hidden neurons.
- M is the total number of hidden neurons in the RBF network.

By using this formula, the value of sigma is scaled based on the maximum distance and the number of hidden neurons. The purpose is to adjust the spread of the Gaussian activation function of the neurons so that it covers the range necessary to capture the input data effectively.

Choosing an appropriate sigma value is important to ensure that the receptive fields of the hidden neurons adequately cover the input space (Lopez-Martin et al., 2021; Meng et al., 2021). If sigma is too small, the receptive fields may be too narrow and may not capture the relevant information from the input data. On the other hand, if sigma is too large, the receptive fields may overlap significantly, leading to redundant or ambiguous representations.

By determining the sigma value based on the maximum distance and the number of hidden neurons, the RBF network can achieve an appropriate receptive field coverage, allowing for accurate and effective processing of the input vectors.

7.1.2 Mathematical Development of RBF Networks

In an RBF network, the output of the *j*th neuron (denoted as g_{ij}) for the *i*th input vector is given by the product of the *i*th row of matrix G and the *j*th column of matrix **W**. Matrix **G** represents the output of the hidden layer neurons, and matrix **W** represents the weights connecting the output neurons to the hidden neurons.

The activation function of the output neuron is linear, meaning that the output is equal to the weighted summation of signals from the hidden layer (Suganthan & Katuwal, 2021). This weighted summation, denoted as **z**, can be calculated as the dot product of the *i*th row of **G** and the *j*th column of **W**:

$$z = G[i, :] \times W[:, j]$$

The result of this calculation is the signal produced by the *j*th output neuron for the *i*th input vector.

To obtain the overall output of the RBF network, the weighted summation signals from the output neurons are collected in a column vector *T*. Each element of *T* corresponds to the target value (actual desired output) of the corresponding training vector. Thus, the matrix equation $\mathbf{GW} = \mathbf{T}$ represents the relationship between the output of the network, the weights, and the target values (Bolandnazar et al., 2020).

By adjusting the weights in matrix *W* during the training process, the RBF network aims to minimize the difference between the predicted output and the target output for each training vector, ultimately improving the network's ability to accurately approximate the desired mapping between inputs and outputs.

The algorithm for training an RBF network can be summarized as follows.

1. Define the number of hidden neurons *K*.
2. Set the positions of the RBF centers using the k-means clustering algorithm. This involves clustering the input data into *K* clusters and determining the center positions based on the cluster centroids.
3. Calculate the value of σ (sigma) using the equation
   $\sigma = \frac{d}{\sqrt{2M}}$, where *d* is the maximum distance between two RBF centers.
4. Calculate the activations of the RBF nodes using the Gaussian activation function, which is given by
   $\phi(X) = e^{\frac{-X - Center^2}{\sigma^2}}$, where X is the input vector and *c* is the center of the RBF node.
5. Train the output layer by adjusting the weights using a supervised learning approach. The weights are adjusted to minimize the difference between the predicted output of the RBF network and the target output for each training vector. The training can be performed using various algorithms such as gradient descent or least squares regression.

By iteratively updating the weights based on the training data, the RBF network learns to approximate the underlying mapping between the inputs and outputs. The training process continues until the desired level of accuracy or convergence is achieved.

7.2 Comparison of RBF and MLP Networks

Both RBF networks and MLPs (multi-layer perceptrons) are popular types of artificial neural networks that can be used for various tasks (Sharafian et al., 2020). Here are some key points comparing RBF networks and MLPs.

- *Data Characteristics:* MLPs are advantageous when the underlying characteristic features of the data are embedded deeply inside high-dimensional datasets. This is often the case in tasks such as image recognition, where key information is hidden within a large number of pixels. MLPs with multiple hidden layers can learn to extract hierarchical features from the data, leading to better performance.
- *Convergence Rate:* RBF networks have a faster convergence rate compared to MLPs. This is because RBF networks have only one hidden layer, and the activation function used (typically Gaussian) allows for a direct mapping from input to output. This simplicity can lead to faster training and convergence on low-dimensional data, where deep feature extraction is not required.
- *Universal Approximators:* RBF networks are proven to be universal approximators, meaning that they can approximate any continuous function to arbitrary accuracy, given a sufficient number of hidden neurons. This property makes RBF networks a powerful tool for function approximation and interpolation tasks.
- *Robust Learning:* RBF networks are known for their robustness in learning. They are less prone to overfitting compared to MLPs, especially when the number of hidden neurons is properly chosen. RBF networks can generalize well to unseen data and exhibit good performance in cases where the training data is limited or noisy.
- *Interpretability:* RBF networks offer interpretability due to their explicit use of radial basis functions as activation functions. The centers of the RBF neurons represent prototypes or centroids in the input space, making it easier to interpret and understand the network's decision-making process.

In summary, MLPs are well-suited for tasks where deep feature extraction is crucial, and the data is high-dimensional, while RBF networks excel in low-dimensional data with direct correlations between input components. RBF networks offer fast convergence, robust learning, and interpretability, making them suitable for various applications where these characteristics are desired.

7.3 Case Study: Client Term Deposit Subscription Prediction

To implement an RBF-based AI model for predicting whether or not a client will subscribe for a term deposit using the Bank Marketing dataset, you can follow these steps.

1. *Download the Bank Marketing Dataset from the UCI Machine Learning Repository:* http://archive.ics.uci.edu/ml/datasets/Bank+Marketing
2. *Load the Dataset into Your Program:* The dataset is available in CSV format, so you can use libraries like pandas to read the data.
3. *Preprocess the Data:* Perform necessary preprocessing steps such as handling missing values, encoding categorical variables, and scaling numerical features. You may also need to split the dataset into training and testing sets.

4. *Implement the RBF Network:* Define the RBF network architecture, including the number of hidden neurons (K), learning rate, and number of epochs. You can use the code provided earlier as a reference for implementing the RBFNet class.
5. *Train the RBF Network:* Create an instance of the RBFNet class and train the network using the training data. Use the features from the dataset as input and the corresponding response ("yes" or "no") as the desired output.
6. *Evaluate the Model:* Once the network is trained, use the testing data to make predictions. Compare the predicted values with the actual response to evaluate the performance of the model. You can calculate metrics such as accuracy, precision, recall, and F1-score to assess the model's performance.
7. *Fine-Tune the Model:* If the model's performance is not satisfactory, you can experiment with different hyperparameters, such as the number of hidden neurons, learning rate, or epochs, to improve the results. You can also explore other techniques like cross-validation or regularization to enhance the model's generalization ability.
8. *Deploy the Model:* Once you are satisfied with the model's performance, you can deploy it to make predictions on new, unseen data. Save the trained model and use it to predict whether a new client will subscribe for a term deposit based on their details.

Note: Always split the data properly into training and testing sets to ensure unbiased evaluation. Additionally, consider techniques like feature selection or dimensionality reduction to improve the model's performance and reduce computational complexity if necessary.

1. Importing required packages:

```
import math
import pandas as pd
from sklearn.preprocessing import LabelEncoder
from sklearn.metrics import accuracy_score
from sklearn.model_selection import train_test_split
from sklearn.cluster import KMeans
from sklearn.preprocessing import StandardScaler
import numpy as np
```

Details of each imported packages:

- **'math'**: The **'math'** module provides mathematical functions and operations. It is used for mathematical calculations in the code.
- **'pandas'**: The **'pandas'** library is used for data manipulation and analysis. It provides data structures and functions for efficient handling of structured data, such as tables or data frames.
- **'LabelEncoder'** from **'sklearn.preprocessing'**: **'LabelEncoder'** is a class from the scikit-learn library that is used for encoding categorical variables into numerical values. It is commonly used to convert labels or target variables into a numeric format suitable for machine learning algorithms.

- **'accuracy_score'** from **'sklearn.metrics'**: **'accuracy_score'** is a function from the scikit-learn library that calculates the accuracy of a classification model's predictions by comparing them to the true labels or target values.
- **'train_test_split'** from **'sklearn.model_selection'**: **'train_test_split'** is a function from the scikit-learn library that splits a dataset into training and testing subsets. It is commonly used to evaluate the performance of machine learning models.
- **'KMeans'** from **'sklearn.cluster'**: **'KMeans'** is a class from the scikit-learn library that implements the K-means clustering algorithm. It is used for clustering data points into K clusters based on their feature similarity.
- **'StandardScaler'** from **'sklearn.preprocessing'**: **'StandardScaler'** is a class from the scikit-learn library that performs feature scaling by standardizing features. It transforms the data such that each feature has a mean of 0 and a standard deviation of 1.
- **'numpy'** as **'np'**: **'numpy'** is a powerful numerical computing library in Python. It provides support for large, multidimensional arrays and matrices, along with a collection of mathematical functions to operate on these arrays efficiently. By importing it as **'np'**, we can use the **'np'** alias to refer to **'numpy'** in our code for brevity.

These packages are commonly used in machine learning and data analysis tasks and provide various functions and tools that simplify the implementation of machine learning algorithms and data preprocessing steps.

2. Get data from the file and encode the labels using LabelEncoder class.

```
Data= pd.read_table("bank-full.csv", sep= None, engine= "python")
cols= ["age","balance","day","duration","campaign","pdays",
"previous"]
data_encode= Data.drop(cols, axis= 1)
data_encode= data_encode.apply(LabelEncoder().fit_transform)
data_rest= Data[cols]
Data= pd.concat([data_rest,data_encode], axis= 1)
```

- **Data= pd.read_table("bank-full.csv", sep=None, engine= "python")**: This line reads the data from the file "bank-full.csv" using the **'read_table'** function from the pandas library (**'pd'**). The **'sep=None'** argument indicates that the separator between values is not specified and will be inferred from the data. The **'engine="python"'** argument specifies that the parsing engine should be the Python engine.
- **cols= ["age","balance","day","duration","campaign","pdays","previous"]**: This line defines a list called **'cols'** that contains the names of the columns to be dropped from the dataset. These columns are "age", "balance", "day", "duration", "campaign", "pdays", and "previous".
- **data_encode= Data.drop(cols, axis= 1)**: This line creates a new DataFrame called **'data_encode'** by dropping the columns specified in the **'cols'** list from the original

'Data' DataFrame. The **'drop'** function with **'axis=1'** indicates that columns should be dropped.

- **'data_encode= data_encode.apply(LabelEncoder().fit_transform)'**: This line applies the **'LabelEncoder'** transformation to the **'data_encode'** DataFrame. The **'apply'** function applies the **'LabelEncoder'** transformation to each column in the DataFrame. The **'fit_transform'** method fits the encoder to the data and transforms the data into encoded numerical values.
- **'data_rest= Data[cols]'**: This line creates a new DataFrame called **'data_rest'** by selecting only the columns specified in the **'cols'** list from the original **'Data'** DataFrame.
- **Data= pd.concat([data_rest,data_encode], axis= 1)**: This line concatenates the **'data_rest'** DataFrame (containing the original columns) and the **'data_encode'** DataFrame (containing the encoded columns) along **'axis=1'** (columns axis). The result is assigned back to the **'Data'** variable, effectively combining the original columns with their encoded versions.

This code reads a dataset from a file, drops specified columns, applies label encoding to the remaining columns, separates the dropped columns into a separate DataFrame, and finally concatenates the original columns with their encoded versions. This preprocessing step is commonly done to convert categorical variables into numerical representations suitable for machine learning algorithms.

3. Split the data into training and testing set.

```
data_train, data_test= train_test_split(Data, test_size= 0.33,
random_state= 4)
X_train= data_train.drop("y", axis= 1)
Y_train= data_train["y"]
X_test= data_test.drop("y", axis=1)
Y_test= data_test["y"]
```

- **'data_train, data_test= train_test_split(Data, test_size=0.33, random_state=4)'**: This line splits the **'Data'** DataFrame into training and testing datasets using the **'train_test_split'** function from the **'model_selection'** module. The **'test_size'** parameter specifies the proportion of the dataset that should be allocated for testing (in this case, 33%). The **'random_state'** parameter is used to ensure reproducibility of the split, so setting it to a specific value (4 in this case) will yield the same split each time the code is run.
- **'X_train= data_train.drop("y", axis=1)'**: This line creates the **'X_train'** DataFrame by dropping the column with label "y" from the **'data_train'** DataFrame. The **'drop'** function with **'axis=1'** indicates that a column should be dropped.
- **'Y_train= data_train["y"]'**: This line assigns the values of the column with label "y" from the **'data_train'** DataFrame to the **'Y_train'** variable. This represents the target variable or the labels corresponding to the training data.

- **'X_test= data_test.drop("y", axis=1)'**: This line creates the **'X_test'** DataFrame by dropping the column with label "y" from the **'data_test'** DataFrame. Similarly to Step 2, the **'drop'** function is used with **'axis=1'** to drop a column.
- **'Y_test= data_test["y"]'**: This line assigns the values of the column with label **"y"** from the **'data_test'** DataFrame to the **'Y_test'** variable. This represents the target variable or the labels corresponding to the testing data.

This code performs a train-test split on the **'Data'** DataFrame, allocating 33% of the data for testing and the remaining 67% for training. It then separates the input features (**X**) and the target variable (**Y**) for both the training and testing datasets. The **X_train** and **X_test** DataFrames contain the input features without the **"y"** column, while the **Y_train** and **Y_test** variables contain the corresponding target values.

4. Scale the data using StandardScaler class.

```
scaler= StandardScaler()
scaler.fit(X_train)
X_train= scaler.transform(X_train)
X_test= scaler.transform(X_test)
```

- **'scaler = StandardScaler()'**: This line creates an instance of the **'StandardScaler'** class, which is used for standardizing features by removing the mean and scaling to unit variance.
- **'scaler.fit(X_train)'**: This line fits the scaler to the training data **'X_train'**. The **'fit'** method computes the mean and standard deviation of each feature in **'X_train'** so that it can be used later for scaling.
- **'X_train = scaler.transform(X_train)'**: This line transforms the training data **'X_train'** by applying the scaling operation. The **'transform'** method subtracts the mean and divides by the standard deviation for each feature, resulting in a standardized version of the data. The transformed data is then assigned back to **'X_train'**.
- **'X_test = scaler.transform(X_test)'**: This line applies the same scaling transformation to the testing data **'X_test'**. It uses the mean and standard deviation computed from the training data **'X_train'** to ensure consistency in scaling between the training and testing datasets. The transformed data is then assigned back to **'X_test'**.

This code snippet performs feature scaling on the input features of both the training and testing datasets using the **'StandardScaler'** class. Scaling is important to ensure that all features are on a similar scale, which can help improve the performance of certain machine learning algorithms that are sensitive to the scale of the input data. By fitting the scaler to the training data and then transforming both the training and testing data based on the learned parameters, we can ensure that the scaling is consistent between the two datasets.

5. Determine σ.

```
max= 0;
for i in range(K_clust):
  for j in range(column):
    d= numpy.linalg.norm(Cent[i]-Cent[j])
    if (max<d):
      max= d
d= max
sigma= d/math.sqrt(2*K_clust)
```

This code snippet calculates the value of the parameter **'sigma'** used in the RBF network. Let's break it down step by step:

- **'max = 0'**: Initialize a variable **'max'** to 0. This variable will be used to keep track of the maximum distance between any two centroids.
- **'for i in range(K_clust)':** Iterate over the range of the number of clusters **'(K_clust)'**.
- **'for j in range(column)':** Iterate over the range of the number of columns (assuming **'column'** is the number of columns in the centroid matrix).
- **'d = numpy.linalg.norm(Cent[i] – Cent[j])'**: Calculate the Euclidean distance between the **i**-th and **j**-th centroids. The **'numpy.linalg.norm()'** function computes the Euclidean norm, which represents the distance between two vectors.
- **'if (max < d): max = d'**: Check if the current distance **'d'** is greater than the current maximum distance **'max'**. If it is, update **'max'** to the new maximum distance.
- **'d = max'**: Assign the value of **'max'** to **'d'**.
- **'sigma = d / math.sqrt(2 * K_clust)'**: Calculate the value of **'sigma'** by dividing **'d'** by the square root of twice the number of clusters **'(K_clust)'**. This formula is commonly used to determine the spread of the RBFs.

In summary, this code snippet iterates over the centroids in the centroid matrix and calculates the maximum distance (**'d'**) between any two centroids. It then uses this maximum distance to compute the value of **'sigma'** for the RBF network. The value of **'sigma'** determines the spread or width of the RBFs, which affects how the RBF network models the input data.

6. Determine the centers of the neurons using KMeans.

```
K_cent= 8
km= KMeans(n_clusters= K_cent, max_iter= 100)
km.fit(X_train)
cent= km.cluster_centers_
```

This code snippet performs K-means clustering on the training data to determine the centers of the neurons in the RBF network. Let's go through each step in detail.

- **'K_cent = 8'**: Specifies the number of clusters or neurons in the RBF network. In this case, **'K_cent'** is set to 8.
- **'km = KMeans(n_clusters=K_cent, max_iter=100)'**: Creates a KMeans object with **'n_clusters'** set to **'K_cent'**, which represents the desired number of clusters. The **'max_iter'** parameter specifies the maximum number of iterations for the K-means algorithm to converge.
- **'km.fit(X_train)'**: Fits the KMeans model to the training data **'X_train'**. This applies the K-means algorithm to the data and assigns each sample to one of the **'K_cent'** clusters.
- **'cent = km.cluster_centers_'**: Retrieves the cluster centers obtained from the K-means clustering. These cluster centers represent the centers of the neurons in the RBF network. Each center is a coordinate point in the feature space.

The K-means algorithm iteratively assigns data points to the nearest cluster center and updates the centers based on the assigned points. After convergence, the final cluster centers are obtained. These centers will be used as the centers of the neurons in the RBF network, enabling the network to model the input data effectively.

7. Determine the value of σ.

```
max=0
for i in range(K_cent):
  for j in range(K_cent):
    d= np.linalg.norm(cent[i]-cent[j])
    if(d> max):
      max= d
d= max
sigma= d/math.sqrt(2*K_cent)
```

This code snippet calculates the value of the parameter **'sigma'** in the RBF network. Here's a step-by-step explanation.

- **'max = 0'**: Initializes a variable **'max'** to 0. This variable will be used to track the maximum distance between cluster centers.
- The following nested loop calculates the distance between each pair of cluster centers **'(cent[i] and cent[j])'**:

```
for i in range(K_cent):
    for j in range(K_cent):
        d = numpy.linalg.norm(cent[i] - cent[j])
        if d > max:
            max = d
```

- **'I'** and **'j'** iterate over the range of **'K_cent'**, representing the indices of cluster centers.
- **'numpy.linalg.norm()'** calculates the Euclidean distance between **'cent[i]'** and **'cent[j]'**, which represents the distance between two cluster centers.
- If the calculated distance **'d'** is greater than the current maximum distance **'max'**, **'max'** is updated with the new value.
- **'d = max'**: Assigns the value of the maximum distance to the variable **'d'**. This step is not necessary since **'max'** already stores the maximum distance.
- **'sigma = d / math.sqrt(2 * K_cent)'**: Computes the value of sigma using the formula **'d / sqrt(2 * K_cent)'**. sigma is a parameter that determines the width of the radial basis functions in the RBF network. It is calculated as the maximum distance divided by the square root of twice the number of cluster centers **'(K_cent)'**.

This code calculates the maximum distance between cluster centers and uses it to determine the value of **'sigma'**, which is a crucial parameter in the RBF network. The choice of **'sigma'** affects the smoothness and width of the radial basis functions, which in turn impact the network's ability to model the data.

8. **Set up matrix *G*.**

```
shape= X_train.shape
row= shape[0]
column= K_cent
G= np.empty((row,column), dtype= float)
for i in range(row):
 for j in range(column):
  dist= np.linalg.norm(X_train[i]-cent[j])
  G[i][j]= math.exp(-math.pow(dist,2)/math.pow(2*sigma,2))
```

This code snippet constructs the matrix **'G'** in the RBF network. Here's a step-by-step explanation:

- **'shape = X_train.shape'**: Retrieves the shape of the **'X_train'** data, which represents the training data. The shape is a tuple that contains the number of rows and columns in **'X_train'**.
- **'row = shape[0]'**: Assigns the number of rows in **'X_train'** to the variable **'row'**. This represents the number of training samples.
- **'column = K_cent'**: Assigns the value of **'K_cent'**, which represents the number of cluster centers, to the variable **'column'**.
- **'G = numpy.empty((row, column), dtype=float)'**: Creates an empty matrix **'G'** with dimensions **'(row, column)'**. This matrix will store the values of the RBF activations.
- The nested loops iterate over each training sample ('i') and each cluster center ('j') to calculate the RBF activations and populate the matrix **'G'**:

```
for i in range(row):
    for j in range(column):
        dist = numpy.linalg.norm(X_train[i] - cent[j])
        G[i][j] = math.exp(-math.pow(dist, 2) / math.pow
(2 * sigma, 2))
```

- **'i'** iterates over the range of **'row'**, representing the index of each training sample.
- **'j'** iterates over the range of **'column'**, representing the index of each cluster center.
- **'numpy.linalg.norm()'** calculates the Euclidean distance between the **i**-th training sample **'X_train[i]'** and the **j**-th cluster center **'cent[j]'**.
- The distance is then used to calculate the RBF activation value using the formula **'math.exp(-math.pow(dist, 2) / math.pow(2 * sigma, 2))'**.
- The calculated RBF activation value is assigned to the corresponding position **'(i, j)'** in the matrix **'G'**.

This code constructs the matrix **'G'** by calculating the RBF activations for each training sample with respect to each cluster center. The resulting matrix **'G'** will be used in subsequent steps of training and prediction in the RBF network.

9. **Find the weight matrix *W* to train the network.**

```
GTG= np.dot(G.T,G)
GTG_inv= np.linalg.inv(GTG)
fac= np.dot(GTG_inv,G.T)
W= np.dot(fac,Y_train)
```

This code snippet performs the calculation to obtain the weight matrix **'W'** in the RBF network. Here's a step-by-step explanation.

- **'GTG = numpy.dot(G.T, G)'**: Performs matrix multiplication between the transpose of matrix **'G'** **'(G.T)'** and **'G'** itself. This results in a new matrix **'GTG'**, which represents the product of **'G'** transposed and **'G'**.
- **'GTG_inv = numpy.linalg.inv(GTG)'**: Computes the inverse of the matrix **'GTG'** using the **'numpy.linalg.inv()'** function. The resulting matrix **'GTG_inv'** represents the inverse of **'GTG'**.
- **'fac = numpy.dot(GTG_inv, G.T)'**: Performs matrix multiplication between **'GTG_inv'** and the transpose of **'G'** **'(G.T)'**. The result is assigned to the variable **'fac'**. This step is an intermediate calculation used to compute the weight matrix **'W'**.
- **'W = numpy.dot(fac, Y_train)'**: Performs matrix multiplication between **'fac'** and the target variable vector **'Y_train'**. The resulting matrix **'W'** represents the weight matrix of the RBF network.

The code calculates the weight matrix **'W'** by performing a series of matrix multiplications and inversions. These calculations involve the transpose of the matrix **'G'** and its product with itself (**'GTG'**), the inverse of **'GTG' '(GTG_inv)'**, and the multiplication of **'GTG_inv'** with the transpose of **'G' ('fac')**. Finally, **'W'** is obtained by multiplying **'fac'** with the target variable vector **'Y_train'**. The weight matrix **'W'** is an important parameter in the RBF network and is used for prediction and classification tasks.

10. **Set up matrix *G* for the test set.**

```
row= X_test.shape[0]
column= K_cent
G_test= numpy.empty((row,column), dtype= float)
for i in range(row):
  for j in range(column):
    dist= numpy.linalg.norm(X_test[i]-cent[j])
    G_test[i][j]= math.exp(-math.pow(dist,2)/math.pow(2*sigma,2))
```

This code snippet calculates the matrix **'G_test'** for the test set in the RBF network. Here's a step-by-step explanation.

- **'row = X_test.shape[0]'**: Retrieves the number of rows in the test set **'X_test'** and assigns it to the variable **'row'**. This represents the number of data samples in the test set.
- **'column = K_cent'**: Assigns the value of **'K_cent'** to the variable **'column'**. This represents the number of centers or neurons in the RBF network.
- **'G_test = numpy.empty((row, column), dtype=float)'**: Creates an empty matrix **'G_test'** with dimensions **'(row, column)'**, where **'row'** represents the number of data samples and **'column'** represents the number of centers. The matrix will be filled with values calculated in the following steps.
- **'for i in range(row)'**: Iterates over each row index **'i'** in the test set.
- **'for j in range(column)'**: Iterates over each column index **'j'** representing the centers in the RBF network.
- **'dist = numpy.linalg.norm(X_test[i] – cent[j])'**: Calculates the Euclidean distance between the **i**-th data sample in the test set **'X_test'** and the **j**-th center in the matrix **'cent'**. This distance is computed using the **'numpy.linalg.norm()'** function.
- **'G_test[i][j] = math.exp(-math.pow(dist, 2) / math.pow(2 * sigma, 2))'**: Computes the Gaussian activation value for the **i**-th data sample and the **j**-th center using the Euclidean distance **'dist'** and the value of **'sigma'**. The activation value is calculated as the exponential of the negative square of the distance divided by twice the square of **'sigma'**. This activation value is stored in the corresponding position in the **'G_test'** matrix.

This code calculates the matrix **'G_test'** by iterating over each data sample in the test set and each center in the RBF network. For each combination of a data sample and a center, it calculates the Euclidean distance and applies the Gaussian activation function to obtain the activation value. These activation values are then stored in the **'G_test'** matrix, which represents the transformed features of the test set in the RBF network.

11. Analyze the accuracy of prediction on test set.

```
prediction= numpy.dot(G_test,W)
prediction= 0.5*(numpy.sign(prediction-0.5)+1)

score= accuracy_score(prediction,Y_test)
print score.mean()
```

This code snippet performs prediction on the test set using the trained RBF network and calculates the accuracy score. Here's a step-by-step explanation.

- **'prediction = numpy.dot(G_test, W)'**: Calculates the dot product between the matrix **'G_test'**, which contains the transformed features of the test set, and the weight matrix **'W'** obtained during training. This multiplication combines the activation values of the RBF neurons with their corresponding weights to generate the predictions for each data sample in the test set.
- **'prediction = 0.5 * (numpy.sign(prediction – 0.5) + 1)'**: Applies a thresholding operation to the predictions. The predicted values are compared to a threshold of 0.5. If a prediction is greater than or equal to 0.5, it is set to 1; otherwise, it is set to 0. This step is often used to convert the output of a binary classifier into class labels.
- **'score = accuracy_score(prediction, Y_test)'**: Computes the accuracy score by comparing the predicted values (**'prediction'**) with the true labels from the test set (**'Y_test'**). The **'accuracy_score'** function from the **'sklearn.metrics'** module is used for this calculation. The accuracy score represents the proportion of correctly predicted samples in the test set.
- **'print(score.mean())'**: Prints the mean accuracy score. Since **'score'** is a single accuracy value, **'mean()'** is not necessary here. The **'mean()'** function calculates the average of a given array, but in this case, the accuracy score is already a single value representing the overall accuracy.

This code calculates the predictions for the test set using the RBF network and applies a threshold to convert the predictions into class labels. It then computes the accuracy score by comparing the predicted labels with the true labels and prints the mean accuracy score.

The provided statement suggests that both the RBF network and MLP achieve a prediction accuracy of 88%. However, it states that the computational cost of training an MLP is much higher compared to the RBF network. As a result, it suggests that using the RBF network is a better choice than MLP in this scenario.

The statement highlights the trade-off between prediction accuracy and computational cost. While both models achieve the same level of accuracy, the RBF network offers an advantage in terms of computational efficiency during the training process. This efficiency can be attributed to the specific characteristics of the RBF network, such as the use of radial basis functions and the simplicity of its architecture.

Choosing between different models often involves considering multiple factors, such as accuracy, computational cost, interpretability, and other specific requirements of the problem at hand. In this case, the statement suggests that the computational efficiency of the RBF network outweighs the marginal difference in accuracy compared to MLP, making it the preferred choice.

7.4 Summary

The chapter introduces RBF networks and provides a comprehensive understanding of their architecture and functioning. It begins by explaining the architecture of an RBF network, which consists of input, hidden, and output layers. The hidden layer is composed of RBF neurons, which play a crucial role in the network's functioning.

The activation function used in RBF neurons is discussed, highlighting the radial basis function itself. The chapter explains how the RBF activation function computes the distance between the input and the center of the neuron, providing a measure of the neuron's activation.

The mathematical development of RBF networks is presented, focusing on the steps involved in training the network. This includes determining the centers and widths of the RBF neurons, as well as computing the output weights using techniques such as least squares estimation or gradient descent.

A comparison between RBF networks and MLP networks is provided, highlighting the differences in their architectures, activation functions, and learning algorithms. The chapter explains the advantages and limitations of both types of networks, enabling readers to understand when to choose an RBF network over an MLP network for specific tasks.

To illustrate the practical implementation of RBF networks, a case study is presented. The case study demonstrates how an RBF network can be used for a specific problem or task, showcasing its capabilities in pattern recognition, regression, or classification. Practical coding examples are provided to guide readers through the implementation process, enabling them to apply RBF networks to their own projects.

Throughout the chapter, the theoretical concepts of RBF networks are accompanied by practical coding examples, allowing readers to understand the implementation details and apply RBF networks in real-world scenarios. The case study serves as a practical demonstration of the capabilities of RBF networks and inspires readers to explore their applications in various domains.

References

Bolandnazar, E., Rohani, A., & Taki, M. (2020). Energy consumption forecasting in agriculture by artificial intelligence and mathematical models. *Energy Sources, Part A: Recovery, Utilization, and Environmental Effects*, *42*(13), 1618–1632.

Bugshan, N., Khalil, I., Moustafa, N., Almashor, M., & Abuadbba, A. (2022). Radial basis function network with differential privacy. *Future Generation Computer Systems*, *127*, 473–486.

Burada, S., Swamy, B. E. M., & Kumar, M. S. (2022). Computer-aided diagnosis mechanism for melanoma skin cancer detection using radial basis function network. *Proceedings of the International Conference on Cognitive and Intelligent Computing: ICCIC 2021*, *1*, 619–628.

Can, Ö., Baklacioglu, T., Özturk, E., & Turan, O. (2022). Artificial neural networks modeling of combustion parameters for a diesel engine fueled with biodiesel fuel. *Energy*, *247*, 123473.

Dhini, A., Surjandari, I., Kusumoputro, B., & Kusiak, A. (2022). Extreme learning machine–radial basis function (ELM-RBF) networks for diagnosing faults in a steam turbine. *Journal of Industrial and Production Engineering*, *39*(7), 572–580.

Joshi, A. V. (2022). Perceptron and neural networks. In *Machine learning and artificial intelligence* (pp. 57–72). Springer.
Karamichailidou, D., Alexandridis, A., Anagnostopoulos, G., Syriopoulos, G., & Sekkas, O. (2022). Modeling biogas production from anaerobic wastewater treatment plants using radial basis function networks and differential evolution. *Computers & Chemical Engineering, 157*, 107629.
Lopez-Martin, M., Sanchez-Esguevillas, A., Arribas, J. I., & Carro, B. (2021). Network intrusion detection based on extended RBF neural network with offline reinforcement learning. *IEEE Access, 9*, 153153–153170.
Mansor, M. A., Mohd Jamaludin, S. Z., Mohd Kasihmuddin, M. S., Alzaeemi, S. A., Md Basir, M. F., & Sathasivam, S. (2020). Systematic Boolean satisfiability programming in radial basis function neural network. *Processes, 8*(2), 214.
Meng, X., Zhang, Y., & Qiao, J. (2021). An adaptive task-oriented RBF network for key water quality parameters prediction in wastewater treatment process. *Neural Computing and Applications*, 1–14.
Pant, A. K., Panday, S. P., & Joshi, S. R. (2012). Off-line Nepali handwritten character recognition using multilayer perceptron and radial basis function neural networks. *2012 Third Asian Himalayas International Conference on Internet*, 1–5.
Pesce, V., Silvestrini, S., & Lavagna, M. (2020). Radial basis function neural network aided adaptive extended Kalman filter for spacecraft relative navigation. *Aerospace Science and Technology, 96*, 105527.
Sharafian, A., Sharifi, A., & Zhang, W. (2020). Fractional sliding mode based on RBF neural network observer: Application to HIV infection mathematical model. *Computers & Mathematics with Applications, 79*(11), 3179–3188.
Suganthan, P. N., & Katuwal, R. (2021). On the origins of randomization-based feedforward neural networks. *Applied Soft Computing, 105*, 107239.

Chapter 8

Self-Organizing Maps

A self-organizing map (SOM) is an unsupervised deep learning technique that enables the visualization and analysis of complex high-dimensional data in a lower-dimensional space. In this chapter, we will delve into the theoretical concepts behind SOM and provide a practical implementation of SOM from scratch.

First, we will introduce the fundamental concepts and principles of SOM. We will explore the structure and functioning of SOM, which consists of a grid of neurons. Each neuron is associated with a weight vector and represents a prototype or cluster in the input space (Delgado et al., 2021). SOM uses unsupervised learning to adjust these weight vectors to map the input data onto the grid, preserving the topological relationships between the data points.

Next, we will discuss the algorithmic steps involved in training a SOM. This includes the initialization of the weight vectors, the definition of a neighborhood function that determines the influence of neighboring neurons, and the adaptation of the weight vectors based on the input data. We will explain how the learning process iteratively adjusts the weight vectors to gradually form a map that represents the input data distribution.

Once the theoretical foundations are established, we will proceed with the practical implementation of SOM from scratch. We will guide you through the process of coding the SOM algorithm using Python. This implementation will involve defining the SOM class, initializing the grid of neurons, implementing the training algorithm, and providing methods for visualizing and analyzing the trained SOM.

Throughout the chapter, we will emphasize the understanding of the underlying principles and concepts of SOM. We will explain the significance of different parameters and hyperparameters, such as the learning rate and neighborhood size, and how they impact the training process and the resulting map. Additionally, we will discuss strategies for evaluating the quality of the trained SOM and interpreting the visualization of the input data.

By the end of the chapter, you will have a solid understanding of SOMs and be able to implement and utilize SOM for various data analysis tasks. This knowledge will enable you to apply SOM to uncover patterns and structures in complex datasets, visualize high-dimensional data in a more interpretable manner, and support decision-making processes in various domains.

DOI: 10.1201/9781003654216-10

8.1 Fundamental Concepts and Principles of SOMs

The SOM, developed by Professor Teuvo Kohonen and also known as a Kohonen map or self-organizing feature map (SOFM), is a popular neural network model that belongs to the category of competitive learning networks. It is an unsupervised learning algorithm, which means it does not require explicit labels or human intervention during the training process.

The purpose of a SOM is to organize and represent complex input data in a lower-dimensional space. It can be used for tasks such as clustering, visualization, and feature detection (Dias et al., 2021). The SOM learns to create a topological mapping of the input data, preserving the inherent relationships and structures present in the data.

The architecture of a SOM consists of a grid of neurons, where each neuron is associated with a weight vector. The grid is typically two-dimensional, although higher-dimensional configurations are also possible (Danielsen et al., 2021). During the training process, the SOM adjusts the weight vectors of the neurons to match the input data. The neurons compete with each other to become activated based on their similarity to the input patterns.

The learning process in a SOM is driven by two main principles: competition and cooperation. Neurons compete to be the best match for the input patterns, and the winning neuron, also known as the best matching unit (BMU), is selected based on the similarity between its weight vector and the input pattern. The BMU and its neighboring neurons undergo an update process, where their weight vectors are adjusted to move closer to the input pattern. By the end of the training process, the SOM forms a map where neighboring neurons in the grid represent similar input patterns. This topological ordering allows for visualization of the input data in a lower-dimensional space, where patterns and clusters can be identified.

The advantages of using SOM include its ability to discover and represent intrinsic features of the input data without prior knowledge or supervision. It can handle high-dimensional data and provide insights into the underlying structure and relationships within the data. Overall, the SOM is a powerful neural network model that enables the unsupervised learning of complex data patterns. It is widely used in various domains, including data analysis, visualization, clustering, and feature detection.

Professor Teuvo Kohonen has found applications of SOM in various fields. The main purpose of SOM is to provide a data visualization technique that helps in understanding high-dimensional data by reducing its dimensionality and mapping it onto a lower-dimensional grid.

By reducing the dimensionality of the data, SOM allows for easier visualization and interpretation of complex datasets. It transforms the high-dimensional input space into a lower-dimensional grid, where each neuron represents a specific location in the grid (Neisari et al., 2021). The arrangement of neurons in the grid is such that neighboring neurons in the grid are more similar to each other compared to those farther apart. Through the competitive learning process, SOM groups similar data together and preserves the topological relationships present in the data. The neurons in the grid compete to become the best match for the input patterns, and the winning neuron (BMU) represents the best match. By assigning similar input patterns to nearby neurons in the grid, the SOM effectively clusters the data based on their similarities.

The reduced dimensionality and clustering properties of SOM make it a powerful tool for exploratory data analysis (Forest et al., 2021). It can reveal underlying patterns,

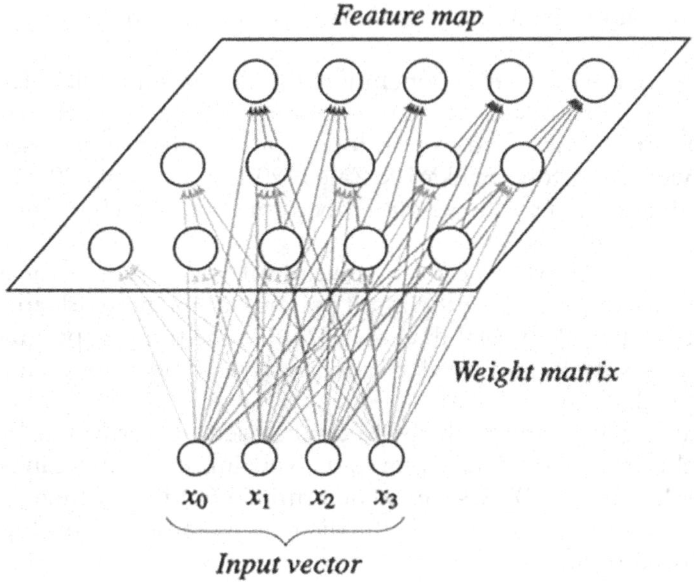

Figure 8.1 The architecture of a SOM.

relationships, and clusters in the data that may not be easily apparent in the original high-dimensional space. This makes SOM useful in various applications such as data mining, pattern recognition, image analysis, and visualization. In summary, the SOM developed by Professor Kohonen provides a data visualization technique that reduces the dimensionality of high-dimensional data, allowing for better understanding and interpretation. It also facilitates clustering by grouping similar data together. Through its unique properties, SOM offers valuable insights into complex datasets and has found numerous applications across different domains.

The architecture of a SOM consists of a grid of neurons, where each neuron represents a specific location in the map as shown in Figure 8.1. The neurons are organized in a two-dimensional grid, although they can also be arranged in higher dimensions or non-grid topologies.

Each neuron in the SOM has a weight vector associated with it, which is the same dimension as the input data. These weight vectors serve as the representation or prototype of the neuron and define its position in the input space (Rivas-Tabares et al., 2020). Initially, the weights are randomly assigned or initialized using specific strategies.

During the training process, the SOM learns to adjust its weights to capture the underlying structure and patterns in the input data. The training is unsupervised, meaning that there is no explicit target or output associated with the training data. The goal is to self-organize the neurons in the map based on the statistical properties of the input data.

The learning process in SOM involves two main mechanisms: competition and cooperation. When presented with an input pattern, the neurons compete to become the best match for the input pattern. The neuron with the weight vector closest to the input pattern, measured by a distance metric (e.g., Euclidean distance), is selected as the BMU.

After identifying the BMU, the cooperation phase comes into play. The neighboring neurons of the BMU are updated to become more similar to the BMU. This encourages the neurons to form clusters and exhibit topological relationships based on the similarity of their weight vectors (Sakkari & Zaied, 2020; Soto et al., 2021). The extent of cooperation is determined by the neighborhood function, which defines the influence of the BMU on its neighbors.

The training of the SOM typically involves multiple iterations, or epochs, where each epoch consists of presenting the input patterns to the network and updating the weights (Guamán et al., 2021; Mahdi et al., 2021). As the training progresses, the SOM gradually organizes itself, and similar input patterns tend to be mapped to nearby neurons in the grid.

Once the training is complete, the SOM can be used for various tasks, such as data visualization, clustering, and data exploration. New input patterns can be presented to the trained SOM, and their BMUs can be determined to identify their closest matches in the map. This allows for visualizing the distribution and relationships of the input data in the reduced-dimensional map.

8.2 Working Paradigm of SOM

The weight update rule in a SOM is a crucial step in the learning process. It determines how the weights of the neurons are adjusted based on the input data to capture the underlying patterns and structure.

The weight update rule can be defined as follows:

- For each training example x, the SOM calculates the distance between the input vector x and the weight vectors of all neurons in the map. The distance can be measured using various metrics, with Euclidean distance being a common choice.
- The BMU is determined as the neuron with the weight vector closest to the input vector x. The BMU is identified by finding the neuron that minimizes the distance between its weight vector and the input vector.
- Once the BMU is identified, the neighboring neurons are updated to become more similar to the BMU. The extent of cooperation is determined by a neighborhood function, which defines the influence of the BMU on its neighbors. Typically, the influence decreases with distance from the BMU, so that closer neurons are more strongly affected.

The weight update rule for each neuron is given by:

$$W_{(t+1)} = W_{(t)} + \eta_{(t)} \times h(c,b) \times \left(x - W_{(t)}\right)$$

- **Where:**
  - $W_{(t+1)}$ is the updated weight vector of the neuron at time $t+1$.
  - $W_{(t)}$ is the current weight vector of the neuron at time t.

  - $\eta(t)$ is the learning rate at time t, which controls the magnitude of the weight update.
  - $h(c,b)$ is the neighborhood function, which determines the influence of the BMU (c) on the neuron being updated (b).
  - x is the input vector.
  - The learning rate $\eta_{(t)}$ and the neighborhood function $h(c,b)$ typically decrease over time as the training progresses. This ensures that the weight updates become smaller and more focused, allowing the SOM to converge to a stable configuration.

- The weight update process is repeated for each training example in the dataset, iterating over the entire dataset multiple times. This process allows the SOM to gradually adjust its weights to better represent the input data and form clusters based on similarities.

The cooperation handle in a SOM involves calculating the BMU, determining the extent of neighborhood cooperation, and updating the weights of the BMU and its neighbors. This iterative process helps the SOM learn the underlying structure of the data and organize itself to capture the patterns present in the input space.

8.3 An Algorithm for SOMs

The algorithm for SOMs, also known as Kohonen maps, can be summarized in the following steps:

1. *Initialize the SOM:*
   - Determine the size and shape of the SOM grid, which consists of neurons.
   - Assign random weight vectors to each neuron in the grid. The weight vectors have the same dimensionality as the input data.
2. *Select an Input Vector:*
   - Randomly choose an input vector from the training dataset.
3. *Find the BMU:*
   - Calculate the distance between the input vector and the weight vectors of all neurons in the grid. The distance can be measured using metrics such as Euclidean distance or cosine similarity.
   - Identify the neuron with the closest weight vector to the input vector. This neuron is referred to as the BMU.
4. *Update the BMU and its Neighbors:*
   - Define a neighborhood function that determines the influence of the BMU on its neighboring neurons. Typically, the influence decreases with distance from the BMU.
   - Adjust the weights of the BMU and its neighboring neurons to become more similar to the input vector. The extent of adjustment is determined by the learning rate and the neighborhood function.

- The weights are updated using the following formula:

$$NewWeight = OldWeight + LearningRate \times NeighborhoodFunction \times (InputVector - OldWeight)$$

5. *Repeat Steps 2–4:*
   - Select a new input vector from the training dataset.
   - Find the BMU and update its neighbors' weights.
   - Repeat this process for a specified number of iterations or until convergence.
6. *Visualization and Interpretation:*
   - After training, the SOM grid represents the high-dimensional input space in a lower-dimensional grid.
   - Each neuron in the grid corresponds to a region or cluster in the input space.
   - The SOM can be visualized to understand the patterns and relationships within the data.
   - The trained SOM can be used for various tasks, such as data clustering, visualization, and data exploration.

The SOM algorithm iteratively adjusts the weights of the neurons based on the input data, gradually organizing the neurons into clusters that reflect the underlying structure of the data. By preserving the topology of the input space, SOM provides a powerful visualization tool and a means of unsupervised learning for data analysis and exploration.

8.4 Learning Algorithms in Detail

The input vectors have three features, and the SOM has nine output nodes. Although it may seem confusing initially, it's important to understand that the three input nodes represent three columns (dimensions) in the dataset, and each column can contain multiple rows or data points.

In a SOM, the output nodes are organized in a two-dimensional grid, typically visualized as a map or grid of nodes (Mallet et al., 2021). Each output node in the SOM corresponds to a specific location in this grid.

To clarify, let's consider an example. Suppose we have a dataset with three features: feature A, feature B, and feature C. Each feature can have multiple values across different data points. In this case, we can represent each data point as a vector with three values: [A_value, B_value, C_value].

When training the SOM, the algorithm maps these input vectors to the output nodes in the two-dimensional grid. The number of output nodes can be determined based on the problem at hand. In this case, there are nine output nodes arranged in a two-dimensional grid (e.g., 3 × 3 grid) presented in Figure 8.2.

During the training process, the SOM algorithm adjusts the weights of the output nodes to represent the patterns and relationships in the input data. The SOM learns to organize similar input vectors close to each other in the grid, creating clusters or regions in the grid that correspond to similar patterns in the data.

By mapping the input vectors to the output nodes, the SOM provides a visualization of the high-dimensional data in a lower-dimensional grid. This visualization helps us understand the underlying patterns and relationships in the data.

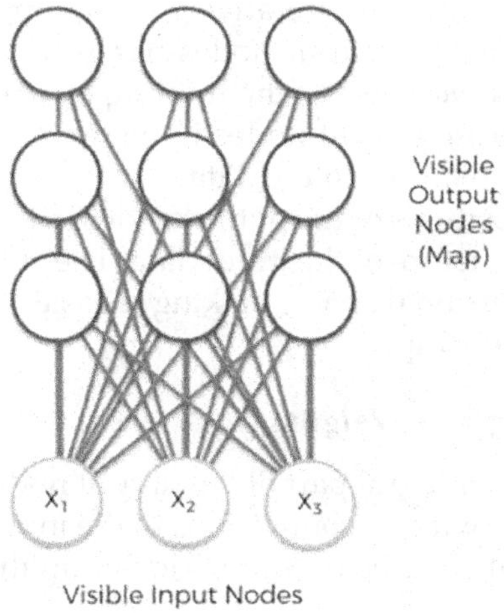

Figure 8.2 Two-dimensional grid of data points.

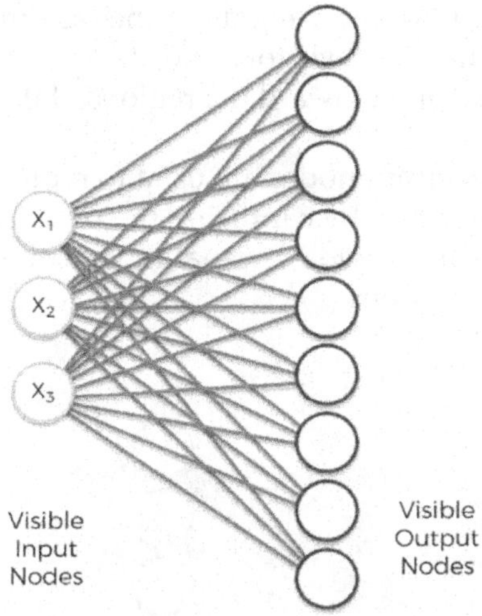

Figure 8.3 Representation of visible input/output nodes.

Let us consider we have a SOM structure with 3 visible input nodes and 9 output nodes. Each of the input nodes represents a specific feature or dimension in the dataset.

In this case, the input node values are:

$X_1 = 0.7; X_2 = 0.6; X_3 = 0.9$

These values represent the input vector that will be fed into the SOM. The SOM algorithm will use these input values to adjust the weights of the output nodes and organize them in a two-dimensional grid presented in Figure 8.3.

The SOM training process involves iteratively presenting input vectors to the SOM and updating the weights of the output nodes based on the similarity between the input vector and the current weights. As the training progresses, similar input vectors will be mapped to neighboring output nodes in the grid, creating clusters or regions that capture the underlying patterns in the data.

By examining the final positions of the output nodes in the grid, we can gain insights into the organization and structure of the input data. The SOM provides a visualization of the data in a lower-dimensional space, making it easier to understand and analyze complex patterns and relationships.

8.4.1 Step 1: Initializing the Weights

In a SOM, the weights are an integral part of the output nodes. Each output node in the SOM has weights associated with its connections to the input nodes. These weights are represented as the coordinates of the output node within the input space presented in Figure 8.4.

Unlike in artificial neural networks, where the weights are separate entities and are multiplied with the input node values, in SOMs, the weights are directly embedded within the output nodes. The weights determine the position of the output nodes in the input space and guide their movement during the training process.

During the training of a SOM, the weights of the output nodes are adjusted based on the similarity between the input vectors and the current weights. As the training progresses, the output nodes move toward the regions of the input space where similar input vectors are located.

The weight vectors in the output nodes are used to represent and organize the input data in a lower-dimensional space. By capturing the underlying patterns and relationships in the data, the SOM can provide a visual representation of the data and enable various analyses and interpretations.

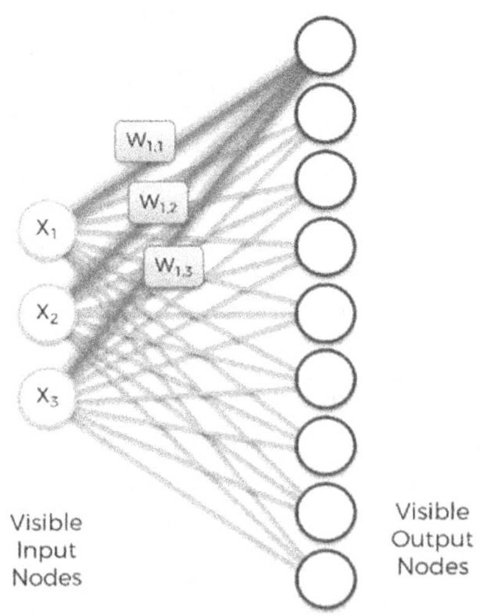

Figure 8.4 Representation of visible input/output nodes with weight.

In the given example, we have a 3D dataset with three input nodes representing the x-coordinate of each data point. The SOM will compress this 3D input space into a single output node, which will have three weight coordinates corresponding to the three dimensions.

If we were dealing with a 20-dimensional dataset, each output node would carry 20 weight coordinates, representing the position in the 20-dimensional input space.

During the initialization of the SOM, the weights are randomly assigned initial values. These initial values are typically close to 0 but not exactly 0. The random initialization ensures that the output nodes start in different regions of the input space and can capture different patterns and structures.

As the SOM training progresses, the weights of the output nodes will be adjusted based on the input data and the learning algorithm. The output nodes will compete among themselves to capture different regions and patterns in the input space. They will develop their own positions and imaginary regions within the input space to best represent the underlying structure of the data.

By the end of the training, the SOM will have organized the input data by grouping similar data points together and forming clusters or "places" within the input space. These clusters can be visualized and used for various purposes such as data exploration, classification, or anomaly detection.

The random initialization of the weights allows the SOM to explore different parts of the input space during training and find meaningful representations of the data.

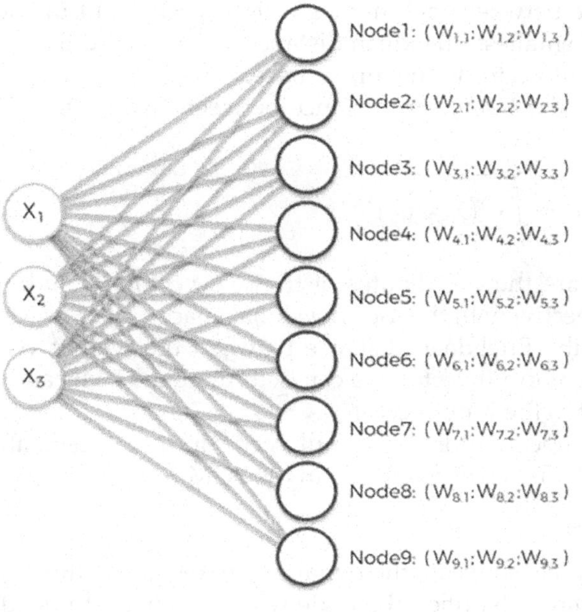

Figure 8.4.a Initialization of weights.

$W_{1,1}$= 0.31	$W_{1,2}$= 0.22	$W_{1,3}$= 0.10
$W_{2,1}$= 0.21	$W_{2,2}$= 0.34	$W_{2,3}$= 0.19
$W_{3,1}$= 0.39	$W_{3,2}$= 0.42	$W_{3,3}$= 0.45
$W_{4,1}$= 0.25	$W_{4,2}$= 0.32	$W_{4,3}$= 0.62
$W_{5,1}$= 0.24	$W_{5,2}$= 0.31	$W_{5,3}$= 0.16
$W_{6,1}$= 0.52	$W_{6,2}$= 0.33	$W_{6,3}$= 0.42
$W_{7,1}$= 0.31	$W_{7,2}$= 0.22	$W_{7,3}$= 0.10
$W_{8,1}$= 0.12	$W_{8,2}$= 0.41	$W_{8,3}$= 0.19
$W_{9,1}$= 0.34	$W_{9,2}$= 0.40	$W_{9,3}$= 0.51

Figure 8.4.b Random weights initialization for SOM.

8.4.2 *Step 2: Best Matching Unit Calculations*

The Euclidean distance is a measure of the straight-line distance between two points in a multidimensional space. In the context of SOMs, we use the Euclidean distance to calculate the similarity between the weight vectors of the output nodes and the current input vector.

To determine the BMU, we iterate through all the output nodes and calculate the Euclidean distance between each node's weight vector and the current input vector. The node with the smallest Euclidean distance is considered the BMU, as it is the closest node to the input vector in the input space.

Mathematically, the Euclidean distance between two vectors can be calculated as follows:

$$Euclidean\ distance = \sqrt{\sum_{i=0}^{i=n} (X_i - w_i)^2}$$

Where X_i and w_i are the coordinates of the two vectors including input vector and weight vector respectively in the n-dimensional space.

By calculating the Euclidean distance between the weight vector of each output node and the current input vector, we can determine the BMU and identify which output node is closest to the input vector.

This process is repeated for each input vector in the dataset, allowing us to assign each input vector to its respective BMU in the SOM.

For 1st node:

For 2nd node:

In a similar way, we compute the remaining nodes using the same method.

Now that you have identified the node with the smallest Euclidean distance as the BMU, which in this case is node number 3, you can proceed with the further steps in the SOM algorithm.

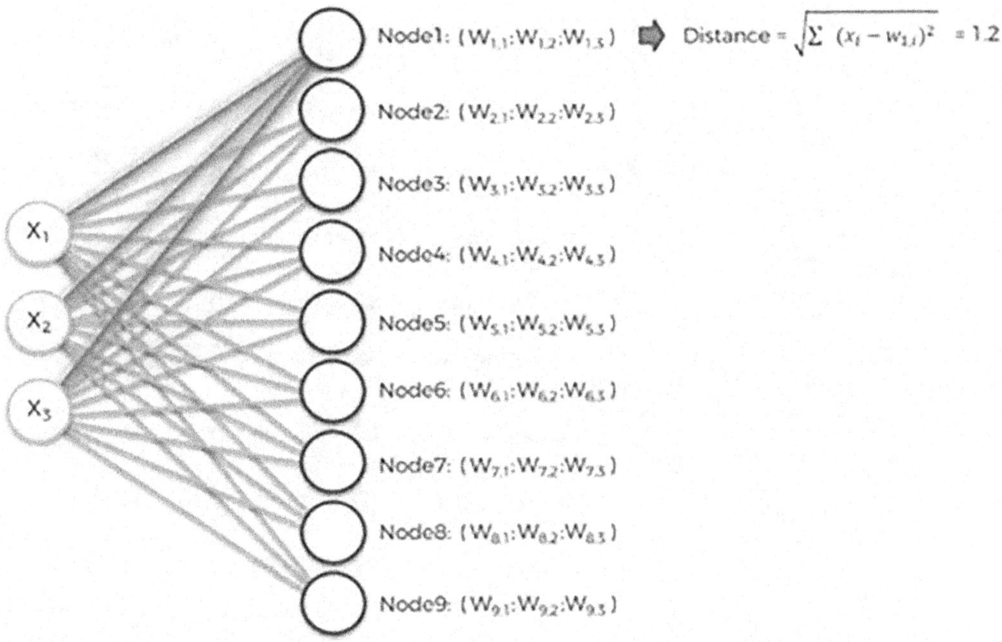

Figure 8.4.c Euclidean distance between the weight vector to 1st output node.

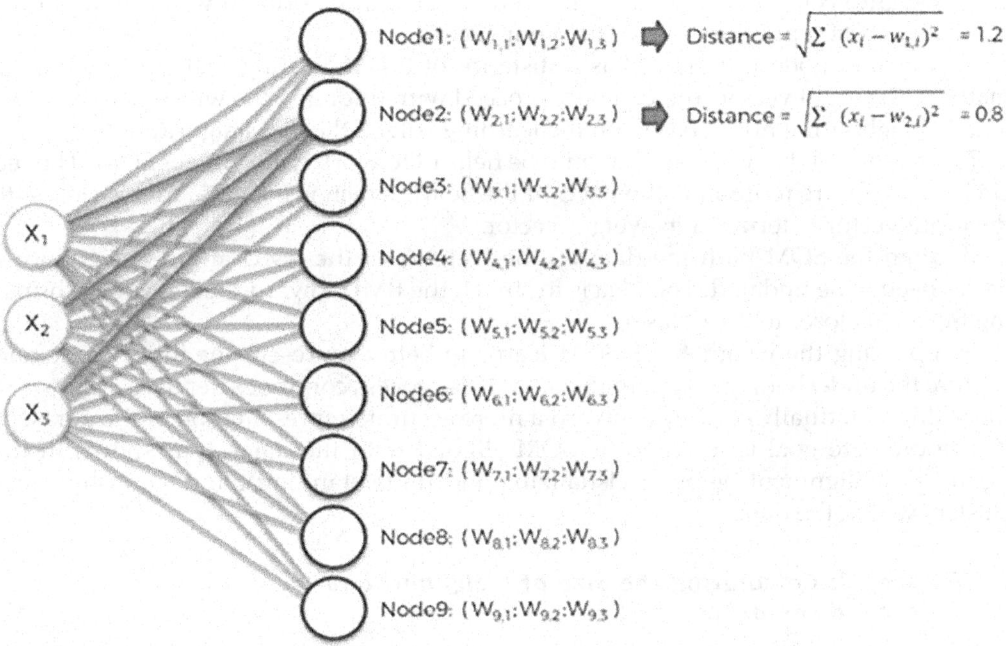

Figure 8.4.d Euclidean distance between the weight vector to 2nd output node.

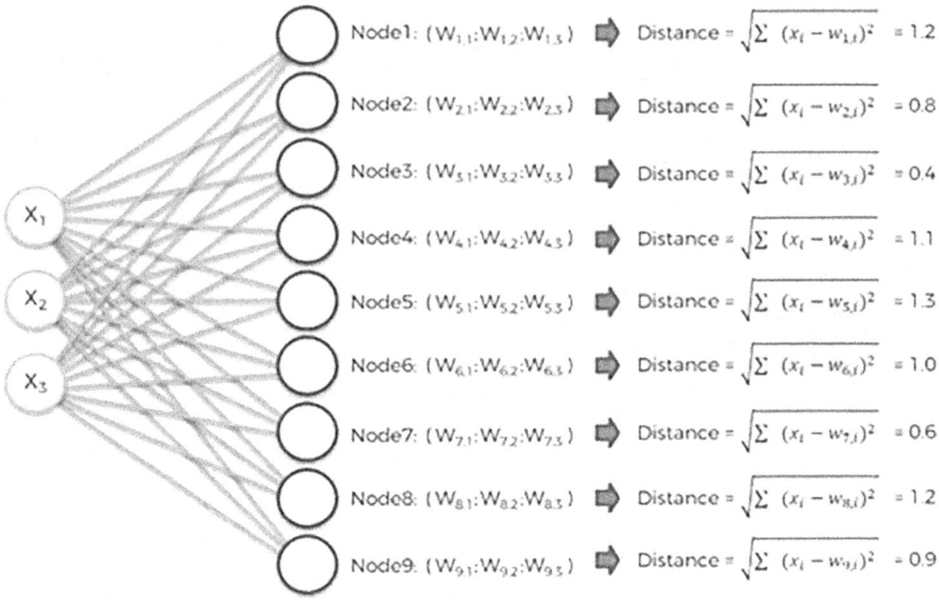

Figure 8.4.e Euclidean distance between the weight vector to each output node.

The BMU represents the output node that is most similar to the input vector in terms of its weight vector. By identifying the BMU, you can determine which node in the SOM is the best representation of the input vector.

In our case, node number 3 has a distance of 0.4, indicating that it is the closest match to the input vector. You can now proceed with updating the weights of the BMU and its neighboring nodes based on the learning rule of the SOM algorithm.

To understand the next part, it would be helpful to work with a larger SOM. The red circle in the figure represents the BMU of the SOM, which is the node that is closest to the input vector in terms of its weight vector.

To align the SOM with the dataset, the weights of the BMU and its neighboring nodes need to be updated. The idea is to stretch the BMU toward the data point, bringing the SOM closer to the dataset.

By updating the weights, the SOM learns to better represent the input space and capture the underlying patterns in the data. This process continues iteratively, allowing the SOM to gradually converge toward a more accurate representation of the dataset.

The ultimate goal is to have the SOM aligned with the dataset, as shown in the figure. This alignment helps in visualizing and understanding the relationships and clusters within the data.

8.4.3 *Step 3: Calculating the Size of Neighborhoods around the BMU*

To determine the size of the neighborhood around the BMU, we need to calculate the radius of the neighborhood. The radius defines the spatial extent within which the weight vectors of the neighboring nodes will be updated.

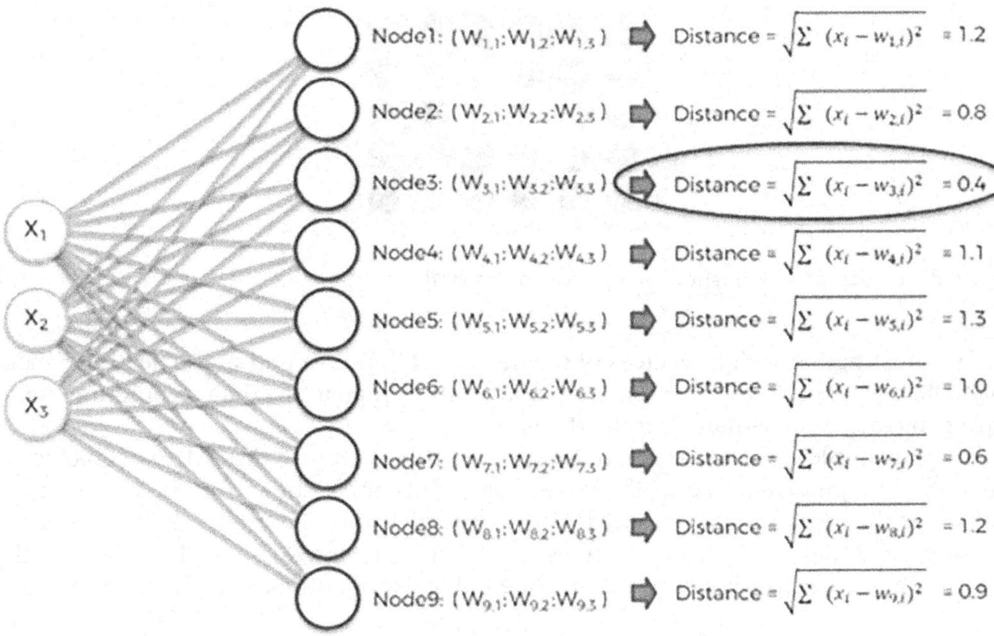

Figure 8.4.f Evaluating minimum Euclidean distance between the weight vector to each output node.

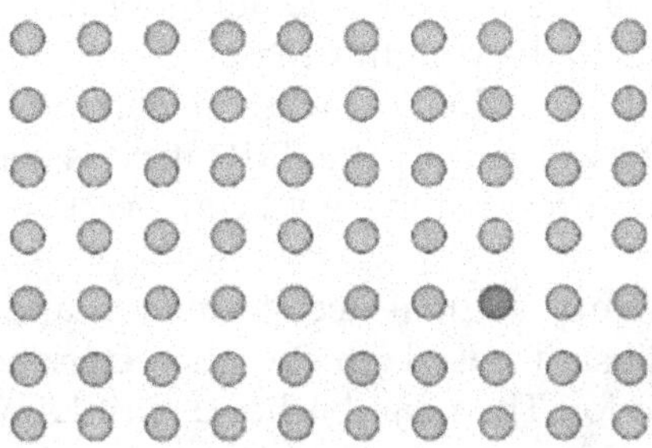

Figure 8.4.g Identifying closest to the input vector in terms of its weight vector.

The size of the neighborhood is typically defined by a decreasing function of time (or iterations) during the training process. As training progresses, the neighborhood size gradually decreases, allowing for finer adjustments and convergence toward a more accurate representation of the data.

To determine if a node is within the radial distance of the BMU's neighborhood, we can use the Pythagorean theorem. This involves calculating the Euclidean distance between the BMU and each node in the SOM. If the Euclidean distance is within the radius, the node is considered to be within the BMU's neighborhood and its weight vector will be updated.

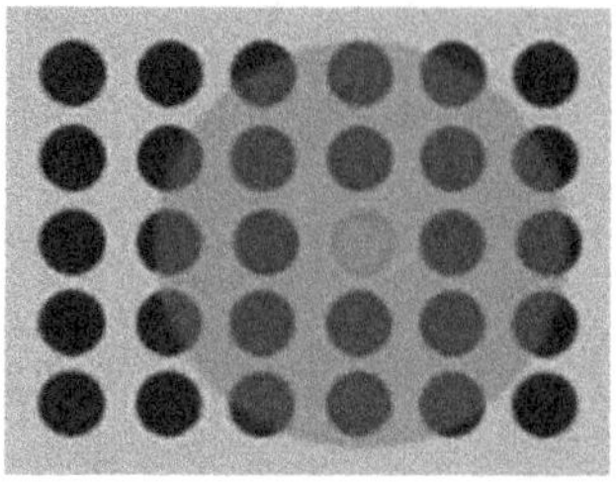

Figure 8.4.h Size of the neighborhood around the BMU.

By adjusting the weight vectors of the neighboring nodes within the neighborhood, the SOM can adapt to the local patterns and relationships in the data, promoting better clustering and representation of the dataset.

In the example shown, the size of the neighborhood around the BMU is depicted by the circular region centered at the BMU (red point) and denoted by the circle with a radius. At the beginning of training ($t = 0$), the neighborhood is relatively large, encompassing a significant number of nodes. As training progresses ($t = 1, 2, 3, \ldots$), the neighborhood size gradually decreases due to the exponential decay function.

$$\sigma(t) = \sigma_0 exp\left(-\frac{t}{\lambda}\right)$$

σ_0= the width of lattice at time 0, t = the current time step, λ = the time constant

The exponential decay function controls the rate at which the neighborhood size decreases. It is typically defined in terms of the number of iterations or time steps during training. As each iteration occurs, the neighborhood size reduces, allowing for more localized adjustments to the weight vectors.

At the later stages of training, when t reaches its maximum value, the neighborhood size diminishes to the point where only the BMU itself is considered within the neighborhood. This final stage ensures that the SOM converges to a more refined representation of the data.

The specific form of the exponential decay function and the rate of neighborhood size reduction can be adjusted based on the characteristics of the dataset and the desired convergence behavior. The neighborhood shrinks with time after each repetition, as shown in Figure 8.4i.

We can easily loop through the lattice's nodes to check whether or not they fall inside the radius given that we are aware of its size. If a node is discovered to be in the neighborhood, Step 4 will update its weight vector as follows.

8.4.4 *Setting the Radius Value*

Setting the radius value in a SOM involves considering the range and scale of your input data as well as the size of your SOM.

Here are some general guidelines to set the radius value.

1. *Scale of the Input Data:* If your input data is mean-zero standardized (zero mean and unit variance), a radius value around $\sigma = 4$ can be a good starting point. If your data

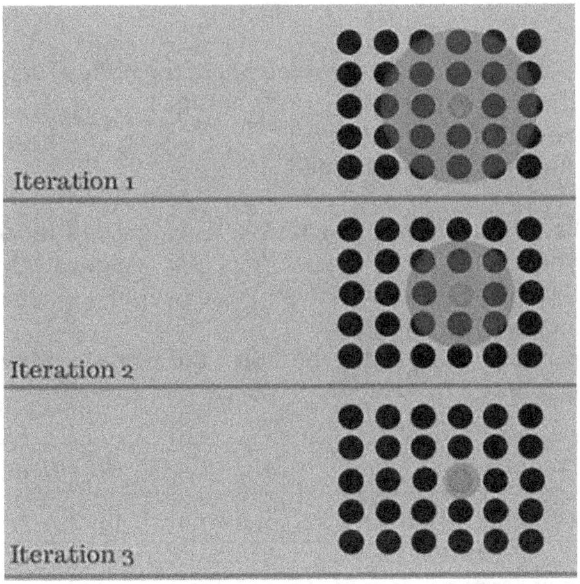

Figure 8.4.i Neighborhood shrinkage with time.

is normalized to a specific range (e.g., [0, 1]), a smaller radius value around $\sigma = 1$ might be more suitable.

2. *Size of the SOM:* The size of your SOM grid also influences the choice of radius. For a smaller grid, such as 10 by 10, a radius value like $\sigma = 5$ can be effective. For larger grids, like 100 by 100, you can increase the radius value accordingly, for example, $\sigma = 50$.
3. *Decreasing Radius over Iterations:* It's important to decrease the radius value as the iterations progress. This ensures that the neighborhood function narrows down gradually, allowing for finer adjustments to the weight vectors. You can decrease the radius along with the learning rate α and the size of the neighborhood function as the iterations proceed.
4. *Consider Cluster Centroids:* In some cases, the radius value can be based on the Euclidean distance between the centroids of the first and second closest clusters in unsupervised classification tasks. This approach can help determine a meaningful radius value based on the structure of the data.

It's worth noting that the choice of radius value may require experimentation and fine-tuning based on the specific characteristics of your data and the problem at hand.

8.4.5 Step 4: Adjusting the Weight

To adjust the weights in the SOM, including the weights of the BMU and its neighboring nodes, the following equation is used:

$$\begin{aligned} New\ Weights\, W(t+1) &= Old\ Weights\, W(t) \\ &+ Learning\ Rate\, L(t) \times \big(Input\ Vector\, V(t) - Old\ Weights\, W(t)\big) \end{aligned}$$

Where:

- $W(t+1)$ represents the newly adjusted weights of the node at time $t+1$.
- $W(t)$ represents the old weights of the node at time t.
- $L(\mathrm{t})$ represents the learning rate at time t.
- $V(t)$ represents the input vector at time t.

In this equation, the new weight for each node is calculated by adding a fraction of the difference between the input vector and the old weight to the old weight itself. The learning rate determines the magnitude of the weight adjustment and is usually a small value that decreases over time.

Based on your example, if Node 4 is the BMU, the corresponding weights for Node 4 can be adjusted as follows:

$W_{3,1} = 0.39$	$W_{3,2} = 0.42$	$W_{3,3} = 0.45$
Input vector: $X_1 = 0.7$	$X_2 = 0.6$	$X_3 = 0.9$

Based on the given learning rate of 0.5 and the provided equations, the updated weights for Node 3,1 (W3,1), Node 3,2 (W3,2), and Node 3,3 (W3,3) can be calculated as follows:

For W3,1:

- New Weights = Old Weights + Learning Rate × (Input Vector1 – Old Weights)
- New Weights = 0.39 + 0.5 × (0.7 – 0.39)
- New Weights = 0.39 + 0.5 × 0.31
- New Weights = 0.39 + 0.155
- New Weights = 0.545

For W3,2:

- New Weights = Old Weights + Learning Rate × (Input Vector2 – Old Weights)
- New Weights = 0.42 + 0.5 × (0.6 – 0.42)
- New Weights = 0.42 + 0.5 × 0.18
- New Weights = 0.42 + 0.09
- New Weights = 0.51

For W3,3:

- New Weights = Old Weights + Learning Rate × (Input Vector3 – Old Weights)
- New Weights = 0.45 + 0.5 × (0.9 – 0.45)
- New Weights = 0.45 + 0.5 × 0.45
- New Weights = 0.45 + 0.225
- New Weights = 0.675

Therefore, the updated weights for Node 3,1, Node 3,2, and Node 3,3 are 0.545, 0.51, and 0.675, respectively.

As the training progresses, the learning rate and neighborhood size gradually decrease, causing the weights to converge and the neighborhoods to shrink. This helps the SOM to create stable zones or clusters that represent patterns in the data.

$$L(t) = L_0 exp\left(-\frac{t}{\lambda}\right)$$

The influence rate determines how much influence the distance from the BMU has on the learning process. Typically, nodes close to the BMU have a higher influence rate (e.g., 1) while nodes farther away have a lower influence rate (e.g., 0). A common approach is to use a Gaussian function to calculate the influence rate, where nodes closer to the BMU have a higher influence.

$$\theta(t) = exp\left(-\frac{dist^2}{2\sigma^2(t)}\right)$$

$\theta(t) = influence\ rate;\ \sigma(t) = width\ of\ the\ lattice\ at\ timet$

Through the iteration of adjusting weights and updating the neighborhood, the SOM can reveal hidden patterns and structures in the data. However, the interpretation of these patterns is ultimately done by humans, as the SOM provides a visual representation of the data that can aid in understanding and analysis.

8.5 Case Studies: Credit Card Fraud Detection using SOMs

The growth of the Fraud Detection and Prevention Market, projected to reach USD 33.19 billion by 2021 according to the report by MarketsandMarkets, highlights the significance of advanced deep learning skills in this industry. As fraud continues to pose a significant threat to businesses, organizations are increasingly turning to innovative technologies like deep learning to enhance their fraud detection and prevention capabilities.

Deep learning offers powerful techniques for analyzing and identifying patterns in complex data, making it particularly well-suited for fraud detection tasks. By leveraging deep neural networks, which are capable of learning hierarchical representations, deep learning models can automatically extract meaningful features from large and diverse datasets, enabling more accurate fraud detection.

The inclusion of a fraud detection case study in this chapter underscores the importance of applying deep learning in real-world scenarios. By developing a deep learning model for a bank to detect potential fraud in credit card applications, the chapter aims to showcase the practical implementation of advanced techniques in the context of a critical industry.

As the market for fraud detection and prevention continues to expand, the demand for professionals skilled in deep learning and related technologies will rise. Deep learning offers the potential to revolutionize fraud detection by improving detection accuracy, reducing false positives, and enhancing the efficiency of fraud investigations.

By exploring this case study, readers can gain insights into the application of deep learning in fraud detection and understand the challenges and considerations involved in developing effective fraud detection models. This knowledge can be invaluable for professionals looking to enter or advance in the field of fraud detection and prevention, as well as organizations seeking to strengthen their fraud detection capabilities using advanced technologies.

To implement SOMs for fraud detection in credit card applications, you can follow these steps.

- *Data Preprocessing:* Start by preprocessing the dataset, which may involve handling missing values, scaling numerical features, and encoding categorical variables.
- *Initialize the SOM:* Set the parameters for the SOM, including the number of nodes or neurons, the learning rate, and the neighborhood radius. Initialize the weights of the SOM randomly or using a specific initialization method.
- *Training the SOM:* Iterate over the dataset and present each credit card application to the SOM. Calculate the Euclidean distance between the input data and the weights of each neuron. Find the winning neuron with the closest weight vector to the input data. Update the weights of the winning neuron and its neighboring neurons based on the learning rate and the neighborhood radius. Repeat this process for a specified number of epochs.
- *Visualization:* After training the SOM, visualize the SOM grid to understand the clustering and distribution of the credit card applications. You can use different visualization techniques, such as heatmaps or scatter plots, to represent the SOM and the fraud/non-fraud labels.
- *Fraud Detection:* Analyze the trained SOM to identify potential fraud cases. You can determine outliers or clusters that have a higher concentration of fraudulent applications. Assign fraud scores or labels to each credit card application based on its distance to the fraud cluster or other defined criteria.
- *Evaluation:* Evaluate the performance of the SOM-based fraud detection model using appropriate metrics such as accuracy, precision, recall, and F1-score. Compare the results with other fraud detection methods or baseline models.
- *Iterate and Refine:* Analyze the results and iterate on the model, adjusting parameters or exploring different feature engineering techniques to improve fraud detection accuracy.

It's important to note that the implementation details may vary based on the programming language and libraries you choose to use. Popular libraries for implementing SOMs include TensorFlow, Keras, or specialized SOM libraries such as MiniSom.

Remember to handle sensitive customer information with care and ensure compliance with data privacy regulations when working with credit card application data.

8.5.1 Description of Dataset

The Credit_Card_Applications.csv dataset presented in Figure 8.5 contains transactions made by credit cards in September 2013 by European cardholders. The dataset covers transactions that occurred over a period of two days, with a total of 284,807 transactions. Out of these transactions, there are 492 cases of fraud, indicating a highly unbalanced dataset where fraud cases account for only 0.172% of all transactions.

The dataset consists of numerical input variables, which are the result of a principal component analysis (PCA) transformation. The original features and background information about the data are not provided due to confidentiality issues. The features V1, V2, . . ., V28 represent the principal components obtained through PCA. The features "Time" and "Amount' are not transformed with PCA.

The "Time" feature represents the number of seconds elapsed between each transaction and the first transaction in the dataset, providing a temporal aspect to the data. The "Amount" feature represents the transaction amount and can be used for example-dependent cost-sensitive learning, where the cost of misclassifying a transaction may depend on its amount.

The target variable is "Class", which indicates whether a transaction is classified as fraud (1) or not fraud (0).

Given the highly unbalanced nature of the dataset, with a small percentage of fraud cases, it poses a challenge for modeling and requires specific techniques to handle class imbalance during analysis and model development.

Overall, the Credit_Card_Applications.csv dataset provides an opportunity to explore fraud detection algorithms and develop models to identify fraudulent credit card transactions.

To build a SOM for credit card fraud detection using the "Credit_Card_Applications.csv" dataset, you can follow these steps using Python.

1. *Import the Necessary Libraries:* Start by importing the required libraries for data manipulation, visualization, and the SOM implementation. In the Data Preprocessing step, we import four libraries to help us with various tasks:

    - **pandas (import pandas as pd):** pandas is a powerful library for data manipulation and analysis. It provides data structures and functions to efficiently handle and process structured data, such as importing datasets, manipulating data frames, and performing various data operations.
    - **numpy (import numpy as np):** numpy is a fundamental library for scientific computing in Python. It provides support for large, multidimensional arrays and matrices, along with a wide range of mathematical functions to operate on these arrays efficiently. It is commonly used for numerical computations and data manipulation tasks.
    - **matplotlib (import matplotlib.pyplot as plt):** matplotlib is a widely used library for creating visualizations in Python. It provides a comprehensive set of functions for creating various types of plots and charts, such as line plots, bar plots, histograms, scatter plots, and so on. It allows us to visualize data and gain insights from the data through graphical representations.
    - **minisom (from minisom import MiniSom):** MiniSom is a Python implementation of the SOM algorithm. SOM is an unsupervised learning neural network that can be used for clustering and visualization tasks. It helps in organizing and understanding complex data by mapping it to a lower-dimensional grid. The MiniSom library provides the necessary tools for building and training SOM models.

By importing these libraries, we ensure that we have access to the required functions and tools for data preprocessing, analysis, visualization, and building the SOM model for the given task.

CustomerID	A1	A2	A3	A4	A5	A6	A7	A8	A9	A10	A11	A12	A13	A14	Class
15776156	1	22.08	11.46	2	4	4	1.585	0	0	0	1	2	100	1213	0
15739548	0	22.67	7	2	8	4	0.165	0	0	0	0	2	160	1	0
15662854	0	29.58	1.75	1	4	4	1.25	0	0	0	1	2	280	1	0
15687688	0	21.67	11.5	1	5	3	0	1	1	11	1	2	0	1	1
15715750	1	20.17	8.17	2	6	4	1.96	1	1	14	0	2	60	159	1
15571121	0	15.83	0.585	2	8	8	1.5	1	1	2	0	2	100	1	1
15726466	1	17.42	6.5	2	3	4	0.125	0	0	0	0	2	60	101	0
15660390	0	58.67	4.46	2	11	8	3.04	1	1	6	0	2	43	561	1
15663942	1	27.83	1	1	2	8	3	0	0	0	0	2	176	538	0
15638610	0	55.75	7.08	2	4	8	6.75	1	1	3	1	2	100	51	0
15644446	1	33.5	1.75	2	14	8	4.5	1	1	4	1	2	253	858	1
15585892	1	41.42	5	2	11	8	5	1	1	6	1	2	470	1	1
15609356	1	20.67	1.25	1	8	8	1.375	1	1	3	1	2	140	211	0
15803378	1	34.92	5	2	14	8	7.5	1	1	6	1	2	0	1001	1
15599440	1	58.58	2.71	2	8	4	2.415	0	0	0	1	2	320	1	0
15692408	1	48.08	6.04	2	4	4	0.04	0	0	0	0	2	0	2691	1
15683168	1	29.58	4.5	2	9	4	7.5	1	1	2	1	2	330	1	1

Figure 8.5 Glimpse of Credit_Card_Applications.csv.

```
import pandas as pd
import numpy as np
import matplotlib.pyplot as plt
from minisom import MiniSom
```

2. *Load and Preprocess the Dataset:* Load the "Credit_Card_Applications.csv" dataset using pandas and perform any necessary preprocessing steps. This may include handling missing values, encoding categorical variables, and scaling the data. To import the dataset and define the dependent and independent variables, you can use the following code:

```
# Load the dataset
dataset = pd.read_csv("Credit_Card_Applications.csv")

# Define the independent variables (attributes)
X = dataset.iloc[:, 1:13].values

# Define the dependent variable
y = dataset.iloc[:, -1].values
```

- In this code, you first import the pandas library as **'pd'**. Then, you use the **'read_csv'** function to read the dataset from a CSV file and store it in the **'dataset'** variable.
- Next, you define the independent variables **'X'** by selecting the columns from 1 to 12 (attributes 1 to 12) using the **'iloc'** function. The **'.values'** attribute converts the selected data into a numpy array.
- Finally, you define the dependent variable **'y'** by selecting the last column (-1) using the **'iloc'** function. Again, the **'.values'** attribute converts the selected data into a numpy array.
- Note that the dataset file path should be provided in the **'read_csv'** function based on the actual location and name of your dataset file.

By completing this step, you have imported the dataset and separated the independent variables (**'X'**) and the dependent variable (**'y'**) for further processing and model building.

To perform feature scaling using normalization in your dataset, you can use the **'MinMaxScaler'** from the **'sklearn.preprocessing'** module. Here's how you can do it:

```
from sklearn.preprocessing import MinMaxScaler

# Create an instance of MinMaxScaler
scaler = MinMaxScaler(feature_range=(0, 1))

# Apply feature scaling to the independent variables (X)
X_scaled = scaler.fit_transform(X)
```

- In this code, you first import the **'MinMaxScaler'** from the **'sklearn.preprocessing'** module. Then, you create an instance of **'MinMaxScaler'** called **'scaler'**, specifying the feature range to be between 0 and 1.
- Next, you apply the feature scaling to the independent variables **'X'** using the **'fit_transform'** method of the **'scaler'** object. The **'fit_transform'** method computes the minimum and maximum values of each feature and scales the values accordingly.
- After executing this code, the **'X_scaled'** variable will contain the scaled values of the independent variables, where all the values will be in the range [0, 1].
- Note that it's important to perform feature scaling on the independent variables to bring them to a similar scale and avoid issues caused by variables with different ranges or magnitudes.

Standardization	*Normalization*
$x_{\text{stand}} = \dfrac{x - \text{mean}(x)}{\text{standard deviation}(x)}$	$x_{\text{norm}} = \dfrac{x - \min(x)}{\max(x) - \min(x)}$

By applying feature scaling, you have prepared your independent variables (**'X'**) by normalizing the values to a common range, which will help in improving the performance of your model.

3. *Initialize and Train the SOM:* Create an instance of the MiniSom class, define the SOM's parameters such as the grid size and learning rate, and train the SOM on the preprocessed data. Here's an example of how you can initialize the SOM model with the specified parameters:

```
# Define the SOM parameters
grid_size = (10, 10) # Adjust the grid size based on your dataset
learning_rate = 0.5 # Adjust the learning rate based on your
dataset

# Initialize the SOM
som = MiniSom(x = grid_size[0], y = grid_size[1], input_len =
data.shape[1], sigma=1.0, learning_rate=learning_rate)
```

Here we create an instance of the **'MiniSom'** class called **'som'** and pass the desired parameters:

- **'x'** and **'y'**: The dimensions of the SOM grid, which determine the number of nodes in the grid. In this example, we have a 10 × 10 grid.
- **'input_len'**: The length of the input vectors. In this case, we have 15 attributes in our dataset.
- **'sigma'**: The radius of the different neighborhoods in the grid. A smaller value means a more focused neighborhood. Here, we set it to 1.0, which is the default value.

- **'learning_rate'**: The learning rate or the step size for updating the weights during each iteration. A higher learning rate can result in faster convergence. We set it to 0.5, which is the default value.

By initializing the SOM model with these parameters, you are setting up the structure of the SOM grid and defining the initial configuration of the weights in the neurons.

To randomly initialize the weights in the SOM model, you can use the **'random_weights_init'** method provided by the **'MiniSom'** class. Here's an example of how you can initialize the weights using your SOM model **'som'** and the input data **'X'**:

```
# Train the SOM
som.random_weights_init(X) # Initialize the weights
```

- In this code, you call the **'random_weights_init'** method of your SOM model **'som'** and pass the input data **'X'** as the parameter. This method initializes the weights of the neurons in the SOM randomly based on the input data. The dimensions of the input data should match the input length specified when initializing the SOM model.

By initializing the weights randomly, you provide an initial configuration for the neurons in the SOM, which will be updated during the training process based on the input data.

To train the SOM model, you can use the **'train_random'** method provided by the **'MiniSom'** class. Here's an example of how you can train your SOM model **'som'** using your input data **'X'** and specifying the number of iterations as 100:

```
som.train_batch(data.values, 1000) # Train the SOM for 1000
epochs or adjust the number of epochs as needed
```

- In this code, you call the **train_random** method of your SOM model **'som'** and pass the input data **'X'** as the **'data'** parameter. You also specify the number of iterations as 100 by passing it as the **'num_iteration'** parameter. This method performs the training process on the SOM model using the input data for the specified number of iterations. During each iteration, the weights of the neurons in the SOM are updated based on the input data.

By training the model, the SOM learns to map the input data onto a grid, organizing similar data points close to each other on the grid. This helps in detecting patterns and clusters in the data.

4. *Visualize the SOM:* Visualize the trained SOM to understand the clustering and patterns within the data. To visualize the results of the SOM, you can use the **'pylab'** library in combination with the **'pcolor'** and **'colorbar'** functions. Here's an example of how you can visualize the SOM map:

```
from pylab import bone, pcolor, colorbar, plot, show

# Create a new figure
bone()

# Plot the distance map of the SOM
pcolor(som.distance_map().T)

# Add a color bar
colorbar()

# Define markers for different classes
markers = ['o', 's']
colors = ['r', 'g']

# Iterate over each customer
for i, x in enumerate(X):
    # Get the winning node for the customer
    w = som.winner(x)
    # Plot the marker on the winning node location
    plot(w[0] + 0.5,
         w[1] + 0.5,
         markers[Y[i]],
         markeredgecolor=colors[Y[i]],
         markerfacecolor='None',
         markersize=10,
         markeredgewidth=2)

# Show the plot
show()
```

- In this code, you first create a new figure using **'bone()'** function. Then, you plot the distance map of the SOM using the **'pcolor'** function, where **'som.distance_map()'** returns the matrix of distances between each neuron in the SOM and its neighbors. The **'colorbar'** function adds a color bar to the plot.
- Next, you define markers and colors for different classes. In the for loop, you iterate over each customer and get the winning node for the customer using **'som.winner(x)'**, where **'x'** is the input data for the customer. You plot a marker on the location of the winning node, with the marker shape and color based on the class of the customer (0 for red circle, 1 for green square).
- Finally, you show the plot using **'show()'** function. This visualization helps to visualize the clustering and distribution of the customers on the SOM map.

The SOM visualization shows (Figure 8.6) the distribution of customers on the SOM map, where the red circles represent customers who didn't get approval and the green squares represent customers who got approval. The white color areas on the map indicate high potential fraud or outliers. By identifying these outliers, you can potentially detect customers who have potentially cheated or committed fraud.

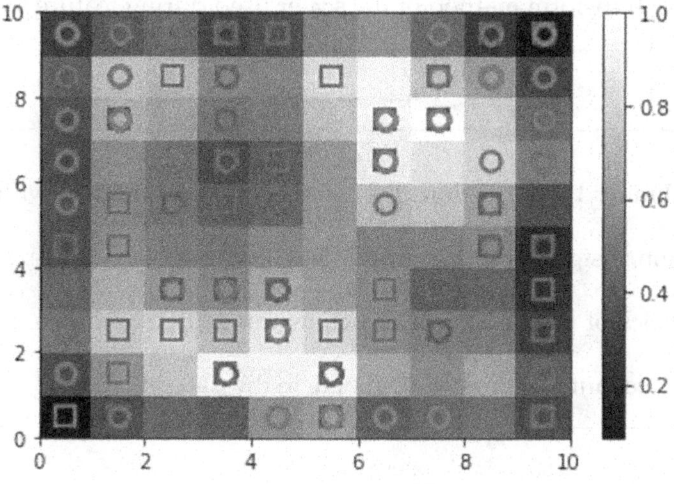

Figure 8.6 SOM visualization.

5. *Catch the Potential Fraud:* To catch the potential fraud from the SOM, you can follow these steps:

1. **Find the Mappings:** After training the SOM, you can use the **'win_map'** method to find the mappings of the input data onto the SOM grid. This method returns a dictionary,
where the keys represent the coordinates of the SOM nodes, and the values represent the
customers mapped to each node.

```
mappings = som.win_map(X)
```

2. **Identify Potential Fraud Nodes:** Analyze the mappings and identify the SOM nodes that have a higher concentration of fraud cases. These nodes represent potential fraud clusters. You can select these nodes based on certain criteria, such as a high percentage of fraud cases or a higher density of fraud instances compared to other nodes.

```
fraud_nodes = mappings[(x, y)] # Replace (x, y) with the coordi-
nates of the potential fraud nodes
```

3. **Inverse Transform the Data:** If you scaled your data during preprocessing, you may
want to inverse transform the data to obtain the original values. This can be done using

the inverse_transform method of the scaler used during feature scaling.

```
fraud_data = sc.inverse_transform(fraud_nodes)
```

4. **Analyze Fraud Data:** Explore the attributes and patterns within the potential fraud
data to gain insights into the fraudulent behavior. You can examine different features or
characteristics of the fraud cases, such as transaction amounts, time of transactions, or
any other relevant information available in the dataset.

```
# Analyze fraud data, for example:
fraudulent_amounts = fraud_data[:, 13] # Assuming column
13 represents transaction amounts
fraudulent_times = fraud_data[:, 14] # Assuming column 14 repre-
sents transaction times
```

By following these steps, you can identify the potential fraud cases based on the SOM and further analyze the specific attributes or patterns associated with those cases. This can help in detecting and preventing fraudulent activities in credit card applications.

8.6 Summary

The chapter provides a comprehensive overview of self-organizing maps (SOMs) and covers various fundamental concepts and principles related to this neural network model. It explains the working paradigm of SOMs, which involves a competitive learning process and topological organization of data.

The algorithm for SOMs is presented, highlighting the key steps involved in training and updating the network. The chapter dives into the details of the learning algorithms used in SOMs, including weight initialization, neighborhood function, and adaptation of the learning rate.

To illustrate the practical implementation of SOMs, a case study on credit card fraud detection is presented. The chapter explains how SOMs can be applied to this specific problem, leveraging the ability of SOMs to capture and represent the underlying patterns in the data. It provides practical coding examples to demonstrate the implementation of SOMs for credit card fraud detection.

Throughout the chapter, the focus is on providing a clear understanding of the fundamental concepts of SOMs and their application in real-world scenarios. The case study on credit card fraud detection serves as a practical example, showcasing the capabilities of SOMs in solving complex problems and detecting anomalies in large datasets.

References

Danielsen, A. S., Johansen, T. A., & Garrett, J. L. (2021). Self-organizing maps for clustering hyperspectral images on-board a cubesat. *Remote Sensing, 13*(20), 4174.

Delgado, S., Morán, F., San José, J. C., & Burgos, D. (2021). Analysis of students' behavior through user clustering in online learning settings, based on self organizing maps neural networks. *IEEE Access, 9*, 132592–132608.

Dias, L. A., Damasceno, A. M. P., Gaura, E., & Fernandes, M. A. C. (2021). A full-parallel implementation of self-organizing maps on hardware. *Neural Networks, 143*, 818–827.

Forest, F., Lebbah, M., Azzag, H., & Lacaille, J. (2021). Deep embedded self-organizing maps for joint representation learning and topology-preserving clustering. *Neural Computing and Applications, 33*(24), 17439–17469.

Guamán, D., Delgado, S., & Pérez, J. (2021). Classifying model-view-controller software applications using self-organizing maps. *IEEE Access, 9*, 45201–45229.

Mahdi, T. N., Jameel, J. Q., Polshchykov, K. A., Lazarev, S. A., Polshchykov, I. K., & Kiselev, V. (2021). Clusters partition algorithm for a self-organizing map for detecting resource-intensive database inquiries in a geo-ecological monitoring system. *Periodicals of Engineering and Natural Sciences, 9*(4), 1138–1145.

Mallet, V., Nilges, M., & Bouvier, G. (2021). quicksom: Self-organizing maps on GPUs for clustering of molecular dynamics trajectories. *Bioinformatics, 37*(14), 2064–2065.

Neisari, A., Rueda, L., & Saad, S. (2021). Spam review detection using self-organizing maps and convolutional neural networks. *Computers & Security, 106*, 102274.

Rivas-Tabares, D., de Miguel, Á., Willaarts, B., & Tarquis, A. M. (2020). Self-organizing map of soil properties in the context of hydrological modeling. *Applied Mathematical Modelling, 88*, 175–189.

Sakkari, M., & Zaied, M. (2020). A convolutional deep self-organizing map feature extraction for machine learning. *Multimedia Tools and Applications, 79*, 19451–19470.

Soto, R., Crawford, B., Molina, F. G., & Olivares, R. (2021). Human behaviour based optimization supported with self-organizing maps for solving the S-box design problem. *IEEE Access, 9*, 84605–84618.

Index